CANADA *in the* GREAT POWER GAME
1914–2014

GWYNNE DYER

CANADA
IN THE
GREAT POWER GAME

1914–2014

Random House Canada

PUBLISHED BY RANDOM HOUSE CANADA

www.randomhouse.ca

Random House Canada and colophon are registered trademarks.

Library and Archives Canada Cataloguing in Publication

Dyer, Gwynne, author
    Canada in the great power game 1914-2014 / Gwynne Dyer.

Includes bibliographical references and index.
Issued in print and electronic formats.

ISBN 978-0-307-36168-4   eBook ISBN 978-0-307-36170-7

    1. Canada—History, Military—20th century. 2. Canada—History, Military—21st century. 3. Canada—History—1914–. I. Title.

FC543.D94 2014   971.06   C2013-906411-7

Cover and text design by Andrew Roberts

Cover photo: © Cathal O'Riada

Printed and bound in the United States of America

10 9 8 7 6 5 4 3 2 1

To Tina—thanks for all the fish

CONTENTS

Introduction   1

CHAPTER 1   Just a Little Precedent   7
EXCURSION 1   The Alliance System   31
CHAPTER 2   A Long Way from Home   39
EXCURSION 2   The Steel Sleet and the Continuous Front   63
CHAPTER 3   The Great Crusade   71
EXCURSION 3   Breaking the Stalemate   99
CHAPTER 4   A Country Divided   105
EXCURSION 4   Would a German Victory
                 Have Been Worse?   133
CHAPTER 5   The Fireproof House   141
EXCURSION 5   The Myth of Appeasement   177
CHAPTER 6   The "No-Ground-Troops" War, 1939–41   183
EXCURSION 6   Blitzkrieg   213
CHAPTER 7   The Real War, 1942–45   217
EXCURSION 7   What If We Had Not Fought Hitler?   249
CHAPTER 8   A Dreadful Mistake   253
EXCURSION 8   Why War Is Hard to Stop   283

CHAPTER 9   Alliances and Peacekeeping   291

EXCURSION 9   The Theory and Practice of
                 Nuclear Deterrence   323

CHAPTER 10   The Space Between   329

EXCURSION 10   All Passion Spent   369

CHAPTER 11   Going with the Flow   371

Photo Permissions   399

Index   403

INTRODUCTION

THE LAST THING THE WORLD NEEDS NOW IS ANOTHER HUNDRED or five hundred histories of the First World War or some locally relevant aspect of it. But 2014 is the centenary of the war's outbreak, and that cataclysmic event is still seen as the turning point where the old world ended and the modern world began, so the avalanche of books is inevitable. And here's another one.

It is not only a history of the First World War, although I am shamelessly using the anniversary as a peg to hang the story on (and the book does actually deal with that war at some length). It is an attempt to make sense of our country's century of involvement in big and little wars, all of them far from home and none of them threatening what strategists like to call our "vital interests." Not just to recount the wars, but to account for them.

Tina Viljoen and I first tried to do this in a book and a television series called *The Defence of Canada* about twenty-five years ago. We argued that the alliances and overseas commitments that Canada had made in the course of the twentieth century were unnecessary for our security and often directly contrary to our interests, even if the politics of the time had probably made them inevitable. And we extended that criticism to include Canada's then-current alliances and overseas military commitments.

1

It was an interesting experience but, with the Cold War still raging at the time, challenges to the prevailing mythology about why we keep sending troops overseas were most unwelcome to the authorities. The project did not end well.

The television series got very good numbers on its first airing, but for reasons that nobody wanted to talk about it never got its scheduled second run, even though the CBC had already paid for it. The publisher was enthusiastic about the book—so much so that when it came in much longer than we had planned, he decided to publish it in two volumes rather than cut the manuscript down. But when the first volume came out there was a concerted howl of rage from the Canadian military history establishment, who condemned it down to the last man. (They were all men at that time, of course.)

The first volume sold well, but the publication of the second volume was cancelled anyway. (Some of the later chapters of the first volume are having a second life in the earlier part of this book.) We didn't know why, but since Tina and I had already been paid, we just moved on to other things. Only many years later was some of the mystery cleared up.

> As big a world as it is, it's astounding how paths cross. There he
> was, in the famous leather jacket, puffing on a smoke just outside
> the doors of the Calgary airport. I had a debt to pay. I walked up
> and introduced myself to Gwynne Dyer. I told him I owed him
> a debt, recounted the whole story, and thanked him for helping
> pay the mortgage and put my kids through university. Gwynne
> graciously accepted my thanks.
>
> Allan Bonner

Allan Bonner is a former CBC journalist turned media adviser whom I had never heard of until the chance meeting in Calgary airport. He told me that he had been approached in 1987 by a film producer with a question. The Department of National Defence was determined to counter the strong perceptions that Dyer and Viljoen had created, so they wanted to do their own film. How could they get their own viewpoint on television?

> I gave more discouraging words. Even if all networks played the DND rebuttal, there was no guarantee it would get the viewership or would have the staying power of Dyer's film. I recommended a more traditional public affairs approach—a speakers' bureau, media interviews, and men and women in Canadian uniforms engaging audiences at conferences, schools and universities. In passing, I asked who had commissioned the producer's study. "Colonel Len Dent" was the response.

Bonner had gone to Ottawa to meet Dent, who turned out to be the director general of information at the Department of National Defence. A team of retired admirals and generals had been assembled at E.A.C. Amy & Sons Management Support Services in Ottawa (founded by retired Brigadier General Edward "Ned" Amy). The rot had apparently spread right into Canada's armed forces, and this group would have the task of convincing serving officers of the value of Canada's NATO commitments. But, as Bonner pointed out, they could also be put to work convincing the general public.

> I was welcomed into this distinguished group and we toured the country setting military officers straight on Gwynne Dyer and his misguided notions. I had a great run for about 14 years, and all the while I was secretly grateful to Dyer for scaring the heck out of DND. I'd regularly see him commenting on TV. . . . I'd watch Gwynne and then look over to see if the phone would ring with another assignment.

Tina and I never realized the ideas in our film would frighten military officialdom so much, but the upper echelons' determination to set things right does suggest that they found a ready audience in the public. The extreme official reaction also suggests how the second broadcast of the television series and the second volume of the book (the one dealing with everything after 1939, including the formation of Canada's current alliances) might have come to be cancelled.

Now we're well into the twenty-first century, and all that bad old history has gone away—or so most people think: the centenary of the First World War has no lessons for us, so we'll just do a national commemoration of Our Glorious Dead and move on to more relevant things. There are two things wrong with that approach. One is that being dead isn't glorious. The other is that the system that produced those old wars and consumed all those lives isn't dead at all. It has been under serious pressure for a long time now and it is in retreat, but it is still capable of tumbling us all into horror. It is right to remember the dead, even if the anguish of the time has dwindled to a distant regret, but it is also necessary to remember what really killed them.

The truth is that this country, a century ago, sent hundreds of thousands of its young citizens to another continent to kill and be killed by strangers who had no designs on Canada, in a war that posed no threat to this country. The reasons that our forebears gave themselves for doing this sound hollow now, but we did it again in 1939, and the reasons for doing that still sound plausible to most of us. And it has got to be a habit: there have been Canadian troops abroad in military (that is, *not* peacekeeping) roles for all but twenty years of the past century.

Because it has actually happened, it seems normal and natural that it should have happened, but in fact *no* other country in the Americas has done this, not even the United States. Since 1945 the Americans, as the world's greatest power, have always had troops overseas, but before that they were much more reluctant to fight in other continents than we were. Canada was involved in both world wars from the start, a total of more than ten years; the United States was at war for only five of those years. In the First World War, the United States lost 116,000 dead; Canada lost 60,000, out of a population that was less than one-twelfth the size.

Faced with these bizarre statistics, the temptation is to lurch to one of two extreme positions. Either you can argue (and lots of people do) that this glorious sacrifice was necessary to preserve our freedom and that the disparity in numbers simply proves that our sacrifice was more glorious than that of the Americans. Or you can denounce Canada's entire military history in modern times as a shamefully stupid blunder into which the naive Canadians were lured by cunning British and American imperialists and/or wicked capitalists. The defect in the former position is that the freedom of Canadians was never at risk, and the fault in the latter position is that it assumes that the people running Canada were as dumb as bricks.

They weren't. They were intelligent, reasonably well-informed people who had to operate, as most politicians always do, within economic, political and legal constraints that they could bend a bit, perhaps, but could not ignore. They were far more reluctant to spend the lives of Canadian soldiers than posterity has admitted. As time passed, they also learned a great deal about the way the great-power game worked, which enabled them to be more effectively reluctant: only two-thirds as many Canadians were killed in the six years of the Second World War as in the four years of the First. And in the end, they acquired the experience and the insight to challenge the very basis of the great-power game, and to take a leading role in the attempt, still underway, to change the way the entire system works. In the course of a century we have been up and down the learning curve a couple of times—at the moment we're a bit down—but it's not a shameful record at all. We're doing the best we can.

Two last things. There are a great many quotes in this book from named people, but with no further source given. In almost all cases, these are taken from one of the hundred-plus interviews that were conducted in the course of making the films and writing the book. And although Tina Viljoen's name is not on this book for contractual reasons, a tremendous amount of the work that went into it is hers. Actually, we originally agreed to do it as an excuse to stay together.

CHAPTER 1

JUST A LITTLE PRECEDENT

To get to our position we had to wade across the Modder River, despite a current that reached nine miles an hour. It wouldn't have been surprising if we had been dragged away; water up to our necks and even over their heads for some; but that was just the start. We had hardly got out of the water and clambered up the bank when we came under the enemy's fire. The bullets came as thick as rain, I'm telling you; you should have seen it. A hundred yards farther on, around seven o'clock, the first Canadian was struck in the shoulder.

Captain J.E. Peltier (Montreal)
(translated from French)

Around ten in the morning, the fire gets heavier; the Boers are dug in on a bend of the river, sheltered by natural trenches; others are up in the trees and fire on us unseen. Only our artillery can hit them. The bullets rain literally over our heads; there's someone killed or wounded every minute. . . . At eleven our line advances four hundred yards; we're now only twelve hundred yards from the enemy. . . .

It's five o'clock and our gallant commander, Major Oscar Pelletier, orders F Company to double up to the first firing line. The company obeys. We can see death coming now, but we run forward like real soldiers. I had hardly gone twenty paces when a bullet struck my right shoulder and I saw the blood gush out of my wound.

Lieutenant Lucien Larue

(died of his wound June 24, 1900)

(translated from French)

IT WAS JUNE 18, 1900, AND IT WAS THE FIRST TIME THAT A CANADIAN military unit had ever gone into battle outside North America—in South Africa, of all places, 13,000 kilometres from home. The temperature did not drop below a hundred degrees Fahrenheit that day until late in the afternoon, and there was no way of getting water to the troops. There was no cover from the lethally accurate fire of the Boers' Mauser rifles except tiny undulations in the terrain and the occasional anthill (and the Mauser bullets went right through the anthills without losing force). On this first day of battle the Canadian battalion lost eighty-three men killed and wounded—one-tenth of its total strength—and the Canadians were only able to withdraw from their exposed position after night had fallen. But what were they doing in South Africa in the first place?

The doctrine is new to me that under the British flag and under the Canadian flag, we should go and broaden people's minds with dum-dum bullets.

Henri Bourassa, House of Commons, *Debates*,

February 13, 1900

Even at the very end of the nineteenth century, the colonial wars that the British army fought from time to time put no serious strain on British manpower or resources. What preoccupied the British government was the growing possibility of a war with its European rivals—and even Britain's thirty-seven million people might be inadequate to meet the demand for military manpower in that kind of war. The ten million people in the white dominions were an extra source of manpower that might be needed in the ultimate crisis, and they had to be accustomed to the idea beforehand. Britain asked Canada to send troops to the South African war because it needed to set a precedent—and the Canadian government, of course, tried to avoid setting that precedent.

> We do not intend to accept any offer from volunteers. *We do not want the men and the whole point of the offer would be lost* unless it were endorsed by the Government of the Colony and applied to an organised body of the Colonial forces.
>
> Joseph Chamberlain, British colonial secretary, to Lord Minto, governor general of Canada, October 4, 1899

> [There was an attempt] to minimize the official appearance of Canada's offer, and to give it as far as possible the character of a volunteer expedition with a small amount of Government assistance.
>
> Lord Minto to Chamberlain, (Secret), October 20, 1899

The war in South Africa was caused by London's decision to bring back under imperial control the Afrikaans-speaking Boers (farmers) who had escaped British rule by trekking inland from Cape Colony in the 1830s. The landlocked Boer republics of the Transvaal and Orange Free State might have been left alone, but then the world's richest gold-fields were discovered in the Rand district of the Transvaal in 1885, and English-speaking miners and speculators poured in. They soon constituted a majority of the local population, but these Uitlanders (foreigners) were denied the vote and heavily taxed by the Transvaal government. They petitioned Queen Victoria for help—and their plea for intervention was backed by powerful British interests eager to gain direct control of the wealth now pouring out of the Rand.

As war approached in 1899, Israel Tarte, Prime Minister Sir Wilfrid Laurier's right-hand man in Quebec, asked in his newspaper, *La Patrie*, why French Canadians should be expected to fight the Boers, who were struggling to preserve "their independence, language and peculiar customs": the analogy with French Canada's own situation was painfully clear. But English Canada was burning with enthusiasm for the empire. On September 30, 1899, less than two weeks before the Boer War began, (militia) Colonel T. Denison, a prominent Toronto lawyer and founding member of the Imperial Federation League, told a special meeting of the Toronto Military Institute (in the presence of the provincial lieutenant-governor) why Canada should volunteer to fight in South Africa. It was not right to depend on Britain for defence without giving anything in return, Denison said—and besides, Canada could hardly expect to succeed in the dispute with the United States over the Alaska boundary "if we had not behind us the power of the empire." So the Canadian government should send a military contingent to South Africa at once: "We have been children long enough, let us show the empire that we have grown to manhood."

Lord Minto, the governor general, had only been in Canada a year, but he already knew too much about the country's politics to imagine that it would be a simple task for Laurier's government to send Canadian troops to South Africa. Moreover, Minto knew enough about South Africa to suspect that "money was playing a large part in the game," and to believe that a war against the Boers, if it came, would be "the most iniquitous we had ever engaged in."

> The fact is, if we fight we fight for Rhodes, Beit & Co, and the speculators of the Rand, and it makes me sick. We shall win, and

get all S. Africa, but how shall we have got it and what a nice heritage of bad feeling we shall have. . . .

From the point of view of a Canadian statesman, I don't see why they should commit their country to the expenditure of lives and money for a quarrel not threatening Imperial safety. . . . Sir Wilfrid [Laurier] told me the other day that if the question were reconsidered he shd [sic] call a cabinet council and ask me to be present. I hope he won't, for I shd be in a nice muddle, my chief at home thirsting for blood, all my friends here ditto, and myself while recognizing Imperial responsibilities, also seeing the iniquity of the war, and that the time for Colonial support has hardly yet arrived.

Lord Minto to Arthur Elliott,
(Private), September 28, 1899

However, Minto knew where his loyalty lay: he kept his doubts to himself and dutifully pressed the colonial secretary's demands for Canadian troops on Prime Minister Laurier. He had an eager accomplice in Major-General Edward Hutton, the British officer commanding the Canadian militia, who as early as July had drawn up a secret draft plan for the dispatch of a Canadian contingent of about twelve hundred men to South Africa.

On October 6 General Hutton wrote confidently to Lord Minto: "Considering that the Laurier Gov'. are expecting the Imperial Gov'. to force the Alaska Boundary Question upon the U.S. Gov'., and that Sir Wilfrid himself referred to arbitration or war (which latter can only mean armed intervention by the Imperial Gov'.), I do not understand how they can hold aloof from giving material support to the Imperial Gov'. in the present Crisis."

Minto applied the screws, sending Laurier a letter warning of the impression that may be produced in the Old Country by a decision on the part of Canada not to offer troops: "It may be taken perhaps to indicate a certain want of loyalty here, which would be all the more unfortunate at a time when we are relying a good deal upon Imperial support in the Alaska question."

J. S. Willison, the editor of the Liberal *Globe*, warned Laurier privately that he had only two alternatives: "either send troops or get out of office." Laurier travelled on to Ottawa and on the evening of October 13 held a meeting with leading members of the Liberal Party to try to find some solution that would not hopelessly alienate either English Canada or French Canada. A federal election was due within a year, and Laurier could not possibly regain office without the support of both Ontario and Quebec Liberals. Yet his Quebec lieutenant, Israel Tarte, and most other Quebec cabinet members were vehemently opposed to sending Canadian troops to the Boer War, while Postmaster General William Mulock, of the Ontario Liberals, stormed out of the meeting in fury when Laurier appeared to be hesitating on the question.

The prime minister had a compromise up his sleeve that he hoped would mollify all the conflicting demands on him—English Canadian, French Canadian and British—though it would not fully satisfy any of them. He proposed that the Canadian government should authorize the formation of a Canadian contingent and pay for its equipment and transportation to South Africa, after which the British government would pick up its costs. Moreover, rather than sending regular troops or an existing militia unit, which would give the proceedings too official a character, it should be a special force made up entirely of volunteers who wanted to go to this particular war. It was pure hairsplitting, of course, but that is what most politicians reckon they are paid to do.

Mulock and the Ontario Liberals accepted Laurier's compromise, and so did Israel Tarte, who had previously been threatening to resign from the cabinet if troops were sent. (Tarte did, however, insist on a public statement that this decision would not constitute a precedent for future Canadian actions.) So Laurier proceeded to authorize a force for South Africa without calling Parliament. The Order in Council, dated October 14, 1899, read:

> The Prime Minister, in view of the well-known desire of a great many Canadians who are ready to take service under such conditions, is of the opinion that the moderate expenditure which would thus be involved for the equipment and transportation of such volunteers may readily be undertaken by the Government of Canada without summoning Parliament, especially as such an expenditure under such circumstances *cannot be regarded . . . as a precedent for future action.* [emphasis added]

Laurier fully understood Britain's long-range purpose in seeking Canada's agreement to send troops overseas to this little war: that was why the announcement stressed that it did not imply any future commitments. But four days later Henri Bourassa, his close friend and political confidant, who quit his seat in Labelle in protest (and was re-elected by acclamation), summed up all the forebodings of French Canada in his public letter of resignation to Laurier. Bourassa wondered, somewhat ironically, whether the British empire was really in danger:

> Or are we face to face with an attempt at military federation of the Empire, a scheme dear to Mr Chamberlain? . . . The Order-in-Council providing for the enlistment and dispatch of our troops seems to state a reservation about the future, and excludes the present action from being considered as a precedent. *The precedent, Sir, is the accomplished fact.* [emphasis added]

Among English Canadians, swollen by "racial" pride and urged on by imperialist propaganda, there was little concern as to where this exciting little war might eventually lead Canada. The real debate was among French Canadians, who knew perfectly well where it was leading and didn't want to go there at all. But most of them still believed that their old bargain with Britain was essential to their national survival, even if the terms were being unilaterally changed by the British and the English Canadians. Laurier was considerably more than just an adroit political fixer, and there was real anguish in his reply to Bourassa's letter of resignation: "Tell me what attitude should the French Canadians take in the Confederation? . . . It is necessary that we choose between English Imperialism and American Imperialism. I see no other alternative. If there is one I wish you would indicate it to me." There probably was no alternative, given the state of English Canadian opinion at the time. But Bourassa was right: a precedent had been set.

As soon as the proclamation had been issued the volunteers flocked in, and 1,061 men on a one-year enlistment sailed for South Africa from Quebec City on October 30, 1899, as the 2nd (Special Service) Battalion, Royal Canadian Regiment. During the month-long voyage to Cape Town on the cramped little ship S.S. *Sardinian* (renamed the "Sardine" by the troops), the battalion commander discovered that few of his supposedly trained militiamen knew more than the rudiments of military drill. Lieutenant-Colonel William Otter, a native-born Canadian regular officer, had commanded militiamen in battle once before, during the North-West Rebellion of 1885, and he was determined not to lead raw troops into battle again. Although the Boer armies had inflicted a number of major defeats on the British by the time the Canadian troops arrived in South Africa, he managed to get two months at Belmont, near Kimberley, to turn his enthusiastic Canadians into soldiers before they were committed to battle. And they did quite well in their first big battle, at Paardeberg.

[Lord Roberts hesitated to attack], but agreed when the Royal Canadians volunteered to lead the action. Commanded by Colonel W. D. Otter, they were made up of "elegant extracts" from the best-known militia units in the Dominion, including a fine French company. . . .

In the dark of early morning they advanced to within sixty yards of the trenches before a withering fire compelled them to lie flat, but they kept up the attack for two hours. . . . Between 5 and 6 a.m. the Boers raised white flags above their trenches facing the Canadians. Other groups followed suit. . . . Roberts at once ordered the cease-fire.

Rayne Kruger,
Goodbye, Dolly Gray (London, 1959)

It was our turn to advance the trench. . . . At two we rose and advanced. Some had shovels and some had bayonets, for we did not know where we would need them. It was very dark, so dark that we were told to advance holding hands. . . . We had gone about 300 yards when orders came whispered along to entrench. We had only been at that a few minutes when again we got whispered word to advance. That order should not have been given.

We had gone about 100 yards when all of a sudden there was a blaze of rifles. We had walked right on top of the Boer trenches. In a flash we were on our faces hugging the ground. We dare not return the fire as it would give us away. To lift one's head would mean sure death.

Had the Boers not been afraid to rise up and fire low, not one of us would have escaped. . . . After a while we crawled or rolled back to our trench. . . . When dawn came the Boers found we had covered their position and so gave in. . . . Leavitt is not expected to live. Boers surrendered to the Canadians. Roberts said we did fine work. . . . Men are horribly shot. . . . Herb. Leavitt walked over four hundred yards after being shot. Anniversary of Majuba thus it was avenged.

Albert Perkins, Royal Canadian Regiment,
Battle of Paardeberg, February 27, 1900

Military historians depict battles in terms of logic and purpose, so Rayne Kruger's version of the final phase of the Battle of Paardeberg, written in 1959, is somewhat different from Albert Perkins's version, written in his diary on the day it happened. In fact, Colonel Otter didn't volunteer his regiment to do anything, and there was no planned attack. The Boer army of five thousand men was outnumbered six-to-one by the British, and it had been surrounded in open country and shelled incessantly for ten days. The Boers were hungry and demoralized by the time the Canadians went stumbling off into the dark to dig new trenches, and General Cronje had already decided to surrender. The Canadians just happened to be in the right place at the right time. But Paardeberg was the first British victory after four miserable months during which the British army had suffered one humiliating defeat after another at the hands of the Boers, so the imperialist press turned the Canadians into heroes, not just in Canada but throughout the empire.

After Paardeberg, the Royal Canadian Regiment took part in the great British advance that captured the capitals of both Boer republics by June 1900. A second contingent of one thousand men, once again raised at the Canadian government's expense, arrived in time to participate in the grim guerrilla war that followed the surrender of the main Boer armies, in which the Boers' farms were burned and their women and children rounded up and put in concentration camps, where about twenty thousand of them died of disease (or from being fed ground glass, according to the version still believed by most Afrikaners). Other Canadian units followed, although these were paid for not by Ottawa but by Britain or by private individuals like Lord Strathcona, the Canadian high commissioner in London, who spent £200,000 of his own money to raise and equip a six-hundred-strong cavalry regiment called (of course) Lord Strathcona's Horse.

In a guerrilla war the whole population is the enemy, including women and children, and like most of the British empire's troops in South Africa the Canadian soldiers frequently indulged in looting.

Small portable items were especially popular: "We had no trouble getting up at the right hour. You could hear alarm clock bells in nearly every heap of blankets and the veldt hummed like a telephone office. (When a soldier loots a house the first thing he grabs is the clock.)" Nevertheless, most of the Canadians felt a certain sympathy for the people they were fighting, and often their rural instinct to help out people in distress mingled strangely with the ruthless nature of modern counterinsurgency warfare. One of the most vivid accounts of the confused behaviour that often resulted was a long letter published in the Ottawa *Citizen* by its editor, Lieutenant E.W.B. Morrison, who was serving in South Africa with the Canadian Artillery. He described an attack on the village of Dullstroom in the northern Transvaal by Canadian troops.

The main street was full of smoke and fiery cinders and as the flames belched out in huge sheets from one side or the other our horses shied and plunged from side to side. The place was very quiet except for the roaring and the crackle of the flames.

On the steps of the church were huddled a group of women and children. The children didn't seem to know whether to cry or to be diverted by the spectacle. The women were white but some of them had spots of red on either cheek and their eyes blazed. Not many were crying. The troops were systematically looking the place over and as they got through with each house they burned it. Our Canadian boys helped to get their furniture out, much as they would do at a fire in a village at home. If they saw anything they fancied they would take it . . . but they had not the callous nerve to take the people's stuff in front of their faces. Of course in the case of shops it was different. . . .

I went into a very pretty little cottage standing in a rose garden on a side street. The C.M.R.'s [Canadian Mounted Rifles] and R.C.D.'s [Royal Canadian Dragoons] were looting it, but really helping the woman out with her stuff more than sacking the place. The woman was quite a good-looking lady-like person and the house was almost luxuriously furnished. She was breathlessly bustling about saving her valuables and superintending the salvage operations. A big dragoon would come up to her and say in a sheepish sort of way: "What you want next, lady?" and she would tell them and they would carry it out. As I stood looking on she turned to me and said: "Oh, how can you be so cruel?" I sympathised with her and explained it was an order and had to be obeyed. She was a good-looking female in distress and had quite the dramatic style of an ill-used heroine.

I certainly was sorry for her—we all were—until the house began to burn and a lot of concealed ammunition to explode and nearly killed some of our men. But all the same it was a sad sight to see the little homes burning and the rose bushes withering up in the pretty gardens and the pathetic groups of homeless women and children crying among the ruins as we rode away.

Lieutenant E.W.B. Morrison,

The Citizen, Ottawa, January 2, 1901

In all, over seven thousand Canadians enlisted for the South African war, of whom about five thousand arrived in time to see active service there. For most English Canadians at home the war began as an exciting distraction and ended at least as a successful demonstration of Canada's military prowess and its unbounded loyalty to the empire. But there were a few nagging details that detracted from this cheery view of the war: of the eight companies of the Royal Canadian Regiment that had enlisted in the first rush of enthusiasm, for example, six flatly refused to extend their service when their year's contract expired in September 1900.

Even in English Canada the war was not without its critics (although the criticism tended to be limited to farmers' weeklies and radical labour journals). Journalist and historian Goldwin Smith, was appalled by the brutalization of Canadian society. He particularly disliked the war toys being given to children: "puppets made by their distortions and squeaking to resemble the agonies of dying Boers." But the mainstream English-language press was overwhelmingly jingoist, and its readers had no quarrel with its view of war as a morally positive and virtually cost-free spectator sport.

In the late afternoon of January 12, 1901, two of the volunteers came home. To greet them, 2,000 citizens of Paris, Ontario, gathered at the Junction Station "to welcome" (in the words of the Paris *Star-Transcript*), "Our Boys who had Done so well—Gunners Arthur Flanagan and Alex Hume."

When the locomotive came puffing and clanking into the station, the band struck up "See the Conquering Heroes Come!" and the crowd raised a series of mighty cheers. Then, "as the Kaki clad heroes alighted, there arose upon the air that familiar refrain, 'Home, Sweet Home'". . . .

After passing along streets of decorated and illuminated houses and through lines of cheering spectators, and after serenading the homes of the heroes and setting off a mass of brilliant fireworks, the procession wound its way to the town hall, [where] a number of long orations were delivered. . . . George Shepherd, John Vine, and John Jefferson, Paris boys who were still in South Africa . . . together with the two returned heroes, were praised for the part they had played in helping to defend "Truth, Justice and Christian Civilization."

Donald A. Smith,
At the Forks of the Grand, vol. 2

But five volunteers was actually not a very impressive total for a town of over four thousand people. In fact, the average native-born English Canadian man was not nearly so eager to go off and die for the empire as his political leaders, his social betters and his newspapers assumed.

Almost 30 percent of Canada's volunteers for the Boer War were British immigrants, though they made up only 7 percent of the total population. Even more significantly, Canada's total contribution lagged far behind that of the other white dominions: it had a larger population than the Australian and New Zealand colonies put together, but they raised over three times as many men for the war. As for French Canadians—the "fine French company" of the Royal Canadian Regiment had francophone officers, but two-thirds of its men were actually English speakers. Only 3 percent of those who served in South Africa were French Canadian, although francophones comprised 30 percent of the Canadian population.

Individual French Canadians went to South Africa for the sorts of personal motives that will induce some men, at certain times in their lives, to go to a war almost regardless of what it is about, and once there they fought just as well as anybody else. But the war was almost universally unpopular in French Canada, where some of the young wore buttons bearing the name of Kruger, the Boer leader, to show where their sympathies lay. In March 1900 there were three days of rioting between English and French students in Montreal, and the militia had to be called out. Meanwhile, the more rabid sections of the English Canadian press called the French Canadians scoundrels and traitors and warned of civil war. Lord Minto, the governor general, reported that some eastern Ontario farmers went to bed at night with guns by their sides because they feared a French Canadian invasion.

Nevertheless, Laurier's compromise had succeeded. He won the 1900 election comfortably, and the country moved on to other concerns. In January 1903 the Alaskan boundary dispute was decided entirely in favour of the United States (because the British representative on the arbitration tribunal voted for the American case in order to avoid a clash with Washington). There was great fury in Ottawa and

across the country, and the two Canadian representatives on the tribunal refused to sign the decision in protest, but Laurier's government
survived. By then the South African War had been over for six months,
and all the Canadian volunteers had come home except for the 224 who
were buried there. It was a gentle enough introduction to the business
of fighting foreign wars—and not too many Canadians were bothered
by a little thing like a precedent.

> Long after the war, John Jefferson, who was then 99 years old, was
> asked why he had been eager to risk his life in South Africa: "I was
> young and foolish," he said, "and I wanted adventure." Then
> thoughtfully he added, "If I'd known then what I know now, I'd
> not have gone. I risked my life so that a few rich men could have
> full control of the gold and diamonds of the Transvaal. I was taken
> in by a lot of propaganda."
>
> *At the Forks of the Grand,* vol. 2

Having persuaded the colonial prime ministers to contribute troops to
the Boer War, Colonial Secretary Joseph Chamberlain invited them all
to another Imperial Conference in 1902. He now wanted to make the
arrangement permanent by getting them to commit some of their forces
to a special "Imperial Reserve" that would be available for service anywhere in the world.

> The weary Titan staggers under the too vast orb of its fate. We
> have borne the burden many years. We think it is time our chil-
> dren should assist us to support it.
>
> Joseph Chamberlain to the colonial prime ministers,
> Imperial Conference, London, 1902

Canada's contribution to the proposed Imperial Reserve would be one infantry brigade and one artillery brigade (about 4,500 men). That was only half the size of Australia's, but Chamberlain charitably explained the discrepancy by observing that Australia didn't have to worry about its own territory being invaded, whereas Canada had the United States next door. However, Laurier objected strongly to the whole idea, and the conference ended with no formal Canadian commitment.

There is a school in England and in Canada, a school which is perhaps represented on the floor of this Parliament, a school which wants to bring Canada into the vortex of militarism which is the curse and the blight of Europe. I am not prepared to endorse any such policy.

Sir Wilfrid Laurier to the House of Commons, Ottawa,
before the Imperial Conference of 1902

Laurier was equally unhelpful to the enthusiastic new British commander of the Canadian militia, Major-General the Earl of Dundonald, who was full of grand ideas for building new training areas and fortifications in Canada and raising the strength of the peacetime militia to 50,000, with provisions for expanding it instantly to 100,000 at the outbreak of war. He also wanted to make cadet corps compulsory in Canadian schools, in order to facilitate the further expansion of the Canadian army to 200,000 men in the early months of a war.

It was all still allegedly in the context of defending Canada against an American attack, but it is hard to believe that Lord Dundonald was not also thinking of other possible uses for a large Canadian army. Laurier was not amused: "You must not take the militia seriously, for though it is useful for suppressing internal disturbances, it will not be required for the defence of the country, as the Monroe Doctrine protects us from enemy aggression." By 1904 Dundonald had been dismissed, ostensibly for trying to stop political interference in militia affairs, but really for showing an excess of zeal. But despite Laurier's refusal to make any overt military commitments to imperial defence, he found it impossible to resist the undertow that was drawing Canada into deeper waters. A new Liberal government in Britain had more success in implicating Canada in imperial defence by subtle means than Joseph Chamberlain had ever had with his direct appeals, and the militia budget crept inexorably upward, more than quadrupling between 1898 and 1911.

It is hard to explain why this happened, for the key Canadian actors did not change. Laurier was prime minister continuously from 1896 to 1911, and his minister of militia throughout all fifteen years was Frederick Borden, a Nova Scotia physician, merchant and politician who combined a gregarious fondness for the social aspects of militia life (he played the fiddle or performed Scottish dances at the slightest provocation) with a stern appreciation of the militia's severely limited military and political value to Canada. There was, it is true, a steady rise in imperialist sentiment in English Canada throughout this period, and any Canadian government concerned to stay in office had to cater to it to a limited extent, but there was certainly no popular demand for a direct Canadian military contribution to the imperial forces.

Yet something must have changed to make Frederick Borden respond more favourably to imperial claims on Canadian resources. His own son had been killed in South Africa, which (as any amateur psychologist will tell you) could have made him more supportive of the empire his son had died for. A less convoluted reason would be simply the warm friendship and easy working relationship that Borden enjoyed with Percy Lake, a British officer with strong Canadian family ties who had already served in Ottawa in the late 1890s, and who returned after Dundonald's abrupt departure in 1904 to serve as Chief of the (Canadian) General Staff until 1908. (He then remained on as inspector general, at Borden's request, until 1910.) At any rate, while there was no sudden and drastic change of direction in Canadian military policy during this period, there was a steady drift.

23

It began with Ottawa's response when Britain began to concentrate its navy in home waters in 1905. As a natural consequence, London decided to withdraw its garrisons from the imperial naval bases at Halifax and Esquimalt. If Canada had not volunteered to take up the slack, the British would simply have abandoned these fortified bases. And that is what certainly would have happened if this withdrawal had occurred as little as a decade before, when Canadian governments had still been quite clear that the whole point of belonging to the empire was that it defended you. But by 1905 this simple formula was getting blurred, and so the Canadian government agreed to replace the British garrisons in Halifax and Esquimalt with its own regular troops, and increased the authorized size of the Permanent Force to four thousand in order to find the men. It was an ambiguous measure—you could argue that these bases were relevant to Canadian defence too, and not just imperial defence, if you really wanted to—and a pretty modest one. Besides, the Canadian government did not really expand its regular forces as promised: in 1908 the Permanent Force still numbered only 2,730 men. But it was the start of a trend.

Five years after Laurier's firm stand in 1902 against Canadian involvement in the "vortex of [European] militarism," there was another Imperial Conference in London, this time orchestrated by the much more congenial Liberal government of Sir Henry Campbell-Bannerman. There was no pushy Joe Chamberlain around in 1907 to queer the pitch with his demands for explicit military commitments from the overseas Dominions; just a soothing resolution that, without committing any of the governments at the conference to any particular action, affirmed the need for "a General Staff selected from the forces of the Empire as a whole, which . . . shall undertake the preparation of schemes of defence on a common principle." Each local section of the General Staff, in Ottawa and the other Dominion capitals, would advise the local government on military matters, but would exercise no powers of command.

There seemed no harm in that, no infringement of Canadian autonomy. Nor was there anything obviously objectionable about the special Imperial Defence Conference of 1909. There were no calls for Canada to earmark troops for overseas service, just a great deal of detailed work by the soldiers on the "standardization" of uniforms, weapons and training throughout the armed forces of the empire. The aim, as Prime Minister Herbert Asquith explained in the British House of Commons that year, was to ensure that "should the Dominions desire to assist in the defence of the Empire in a real emergency, their forces could be rapidly combined into one Imperial Army."

It was all carefully couched in conditional phrases, so as not to startle the prey, but in fact this was how Canada effectively became committed to defending Britain in Europe, even though there was never a parliamentary debate or a cabinet discussion of the question. After 1909 Canadian officers regularly attended Staff College courses in Britain, and British officers in Ottawa organized a Canadian branch of the General Staff. Even in English Canada, however, there were some alert observers who understood the implications of all this and had the gravest reservations about where it was leading. Dr. O.D. Skelton, then a professor at Queen's University and later the founder of the modern Department of External Affairs, wrote to a friend in a public letter of 1909:

> You calmly assume that in all the wars in which Britain is engaged she is "assailed" rather than "assailing." A recollection of the process by which the British Empire has expanded . . . might suggest that she has had at least her share of attacking. . . . There are real difficulties in any plan of Canadian neutrality while Britain is at war, I admit, but they are not so serious as the problems presented by the proposal to accept all Britain's wars as ours.

But voices like Skelton's were very scarce in English Canada. For most English Canadians, allegiance to Britain, even to the extent of automatic involvement in her wars, was not something to be weighed rationally. It was instinctive.

Politics wore a complexion strictly local, provincial or Dominion. The last step of France in Siam, the disputed influence of Germany in the Persian Gulf, the struggle of the Powers in China were not matters greatly talked over in Elgin; the theatre of European diplomacy had no absorbed spectators here. Nor can I claim that interest in the affairs of Great Britain was in any way extravagant. . . .

It was recognised dimly that England had a foreign policy, more or less had to have it, as they would have said in Elgin; it was part of the huge unnecessary scheme of things for which she was responsible—unnecessary from Elgin's point of view as a father's financial obligations might be to a child he had parted with at birth. It all lay outside the facts of life, far beyond the actual horizon. . . .

[But] belief in England was in the blood. . . . Indifferent, apathetic, self-centred—until whenever, down the wind, across the Atlantic, came the faint far music of the call to arms. . . . The sense of kinship, lying too deep for the touch of ordinary circumstance, quickened to that; and in a moment, "we" were fighting, "we" had lost or won.

Sara Jeannette Duncan,

The Imperialist, 1904

Sara Duncan's "Elgin" was actually Brantford, Ontario, where she grew up. Her novel was a fair representation of what people felt in the small towns of English Canada (and Canada was still a country of small towns): a sentimental loyalty to Britain that didn't count the cost, and never even imagined there might be much cost. Their only example, after all, was the Boer War, which had been cheap and glorious. The unobserved drift toward a European military commitment in the Militia

Department in Ottawa coincided with the drift of sentiment in English Canada, and would not rouse strong conflicting emotions in French Canada until and unless Canadian forces were actually sent to Europe.

If Laurier had realized what was happening, perhaps he could have stopped it. But as his prime ministership entered its second decade his political troubles began to mount, and he wasn't looking for any extra fights. Besides, it was hard to put your finger on exactly what was happening unless you immersed yourself in the flow of paper across the militia minister's desk.

So it is much to be doubted that Sir Wilfrid Laurier, preoccupied with preparations for an imminent election, even knew that in July 1911 his minister of militia approved the assignment of a staff officer to draw up plans for sending overseas a Canadian expeditionary force of 25,000 men—six times larger than the one Laurier had rejected a decade before. Let alone the fact that the staff officer in question was specifically instructed to assume that the force would be going to a war "in a civilized country with a temperate climate."

The election Laurier was preparing for in 1911 was precipitated by another defence-related issue: the British request for financial contributions from the dominions and colonies to keep the Royal Navy ahead of the Germans in the battleship race, and Laurier's preference for a modest Canadian navy under Canadian control. The Conservative leader, Robert Borden, mocked Laurier's "tinpot navy," and won the election by a landslide. But when he then gave Britain $35 million to buy new battleships in 1912, he at least hoped that Canada would in return have an increased influence on British foreign policy in the form of a permanent representative on the Committee of Imperial Defence. He was being naïve. In December 1912 the secretary of state for the colonies gently explained to Prime Minister Borden that imperial defence policy "is and must remain the sole prerogative of [the British] Cabinet, subject to the support of the House of Commons." In other words: We asked for your money, not your advice.

That was as far as British frankness went, however. The assumption that imperial defence included the defence of Canada itself was still accepted almost universally in Canada, but the old bargain was really long dead and starting to smell. By now the British had brought themselves to the point of admitting explicitly (but only in their secret documents) that they had no intention of helping Canada in the event of an attack by the United States, the only plausible military threat to Canadian interests.

The question of Britain's responsibility for Canadian defence had been repeatedly discussed (and generally fudged) by the Committee of Imperial Defence (CID) in London during the preceding decade, but in 1905 the decision never to send military help to defend Canada against the United States became explicit. In this year Sir Edward Grey, the foreign secretary, prevented the CID from discussing American infringements of the Rush-Bagot Treaty that limited the number and size of warships on the Great Lakes by stating that "he had no desire to discuss the question of what action would be taken by us in the event of a war with the United States."

The same conscious distortion of strategic realities was becoming British policy in personal contacts with Canadian politicians. In the summer of 1912, for example, when a joint CID meeting with Canadian ministers was being considered, Maurice Hankey, secretary of the CID, warned Prime Minister Asquith that they must at all costs avoid discussing the possibility of war with the United States with the Canadians:

The peculiar delicacy of this question is that in 1905 the Committee of Imperial Defence came to the conclusion that the Admiralty could not either themselves undertake the Defence of the Canadian Lakes, nor recommend any measures by which Canada could herself undertake their defence (a conclusion which vitiates any measure of military defence)—and *this conclusion was not discussed with Canada, nor communicated to her Government.* [Emphasis in original.]

This was a perfectly reasonable foreign policy for Britain; nor was it particularly bad for Canadian interests, since in fact the United States was very unlikely to embark on the conquest of Canada. But the British were guiltily conscious of the fact that many Canadians had not yet figured that out, and that they were exploiting obsolete Canadian fears of American attack in order to get Canadian support in *their* wars. Thus, for example, Sir William Nicholson, the chief of the Imperial General Staff, objected to sending Ottawa a document in 1912 saying that war with the United States was "in the last degree unlikely," and that Canadian coasts were safe from attack by any other power because *America* would intervene to protect them, on the grounds that this was inconsistent with London's continual encouragement to the Canadians to build up their own military power. That power was wanted for imperial defence purposes, and so the offending admission was deleted from the document sent to Ottawa.

However, apart from French Canada and a handful of English Canadians, few "colonials" were willing to question the imperial government's judgment on questions of war and peace. Moreover, Borden had to deal with the political realities of English Canada. It was the fantasy world of the *Boy's Own Annual*: the great majority of English Canadians were convinced that any war Britain got involved in would be just, and very many believed that war, or at least militarism, was a positive moral good. And although Borden himself was not a militarist, he had little choice but to give the portfolio of militia and national defence to Colonel Sam Hughes, a Conservative politician and part-time soldier who most certainly was.

Hughes had funded an entire political career on being an enthusiastic promoter of the militia. During the Boer War, when his offer to raise a volunteer force was rejected by the British, he had invented a job for himself with the railway line of communications forces there. The British commander-in-chief, Field Marshal Lord Roberts, tried beyond endurance by Hughes's bumptious and loudly stated conviction of his own inestimable military worth (especially compared to the plodding and limited intellects of mere professional soldiers), eventually sent Hughes home, but that rebuff simply confirmed Hughes in his lifelong belief that the only thing wrong with the British empire was the fact that it was run by the English. It was, nevertheless, the best game in town for a militarist, and in 1913 Hughes told an audience in Napanee, Ontario, why Canada needed a strong militia and an unconditional commitment to take part in the wars of the empire:

> To make the youth of Canada self-controlled, erect, decent and patriotic through military training, instead of growing up as under present conditions of no control, into young ruffians or young gadabouts; to ensure peace by national preparedness for war; to make the military camps and drill halls throughout Canada clean, wholesome, sober and attractive to boys and young men; to give that final touch to imperial unity, and crown the arch of responsible government by an inter-Imperial Parliament dealing only with Imperial affairs.

In 1913 an unprecedented three-quarters of the 74,000 men enrolled in Canadian militia regiments actually received a couple of weeks' training in camp—and Sam Hughes (who had recently promoted himself to major-general) was not in the least ambivalent about the fact that they would almost certainly be sent to fight overseas if war came. He delighted in sub-Nietzschean formulas that exalted mass action and war: "The old Saxon days have returned," he was wont to exult, "when the whole nation must be armed." And his audiences lapped it up; English Canada was ready to "fight the good fight." Like the hymn, however, that was an English, Protestant view of things—and the larger forces in the world were moving strongly against England.

THE ALLIANCE SYSTEM

MOST OF THE PEOPLE WHOSE LIVES WERE CHANGED OR ENDED BY what we now call the First World War believed they were taking part in a unique event of great moral importance, and the name we subsequently gave it strengthens that impression. Indeed, they were soon calling it "the war to end all wars." But the First World War was not an unusual political event, nor did it have any moral significance. It was just another turn in the cycle of "world wars" that stretched back to the beginning of the modern international system in seventeenth-century Europe. The list of principal players had changed over the centuries, but the basic rules of the alliance game had not.

During the 1400s and 1500s, powerful centralized governments began to extend their control over large parts of Europe. At the same time, rising wealth and better communications made it easier for large armies to operate far from home. Local wars had been constant in medieval Europe, but now a new pattern was superimposed on the old: the entire continent was transformed into a unified political and military arena.

Governments have always sought allies in their quarrels—it is an obvious way of increasing your own side's power—but they could now make useful alliances with distant states. The ideal allies were countries that also had a quarrel with your own enemy, but it was almost as good if they had a quarrel with one of your enemy's allies. So gradually, all the local rivalries coalesced into an interlocking political and strategic system that incorporated every great power in Europe—which soon came to mean, in practice, every great power in the world, since by the seventeenth century Europe already effectively dominated the entire globe. The modern international system was born, and in 1618 it produced the first "world war": the Thirty Years' War (1618–48).

If you find the phrase jarring in this context, it's because the images we normally associate with a "world war" are trenches, tanks, bomber fleets and nuclear explosions. Those are the things that make the world wars of the twentieth century different *technologically*. But as a *political* phenomenon such wars have a much longer history. In political terms, a world war is a war in which every recognized great power of the time is simultaneously involved, and in that very important sense the Thirty Years' War was indeed the first world war. By the 1630s Swedish troops were fighting Spaniards in the centre of Germany, and Catholic France was allied to Muslim Turkey.

> The use of alliances, Sir, has in the last age been too much experienced to be contested. . . . By alliances, Sir, the equipoise of power is maintained, and those alarms and apprehensions avoided, which must arise from daily vicissitudes of empire, and the fluctuations of perpetual contest.
>
> Sir Robert Walpole,
> House of Commons, London, 1741

The alliances that organized the great powers into a system were generally governed by the principle known as the "balance of power," a dynamic process in which coalitions were created against whichever state was seen as the most dangerous (the most powerful, or the most rapidly growing) in the system. In the early centuries of the system, alliances often had no formal existence in peacetime, although most states had a clear idea of whom they would be allied to when the next war came. But the absence of formal alliance structures meant that the "world wars" generally got off to a ragged start, with the various great powers joining in over a period of a number of years. Indeed, in the Thirty Years' War, there was no single year when *all* the European powers were involved, although all of them were active in the war for substantial periods of time.

In the next three world wars, the aspirant superpower was France, which had become by far the richest and most populous of the European states. The Thirty Years' War was followed at intervals of about half a century by the War of the Spanish Succession (1702–13); the Seven Years' War (1756–63); and finally by the Revolutionary and Napoleonic Wars (1792–1815). France was ultimately thwarted by alliances between all the states it threatened to dominate, but the game did not stop; after 1815 Britain emerged as the dominant power in the system. As an island country with no significant possessions on the European continent, Britain was considerably less threatening to the other great powers, but eventually, inevitably, a new challenger emerged: Germany. The result was the fifth world war—or, as it is more familiarly known, the First World War.

None of these transient superpowers and would-be superpowers was out to conquer the world, or even to rule all of Europe. They usually had specific, limited territorial goals, plus a general desire to become so powerful that they would be invulnerable to any challenge. But invulnerability for one state meant an unacceptable degree of vulnerability for everybody else in the game, so the alliance-forming process never lacked fuel. Nor were the world wars necessarily fought all over the world (though most of them affected several continents). The key criterion is simply that all the great powers are involved. And that being the case, world wars are unlike wars between two individual countries in the sense that they are not really about anything in particular. They are about everything in general.

As soon as continent-spanning alliances became the European norm, the possibility existed for wars in which there would be a general settlement of accounts. In theory, all the members of the winning alliance would achieve their particular national objectives, while all the members of the losing alliance would have to grant the victors' demands. It was never quite that simple in practice, but these wars invariably brought about a general reshuffle of the cards—and even in the long intervals of relative peace, the next general war became the implicit focus of the great-power competition. International politics became and remained a zero-sum game in which any gain in power by one state is automatically a loss for all the others in the system. As to why these "world wars" recurred with an interval of about half a century—that had to do, curiously enough, with the peace treaties.

> *Utrecht, Peace of*: a series of treaties (1713) concluding the war of the Spanish Succession. Philip V kept Spain . . . and Charles VI obtained Milan, Naples, Sardinia and the Spanish Netherlands. Britain gained Gibraltar, Minorca, Newfoundland and Acadia. . . . French expansion was halted.
>
> Longman's *Modern English Dictionary*

> Treaties are like roses and young girls. They last while they last.
>
> Charles de Gaulle, 1962

Once upon a time, schools taught European history as a succession of peace treaties at which everything was settled: the Treaty of Westphalia (1648), the Peace of Utrecht (1713), the Treaty of Paris (1763), the Congress of Vienna (1815), and so on. Fashions in teaching history have changed now, but as far as the causes of world wars are concerned, the old-fashioned history teachers were right—peace treaties did matter. They were the indisputable record of what territories the victorious side had won and what the defeated alliance had lost. Equally important, they were an implicit statement of each state's power, and therefore its position in the international pecking order. However, there was always the prospect of a rematch.

At the end of each world war the relative rank of the great powers, together with all the borders that depended on that, were defined and frozen. But afterward, as the years passed, some countries would grow more quickly than others, and some would change sides. At first the winners of the most recent world war would still be powerful enough to enforce the peace treaty, but gradually the chance would grow for another roll of the dice. The interval of around fifty years between world wars was simply the average time it took for enough changes to take place that the most recent peace treaty was no longer enforceable.

By then, some countries would reckon that their strength entitled them to more status, influence and territory than they were allocated in the last treaty, and others no longer had the strength needed to defend their gains under that treaty. The international system would become increasingly unstable, and at that point it took a deliberate decision by only one country to attack a neighbour, or even just a bluff that misfired, to start the slide into another general war. It would end in another treaty that readjusted everybody's "prestige" (in plain English, the ability to frighten their rivals) and changed a good many borders.

This system was well understood and generally accepted by educated Europeans down to the early nineteenth century. They lived, as Walpole said in 1745, amid "the fluctuations of perpetual contest." Yet by 1914 almost everybody had forgotten how the system worked. There had not been another world war on schedule in the mid-nineteenth century, so they saw themselves as the heirs of the "long peace" that had lasted, by then, just one year short of a century.

History does not run on rails. The mid-nineteenth-century world war almost happened several times, but it never quite got going. Instead, there was a series of smaller wars in which the great powers fought each other not all at once, but in rotation: Britain, France and Turkey against Russia in 1854, France and Italy against Austria in 1859, Austria against Germany in 1866, and Germany against France in 1870. They were quite big wars, but mostly quite short—which may partly explain why they didn't expand into a general war: there just wasn't enough time. It may also have helped that Britain was so powerful compared to all the others (at mid-century half the industrial capacity of the entire world was in the United Kingdom), and so safe from its rivals because of its complete domination of the seas, that it simply didn't feel the need to become involved in most of these wars. Whatever their outcomes, Britain would remain the undisputed superpower.

This series of short European wars, a string of firecrackers rather than a single great explosion, nevertheless had the cumulative political effect of a world war. It was in these wars that the Austrian empire ceased to be a power of the first rank, and the newly united German empire became one. Italy emerged as a power (albeit a minor one), and France dropped down a peg. Various territories changed hands: Venetia, Alsace-Lorraine, Schleswig-Holstein and Romania, among others. Political realities having been adjusted to conform to the actual strength of the various great powers, stability then returned to the system for around another half century. But not forever, of course.

In the last decades of the nineteenth century Germany grew very fast, Russia grew even faster (although from a lower starting point) and British power went into relative decline. By the beginning of the twentieth century, world war was in the air again, and the alliances that would fight it were solidifying fast. Between 1898 and 1914, a crisis that brought Europe to the brink occurred almost every other year.

> If there is ever another war in Europe, it will come out of some damn silly thing in the Balkans.
>
> Prince Otto von Bismarck, 1898

There is a grand old tradition, when writing about the outbreak of the First World War, to start with the assassination of Archduke Franz Ferdinand of Austria by a nineteen-year-old Serbian called Gavrilo Princip in Sarajevo in June 1914, and follow the escalating diplomatic crisis of the following month in simulated astonishment at how such a huge event could have grown from such a little cause. The writer can then, according to taste, castigate the statesmen and generals of the time impartially for letting this needless calamity happen, or try to fasten the blame on some specific player (usually Germany, if you're writing in English or French) who allegedly *wanted* the war and made it happen. People want a big disaster to have a big cause and a recognizable villain. But if you really want to understand how such a great war grew out of such petty events, you would do better to consider the Power Law.

The Power Law describes how so-called critical systems like those that produce earthquakes and forest fires are completely undiscriminating about the scale of the event. Most events will be on the smaller side, of course, but you don't need special causes to get a huge one: an event of any size can happen literally at any time.

A critical system is one that is inherently unstable, and locks in more and more instabilities as time goes by. Think of the accumulating stresses along a fault line between two continental plates, or the accumulation of inflammable debris on the forest floor. From time to time there will be earthquakes and forest fires, but most of them will be small. The Power Law says that any one of them could be the Big One.

To know if a particular class of events is subject to the Power Law, you just graph the scale of the events against their frequency. If it turns out to be a straight relationship where doubling the size of the event decreases the frequency by half—or makes it four times less likely, or sixteen times, or any other power of two—then you are dealing with a critical system, and you can forget about seeking major causes for bigger events. A random pebble is sixteen times less likely to cause a huge avalanche than a little one, but it *can* cause either.

British physicist Lewis Richardson was the first to notice that wars are subject to the Power Law, and it was confirmed in 1983 by Jack Levy, currently Board of Governors' Professor of Political Science at Rutgers University, in a massive study entitled *War in the Modern Great Power*

System, which spanned the entire period 1495–1975. If you measure the size of every war by its casualties, then doubling the size exactly halves the frequency. This means that great wars do not need great causes. Once sufficient strains have accumulated in a critical system, a world war can strike out of a clear blue sky, as it did in the summer of 1914.

All that stuff you read in conventional accounts of 1914 about the interlocking military alliances and the even more intricately interlinked railway timetables that delivered millions of mobilized troops to the frontiers of the great powers is perfectly true: the great powers really had built a system that was bound to fail catastrophically sooner or later. But those were precisely the instabilities and strains that made international politics into a critical system in the early twentieth century. The question of whether we still live in a critical system today will have to wait until later.

CHAPTER 2

A LONG WAY FROM HOME

PARIS, ONTARIO WAS, IN 1914, A STEPHEN LEACOCK SORT OF TOWN: credulous, not too wise in the ways of the world, but enthusiastic and eager to please. It would be wrong to say that the news of the outbreak of war that August struck Paris like a bolt from the blue. That would imply threat. Rather the war in Europe (not yet the Great War, let alone the First World War) came as a welcome diversion at the end of the summer.

A crowd began to mill around Grand River Street. Prominent citizens trumpeted their considered opinions. One said: "The war will be over within three months. The Russians will roll in from the east and the British and French from the west, and they'll meet in Berlin before Christmas." The crowd vigorously cheered his perspicacity.

Then the Citizens' Band formed up in front of the fire hall and began to play martial music. The crowd grew larger. It sang "The Maple Leaf Forever," "Rule Britannia," and "God Save the King." Members of the Scout Bugle Band ran home for their bugles. As Bugler Grenville Whitby rushed from the house, his father said: "War's a serious thing. You shouldn't be out tonight making a noise." Grenville heedlessly ran down the street, blowing shrill blasts. The crowd formed itself into a procession, and led by blaring bugles and thumping drums, paraded along William, Willow and Dundas Streets. Torches smoked and flared, and in their light, eyes gleamed with exultation.

Donald A. Smith,

At the Forks of the Grand, vol. 2

In Montreal on 1 and 3 August, when it was already clear that France, at least, was going to be fighting Germany, huge crowds paraded in the streets waving British and French flags and singing "La Marsellaise" and "Rule Britannia." When Britain formally declared war on Germany on 4 August (automatically taking Canada with it), thousands of people came out to cheer in Winnipeg, Regina, Edmonton, Vancouver and Victoria. In the other Paris, in France, the newspaper *Le Temps* saw something deeply poetic in the fact that English Canadian blood would now be shed for France, while French Canadians bled for England.

Two weeks later in the House of Commons in Ottawa, Sir Wilfrid Laurier, the former prime minister, stood up and declared: "We are British subjects, and today we are face to face with the consequences which are involved in that proud fact." By then the Conservative government of Prime Minister Sir Robert Borden had already offered to send one division (22,500 men) to Europe. It had secretly bought two submarines that had just been built for the Chilean navy, and had placed Canada's two decrepit training cruisers at the disposal of Britain's Royal Navy. Maybe Borden's government could have responded a little less eagerly, but it could not really have stayed out of the war unless it had decided to declare Canada independent then and there. Nobody had that in mind, not even the most ardent of Quebec Nationalists.

Canada, an Anglo-French nation, tied to England and France by a thousand ethnic, social, intellectual and economic threads, has a vital interest in the maintenance of the prestige, power and world action of France and England.

Henri Bourassa, *Le Devoir*, September 8, 1914

Canada was a very different country a century ago: the great majority of its eight million people were actually of British or French descent, and few English Canadian families had been in the country for more than two or three generations. Nevertheless, sentimental ties are not the same as "vital interests," and there were no practical reasons why Canada's long-term interests depended on the maintenance of British power and prestige (except for the old but fading concern about American expansionism). However, plenty of short-term interests were in play—many Canadian and British business interests were linked, for example—and in any case Canada was not a fully independent nation in 1914. Henri Bourassa, whose newspaper was the strongest public voice of French Canadian nationalism, would probably have preferred to copy the policy of the United States and declare Canada neutral in the war, but he understood that emotional, commercial and legal factors meant that Canada had to support the Entente powers (Britain, France and Russia). However, he stressed that it should do so "to the measure of its strength, and by appropriate means"— which did not, in his opinion, include sending Canadian troops to Europe.

The Canadian territory is nowhere exposed to the attacks of the belligerent nations. As an independent nation, Canada would today enjoy perfect security. . . . It is then the duty of England to defend Canada and not that of Canada to defend England.

Henri Bourassa, *Le Devoir*, September 8, 1914

But it was no use arguing. The national mood, at least in English Canada, would not have stood for anything less than full Canadian military commitment to the war. There was probably not a single person in Canada in August 1914 (indeed, there were not even very many in

Europe) who genuinely understood how the war had come about, but that didn't make any difference.

————

Q. Do you remember why you joined up?

Spirit of adventure, mostly, I think, at that time. Because I don't think one knew, had any idea what was ahead, you know. And I think that was the only thing that interested me then, was to see the world.

Nursing Sister Mabel Rutherford, Toronto

Q. Did you feel at the time that there was any distinction between Canada and Great Britain?

No, no. The Empire was at stake. . . . They were peace-loving people, but the thing was on the barrel-head, and you almost unquestioningly said: "Well, if they need me, I'll go."

Ted Watt, Victoria, Royal Canadian Navy

Although there was a tiny handful of pacifists in Canada, English Canadian popular culture was quite overtly militarist and jingoist. The young had no doubts about the war; nor did most of their elders. In 1914 they were not just English Canadians; they were *British* Canadians.

But the response of ordinary French Canadians was another story entirely. It was not a question of language or culture, basically, but simply of geographical perspective—of where people thought they lived in the world. When the call for volunteers went out, recent immigrants from France enlisted just as readily as the most enthusiastic English Canadians: the town of Trochu in Alberta, which had been settled by French ex-cavalrymen in the years before the war, virtually emptied in 1914 as the men went back to fight for their mother country. But French Canada itself had long ago abandoned the delusion that it was part of Europe, and few

French Canadians saw any reason to fight in its wars. They also soon became aware of a particularly good reason for remaining civilian: the minister of militia and national defence, Colonel Sam Hughes.

Hughes was a bullying Ontario Orangeman who neither knew nor trusted French Canadians. Colonel Willoughby Gwatkin, on loan from the British army as chief of the General Staff, had prepared careful mobilization plans in 1912 that would have included French Canadian participation, but Hughes was determined to do everything his own way: finally he had a real war and the power to run it.

Casting aside the existing mobilization plans, which would have carried out the first phase of the process at the local militia centres, Hughes simply sent telegrams directly to every battalion in the militia, inviting the hundred-odd part-time colonels who commanded them to show up with as many volunteers as they could find. They were invited to bring them, moreover, not to the perfectly adequate training area already in existence at Camp Petawawa in the Ottawa valley, but rather to a wilderness area at Valcartier near Quebec City. (This served no military purpose, but it did serve the business interests of Sir William Mackenzie and Donald Mann, two good friends of Hughes who happened to own the only railway link to Valcartier.)

Hughes personally supervised the creation of a central training depot at Valcartier, transforming woods and sandy valleys into a huge training camp with streets, buildings, telephones and four miles of rifle ranges in about three weeks: his ability to bring order out of chaos was almost as great as his propensity for creating chaos in the first place.

Hughes considered himself a military genius, despite the fact that he had no serious military training or experience. Indeed, he considered his ignorance of conventional military procedures and practices to be a positive virtue, since he completely believed the southern Ontario myth, a hallowed relic of 1812, which maintained that the sturdy, independent-minded Canadian volunteer, however lacking in training, was intrinsically superior to the over-trained and unimaginative regular soldier.

43

Throughout his career he seized every opportunity to demean and publicly humiliate Canada's relatively few professional soldiers—so in 1914, instead of using the Royal Canadian Regiment, which contained most of the trained infantrymen in Canada's three-thousand-strong Permanent Force, to train the flood of volunteers, he immediately sent it to Bermuda to replace a British regiment heading for France. (It did not reach France itself until 1916.)

At Valcartier, therefore, it was the blind leading the blind, and Hughes largely ignored even the structures and skills that were available in the militia. He simply disregarded the existing militia units and their traditions, creating entirely new battalions for the Canadian Expeditionary Force (CEF) that were identified solely by their numbers and trained from scratch at Valcartier. In his appointments of commanders, personal favouritism was the only visible criterion: at least one-third of all the officers who went overseas in 1914–15 had not yet met even the very modest militia training standard for their rank. And since many more militia officers and men had shown up at Valcartier than would be needed for the single infantry division that was to sail for Europe in October, there was tremendous chaos.

In fact, one rather suspects that it was Sam Hughes's instinct to create chaos quite deliberately, since that was the environment that afforded the greatest scope for the kind of behaviour he revelled in. The autumn of 1914 presented him with the opportunity to dispense patronage on a scale that he had never previously dared to imagine, and he seized it with both hands. The relatively scarce jobs for officers in the First Canadian Division were allocated almost entirely on the basis of friendship rather than professional competence (with the inevitable result that "everybody was at everybody's throat," as one militia officer put it), and Hughes even created an entire parallel structure of "supernumerary officers" who would go overseas with the division although they had no jobs to do. He spent most of his time at Valcartier, and when he wasn't holding court to receive the petitions of officers seeking posts of command he was often to be found galloping around the camp, shouting orders and impartially cursing everybody as he went.

> From time to time during the mobilization and training of the First Contingent at Valcartier, there were disturbing reports as to the conduct of the Minister of Militia at Valcartier. On September 16, the Governor-General reported to me that Hughes' language to his officers had been violent and insulting.
>
> Prime Minister Sir Robert Borden, *Memoirs*, vol. 1

> Mr Borden is a most lovely fellow, as gentle-hearted as a girl.
>
> Minister of Militia Sam Hughes, 1914

Borden did not have a high opinion of Hughes: "while he was a man of marked ability and sound judgement in many respects, his temperament was so peculiar, and his actions and language so unusual on many occasions, that one was inclined to doubt his usefulness as a Minister." But whether because of his gentle heart or his fear of Hughes's powerful allies in the "militia lobby" and the Ontario wing of the Conservative Party, Borden did not remove Hughes. Instead the "general" was left free to swagger around in uniform, blustering and posturing—and he did not even consent to organize the relatively few French-speaking volunteers who risked placing themselves in his power into a single francophone battalion. Out of some 33,000 men who sailed for Europe in the First Contingent on October 3, 1914, only 1,245 were French-speaking, and by the time the contingent reached France as the First Canadian Division, only one of its forty-eight infantry companies was French-speaking. French Canadians were profoundly unimpressed.

Out of personal conviction or self-interest, individual French Canadians tried to swim against the tide. Dr. Arthur Mignault of Montreal, for one, offered to contribute $50,000 toward raising a

French-speaking regiment. Borden's government went along with the proposal, and Mignault's efforts were blessed by Sir Wilfrid Laurier and a number of other French Canadian politicians. But it wasn't quite enough. When the 22nd Battalion sailed from Quebec in 1915 with the Second Contingent, it had to be brought up to strength by drafting in French Canadian recruits from other units raised in Quebec.

But it wasn't just the French Canadians who were reluctant. Right from the start, there were very big differences in the rate of volunteering: far more volunteers came from English-speaking areas than French, of course, but also more from the West than the East, and more from the rootless cities, where the newspapers had the greatest influence, than from the settled rural areas. In fact, native-born Canadians of every sort, apart from the very young, the adventurous and the economically desperate, seemed somewhat reluctant to go and fight the Germans.

At the start, too, it was easy to find socially acceptable reasons not to volunteer. In 1914, for example, farmers still needed their children's labour, and since Britain depended heavily on Canadian agricultural products, they could always argue that their sons were more valuable to the war effort at home. And if all else failed, you could pretend you wanted to enlist and then get your mother to write you a note. In the early days of the war, volunteers would be turned away if their wives or mothers wrote a letter proving that their menfolk were needed at home.

> Our Canadian women should realise that their objections, unless made for good cause, are highly unpatriotic. The privilege of objection was granted to prevent abuse in enlistment by married men, but if Canada is to maintain her independence the Canadian soldier must do his duty and his wife should not restrain him from selfish motives.
>
> Colonel E.W.B. Morrison,
> in a public protest, August 19, 1914

But many Canadian women, blinded by selfishness, did not want their husbands and sons killed in order to protect Canada's "independence." Despite all the public oratory and flag waving, the imperialist *Montreal Star* noted with some dismay on August 10 that only 20 percent of the volunteers so far were Canadian-born. A month later the *Canadian Military Gazette* somewhat peevishly complained that there were 800,000 men eligible for military service in the country, so there should have been hundreds of thousands volunteering. There weren't. In the Toronto area one regiment, the Mississauga Horse, was said to have only one native Canadian for every six or eight British-born volunteers. Montreal couldn't meet its quota for the First Contingent at all and the difference had to be made up with men from Winnipeg and the West. And the pro-British establishment's fears were correct: a large majority of those who joined the First Contingent were not Canadian-born.

I came from England, Folkestone, down in Kent. I came in '12.

Q. And when did you join the army?

In '14.

Q. Did you go overseas at once?

At once, yes, the First Contingent. We went down to Montreal and we shipped from Quebec—thirty-two boatloads. At that time, we were one of the biggest convoys that had ever crossed the Atlantic.

Q. Why did you join in '14?

Well, I think it was, as I look back at it, genuine patriotism. Maybe I changed my mind afterwards, after we got there. But at the time it was genuine.

Q. But you'd only been in Canada two years.

Two years, yes. So I was looking at it probably from an English point of view.

George Turner, Edmonton, Canadian Army

George Turner survived the trenches and came back a devout Canadian (there's nothing like a war for moulding a national identity), but people like him formed a very high proportion of Canada's volunteers, especially in the early years. In fact, during the three years to October 1917, when all enlistments were voluntary, 49 percent of the people who joined the Canadian forces were British-born immigrants, although they were only 11 percent of the population. And that was why the West bore such a huge burden in the war. In 1914 there were barely a million and a half people in the four western provinces, a mere fifth of Canada's total population, but almost two-fifths of the soldiers who served overseas came from the West: that was where the bulk of the recent British immigration had gone, so that was where the volunteers were.

> Yes, I was at the station, because I can remember how far they leaned out of the windows, waving to the people. And the way the mothers and the wives tried to clasp their hands as they went, as the train drew out very slowly, and this lament going on in the background: "Will ye no' come back again?"
>
> Naomi Radford, Edmonton

The most extreme case was Alberta, which had been settled almost entirely during the preceding fifteen years. In the first year of the war Alberta contributed 22,325 men to the Canadian army (in addition to 5,600 British, French and Belgian reservists who went back to fight for the Old Country in its own army), out of a total population of less than half a million. From the Edmonton city area alone, seven thousand men enlisted, and the little town of Strathmore, east of Calgary, gained the distinction of being the most patriotic town in Canada. There, *every* eligible man joined the army in the fall of 1914, except one—and he went as soon as the harvest was over. But then Strathmore had only been settled nine years before, and most of the settlers were from Britain.

I remember the start of it. I remember when they assassinated the Archduke. And I remember all the boys around, you know, joining up—the older ones.

There were an awful lot of people from the town went . . . . My people were all very patriotic about the whole thing, and that. But I don't think anyone expected it to go on as long as it did. I think, you know, in those days people thought the British Empire was pretty well invincible.

Serres Sadler, Strathmore, Alberta
(too young for the First World War, so he went next time)

There was, in fact, a fairly consistent pattern in the rate of volunteering in Canada, a curve sloping down from west to east. The longer a region had been settled, the more aware people were of their own separate identity and interests as Canadians, and the less they tended to see Britain's war as their own (however many flags they waved). The split between immigrants and native-born was very noticeable in a town like Paris, Ontario, where just about half the population was Canadian-born, while the remainder were English immigrants attracted by the booming textile industry there. By mid-1915 the English-born in the town were openly accusing the Canadian-born of being "slackers." One person wrote to the local paper:

In the present great war for the freedom of our beloved Empire, it behooves us in Canada to spring up from this drowsy slumbering attitude that the Canadian born are assuming towards our Motherland . . . . What is our little town of Paris doing in its share to win from the uncivilized, barbarous Hun? They, if we are beaten in this war, would come over from the United States and Germany in their millions, to take everything over from a pin to our federal government.

If the Germans are victorious, the very first thing they would do would be to take over Canada. . . . They would fill every city,

town and village, and hold drunken, debauching orgies, in cele-
brating their victory, and our women and children would be the
victims of these drunken, barbarous wretches.

Every minister of the church, every woman and girl, should
do all they can to encourage all young men who have any grit in
them to put on the King's uniform. . . .

At the Forks of the Grand, vol. 2

The clergymen of the Paris Ministerial Association did their best,
organizing a great public rally as part of an approach that became
known as "coercive recruiting": coercion by public opinion. The drums
banged, the buglers played, and the speech makers orated, but only
twenty-eight more recruits marched up to the platform "as though at a
revival meeting," to be sent off with the usual "crisp 10-dollar bill" and
a parcel of comforts from the Ladies' Patriotic League.

Further east in the Maritimes, where there were virtually no recent
English immigrants, recruiting was even harder.

Must we say hereafter with bated breath that this is the city and
Province of the Loyalist? Must we say at this momentous period,
fraught with the gravest responsibilities ever cast upon British people, that there exists within the borders of this Province at least
5,000 men, physically fit, and from whom a bare 800 have displayed sufficient courage and patriotism to unsheath the sword in
defence of their homes?

M. Frink, Charlottetown, Prince Edward Island,
June 29, 1915

Prince Edward Islanders might be "Loyalist" by tradition, but by
1914 they had been there long enough to notice which continent they
lived in, and they did a lot less volunteering than British Columbians.
As for the one big dip in the curve, Quebec—as Laurier said in Parliament,

defending the French Canadians' evident reluctance to die for Britain: "Enlistment [varies inversely] with the length of time that the men have been in the country. . . . French Canadians . . . have been longer in the country than any other class of the community."

Q. Were you excited at the time, about going to war?
Oh yes, it was an adventure, you know. We were all a bunch of young people, eh? I was about the youngest in the crowd, but I took it as an adventure, you see. Because the story was that we'd never see the war, because it would be all over by the time we got to England.

Leslie Hudd, Sherbrooke, Quebec, Canadian Army

After three months of training in England in the winter mud of Salisbury Plain, the Canadians began to move to France. The first unit to enter the trenches, in January 1915, was "Princess Patricia's Canadian Light Infantry" (named after the daughter of the governor general). It was a special battalion made up mainly of ex-British regulars and Canadian veterans of the Boer War, which had been raised and equipped with $100,000 donated by Captain A. Hamilton Gault, a Montreal millionaire and militia officer who had fought in South Africa. (Gault served in France with the battalion himself, and eventually lost a leg in battle.) But even the large number of experienced soldiers in the PPCLI were at a loss for how to deal with this very new kind of battlefield, with its barbed wire and machine guns and crushing artillery barrages.

Of course you have read about the trenches in the papers. Well, our battalion has had four spells in them. Three or four days is usual. No charges made or repulsed, but we have had a number of casualties. . . .

Our trenches are from 75 to 120 yards from the German trenches. Wise lads, too. The first night in, they called out to know if we were Canadians. How are things on Hastings Street? They also sang an English song or two.

The English Tommies that were here last fall are the ones who had it bad. We have come to trenches all prepared and drained, and in some places, paved with boards, brush, galvanized iron or even bricks. There are dugouts built and floored with straw.

The cooking and smoking, with a little would-be witticisms with Fritzies across the way . . . while away the tedious hours.

Jairus Maus (Paris, Ontario)

Enlisted in PPCLI in Vancouver, January 1915

At the Forks of the Grand, vol. 2

During the wettest English winter in living memory, the Canadian troops had already got rid of some of the more useless bits of equipment foisted on them by the political patronage that infested the Canadian militia organization (such as boots that disintegrated in the wet). But when the battalions of the First Canadian Division began to cross over to France in mid-February, their men were still carrying the Ross rifles that were Sam Hughes's pride and joy. He'd been warned by the British army that they were excellent target rifles but useless for sustained fire in combat—but nobody could ever tell Sam Hughes anything. The Canadians first saw heavy fighting at Ypres in March:

How the Germans knew a bunch of green Canadians were going to take over this part of the Ypres front, I don't know, but . . . they opened up on us, and that was our first baptism of fire as a unit.

So the troops on our right, the British, put up this rapid fire with their Lee-Enfields. They were so disciplined that it sounded like a hundred machine-guns going off at one time. So at our front, the Canadian front, we tried to do the same thing [starts to cry].

Q. What happened?

Well, the boys were fighting away there and trying to do the rapid fire, but you see the Ross rifle had a lock bolt with grooves in it. So it went all right for a while, but then we noticed that we couldn't bring the bolt back. When the rifles got hot, they jammed.

So what did we do? 'Course we were under cover, eh? We'd sit up and try to use our foot to push the bolt down. That's when it started. Over that rifle I bet we lost about 1500 or 2000 men either wounded or killed, just over that silly damn thing. It was a lovely target rifle, but as an active service rifle, no, no.

Leslie Hudd

I have been seeing a bit of real warfare recently. Three nights ago we charged and took a German trench.

Under the flare of rockets they put up, they sent a terrific rifle fire into us. But almost immediately on our reaching their trenches, they fled. Our Battalion, the 16th, was only supposed to be supporting another battalion, which was to do the charging, but a great many of our boys reached the trench as soon as any. When we were first told to take a German trench, my nerves were a bit jumpy, otherwise one is warmed up and excited and doesn't care. But it was a sad, sad roll-call. Half or more of my chums were missing. Some, no doubt, will recover.

After getting through this bout alright, I was mug enough to volunteer yesterday morning to leave a trench for a building some distance off, where the cook had some soup for our boys, who needed something bad enough. The shell fire was heavier than I anticipated, and so I'll have a little holiday. . . . One in my right forearm and two in my left leg, but all clean wounds, although my leg is broken. . . . In all probability, I will convalesce in England.

Jairus Maus, letter home of April 1915
At the Forks of the Grand, vol. 2

Maus left the line just before the Canadians came to be among the first troops in the world to experience a new horror. From the middle of April there had been persistent warnings that the Germans were going to use poison gas. There were reports of a German rush order in Ghent for twenty thousand mouth protectors "to protect men against the effects of asphyxiating gas," and Belgian intelligence estimated that the attack would come on the front where the German 26th Reserve Corps were dug in. "All this gas business need not be taken seriously," replied French headquarters. And it wasn't.

Facing the German 26th Reserve Corps were colonial troops: Canadians of the First Division and Algerian troops of the French African Light Infantry. When the Germans released the greenish-yellow gas on 22 April, the Algerians fled and the Canadians had to stretch their line out to cover that part of the front, too.

> Instead of being two or three men every two or three feet, we were one man to about four or five feet. . . . I was gassed, but you see, we had no idea what it was.
>
> We saw this stuff coming over, it was sort of mist. The wind was blowing our way, towards the trenches. So next we knew it was gas, chlorine gas. The only thing we could do, we covered our mouths. So we took a piece of shirt, anything you could get, and wet on it. I don't know if I should say how we wet on it, but we wetted it, anyway, and wrapped that around our faces, and we had to take a chance on our eyes.
>
> Anyway, it worked some, but we lost a lot of men over that. It was hell, that gas. . . . We did what we could, and when we were taken from the trenches, we got a big name over in England over this. . . . The papers were full of what the great, brave Canadians . . . [cries].
>
> Leslie Hudd

It was a screeching of shells, men falling on all sides, Frenchmen retreating in disorder, yelling all kinds of things we could not understand, until they saw our gallant boys in khaki advancing in one thin line at the double, and they rallied with shouts of "Brave Anglaise". . . . We drove the Germans back, a few hundreds of Canadians against thousands of Germans. But I don't think they knew there was only such a small number of us. It was getting dark . . . anyhow, we gained the situation and dug holes into the ground, and neither the Germans nor their terrible shelling could move us, and wasted out and tired as we were, doing without sleep and not much food, we stuck to them five days and nights, until we were relieved . . . . We have now got pads to put over our nostrils and mouth, ready for the poisonous gas that those German curs use. . . .

You would hardly know me now. I have aged quite a bit in looks, also in feelings, and got very thin. It is all with the continued hardships and nerve-racking things we have to endure. Well, dear mother, I will close, hoping I am alive to receive your answer to this letter.

John Carroll (Paris, Ontario),
machine-gunner, 3rd Brigade, CEF

The 1st Canadian Division did all that was asked of it and finished with a desperate bayonet charge. But the cost was terrible. Hundreds of good, willing lads gave up their lives without a murmur. Personally, I suffered from a bullet wound in the right side of my body and two in my right leg. Those in my leg are healing fine, but the one through my body, of course, is not doing well. . . . I was lying on my side firing when I got the first bullet through my leg, followed shortly after by another in the right side, and a second in the leg. . . .

Ask Lorne to find out for me how Knill, Larin, Cullum and Murray are. Never saw any of them after the fight started, and am anxious about the fellows. I do hope that the Paris boys come through alive, for it was terrible work.

I heard a good joke while lying on the road at Ypres. One of our stretcher bearers asked a severely wounded Irishman if there were many dead on the field, and he answered, "Sure, it's alive with dead men."

A.D. Fraser (Paris, Ontario), April 1915
(Napoleon Larin and A.E. Cullum were wounded,
and Ivor Murray was dead. Fraser survived the war.)

The Canadians lost 6,341 men at Ypres, and two weeks later, at Festubert, they were asked to do it again. They were short of high-explosive shells and the map of the objective was printed upside down, so Brigadier-General Arthur Currie, the ranking Canadian officer, asked for a postponement of the attack. He was refused. The Canadians managed to advance six hundred yards and captured the eastern hedge of an orchard. Their casualties were 2,468.

Prime Minister Borden stood up in the House of Commons and said: "They have proved themselves equal to any troops in the world, and, in doing so, they have brought distinction and renown to the Dominion." It was all true, but the gap in comprehension between those at home and those at the front was growing as wide as the Atlantic. Talbot Papineau (grandson of the leader of the 1837 rebellion), who was serving in Princess Patricia's Canadian Light Infantry, did not think in terms of distinction and renown any more:

I hate this murderous business. I have seen so much death—and brains and blood—marvellous human machines suddenly smashed like Humpty Dumpties. I have had a man in agony bite my finger when I tried to give him morphine. I have bound up a man without a face. I have tied a man's foot to his knee when he told me to save his leg and knew nothing of the few helpless shreds that remained. He afterwards died.

I have stood by the body of a man bent backward over a

shattered tree while blood dripped from his gaping head. I have seen a man apparently uninjured die from the shock of explosion as his elbow touched mine. Never shall I shoot duck again or draw a speckled trout to gasp in my basket—I would not wish to see the death of a spider.

Talbot Papineau letters,

Public Archives of Canada

In early December 1915 Jairus Maus died of the "clean" wounds he had received at Ypres about seven months earlier while going for soup. His mother and sister, who had gone over to Britain to be with him, brought his body home to Paris, Ontario, for burial.

———

On the 9th. January [1916] the final evacuation took place off Cape Helles. Thirty-two of the Newfoundland Regiment were honoured as rear-guard to remain in the trenches, and rifles and flares continued to go off at intervals. But it was recognised that the element of surprise would not serve and the rear-guard was thought doomed. The Turks would be apt to take toll for their former napping. But they proved sportsmen.

Our men said they stood four ranks deep on a narrow strip of beach which could have been enfiladed from the heights with great slaughter. Not a shot was fired, however. The Turks had called across the hill the previous day: "Goodbye. We know you're going. So are we. Good luck!" . . . They were a decent foe. They cared for British graves and there were no atrocities. Of the 32 [Newfoundlanders] who had been dedicated to an almost certain fate, all escaped.

Nursing Sister Mabel B. Clint, No. 1 Canadian Field

Hospital, Lemnos (near Gallipoli), 1916. (*Our Bit*)

The traditional role of Newfoundland politics has been to make Canadian politics look good by comparison, and it positively shone in that role in the First World War. Not all of Sam Hughes's pals profited directly from their work in recruiting and equipping the Canadian Expeditionary Force, although one of the honorary colonels, J. Wesley Allison (whose shady business activities were partly responsible for Hughes's ultimate downfall), boasted publicly of the wonderful profits he had made in his dealings with the British government. In most cases, Canadian business-men and politicians who exhorted other men to join up for the war (and sometimes spent their own money to help found new regiments) were not so much out for profit, but just aware that their efforts might be rewarded with British knighthoods, honours and distinctions, which still played a large part in social advancement in Canada at the time. Not one of them, however, could match the social-climbing ambitions and skills of Sir Edward Morris, the prime minister of Newfoundland.

Newfoundland was an independent country then, of course, but it had not had any military forces for almost a century. Nevertheless, on 7 August 1914 Prime Minister Morris sent a telegram to London offering an entire regiment for service overseas. Two days later London accepted Newfoundland's offer. Morris and the British governor, Sir Basil Davidson, then created the Newfoundland Patriotic Association to raise, equip, and finance the contingents dispatched from Newfoundland. The governor made himself chairman of the association and controlled committee appointments: in effect, he directed Newfoundland's war effort. It was a highly unusual arrangement for a self-governing dominion, but Morris needed the Governor's support to stay in power, and Davidson needed an eminent Newfoundlander who was willing to trade colonial soldiers for imperial honours. As he explained in a dispatch to London in 1914:

> The bulk of His Majesty's subjects in Newfoundland had then been steeped in ease for hundreds of years and imbued with an instinctive aversion to war, albeit the bravest of people in their

own seafaring conditions. Neither did they understand the causes which compelled His Majesty's Government to declare war, nor did they consider themselves directly interested in the issue.

The larger part . . . were on the whole inclined—living in the misty atmosphere of past centuries—to side with the King of Prussia, as the champion of Protestantism, and they remembered France only as the traditional enemy. The old memories of the press-gang still lived in the outports, and the recollection of soldiering was that the wastrels of the hamlets enlisted for life and never returned home.

Sir Edward Morris, it seemed to the governor, was the man who could get past all that: an Irish Catholic politician who had prospered mightily by trimming his sails to catch the prevailing wind from Britain (he had a standing order in London for the latest guide to the British peerage), but who knew how to play the local game. And the war looked a lot like salvation to Morris: if he played along with Governor Davidson, he might be able to use the war as a stepping-stone to better things than Newfoundland politics.

So the Newfoundland Patriotic Association duly raised a contingent for overseas service, and the "First Five Hundred," recruited mainly from St. John's—baymen tended to be more doubtful about the whole enterprise—sailed for England in the steamship *Florizel* in October 1914. They then spent ten months training in England—and they had only volunteered for a year. In August 1915, as they were being reviewed by the king and by Lord Kitchener, the British war minister, they were given the option of returning home or enlisting for the period of the war. Most of them, unable to face the social disgrace of quitting, chose to stay, whereupon Kitchener announced that they were just the people he needed in Turkey. A week later they were sent to the Gallipoli peninsula, where imperial forces had landed earlier in the year in an attempt to break through the straits at the Dardanelles and capture Istanbul.

By now, the legendary early battles between the Turks and the Anzacs (Australians and New Zealanders) were largely over. What the Newfoundlanders had to face was four months of grinding, stalemated trench warfare where more men died from disease and exposure than from enemy action.

> All over the Peninsula disease had become epidemic, until the clearing stations and the beaches were choked with sick . . .
>
> By sickness and snipers' bullets we were losing thirty men a day. Nobody in the front line trenches or on the shell-swept area behind ever expected to leave the Peninsula alive.
>
> John Gallishaw, Royal Newfoundland Regiment,
> *Trenching at Gallipoli*

Those who survived Gallipoli and were unlucky enough still to be fit for war were then sent to the Western Front, where the Royal Newfoundland Regiment was virtually wiped out at the battles of Beaumont Hamel and Gueudecourt in 1916. But Morris survived: aware that public opinion was turning against the war and that he had no chance of winning the 1917 election, he postponed the election on the grounds that he would be absent attending the Imperial War Cabinet in London. But his real reason for being in England was rather different. Sir Basil Davidson had written a letter for him.

> Sir Edward Morris . . . now feels weary of the burden of leadership . . .and he has expressed to me his hopes that he may shortly retire from public life and reside in England.
>
> [By 1914, in Newfoundland], the proud tradition of attachment to the King and the Royal House had become almost lip service, not involving the conception that loyalty might involve sacrifice. Despite these discouraging conditions Sir Edward never hesitated, but offered his people to the Army and Navy and pledged the Colony's credit for their maintenance.

[I wish] to press for your advocacy before the King in granting to Sir Edward Morris the unprecedented Honour of a Peerage,
as a fitting reward for a man who has so well served the Cause of
the British Empire. Sir Edward has sufficient means to maintain
the Dignity of a hereditary title and a seat in the House of Lords.

Governor Davidson to the colonial secretary,

September 1917

Morris was already in London by September of 1917. On Christmas
Eve he finally wrote to two of his former colleagues to announce his
resignation as prime minister of Newfoundland. A few days later he
received his peerage, and a grateful imperial government arranged for
him to be appointed to the boards of a British insurance company and
an aircraft-building firm. His heir still sits in the House of Lords today.

"I'd like to know," said one chap, "why we all enlisted."

"I wish you fellows would shut up and go to sleep," said a
querulous voice from a nearby dug-out.

"It doesn't do any good to talk about it now," said Art Pratt, in
a matter of fact voice. "Some of you enlisted so full of love of country that there was patriotism running down your chin, and some of
you enlisted because you were disappointed in love, but the most of
you enlisted for love of adventure, and you're getting it."

Again the querulous subterranean voice interrupted: "Go to
sleep, you fellows—there's none of you knows what you're talking
about. There's only one reason any of us enlisted, and that's pure,
low down, unmitigated ignorance."

John Gallishaw, *Trenching at Gallipoli*

THE STEEL SLEET AND THE CONTINUOUS FRONT

At first there will be increased slaughter—increased slaughter on so terrible a scale as to render it impossible to get troops to push the battle to a decisive issue. They will try to, thinking that they are fighting under the old conditions, and they will learn such a lesson that they will abandon the attempt forever. Then . . . we shall have . . . a long period of continually increasing strain upon the resources of the combatants . . . Everybody will be entrenched in the next war.

J.S. Bloch,

Budushchaya Voina [Future War], 1897

THESE PREDICTIONS ABOUT THE NEXT WAR BETWEEN THE GREAT powers were first published in Russian by Jan Bloch, a Polish financier who had never been a soldier. But he got it all right: the trenches, the unprecedented scale of the slaughter, the enormous industrial resources that would be mobilized for the struggle—even the detail that most of the countries fighting the war would ultimately face revolution at home. He got only one thing wrong: he thought that so horrifying a prospect would deter the great powers from embarking on such a war.

Bloch was born in the part of Poland that then belonged to the Russian empire. He studied at the University of Berlin and returned home to pursue a financial career in a Warsaw bank, but he found time to conduct a fourteen-year study of modern warfare in his spare time. He published his conclusions in a six-volume, 3,084-page work in Russian in 1897, but it became famous across Europe only with the publication of the one-volume English translation, *Is War Now Impossible?*, in the following year.

By the time of Bloch's study, all the countries of mainland Europe (but not the British) had created mass armies: their young men were conscripted into the army for two or three years in order to train them for war, and then they were sent home—but they remained in the reserve for another fifteen or twenty years, with an obligation to train annually and rejoin the army full-time if there was a war. Bloch's analysis, based on an examination of modern military technologies (such as smokeless gunpowder, rapid-firing rifles, Maxim machine guns and long-range artillery), showed that these mass armies would not be able to wage battles in the old, decisive way because the sheer amount of firepower would force men to go to ground. An entrenched man would then, on average, be able to stop four men advancing against him across open ground, so the armies would have to stop moving, and the rest of the war would be conducted along an enormous battlefront like a siege operation on a continental scale. Armies of millions of men would inhabit these trenches year in, year out, and immense industrial resources would be consumed in attempts to break the resulting stalemate. The struggle might eventually be decided by attrition, if one side ran out of men and industrial resources before the other, but a likelier outcome was that the economic and social strains would be so great that they would lead to the "break-up of the whole social organization" and revolutions from below.

The book caused a sensation, and was partly responsible for the convening of the world's first peace conference at The Hague in 1899.

However, the people who should have taken most interest in it, the professional military officers who served the various great powers, dismissed it out of hand as the ravings of an amateur. Why, if Bloch were right, the cavalry would even have to give up their horses! Reflecting on this obstinate ignorance shortly before his death in 1901, Bloch wrote: "The steadfastness with which the military caste clings to the memory of a state of things which has already died is pathetic and honourable. Unfortunately it is also costly and dangerous." Dangerous because if the armies refused to recognize that that was the future of war, then war was indeed still possible. Thirteen years later, it duly came.

The general staffs of all the European armies had prepared elaborate plans for the first moves in the war and not much for later phases because they thought that there wouldn't be any later phases. They assumed that the war would be like those of the mid-19th century, which in most cases were settled swiftly after a few decisive battles. The French and the Russians planned headlong attacks on Germany from the west and the east, while Britain, although a member of the Entente, had not formally committed itself to sending troops to the continent at all. The Germans, outnumbered by at least two-to-one and facing attacks on two fronts, adopted a gambler's strategy: the Schlieffen Plan.

Count Alfred von Schlieffen, chief of the Imperial German General Staff from 1891 to 1906, reckoned that Germany would have six weeks to knock France out of the war before the Russian army was fully mobilized and ready to attack, but that it was unlikely to succeed in doing that by a frontal attack against the French army along the Franco-German border. The German army might push the French a long way back, but France would still be in the war, and most of Germany's troops would still be tied up in the west when the massive Russian army finally moved into Germany from the east. So the German plan was to surprise the French by marching west into Belgium before swinging round and advancing south past Paris, and finally swinging back east to envelop the French army and force France to seek peace.

The whole operation, Schlieffen reckoned, would take precisely forty-two days, and then the German troops would be transferred east to stop the "Russian Steamroller."

There were only two problems with the Schlieffen Plan. One was that Belgium's neutrality was guaranteed by Britain, and attacking it was likely to result in a British army being sent to France to fight the Germans (although the Germans went on hoping that it wouldn't until the last minute). The other was that the German army just couldn't march fast enough to get all the way around to the rear of the French army—for it had a long way to go—before the French and the British moved enough troops into northern France and western Belgium to stop them.

At first, the mobilization of the new mass armies went exactly according to plan: the German army, for example, grew sixfold in size in the first two weeks of August 1914 as all the reservists joined their regiments, and the trains then delivered them swiftly and efficiently to the various fronts. By the middle of the month there were 1,485,000 German soldiers on the borders with France and Belgium, ready to march and fight as soon as they got off the trains. The French, the Russians and lesser players like the Austrians performed similar miracles of organization—but then everything went wrong.

The French attacked straight across the frontier into Germany in massive force in accordance with Plan XVII. Their doctrine was *offensive à outrance*: by sheer élan the French infantry would charge through machine-gun fire and shrapnel, and sweep the German defenders aside. Indeed, the French soldiers were still wearing blue coats and red trousers in August 1914, despite the fact that this made them highly visible to the German machine-gunners. The offensives all failed amid great carnage, and by the end of August the French were on the defensive everywhere.

But the Schlieffen Plan failed too. When the French and the small British Expeditionary Force went over to the defensive in late August they were able to stop the German attack well short of Paris—and then something happened that took the soldiers completely by surprise (although Bloch had predicted it fifteen years before). As soon as the exhausted armies stopped moving, they began entrenching to protect themselves from the lethal firepower of the enemy soldiers facing them, and those trenches quickly became a "front line" that made any further movement or manoeuvre virtually impossible. General Foch, later commander of the whole French army, was one of the first to notice what was happening. Sent to the western end of the front line after the armies had fought each other to a standstill north and east of Paris, he complained: "They have sent me here to manoeuvre, but things are not going very brightly. This eternal stretching out in a line is getting on my nerves."

As the Allies and the Germans repeatedly tried to get around the remaining open end of this peculiar new obstacle, the armies would collide, halt and end up digging new stretches of trench, and within a few more weeks the front line reached the sea near Nieuwpoort in Belgium. Suddenly there were no more enemy flanks that you could hope to get around, just an endless front line. It was theoretically possible to walk 750 kilometres from the English Channel to the border of neutral Switzerland along either of two parallel lines of trench, sometimes as close as ten or twenty metres apart but more usually several hundred, without ever setting foot on the surface. The "Western Front" (from the German *Westfront*) was born.

The same thing happened in the east. The Russians mobilized far faster in 1914 than the German General Staff expected, and invaded eastern Germany in four weeks, not six, while the bulk of the German army was still committed to battle in France. So the Schlieffen Plan would have been a failure strategically even if it had gone exactly according to plan: in theory, the Russian army could have been nearing Berlin by the time the German army was enveloping Paris. But in practice it didn't much matter, because the much smaller German army defending in the east was nevertheless able to stop the Russian offensive cold. By winter another "front line" of trenches had come into existence in Eastern Europe, this one 1,600 kilometres long, and the war of rapid movement and decisive victories that the generals had foreseen was over. Everywhere, it had just become much easier to defend than to attack.

The reason for burrowing down into the trenches was obvious: industrial weapons—quick-firing artillery and machine guns that spewed out six hundred bullets a minute—filled the air with a lethal steel sleet, and anybody trying to move above ground was almost certain to be hit. In the first month of the war France lost 75,000 men killed and another 175,000 wounded. Had the French army continued to fight that kind of war, it would have run out of men entirely in about one year. The act of killing had been mechanized, and the trenches, however dreadful, were the only way to keep losses down to a (barely) tolerable level. Men became the prisoners of machines, trapped below ground level—except, of course, when they were ordered to attack, and had to stand up into the machine-gun fire.

The essence of the general's art had always been to manoeuvre his forces, but now no movement at all was possible until he had broken through the trench line facing him—and the continuous front meant that *every* attack had to be a frontal attack. Since infantrymen could not hope to survive the hail of fire that would greet them if they tried to advance unaided—that was why they had dug the trenches in the first place—the only way to break through was to eliminate the sources of that fire by shelling the enemy's barbed wire, trenches and gun positions into ruin before the attack. At least that was the theory.

So the trench war became a war of artillery, and over half the casualties were now caused by shellfire. The greatest problem of 1915 for every country was not at the front but at home, where shell production could not keep up with demand. Even in Britain, the world's most industrialized country, there was a critical shell shortage in 1915, and the demands went on mounting: at the Third Battle of Ypres in 1917, the nineteen-day British bombardment used 4.3 million shells, weighing 107,000 tons. Battles had become an industrial operation in reverse, in which the rate of destruction at the front matched the rate of production at home.

But still the infantry could not break through, though they died in their millions trying. The shells could destroy most of the enemy's machine guns in the first-line trenches, and even the enemy's guns behind the lines, but enough defenders always survived to make the advance a slow and costly business, and the bombardments turned the ground into a wilderness of shell holes across which any movement was very difficult. Eventually the attackers might take the enemy's first-line trenches—and by the middle of the war these alone could be a belt up to three thousand metres wide—but by that time the enemy's reserves would have arrived and manned a whole new trench system just to the rear. There was no way around the trenches, and seemingly no way through them either.

Trapped in a two-front war and seriously outnumbered, the Germans went over to the defensive on the Western Front in early 1915. It was the British and French who launched almost all the great offensives on the Western Front, which is why they usually lost more men attacking the German trenches than the Germans did in defending them. Yet in coldly rational terms it made sense, because they had more men to put into the field than the Germans. If enough people were killed, the Germans would eventually have to stop fighting because they would run out of men first.

This was such a horrifying concept that it was rarely articulated, but it is impossible to believe that the planners and managers of the battles did not understand it at some (perhaps unadmitted) level. What else can explain the grim determination with which British and French generals pursued apparently futile enterprises like the Battle of the Somme, in which the British imperial forces captured only 115 square kilometres in five months of fighting at a cost of 415,000 men killed and wounded, including 24,000 Canadians, 30,000 Australians and New Zealanders, 3,000 South Africans and 2,000 Newfoundlanders—3,600 men for each square kilometre? The territory gained and lost was not of any value, nor did any of these offensives ever come near to a decisive breakthrough. What really mattered was that the Germans were compelled to sacrifice men and equipment at a comparable rate, although their total human and material resources were much smaller. And this extraordinary war of attrition continued for about forty months, from the end of 1914 to the spring of 1918.

CHAPTER 3

THE GREAT CRUSADE

MOST CANADIAN TROOPS WERE SENT TO THE WESTERN FRONT IN
France and Belgium, but as part of the British imperial forces, Canadians
ended up in every theatre of the war: there were Canadian fighter pilots in
Italy, Canadian river pilots and marine engineers in Mesopotamia (Iraq)
and Canadian sailors on all the world's oceans. In October 1915 Private
Lester B. Pearson, #1059, Canadian Army Medical Corps (who would one
day become secretary of state for external affairs and then prime minister
of Canada), landed in Macedonia in northern Greece with a new British
expeditionary force. Britain and France had decided to violate Greek neutrality (rather like the Germans violated Belgian neutrality) in order to
bring help to their Serbian allies against the Austrians and the Bulgarians,
and Pearson was part of the help. He was eighteen years old.

> My impressions of those first few days are of a vast muddy plain
> with our half dozen tents the only sign of human habitation; of
> ceaseless rain and fierce winds; of horse ambulances coming
> down the road with their loads of human agony; of the bugle blow-
> ing the convoy call; of the boom of guns; of struggling in the mire
> with wounded soldiers of the Tenth Division slung over our

shoulders—we had no stretchers as yet. . . . They had been under-going terrible experiences up in the hills. The weather was below freezing, but through official mismanagement, they had only tropical clothing. Practically all of them were frostbitten and some in addition badly wounded, but not one complained.

We pitched our tents, spread straw over the mud and laid the casualties down on that, till there would be forty or fifty in a tent. Then the medical officer would come around with his lantern, the dead and dying would be moved to one side, the dangerous cases would be attended to at once and the less serious ones simply cheered up. All the while the wind whistled over the Macedonian plain and the sleet beat against the canvas. Nightmare days when we all worked till we dropped . . . but the chance for real service, the goal of our months of training.

Letters home, October 1915,
quoted in Lester Pearson, *Mike: Memoirs*, vol. 1

For the first time in Canada's history, there were also women in uniform: 2,504 Canadian nurses served in every theatre of the war. The first Canadian women arrived behind the lines in France in early 1915, and by the autumn of that year hundreds of Canadian nurses were struggling to keep sick and wounded soldiers (and themselves) alive in the pestilential conditions of the Eastern Mediterranean theatres of war as well. In August Mabel Clint of No. 1 Canadian Field Hospital arrived on the island of Lemnos, just off the Gallipoli battlefield, to find "sani-tary conditions appalling, food scarce and bad, heat great, small quan-tities of water, and a frightful plague of flies."

Then one by one the Officers, sisters and orderlies succumbed to dysentery, till only three out of thirty-five nurses were on duty in No. 1. Canadians seemed to feel the change of climate particularly, but lack of food, water and the general environment was the determining factor. . . . No. 3 suffered still more. . . . Within a few days of each other, their Matron and a sister fell victim to the scourge. As the little cortège of those well enough to attend followed the flag-draped coffins on wheeled stretchers, with the Sisters' white veil and leather belt laid on them, some of the patients in my ward were moved to tears. . . . It was expected that other nurses would die, and . . . the order went forth that other graves must be ready. . . . A trench to hold six was dug in the Officers' lines. A laconic notice-board bore the legend: "For Sisters only." At the moment, as one of our Mess remarked, you could almost "pick the names of the six."

Nursing Sister Mabel Clint, Lemnos, 1915, *Our Bit*

In the end, only thirty-nine Canadian women died overseas, but it was nevertheless a sign of the times. Even the strict rules of a traditional male-dominated society were collapsing before the war's voracious demands for manpower and, even more important, for total commitment.

They would have little flags in the window. I can remember one house with three flags, that they had sent people overseas. One flag for each son or husband.

Naomi Radford, Edmonton

It is difficult to place a limit on the numbers of men that may be required in this devastating war. No numbers which the Dominion Government are willing and able to provide with arms and ammu-nition would be too great. . . .

British War Office to Ottawa, May 1915

In July 1915 Prime Minister Robert Borden went to England to try to find out a bit more from the British about their war plans. They were vague.

The war was consuming munitions in quantities far greater than anybody had anticipated in peacetime, and nobody was sure when the factories would be geared up to produce enough ammunition for a decisive offensive. Estimates of when the British would be ready to exert their full force ranged from a year to eighteen months, but it was clear that the numbers of men required for that great offensive would be far beyond anything that had been previously envisaged. So in October 1915 Borden passed an Order in Council increasing the Canadian force to 250,000 men.

In return for this great contribution to the imperial war effort, however, Borden wanted Canada to have a voice in determining the conduct of the war. After his visit to Britain in mid-1915 and his shock at the confusion that reigned there, he noted that the old relationship between Britain and Canada had "in some measure passed away. Once for all it has been borne in upon the hearts and souls of all of us that . . . the issues of war and peace concern more than the people of these islands." The British colonial secretary, the Canadian-born Andrew Bonar Law, complacently informed Borden in late 1915 that he fully recognized "the right of the Canadian government to have some share in the control of a war in which it is playing so big a part. I am, however, not able to see any way in which this could practically be done. . . . If no scheme is practicable, then it is very undesirable that the question should be raised."

Bonar Law's reply drove the normally gentle Borden to fury, but his method for forcing the British to reconsider was quixotic. In his 1916 New Year's message, Borden doubled the planned strength of the Canadian Expeditionary Force to 500,000. Among the people who were astonished by this move (Borden had decided on it alone while bedridden with the flu) was the governor general: "His Royal Highness cannot but feel considerable doubt as to the possibility of increasing the Canadian Forces to 500,000 men. His Royal Highness understands that of the 250,000 men at present authorised some 50,000 are still deficient and he fears that the magnificent total of 500,000 may be beyond the powers of the Dominion of Canada to provide under voluntary enlistment."

The Duke of Connaught was quite right in his assessment: Borden's target, if maintained, would eventually require conscription. On the other hand, the prime minister was sure that the men would be needed, since the monthly "wastage" of troops showed no sign of decreasing. He also hoped that his announcement would end the criticism of his government by those English Canadians who didn't think he was doing enough for the war. But above all, Borden believed that it would compel the British to give Canada a share in the direction of the war: "It can hardly be expected that we shall put 400,000 or 500,000 men in the field and willingly accept the position of having no more voice . . . than if we were toy automata. . . . It is for [the British] to suggest the method and not for us. If there is no available method and we are expected to continue in the role of toy automata the whole situation must be reconsidered."

But in practice it could not be reconsidered. By announcing that Canada would raise half a million troops before London had even asked for them, Borden had given the imperialist establishment in English Canada a pledge from which it would never release him—and since Canada had offered the troops of its own accord, he had not really strengthened his bargaining position with London. The gesture was in any case unnecessary: by December of 1916 the new British prime minister, David Lloyd George, had realized that the Dominions must be granted a share in policy making. "We want more men from them," he told the colonial secretary. "We can hardly ask them to make another great recruiting effort unless it is accompanied by an invitation to come over and discuss the situation with us." He then invited the dominions and India to send representatives to London for an Imperial War Conference at which they could "discuss how best they could cooperate in the direction of the war. They were fighting not for us, but with us."

What was never seriously discussed at these meetings of the Imperial War Cabinet, however, was the question of a compromise peace. The sheer scale of the losses incurred by all the combatants had changed the war into something new: a "total war" in which all the available manpower and resources were devoted to the sole aim of achieving military victory. The entire workforce of wealthy industrial societies—including millions of women who were drawn into industry for the first time—was mobilized for war production. And since everyone was at least theoretically involved in the war effort in one way or another, everybody, whether in uniform or not, soon came to be treated as a legitimate military target: the first air attacks on civilians came in 1915, with the Zeppelin raids on London.

It was not the supreme importance of the issues at stake that made the First World War the first total war: as a political phenomenon it was no different from all the preceding great-power world wars. It was simply the first time that that kind of war had occurred since the great powers had acquired the vast resources and the technological and organizational capabilities of fully industrialized states. Once these capabilities existed, it was inevitable that they would be used, since the side that showed restraint would surely lose. But the mass slaughter had such a powerful psychological effect on the combatants that it became impossible to end a world war in the old way.

After millions of ordinary citizens had died (most of them in uniform, but some not), the traditional outcome of such wars—a fairly modest reshuffle of territories and a readjustment of influence among the great powers—was no longer acceptable to the populations of the warring countries. It became necessary to elevate the war to the status of a moral crusade, or at least to define it as a struggle for sheer national survival, in order to justify the sacrifices that were being demanded. This was in the nature of a self-fulfilling prophecy: as the only war aim acceptable to the people of each nation became total victory, the war did become something close to a life-and-death struggle for the European great powers, or at least for their governments. It was nothing of the sort for Canada, of course, but a great many English Canadians were also swept away by the rhetoric of the time.

———

Of the Mathieson family of Victoria, five brothers were on active
service, and . . . Arthur Green and three sons of Victoria . . . seven
boys of the Kerridge family of Vancouver were all at the Front. Of
the George family, Victoria, in 1916, three were killed, one was
missing, one a prisoner, two were at the Front, and two waiting till
they were old enough to go. . . .

Canadian Annual Review, 1916

It was the English Canadian families whose sons and husbands had
already volunteered in large numbers who welcomed Borden's call for
500,000 men at the beginning of 1916: they rushed out and enlisted in
even larger numbers. During the first three months of 1916, men were
joining up at the rate of almost a thousand a day. The government
heaved a sigh of relief: Canada might be able to raise half a million men
without having to resort to compulsion. But then enlistment began
dropping rapidly: in December 1916, there were only 5,791 enlistments
for the entire month. At that rate the country would fall far short of the
target of enlisting 30 percent of all males of military age.

By now the unemployment of 1913 was long forgotten. Farmers
needed all the help they could get, and munitions factories were employ-
ing a quarter of a million workers. The war had stimulated an unprecedented growth in Canadian industry: in 1914 Canadian arms manufacturers produced little other than small arms and ammunition, but in the
last two years of the war the Imperial Munitions Board, created by
Borden in late 1915, was spending more than the Government of
Canada itself, and had 675 factories working for it in 150 different towns
in Canada. By 1917 Canadian industries were turning out warships,
military aircraft and between a quarter and a third of all the shells fired
by British guns on the Western Front: twenty-four million shells were
shipped to Europe that year. Arms production was probably the most

effective use that could be made of Canadian manpower, but it caused great difficulties for the army recruiters.

Brigadier James Mason, the director of recruiting, presented the senate with a mass of statistics and a very depressing conclusion for the government. There were, he reported, one and a half million eligible men in Canada (half of them unmarried). By February 1916, 249,000 men had enlisted, but it was going to be much more difficult to get the next quarter-million:

> Moreover, this large number, if and when sent to the Front, must be maintained, and it has been estimated that the casualties will not be less than five percent monthly of the total force. This means that we shall have to provide each month, to maintain our Army's strength, at least 25,000 new men—or 300,000 a year.
>
> There can be no question that the additional 250,000 to bring our quota up to 500,000, and the 300,000 required annually to keep it at that figure, will not be obtained under the present system of enlistment.
>
> Brigadier James Mason, March 1916

By now the British tradition of voluntary enlistment was falling by the wayside elsewhere: in January 1917 Great Britain introduced conscription, and New Zealand had already done so. The feeling persisted in Canada that there was a great untapped mass of men of the right age, but no actual data existed: some parts of the country had only recently been settled, and until the war there had been no need for this detailed information. The obvious solution was a national registration system, so two million large cards were printed and distributed to all the post offices in the country. (Originally they were going to be mailed to every male citizen in the country, until somebody realized that if you already had the name and address of every male in Canada, you might not need a registration system.) But the government shrank from making registration compulsory, and it was estimated that about 20 percent of the males between eighteen and sixty-five didn't fill in the cards. There was a strong suspicion that the government was moving toward conscription, even if it said it was not, and many men felt it prudent not to draw themselves to the army's attention.

> You have asked for an assurance that under no circumstances will Conscription be undertaken or carried out. . . . I must decline to give any such assurance. I hope that Conscription may not be necessary, but if it should prove to be the only effective method to preserve the existence of the State and of the institutions and liberties which we enjoy, I should consider it necessary and I should not hesitate to act accordingly.
>
> Prime Minister Sir Robert Borden to labour leaders,
> December 27, 1916

Not only did many men not fill out the cards, but when the army, seeking volunteers, canvassed the men who had registered, most of them felt that they were doing their duty by working in industry. By now even the West had run out of young, single, unemployed men with strong British loyalties, and nobody thought the war was an adventure any more. In Winnipeg, out of 1,767 men registered, nobody was willing to volunteer. Out of a pool of 4,497 men registered in Quebec, four enlisted. Most eligible Canadian men seemed curiously unconvinced that there was any threat to "the existence of the State and the institutions and liberties" they enjoyed.

Meanwhile, nothing had improved in the management of the Canadian forces. Sam Hughes, now "Sir Sam," emphasized that the goal of 500,000 men was a target for which the prime minister alone had to take responsibility, but he was scarcely a model of responsibility himself. In August 1916 he cabled Borden from England to suggest that Canada should put eight or ten divisions in the field (it then had four). His motive appeared to be the pure spirit of competition: Australia, with a much smaller population than Canada, already had five divisions in France, and it was rumoured that there were enough Australian troops in England and Egypt to form four more.

On the same day, as an afterthought, Hughes cabled asking to have "sixty or eighty thousand troops sent over immediately." He assured Borden that this would still leave over one hundred thousand troops in Canada. Besides, Hughes added helpfully, more men could easily be made available if clergymen helped out in the fields to release more farmers' sons for military service.

The worst thing about Sam Hughes—worse even than his venal "friends" in commerce and industry, his absurd pretensions to military genius, or his random enthusiasms for new models of service rifle or entrenching tool—was his relentless, reflexive determination to do favours for his friends in the militia. He was the epitome of the "good ol' boy" politician whose sole method for extending his influence over his political environment is to create an ever-widening network of people who are indebted to him for their jobs. Professional military competence was therefore quite irrelevant to Hughes when he appointed officers to positions of command (and he had his "militia" ideology to rationalize his disdain for formal military qualifications). In the Post Office, this kind of management policy means that the mail gets delivered late and the organization runs a deficit; in an army at war, it means that large numbers of people get killed because of the incompetence of their superiors.

All the officers selected for the First Contingent of the Canadian Expeditionary Force were appointed by Hughes more or less as a personal favour, and many of them were not capable of organizing a piss-up in a brewery: the subsequently famous British military critic J.F.C. Fuller, then a young officer, remarked on seeing the 1st Canadian Division debark at Devonport in England in 1914 that they would be fine soldiers only "if the officers could all be shot." Most of the officers of the 2nd Canadian Division, and many of those commanding sub-sequent contingents, also got their jobs through Hughes's reflex crony-ism: if you were a Canadian who wanted a combat command in the war, there was no other way. And yet, once they had actually seen battle, Hughes's own appointees tended to turn against him.

From mid-1915 on there was unremitting guerrilla warfare between the Canadian divisions in France and the tangled web of competing Canadian military authorities in England that Hughes had created to administer them. It was much more than the usual friction between the front and the rear: the key question was always whether the commanders in France had the right to choose their own replacement officers (mainly by promoting them from the ranks of their own battle-wise troops), or whether they must accept replacements from among the horde of "super-numerary" officers—all promised a job by Sir Sam but utterly lacking in combat experience—who languished in England waiting for the call.

Combat experience changes people—and it also winnows them. The men whom Sam Hughes had chosen as officers for the Canadian divisions in France in 1914 and 1915 were almost all deficient at the start in the military knowledge they would need to do their jobs well, and there was a disproportionate number of sycophants among them. But time and battle weeded out the weak (there are almost always ways for an officer to escape the front, if he is determined to avoid it) and taught the survivors to act and think like real officers. The ex–lawyers and farmers and insur-ance salesmen turned into competent majors and colonels who under-stood exactly what it means to be responsible for your countrymen's lives—and that while it is your duty as an officer to spend the lives of some of them in order to achieve your country's objectives, the rate at which they die will be determined largely by your own military competence.

The toy soldiers turned into professionals, and they became con-temptuous of Hughes's bluster. More than that, they became determined to stop him from parachuting his new crop of patronage appointments (ironically, "officers" who had the very same defects they themselves had

had a year or eighteen months before) into positions of command where by inexperience they might waste the lives of veteran Canadian soldiers who had survived the battles of Ypres and the Somme.

The first evidence of this transformation of perspective among Canadian officers at the front came right at the end of 1915, when Hughes made one of his typical gambits for finding more jobs at the front for his cronies. He proposed that all the British staff officers serving with the Canadian Corps should be replaced by Canadians, even though his own bias against professional military education for militia officers had prevented all but a handful of Canadian officers from being properly trained for staff appointments. Faced with the prospect of having incompetent Canadians replace the trained British officers who were currently doing the vital planning jobs in the Canadian divisions, however, the Canadian senior commanders at the front unanimously backed the British corps commander, Lieutenant General Sir Edwin Alderson, in protesting against it. Hughes's proposal was dropped.

Hughes's persistent meddling with the Canadian forces in England—he regarded them as his personal empire—was the biggest factor in finally bringing him down. He was so seldom in Ottawa that Borden was gradually able to hand over more and more of the administration of Hughes's own department to other, more competent people. The final confrontation came when the prime minister decided to order Hughes home and create a new ministry for overseas service, to be run by Sir George Perley in London. Hughes was furious. In his own mind he was perpetually beleaguered by the plots of jealous rivals and incompetent subordinates, and now he accused Borden of being a plotter too. Borden had had enough: on November 9, 1916, he demanded Hughes's resignation as minister of militia and national defence.

All of the men seemed to have gone. You had a tremendous rate of enlistment here, and my father at the newspaper was working over-time all the time, and he would come home absolutely exhausted.

You have to remember there was no TV, there was no radio, but a dispatch would come through that, say, the Somme Battle was in progress. . . . And the phone rang incessantly—these poor, anxious voices: "We're so sorry to bother you, but is there any news?"

So at the age of, I suppose about eight or nine by then, I was part of the chain of communication, because I would let my father rest. And I remember what a dreadful time I had pronouncing the names of these various battles. And Daddy would tell me what dispatch had come through, and I'd just repeat it.

Naomi Radford, Edmonton

By the end of 1916 Canada was a divided country: divided between those families who had a son, a husband, or a brother serving overseas and those who were still essentially living in the atmosphere of peacetime. The latter group might follow the progress of the European war in the newspapers, but they could not share the quiet terror of those who spent their days waiting for the official message that it was time to dress in mourning.

The sight of a telegraph boy was a thing of horror . . . because they were never allowed to phone bad news. And you'd see the boy come down the street on his bicycle, and you'd watch what house he stopped at. And then, later, probably my mother would go over, one of the neighbours would go over.

Naomi Radford

The resentment against men who had not volunteered was greatest in the West, where a large majority of families had a close relative in the trenches. At times it had a very bitter edge.

The odd person, mostly old people, would go around, and they'd see a chap that they felt should be overseas, and they would bounce up and put a white feather on him.

And of course, as the war went on these were often chaps who'd come back wounded, or had a heart condition or something. It was a very cruel thing to do. . . .

Oh no, there was no organisation as far as I know. They were just "public-spirited" people.

Naomi Radford

But far more than for the "shirkers" in their own communities, English Canadians with relatives in the forces reserved their deepest feelings of resentment for French Canadians. It was universally felt in English Canada that French Canadians were not carrying their share of the burden—and of course they weren't, for they didn't think it was their burden.

———

Canada being part of the British Empire, it is the sacred duty of the Canadian people to assist Great Britain in her heroic defence of liberty. This was the position taken by the Episcopacy of French Canada at the outbreak of the War, and this is the attitude Bishops . . . will continue to maintain to the very end. The obligations we owe the British Crown are sacred obligations.

Archbishop Bruchési of Montreal, Laval, January 7, 1916

The Catholic hierarchy in Quebec almost unanimously supported the British cause during the war, in fulfilment of the church's part in the old bargain: you don't meddle in our empire, and we'll support yours. However, it was fighting an uphill battle against its own *curés*, who shared the general conviction that the Kaiser was not casting lascivious eyes on Trois-Rivières and that the war was none of French Canada's business. But there were some French Canadians who joined up anyway.

4.15 a.m.

Only ten minutes now before zero. The horizon shows a line of grey. Dawn is coming; and my heart is filled suddenly with bitterness when I realize that the day may be my last. . . . A shell bursts in our trench, breaking the leg of a man a few yards away. Stretcher-bearers apply a dressing and carry him to the rear. "There goes one man who won't die in the attack," remarks a soldier, almost enviously.

Our company commander, Capt. J.H. Roy, appears. "Ten rounds in your magazines and fix bayonets!" he orders. There is a click of steel on steel. Only two minutes now remain. . . . Yesterday, I believed I could die with something approaching indifference. Now I am aware of an intense desire to live. I would give anything to know beyond doubt that I had even two whole days ahead of me. . . . I see things—differently than I did yesterday.

Signaller Arthur Lapointe, 22nd Battalion, CEF,
Soldier of Quebec: 1916–1919

At one time or another thirteen battalions destined to join the CEF strove to attract French Canadian recruits in Quebec, but apart from the 22nd Battalion, only the 163rd "Poil-aux-Pattes" and the 189th (recruited mostly in the Gaspé) reached Europe—and after the dreadful losses suffered by the 22nd Battalion at Courcelette in September 1916, the others were broken up to refill its ranks. The 22nd was a remarkable formation, with possibly the most distinguished fighting record in the entire Canadian army, but there were scarcely enough French Canadian volunteers to keep that single battalion up to strength.

4.25 a.m.

Zero hour! A roll as of heavy thunder sounds and the sky is split by great sheets of flame. . . . Through the deep roaring of the guns I can hear the staccato rat-a-tat of machine-guns. I scramble over the parapet and, with Michaud, am one of the first in No Man's Land. Our company is forming up and the moments of delay seem endless. . . . A shell strikes a few yards away, and Lieut. Gatien is seriously wounded. We are not allowed to help him; that is the stretcher-bearers' duty. The noise of the barrage fills our ears; the air pulsates, and the earth rocks under our feet. I feel I am in an awful dream and must soon awake. . . .

We reach the enemy's front line, which has been blown to pieces. Dead bodies lie half buried under the fallen parapet and wounded are writhing in convulsions of pain. . . . Through clouds of smoke, I catch sight of German soldiers running away. Shall I fire at them? I pity the poor devils and have seen enough dead lying in the mud; but this is war, so I open fire. A German soldier falls. Did one of my bullets find a mark, or was he struck down by a shell? I shall never know.

Soldier of Quebec: 1916–1919

There were some practical reasons why so few French Canadians joined the forces: they tended to marry younger, and the army that was seeking their services had become an almost entirely "English" institution (among some eighty Canadian brigadier generals in the First World War, only four were French Canadian). But these obstacles were unimportant compared to the fundamental French Canadian disinclination to die for the British empire.

As far as most French Canadians were concerned, the sentimental tie to France was not strong enough to justify dying for her, and loyalty to the British empire did not oblige its Canadian subjects to die in Britain's wars in other continents. So English Canadians were coming to see all French Canadians as cowards or traitors, while French Canadians who had enlisted found themselves regarded as dupes by many of their own people. After a year at the front Talbot Papineau sent an open letter to his cousin, Henri Bourassa:

> Can a nation's pride be built upon the blood and suffering of others? . . . If we accept our liberties, our national life, from the hands of the English soldiers, if without sacrifices of our own we profit by the sacrifices of the English citizen, can we hope to ever become a nation ourselves? . . . Yet the fact remains that the French in Canada have not responded in the same proportion as have other Canadian citizens. . . . For this fact . . . you will be held largely responsible. You will bring dishonour and disfavour upon our race, so that whoever bears a French name in Canada will be an object of suspicion and possibly of hatred.
>
> Talbot Papineau to Henri Bourassa, March 21, 1916

But Papineau was as much English Canadian as French Canadian (his father, like Henri Bourassa's, was descended from Louis-Joseph Papineau, but his mother was American and he was brought up in Montreal mainly in English). Bourassa replied in another open letter, pointing out that even in English Canada it was the relatively recent arrivals, the "blokes" from Britain, who had done much of the volunteering. Moreover, he added, "the floating population of the cities, the students, the labourers and clerks, either unemployed or threatened with dismissal, have supplied more soldiers than the farmers," whose roots were in the land. Even if he changed his personal position, Bourassa said, he could not persuade French Canadians to enlist. French Canadians "look upon the perturbations of Europe, even those of England or France, as foreign events. Their sympathies go naturally to France against Germany, but they do not think they have an obligation to fight for France."

I have just found Michaud safe and sound. . . . We have taken the German second support line and captured about fifty prisoners, all haggard and wild-eyed, as though they had traversed a hell on earth. Most of them are wounded. One young lad with a badly torn face is raising awful cries. Another, with a leg torn away, is groaning; and his moans rend one's heart. Further away lies one of our men, a young soldier, a comrade of mine from the old 189th. He is terribly wounded, and holds his beads in his one remaining hand. Time and again he calls for his mother, and when his sufferings are more than he can endure prays for death. I can't stand the sight of his suffering, and walk away, with a great lump in my throat.

Soldier of Quebec: 1916–1919

Apart from the 22nd Batallion, however, it had become an almost entirely English Canadian war, and as the casualties mounted, so did the pressures from English Canada to compel French Canadians to "do their share." Only a few English Canadian politicians, like R.B. Bennett, the director of national service, whose recruiting work brought him into regular contact with French Canadians, were fully aware of the dangers this entailed. Bennett frankly told his English Canadian audiences that for the sake of national unity it might be better if the burden of sacrifice remained unequal: "We don't want to have our forces spent in quelling riots at home." But that was not what the audiences wanted to hear, nor were there many English Canadian politicians with the wisdom or the courage to say it to them.

————

The Canadians played a part of such distinction [on the Somme in 1916] that thenceforward they were marked out as storm troops; for the remainder of the war they were brought along to head the assault in one great battle after another. Whenever the Germans found the Canadian Corps coming into the line they prepared for the worst.

David Lloyd George, War Memoirs, vol. 6

Once we got there we were strictly Canadian—there was no fooling around at all. We thought we were quite superior to everybody else, you know.

George Turner, Sergeant, CEF

By the end of 1916, despite all the political infighting and the disastrous losses (the Canadians had 24,029 casualties during the Battle of the Somme), the Canadian Corps in France had become a competent, highly professional army—and despite the very large proportion of English-born volunteers in its ranks, everybody in the corps developed a strong Canadian identity. But as the politicians at home struggled to find enough men to send to the front as replacements, the Canadians in the field ran into a new problem. The reinforcements were sent out so hastily that they were sometimes virtually untrained.

I found myself in a shell hole with some infantryman, and looking over a hundred yards or so away there was a German who was standing up out of a shell hole and shooting as if he was shooting at rabbits. I don't know whether he hit anybody, but any rate he was there. And I sort of said: "Why don't you shoot? Why don't you fire at that man?"

"Oh, I don't know how to fire. . . ."

He just couldn't use a rifle. So I took the rifle from him and took a shot, and the man disappeared. I don't suppose I hit him, but at any rate he wasn't there anymore.

"Tommy" Burns (later general,
then a junior officer in the 11th Brigade)

The rate of losses in the Canadian army was already the major problem, and in 1917 it became critical. The last straw, ironically, was the most famous Canadian success in the war, the capture of Vimy Ridge. It was a long escarpment dominating an industrial plain, from which "more of the war could be seen than from any other place in France," and no significant advance was possible along the most important part of the British front as long as it stayed in enemy hands. The Germans had held most of the ridge since October 1914, and 200,000 had already been killed or wounded in previous British and French attempts to capture it. In April 1917 the job of taking it was given to the Canadian Corps.

It was the first time that all four Canadian divisions had fought together as a corps, and the Canadians prepared for the assault with the meticulous care that was becoming their trademark in battle. They spent weeks studying a scale model of the battle area and practising the planned manoeuvres. More than a million artillery shells—50,000 tons—fell on the Germans in the week before the attack (they called it "the week of suffering"). Even now Vimy looks like a partially reclaimed moonscape, and signs still warn of unexploded shells.

Very early on April 9, Easter Monday (having spent Sunday at church services), the men of the four Canadian divisions were given a stiff tot of rum and began moving forward under cover of a heavy barrage. For once the weather was in their favour: the snowstorm in which the Canadians crept forward across no man's land was unusual for April, but the snow was flying into the Germans' faces, concealing the Canadian advance. The Canadian Official History says the attack "went like clockwork," but nothing in battle goes like clockwork: some regiments in the 11th Brigade, which had suffered heavy losses in other recent fighting, had just "lost their confidence" (as the saying went):

When they were supposed to get up, out over the top and go forward, they tended, after some casualties had occurred, to just not go on any further. And actually, with many of the troops being quite green, you couldn't expect them to do any better than that. When you got a bit forward, you found that the advancing troops had sort of stuck in the mud, somehow or other, and the attack as planned just fell apart.

"Tommy" Burns

Nevertheless, the bulk of the Canadian army swarmed up over the ridge and seized the German trenches. Although the Germans were very well dug in, a lot of the forward positions were taken by surprise, but the attackers were taking heavy losses.

I got bowled over nearly at the start, but picked myself up and ran on with the boys towards the German trenches, and believe me it was some fighting. It was like hell let loose. I was through the Somme but that was nothing compared to this one. . . . It was at the second line that I was knocked out by the concussion of a high explosive shell that burst right near me. By this time there were only two of us left of our machine gun crew.

The shock of the explosion threw me into a shell hole. Corporal Lang . . . came into the hole after me and gave me a drink of rum and water, which soon pulled me around and we started off for Fritz's third line. By this time the enemy were calling for quarter and surrendering fast.

J.M. Thompson, Paris, Ontario, April 1917

We went over Vimy Ridge just at dusk. The Canadian attack . . . had left it a jungle of old wire and powdered brick, muddy burrows and remnants of trenches. . . .

Two hours later we found Fourteen Platoon, hardly recognising it. The sergeant was there, and MacDonald, but most of the others were strangers. . . . MacDonald told us our company had gone straight through to the objective in spite of sleety snow and mud and confusion, but a flanking fire from the left, where the 4th Division had been held up, had taken a heavy toll. Belliveau and Jenkins and Joe McPherson had been killed in one area. One shell had wiped out Stevenson and two others.

MacMillan had been shot in the stomach and had died after waiting hours in the trench. Gilroy and Westcott and Legge had been killed by machine-gun fire. Herman Black had run amuck. They found him almost at the bottom of the Ridge, near a battery position, with eight dead Germans about him, four of them killed by bayonet.

Will R. Bird, *Ghosts Have Warm Hands*

After two days of futile counterattacks the German commander, Crown Prince Rupprecht, ordered the withdrawal of his troops onto the plain below. He had lost a dominating position, and 4,000 Germans had been taken prisoner. But the Canadians had suffered 10,602 casualties, including 3,600 dead.

On April 10, word reached us of the splendid victory of the Canadians in taking Vimy Ridge on the preceding day.

Fine tribute from Haig [the British commander-in-chief]. Some mention in editorials, but none in "Times," which is disgraceful. . . .

Dispatched telegrams of congratulations to General Byng.

Robert Borden, *Memoirs*, vol. 2

It was partly in recognition of the Canadian Corps' achievement at Vimy that it was finally given a Canadian commander in the early summer of 1917, and so became the first completely Canadian field army in the country's history. But while Lieutenant General Sir Julian Byng, the British officer who had commanded the Corps since May 1916, was well liked by the troops, his Canadian successor, General Sir Arthur Currie (who had been an insurance agent and part-time militia officer when the war broke out), was not. Leslie Hudd, by now a seasoned veteran, met Currie after he was recommended for a French Croix de Guerre and a British Military Medal for single-handedly taking a German machine-gun post.

> I was just a buck private. So the [French] General came down and he embraced us all, and I was kissed on both cheeks. Currie came, and he shook hands with the officers and sergeants, but he just pinned it on the privates. . . . I never had much use for Currie. I thought it was his job to congratulate us the right way. All the privates thought that; thought they were worth a handshake from their commander. Not that I've got anything against him as a general, but you could say he wasn't too popular.
>
> Leslie Hudd

Currie was a shy, ungainly man who had none of the actor's skill at currying favour with the troops that is cultivated by so many successful generals. But although his later life was blighted by a campaign of slander directed by Sam Hughes and his cronies, who claimed that he wasted men's lives needlessly, Currie actually worked very hard at keeping them alive. He was an excellent and conscientious commander who was once considered by Prime Minister David Lloyd George as a possible replacement for Sir Douglas Haig, the British commander-in-chief in France.

However, despite Currie's success in his unending struggle to keep the Canadian Corps together and prevent it from being frittered away in small packets by the British High Command to plug weaknesses in various sectors of the front, he could exercise little control over the way the Corps as a whole was actually used. Nor was there any senior Canadian military voice in Ottawa to give Prime Minister Borden strategic advice from the point of view of Canada's own interests: during the entire war the chief of staff of the Canadian army was a British officer, Major General Sir Willoughby Gwatkin. As in all Canada's wars down to the present, the strategic thinking was being done elsewhere.

———

The victory at Vimy Ridge confirmed Borden's belief that the Canadian army was the finest of the allied armies and made it even more difficult for him to contemplate reducing the Canadian commitment. However, no army could afford to go on taking such losses unless it received a steady flow of reinforcements, and voluntary enlistments were drying up. The prime minister had also been much affected by his visit to the front, where he was shocked by what he saw, and by the nerve-racking visits he insisted on paying to all the Canadian military hospitals. (He visited fifty-seven during his 1915 trip.)

> On the one hand, I was inspired by the astonishing courage with which my fellow-countrymen bore their sufferings, inspired also by the warmth of their reception, by a smile of welcome, by the attempt to rise in their beds to greet me. In many cases it was difficult to restrain my tears when I knew that some poor boy, brave to the very last, could not recover.
>
> On the other hand, the emotion aroused from these visits had an exhausting effect upon one's nervous strength: and frequently I could not sleep after reflecting upon the scene through which I had passed.
>
> Robert Borden, *Memoirs*, vol. 2

He felt a tremendous obligation to the troops in this army. . . . He thought that having "his boys" reinforced was necessary for Canada's defence, which he regarded as being across the ocean.

On the other hand, he also, being the man he was, felt what a terrible disgrace it would be to Canada and the people of Canada if this wonderful army that had been built up, that had fought at the Somme, at Ypres and Vimy, and so forth, had to be disbanded, in effect, because of the terrible casualties which they had suffered.

Henry Borden (nephew of Robert Borden)

As much as Borden's solicitude for "his boys," the deteriorating military situation of the Allies in general was now pushing him very strongly toward conscription. He spent from the middle of February to early May 1917 in England attending the first Imperial War Cabinet meetings. He was appalled by what he learned. The Allies' situation was growing worse: they might even be losing the war.

Astonishing news of the abdication of Czar and revolution in Russia. Evidently due to dark forces, the Monk Rasputin, the pro-German Court and bureaucratic influences, the meddling of the Empress, the weakness of the Czar, and his inability to realize or comprehend the forces of liberty and democracy working among the people.

Robert Borden, *Memoirs*, vol. 2

The early optimism that the Russian Revolution would improve matters soon turned to fears that Russia would withdraw from the war. If that happened the whole weight of the German army could be concentrated on the Western Front, and things were bad enough there already. The French offensive that had begun at the same time as Vimy Ridge in the spring of 1917 had pushed their army past the breaking point. One French regiment went to the front making bleating noises like lambs being led to slaughter, and when the offensive collapsed, fifty-four divisions—almost half the French army—mutinied. It took 100,000 courts martial to restore discipline, and even after that the French army seemed to be finished as an offensive weapon, perhaps for years.

Meanwhile, German submarines were sinking a million tons of Allied shipping a month, and the first sea lord, Admiral John Jellicoe, had concluded: "It is impossible for us to go on with the war if losses continue like this." Only one bright spot loomed on the horizon: the German campaign of unrestricted submarine warfare, by sinking neutral shipping, was pushing the United States into the war on the side of the Allies. (Washington declared war on Germany on April 6, 1917.) But it would take almost a year before American troops reached Europe in large numbers, and meanwhile France, Britain and the colonies had to hold out somehow on the Western Front. There was only one solution, and Lloyd George put it very bluntly to the Imperial War Cabinet on March 20, 1917:

> Let us look quite frankly at the position. [Germany] has more men in the field than ever she had. . . . She is in a very powerful military position. . . .
>
> The Allies are depending more and more upon the British Empire. . . . We started with 100,000 men, we now have 3,000,000 in the field. . . . What is it necessary for us to do in order to achieve the very sublime purpose which we have set before us? The first thing is this: we must get more men.

Lloyd George's "very sublime purpose," of course, was to make sure that the British empire won the war—no matter what the cost to Britain or anybody else. By 1917 the first total war had brought a new breed of men to power in Britain, France and Germany: Lloyd George, Georges Clemenceau and Erich Ludendorff owed their positions to promises that they would wage the war unrelentingly and uncompromisingly until total victory. In fact, there was probably no choice by 1917: it was not only in Russia that revolution was a danger. After so much sacrifice, any major European government that stopped the fighting short of victory now faced the risk of overthrow by an angry and disillusioned populace: only victory could make them safe. Even in Britain the cabinet was seriously worried about domestic political stability.

In Canada there was no danger of revolution, but the English-speaking majority would not forgive any government that failed to prosecute the war to the utmost, while the French-speaking minority would not forgive any government that resorted to compulsion. Four days after he returned to Ottawa from the Imperial War Cabinet meeting, Borden made his decision: he announced that the government would impose conscription.

EXCURSION 3

BREAKING THE STALEMATE

Ludendorff: The English soldiers fight like lions.
Hoffmann: True, but don't we know that they are lions led by
donkeys.

Falkenhayn: *Memoirs*

"LUDENDORFF" WAS GENERAL ERICH LUDENDORFF, EFFECTIVELY
the supreme commander of the German army in 1917–18.
"Hoffmann" was General Max Hoffmann, who was an old associate of
Ludendorff's and chief of staff on the Russian front for much of the war.
"Falkenhayn" was General Erich von Falkenhayn, the chief of the
German General Staff for the first two years of the war. The conversa-
tion is quoted at the beginning of *The Donkeys*, a book published by
British military historian Alan Clark in 1961 which ruthlessly dissected
and analyzed the shortcomings and failures of the British army's senior
officers in the battles of 1915.

Clark's book set the fashion for blaming the slaughter of the First
World War on arrogant, stupid and callous commanders that has largely
dominated popular accounts and dramatizations of the war ever since.
Indeed, *The Donkeys* was the principal inspiration for the satirical

musical *Oh, What a Lovely War!*, which spread the fashion even more widely. (Clark, later a maverick Conservative Member of Parliament and cabinet member under Margaret Thatcher, even took the play's authors to court in order to obtain proper credit and a share of the royalties.) So it's a pity, really, that the whole conversation between the German generals that gave Clark his title never happened. Clark simply made it up.

It's also a pity that the military profession is dismissed as hidebound and unimaginative in its conduct of the First World War, when in fact it responded quite quickly to the unprecedented tactical and strategic problem that had been presented to it by the continuous front. It took only three years, from January 1915 to late 1917, for the combatants to come up with the technologies and the techniques that would ultimately break the trench stalemate and restore mobility to the battlefield, although none of them had yet reached maturity when the war ended twelve months later.

In broad terms, only two things were necessary for an attacking army to achieve breakthroughs: surprise, and the ability to move faster than the defenders. The crux of the problem was that the attacker could never get through the lines of enemy trenches and out into open country before the defender brought up his reserves and created new defences behind them. But the defender wouldn't bring his reserves up before the battle if the attack came as a complete surprise—and he wouldn't have time to do so during the battle if the attacker could keep up his speed of advance through the enemy's defences: as little as one kilometre an hour would probably do it. So various professional officers (and civilian engineers) began casting around for ways to achieve both surprise and speed.

Panic spread like an electric current, passing from man to man along the trench. As the churning tracks reared overhead the bravest men clambered above ground to launch suicidal counter-attacks, hurling grenades onto the tanks' roofs or shooting and stabbing at any vision slit within reach. They were shot down or crushed, while others threw up their hands in terrified surrender or bolted down the communication trenches towards the second line.

German infantryman's first encounter with a tank, 1916

No sooner had the obstacle of the trenches suddenly appeared in 1914 than the solution occurred to a British staff officer, Colonel E.D. Swinton of the Royal Engineers. What was needed, obviously, was a vehicle armoured against machine-gun bullets and carrying its own guns, which could roll over shell holes, barbed wire and trenches on caterpillar tracks. Against much opposition from military conservatives, the idea was adopted by Winston Churchill (even though he was then First Lord of the Admiralty, and not in charge of the army at all). The earliest production models of the "landships," as they were first called, reached the Western Front in the autumn of 1916.

They were huge, primitive and horribly uncomfortable vehicles. The eight-man crew, stripped to their waists in the forty-degree heat, shared the interior with an exposed 105-horsepower Daimler engine. The fumes from the engine and from hot shell cases rolling around on the floor made the atmosphere inside almost unbreathable in combat. There were no springs in the suspension, the noise made voice communications impossible, and it was hard to see hand signals in the semi-darkness, as the only light came through the vision slits.

But the first time the tanks went into battle in really large numbers, at Cambrai in November 1917, where 476 were committed, they enabled the British army to advance ten kilometres in six hours, at a cost of just four thousand dead and wounded. Earlier the same year, at the Second Battle of Ypres, the British had taken three months to advance a similar distance, and they had lost a quarter of a million men doing it. But there was more to the success at Cambrai than just tanks. There was also, for the first time ever on the Western Front, a comprehensive plan for indirect artillery fire to engage the German defences simultaneously through the full depth of the defended zone, all the way back to the furthest reserve positions.

At Cambrai, there was no prolonged bombardment in the old style to destroy the wire and soften the defenders up. Indeed, to preserve secrecy and the possibility of surprise, the one thousand British guns that were deployed on a ten-kilometre front at Cambrai did not open fire, even to observe and adjust the fall of their shells, until the moment of the attack. It was the first large-scale use of "predicted fire," relying on aerial reconnaissance, accurate mapping of the targets, equally accurate surveying of your own gun positions and ballistic calculations instead of on direct observation. With the help of the tanks, and the 289 aircraft used as artillery spotters, ground-attack aircraft and bombers, the attack almost broke through the German lines completely. Only a very rapid and ferocious German counterattack closed the breach, but that was unlikely to happen every time.

The old trench stalemate was over, for the Germans had just solved the breakthrough problem in the same way, although with less reliance on tanks. (Curiously, the Germans put far less effort into developing tanks than the British and the French, although they did develop the first effective anti-tank rifles.) Beginning with an offensive at Riga on the Russian front in September 1917, a German artillery officer named Colonel Georg Bruchmüller independently came up with the same formula for surprise and rapid penetration: massive amounts of indirect and predicted artillery fire that gave no warning beforehand, and infantry "storm-troops" who were instructed to bypass enemy strongpoints that were still resisting and just keep moving ever deeper into the defended zone, spreading confusion and dismay and ultimately driving the enemy into flight. He gained the nickname "Durchbruchmüller" ("break-through"-müller) for his successes, and can claim a significant amount of credit for the offensive that smashed what was left of the Russian army and triggered the Communist coup against the democratic government in St. Petersburg in November 1917.

Three years after the failure of the Schlieffen Plan, the Russian collapse seemed to be giving Germany an unexpected second chance to win the war, and Bruchmüller was promptly moved to the Western Front. His tactics worked well there, too, in the great German offensives of spring 1918, but not so well that the Allied armies collapsed. After a series of major retreats in the spring, the Allies returned to the offensive in mid-1918, using quite similar tactics. The French and British armies were almost as exhausted as the Germans, but freshly arrived American troops took point in the French part of the line and the Canadian Corps and the Australians spearheaded the attacks in the British sector. Like the Germans, they were now able to gain ground consistently with their attacks.

Tanks never did play a decisive role in these battles, but the plans for 1919, had the war continued, called for a force of several thousand tanks supported by aircraft to smash through the enemy's front, with infantry following closely in armoured personnel carriers. Confronted with an unprecedented military problem, the soldiers of the First World War had solved the trench stalemate about as fast as you could reasonably ask. This begs the question of why anybody should ever be required to solve such a problem, of course, but from a professional point of view they did quite well.

CHAPTER 4

A COUNTRY DIVIDED

Bullets went through my main spar on the lower starboard wing and before I knew it I was in a steep dive but upside down, hanging onto the cowling openings beside the guns with both hands and my toes pressed up against the toe straps on my rudder bar for all I was worth. My seat belt had too much elasticity and did not hold me fast.

German machine guns were rat-tat-tatting away as the different pilots took turns shooting at me.

I went from 12,000 to 3,000 feet in this position, swearing at the Huns for shooting at me when I was obviously going to crash in a few minutes. I was panicky. At about 3,000 feet I went into heavy cloud, collected my panicked brains, reached up into the cockpit with one hand, caught the spade grip on the joystick, pressed the blip switch cutting the engine and slowly pulled back on the stick, coming out of the cloud right side up with no German pilots around.

I was over the German lines, did not want to be a prisoner, did not know whether the wing would stay together if I put the engine on or not but decided it was the only thing to do. . . . I put the engine on slowly, the wing held together, and with no one shooting at me from the air I stooged back home, a very thankful and less cocky fighter pilot.

Flight Sub-Lieutenant W.A. Curtis, Toronto, Ontario

THE ONE ASPECT OF THE WAR THAT STILL RETAINED SOME GLAMOUR for Canadians by 1917 was the war in the air. Once aerial warfare really got into high gear in 1916 and the British air services began to expand at a breakneck rate, Canadians flocked to join. Many young men already overseas wanted to escape the impersonal slaughter of the trenches, even if it just meant a lonelier death in a burning airplane a few months later, and many in Canada simply joined for the adventure. They were all slightly crazy.

A French squadron had its airfield not far from our hospital camp [in Macedonia, and] one or two of us had struck up an acquaintance with a young pilot of this French squadron. . . . On one visit . . . my friend was getting ready for a flight, and asked me if I would like to come along; there was room for one passenger. So I left my heart and courage on the ground and he took the rest of me up into the air.

After the first spasm of fear passed, I found that I liked flying. . . . My pilot friend may have sensed this, for he . . .gave me more flying than I expected, heading his machine, a Voisin monoplane, all canvas and string and wooden struts and a 90 hp engine, northwards to where the enemy were. When he indicated that he was going to do a little reconnoitring of the Bulgarian positions, my exhilaration diminished . . . [but] I have always claimed since that I was the only man in the history of military aviation whose first flight was over enemy territory.

Lester Pearson (who applied to join the Royal Flying Corps as soon as he landed), *Mike: Memoirs*, vol. 1

Ten of the top twenty-seven aces in the British forces were Canadians, and they included four of the twelve leading aces in the entire war. This extraordinarily high Canadian quotient was partly a reflection of the Canadians' remarkable enthusiasm for flying: by the time the various British air services were amalgamated into the Royal Air Force on April 1, 1918, there were 22,000 Canadians serving in them. (Indeed, the main reason that a separate Canadian Air Force was not created until the closing months of the war was the British concern that hiving the Canadians off would decimate their own squadrons. "Thirty-five per cent of our total strength in pilots is Canadian," remonstrated a British officer, Lieutenant Colonel R.C.M. Pink, in May 1918. "Under the Air Force Act every one of these can walk out of the door tomorrow and return to the Canadian service unless this service is definitely part of the Royal Air Force.") But the pilots themselves mostly didn't care what flag they saluted: they lived in an intense, closed world where the only thing that counted was the respect of their peers.

> Major W.G. Barker, DSO, MC, and the officers under his command, present their compliments to Captains Brumowski, Ritter von Fiala, Havratil and the pilots under their command, and request the pleasure of a meeting in the air. In order to save Captains Brumowski, Ritter von Fiala and Havratil and the gentlemen of their party the inconvenience of searching for them, Major Barker and his officers will bomb Godega Aerodrome at 10 a.m. daily, weather permitting, for the next fortnight.
>
> Leaflets dropped over the Austrian lines in Italy by No.
> 139 Squadron (Major Barker commanding) in mid-1918

In late 1918 Major William Barker of Dauphin, Manitoba, was already one of the leading aces of the war, with forty-six confirmed victories accumulated in two and a half years of fighting over the Western

Front and in Italy. (The Austrian Air Force sensibly kept its leading aces on the ground during the daily bombing of Godega airfield despite Barker's generous invitation.) But Barker was also, at the age of twenty-three, a man living on borrowed time, for even very good pilots rarely survived as long as he had in combat.

By late 1918 the Allied authorities well understood the propaganda value of live aces in boosting their populations' flagging morale, so Barker was eventually posted to command an air-fighting school in England in order to keep him alive. His protests were unsuccessful, but he did manage to get himself appointed to a squadron in France for ten days on the way home, on the grounds that German aerial tactics over the Western Front were now different from those he had become familiar with in his more recent experience against the Austrian Air Force over Italy. He had still seen no enemy aircraft when he took off alone for England on October 27 at the end of his ten days' stay in France, however, so he decided to take one last peek over the front.

He was in luck, sort of. As his Snipe fighter climbed to 21,000 feet over the Forêt de Mormal he spotted a Rumpler two-seat observation aircraft on a reconnaissance flight high above the British lines. But as he concentrated on the Rumpler he failed to notice the entire "flying circus" of sixty Fokker D-VIIs, the latest and fastest type of German fighter, that was flying beneath him stacked up in three or four echelons. As the Rumpler broke up before Barker's guns, one of the German fighters, climbing in a near stall, raked his plane from below with machine-gun fire and shattered his right thigh with an explosive bullet. Barker threw the Snipe into a spin and levelled out several thousand feet below, only to find himself in the midst of fifteen more Fokker D-VIIs. He got in quick bursts at three of them, setting one on fire at ten yards' range, but then he was wounded in the other thigh and fainted.

Barker spun down to fifteen thousand feet before he recovered consciousness and pulled his fighter out of its dive once more—only to find himself in the middle of a lower echelon of the same German formation. By sheer instinct he got on the tail of one of them, but by the time it burst into flames his own aircraft was being riddled with bullets from behind; one bullet shattered his left elbow and he passed out again, dropping to twelve thousand feet before he came to amidst the lower echelon of the flying circus. As the German fighters milled around his smoking machine, taking turns to attack from every point of the compass, it was clear to the thousands of British and Canadian troops watching from the trenches below that Barker was finished.

He must have thought so too, because he aimed his tattered Snipe at one of the D-VIIs and flew straight toward it as if to ram, firing as he went. But at the last instant it disintegrated and Barker hurtled through the wreckage; in the clear for a moment, he dove for the British trenches and crossed them at treetop height, finally crashing into the barbed-wire entanglements around a British balloon site just behind the lines.

"The hoarse shout, or rather the prolonged roar, which greeted the triumph of the British fighter, and which echoed across the battle front, was never matched . . . on any other occasion," recalled Colonel Andy McNaughton, a militia officer who had risen to command the Canadian Corps Heavy Artillery and watched the fight from his advanced headquarters near Valenciennes. (McNaughton became commander of the entire Canadian army in the next war.)

Billy Barker's lonely last fight, in which he added four more aircraft to his score, won him the Victoria Cross and failed to dampen his ebullience even slightly. "By Jove, I was a foolish boy, but anyhow I taught them a lesson," he told the newspapers from his hospital bed near Rouen ten days later. Although his leg wounds never properly healed and he had to walk with canes for the rest of his life, Barker stayed in aviation after the war, founding Canada's first (spectacularly unsuccessful) commercial airline in collaboration with another Canadian ace and Victoria Cross winner, Billy Bishop, briefly becoming director of the new Royal

Canadian Air Force, and continuing to fly personally until he was killed in a crash at Ottawa's Uplands Airport in 1930.

The exploits of Barker and men like him, in a kind of combat that seemed to retain some of the honour and glory that had traditionally been associated with warfare, provided Canadians with virtually the only relief from the bitter news arriving daily from the trenches. But it was on the ground that the war would ultimately be won or lost, and by late 1917 the demand for fresh cannon fodder had become so great that the government was knocking on the door of every family in Canada.

———

Prime Minister Borden's decision in May 1917 to bring in conscription was greeted with grim satisfaction in much of English Canada. The enthusiasm of the early days was long gone—too many families had already lost a son or a husband—but in its place, especially in the homes of the bereaved, was an inflexible determination to win the war and to make sure that the suffering was shared by all.

> The casualty lists were never printed until during the next week, and I can remember the appalling lines down the paper. And you'd look at it, you know, watching for the names that you knew. Q. How did people in the West feel about conscription? Well, I think they were all for it. Because after all, the flower of the flock had already been taken.
>
> Naomi Radford, Edmonton

Borden could in all honesty argue that the voluntary system was no longer working. In the fighting of April and May 1917 the Canadian Corps in France suffered 24,000 casualties, and recruitment at home was only 11,000. At that rate the army would run out of men fairly soon, so compulsion seemed to him the only solution. But Borden's problems were greatly eased by the serious split over conscription that now began to tear the Liberal opposition apart.

French-speaking Liberals unanimously opposed conscription, but most of the prominent English-speaking Liberals were conscriptionists by conviction, and the rest were hedging out of political necessity. Even William Lyon Mackenzie King, Laurier's protégé and likely successor, who had opposed conscription all along precisely because it would split both the Liberal party and the country, was starting to waver, fearing that there might be no future for an English-speaking politician who didn't line up with the English-speaking majority on this issue. "I have changed my views on conscription as the war has progressed and I have seen freedom threatened," he announced.

Borden's Conservatives split on English-French lines over conscription, too: the few remaining prominent French Canadian Conservatives in his cabinet warned him that if the Conservative Party brought in conscription, it would be destroyed in Quebec for twenty-five years. But the Conservatives depended much less heavily than Laurier's Liberals on French Canadian votes, and Borden was under too much pressure from conscriptionists in the rest of the country—and from the war itself—to back down. Moreover, he was convinced that conscription was what the men at the front wanted. Indeed, that *may* have been his most powerful motive:

> If we do not pass this measure, if we do not provide reinforcements, with what countenance shall we meet them on their return? . . . If what are left of 400,000 such men come back to Canada with fierce resentment and even rage in their hearts, conscious that they have been deserted or betrayed, how shall we meet them when they ask the reason? I am not so much concerned for the day when this Bill becomes law, as for the day these men return if it is rejected.

Both Borden and Laurier realized that the country was heading into a crisis, and Borden hoped to weather it by forming a coalition government. However, Laurier's unwavering opposition to conscription made that impossible, and he demanded a referendum on the issue (like the one that had recently rejected conscription in Australia).

> The law of the land, which antedates Confederation by many generations, and which was reintroduced at the time of Confederation, emphatically declared that no man in Canada shall be subjected to compulsory military service except to repel invasion for the defence of Canada. My honourable friend says the first line of defence for Canada is in France and Flanders. I claim there never was any danger of invasion on the part of Germany. Nobody can say that Canada, for one instant during the last three years, was in danger of invasion.
>
> Sir Wilfrid Laurier

In English Canada, there was an impression that if the French Canadians would only stop listening to Bourassa—if only Laurier would give them a lead—then they would see the error of their ways and start joining the army in large numbers. But that was nonsense: Laurier was compelled to oppose conscription both by his own long-held political principles and by the urgent need to provide some legitimate political voice for the very large number of Canadians (not all of them French Canadians, by any means) who vehemently disapproved of conscription. It was a bitter end to Laurier's lifelong role as a bridge between English and French Canada, but it was perhaps the greatest service he ever did for the country.

> Now if I were to waver, to hesitate or to flinch, I would simply hand over the Province of Quebec to the extremists. I would lose the respect of the people whom I thus addressed, and would

deserve it. I would not only lose their respect, but my own self respect also.

Sir Wilfrid Laurier, letter to Newton Rowell, June 8, 1917

Even with Laurier's Liberals providing a legitimate political vehicle for opposing conscription, the customary Quebec phenomenon whereby political moderates are outflanked in public by Nationalist extremists soon made itself felt with a vengeance at the anti-conscription political meetings and demonstrations that proliferated in Quebec's cities. From the start these were marked by blood-curdling threats and occasional street violence. On May 25 Colonel Armand Lavergne, a former commander of the militia regiment at Montmagny and a well-known Nationalist, told a great throng in Quebec City: "I will go to jail or be hanged or shot before I will accept [conscription]. The Conscription of 1917 had its origin in 1899, when Canada sent men to assist in crushing a small nation in the Transvaal. . . . It is not for Canada to defend England, but for England to defend Canada." The crowd cheered lustily, and then went and smashed the windows of the *Quebec Chronicle* and *L'Événement*, the two pro-government papers in the city.

Throughout the long summer of 1917, as the Military Service Bill dragged its slow way through Parliament, the political atmosphere in Quebec grew steadily more poisonous. Almost every warm evening during June and July, crowds of young men surged through the streets in the French-speaking quarters of Montreal breaking windows, firing off blank rounds and shouting "À bas Borden" and "Vive la Révolution."

Tancrède Marsil, whose antiwar newspaper *Le Réveil* had closed down in March 1917 after a warning from Ottawa, got his second wind from the government's decision to bring in conscription, and soon exercised a powerful influence through his new paper *La Liberté* and his impassioned speeches. In late June in Waterloo, in the Eastern Townships, he told the crowd: "before we have conscription, we will have revolution," and added that the people of Quebec would prefer to see "two or three thousand men killed in the streets rather than send three hundred thousand men to Europe." His angry audience responded by breaking nearby windows and cursing the Quebec Conservatives.

Talk like that made people very nervous in 1917, when real revolutions were breaking out in some other parts of the world: it was scarcely a year since the Easter Rising in Dublin, and only a couple of months since the Russian Revolution in Petrograd in February. And the pressure in Quebec just went on building: on July 15 Colonel Lavergne declared before fifteen thousand people at Quebec City:

> If the Conscription law is enforced (French) Canadians have only one choice—to die in Europe or to die in Canada. As far as I am concerned, if my body is to fall in any land, I want it to be on Canadian soil.

On July 24 Ottawa moved to close down Marsil's newspaper *La Liberté* after it had called for a general strike, a run on the banks and, if necessary, a revolution—but by that time a certain Élie Lalumière, a dealer in electrical fixtures and one of Marsil's many rivals in street rhetoric, was claiming to have five hundred men under training in Montreal to resist conscription by force of arms.

The first phase of the crisis peaked in August, as Borden's Military Service Bill finally passed into law with the support of more than twenty English-speaking Liberals who had deserted Laurier to vote for it. Lord Atholstan, the publisher of the *Montreal Star* and a vocal supporter of conscription, had received numerous threats, and at four o'clock on the morning of August 9 his house at Cartierville, a rural part of Montreal Island, was dynamited. It was a large stone house and none of the family or servants was hurt, but the explosives were found to be from a load of 350 pounds of dynamite that had been stolen from a quarry by a gang of masked men at the beginning of the month. A terrorist campaign was feared, and so the Dominion Police* were brought in. They offered a large reward for the culprits, twelve men were arrested—and one of them turned out to be the regular anti-conscription speaker, Élie Lalumière.

Lalumière detailed plots to blow up the *Star* offices, the *Gazette* and the Mount Royal Club, and to assassinate Sir Robert Borden and other well-known political figures. The English-language press described his associates as "desperadoes, cocaine fiends, wanted for several murders and crimes." By the end of the summer of 1917 many members of the public in Montreal were signing an anti-conscription "Declaration" which warned that "if the Bill is enforced Borden and his men will have to suffer the penalty of death," and on August 30 the city was swept by demonstrations, marches, outbreaks of looting and clashes with the police during which revolvers were freely used and at least seven men were wounded.

But the proto-insurrectionary character of the street violence and the growing number of attacks on property in the anti-conscription protests began to worry the French Canadian establishment. The higher clergy of the Catholic church in Quebec, in accord with tradition, had supported the British from the start and now reluctantly backed conscription too, but hitherto the French Canadian political and cultural elites (and the business elite, such as it was) had mostly turned a blind eye to what was happening in the streets because of their sympathy for the anti-conscriptionist cause. Matters were now clearly getting out of hand, however—and at the same time they were offered a safer and more moderate way of opposing conscription, in the form of an imminent federal election. For there did, after all, seem to be a chance of defeating conscription through the ballot box.

---

* The Dominion Police were founded in 1867 to provide security in Ottawa, but they were pressed into service during the First World War to supervise the enforcement of conscription. They were ultimately amalgamated with the RCMP in 1921.

By October 1917 Prime Minister Borden had succeeded in forming a "Union" government, which incorporated most of the English-speaking Liberals, especially from Ontario and the West, as well as his own Conservatives. However, he had failed to win bipartisan support for an extension of Parliament past its normal term. That meant he had to call an election before the end of 1917, and he was by no means certain of winning that election. Even in English Canada, organized labour and farmers were dead against conscription, and the popular magazine *Everywoman's World* found that a six-to-one majority among its readers opposed it (although that mattered less, since women didn't have the vote). What worried Borden's government most, however, was "French, foreigners, slackers."

Quebec was a lost cause for the Conservatives: the entire Nationalist movement, with Henri Bourassa in the lead, placed itself at the service of the Liberal opposition. "We ask nothing better than to assist Laurier to throw out of power the Government which has proved itself a traitor to the Nation," Bourassa wrote in *Le Devoir*—and the Nationalists ran practically no candidates of their own in Quebec in order not to split the anti-conscription vote.

The Conservatives had good reason to worry about the Prairie provinces, too. They could more or less count on the "British" element of the Western population, but the great surge of immigration that had rapidly populated the Prairies in the two decades before the war had also included a high proportion of "foreigners"—particularly Ukrainians—who felt even less enthusiasm than French Canadians for sending their sons to die for Britain: all three Prairie provinces had voted Liberal in the most recent provincial elections.

But in the West (unlike Quebec), the Union government had an opportunity to shift the voting balance radically by disenfranchizing the Ukrainians, most of whom came from Austrian-controlled Galicia and therefore technically counted as enemy aliens. Nor would such a flagrant act of electoral manipulation alienate those Prairie voters, mostly

"British," who were potential Conservative supporters. The Ukrainians were not actually sympathetic to their former Austrian imperial masters, of course, but Anglo-Saxon jealousy at the growing prosperity of Ukrainian homesteaders, and fury at the refusal of Ukrainian farm labourers to accept the low pre-war wages at a time of booming grain prices, easily translated into racism.

One Alberta MLA told the *Toronto Telegram* how sad it made him to see the country "being cleared of our fine Anglo-Saxon stock and the alien left to fatten on war prosperity." The Wartime Elections Act of 1917 adroitly exploited this prejudice—and destroyed the mainstay of Liberal anti-conscriptionist sentiment in the West—by taking the vote away from all naturalized Canadians born in enemy countries who had arrived in Canada after 1902. It was election-rigging on a breathtaking scale. Borden's government also generously gave women the vote—but only to women who might be expected to support conscription: those serving as nurses with the Canadian forces, and the far larger number of female relatives of serving soldiers. (One angry suffragette leader wrote to Borden suggesting that it would have been simpler if he just disqualified everyone who didn't promise to vote Conservative.)

> Our first duty is to win at any cost the upcoming elections, in order that we may continue to do our part in winning this war and that Canada not be disgraced.
>
> Robert Borden, diary, September 1917

The election was held in December, six months after conscription had been introduced. The pro-Borden *Colonist* in Victoria warned voters against "Bolsheviki intoxicated with the hope of power" (the Liberals, presumably), and Toronto's *Daily News* printed a map of Canada with Quebec outlined in black, labelled "The Foul Blot on Canada." Meanwhile it was practically impossible for Union government candidates to get their views heard in Quebec. Albert Sévigny, a Quebec

Conservative Party Member, was shot at, stoned, and unable to say a word at Saint-Anselme, in his former riding of Dorchester, and he was howled down even in Westmount. Another Union government meeting, this time in Sherbrooke, turned into a three-hour riot.

All the careful stacking of the deck paid off. In the December 1917 election, most of the female relatives of serving soldiers (who had been promised that none of the remaining men in their families would be conscripted) voted for the government. In the Prairie provinces, where most voters of Ukrainian, German, Austrian, Hungarian and Croatian descent had been disenfranchized, Unionist candidates swept the board, winning forty-one out of forty-three seats. Despite all Borden's massaging of the voting lists, the Conservative majority among civilian voters was still barely a hundred thousand votes. But soldiers voted almost twelve-to-one for the government, tripling its majority and changing the outcome in fourteen ridings. In the end, Borden's Union coalition of Conservatives and Liberal defectors took 268 seats—but only three of those seats were in Quebec. Laurier's Liberals took 62 seats in Quebec, and only 20 in all the rest of the country. Canada had never been so divided.

Only one Liberal did well out of the 1917 election, and it would have taken some foresight to realize it at the time. Mackenzie King had wavered on the conscription issue for a time: he rebuffed an approach from the Union government, which was having great success at recruiting pro-conscriptionist Liberals, but did consider simply not running. But he finally returned to his original convictions and waged an apparently suicidal anti-conscription campaign in North York (the old seat of his grandfather, William Lyon Mackenzie, before the 1837 rebellion). Election day was the worst of King's life: he was overwhelmingly defeated and his beloved mother died. But as he watched Laurier's political destruction spelled out in the election returns, he was also aware that Quebec would remember the Conservative imposition of conscription long after the war was over: "This will make me prime minister," he told a friend.

Just after the election, Sir Wilfrid Laurier wrote to a Liberal friend commanding a regiment in France to explain why the English-speaking Liberals who had deserted him had been wrong: "Your reason to take the stand which you took is: 'To us speedy reinforcements seem to take precedence of all else.' I appreciate the point of view, but you will see how far wrong you were. The conscription measure was introduced in the first week of June [1917]. We are now in the third week of January [1918] and not ten thousand men, if indeed half that many, have been brought into the ranks by this measure."

The defect in the Military Service Act was the high number of exemptions that could be applied for—but without those exemptions, Borden would probably never have won the election. Of the 400,000 unmarried men in Canada aged between twenty and thirty-four—the "first class"—380,000 had claimed exemptions by the end of 1917 (and Ontario, for all its electoral support of the government, claimed more exemptions than Quebec: 118,000 for Ontario, 115,000 for Quebec). Exemption tribunals were staffed by local people and reflected local loyalties and prejudices. The Quebec tribunals were accused of granting almost blanket exemptions to French-speaking applicants, while "they applied conscription against the English-speaking minority in Quebec with a rigor unparalleled," according to the chief appeal judge, Mr. Justice Lyman Duff of the Supreme Court. Military representatives took to appealing virtually every exemption, and in early 1918 the Military Service Act was toughened. Nineteen-year-olds were ordered to report for service, and men between twenty and twenty-two were exempted only if they were the sole remaining son of military age in the family. Every young man in the first class had to carry a written proof of exemption or be liable to arrest. All over the country, young men vanished into the woods:

> A mounted policeman once told me of the men who had gone way
> deep into the Peace River country or the Athabaska country and
> hid out. He would be searching around, and find them in a cabin
> someplace or other. And I remember him telling me of a mother

that practically scratched his eyes out—she had three sons hidden around the country, and saw that they got food.

Naomi Radford

In Quebec opposition to the new regulations was spectacular, especially since a hasty marriage was no longer a way out of the draft (men now had to have been married prior to July 6, 1917, to claim exemption). There were still thirty thousand appeals before the courts, but the minister of justice was making arrangements to speed up the process and feelings were reaching fever pitch: the popular resistance that seemed to have crested in August 1917, and to have been almost completely dissipated by the December election, came roaring back to life.

The delayed-action conscription crisis of 1918 was quite inevitable. During all the protests of 1917, the subject had been emotional but almost entirely theoretical: the machinery ground into action so slowly that few conscripts actually disappeared into the army before the end of that year. By early 1918, however, everybody in Quebec knew someone who had already been conscripted, or who was facing the near-certainty of conscription at any moment. It put the issue in a very different light, and things came to a head at the beginning of Easter weekend in Quebec City, when the Dominion Police detained a young man named Mercier who was unable to show proof of an exemption.

Mercier finally managed to get permission to go home and produce his papers, and he was then duly released—but meanwhile a crowd of several thousand had gathered, angered by "the tactless and grossly unwise fashion in which the Federal Police in charge of the Military Service Act did their work" (as the jury put it at the subsequent inquest). To vent their anger, the crowd proceeded to burn down the police station. The mayor tried to get them to disperse—but the mob, singing *O Canada* and *La Marseillaise*, attacked the offices of the *Quebec Chronicle* and *L'Événement* instead. The following evening another mob attacked the offices of the registrar of military service and burned all the files.

In an act of singular ineptitude, the local military authorities then brought in a battalion of Toronto soldiers as reinforcements. The officer in charge of the operation was one of the army's few senior French Canadians, Major General E.L. Lessard, but mutual incomprehension and suspicion between francophone crowds and anglophone troops did not help matters—nor did charging at the crowds with bayonets. On Sunday, March 31, the army also resorted to cavalry charges, driving back the crowds with axe handles. By then, military discipline was breaking down and some soldiers were firing at the mobs. Charles "Chubby" Power, the young Liberal MP for Quebec South, a veteran who had served overseas, reported hearing an officer from his own regiment admit that he had been unable to prevent some of his soldiers from opening fire. He had not seen any wounded, he said.

On Easter Monday, the Old Town looked like a battlefield. Using snowbanks and ice barricades for shelter, the crowds were throwing bricks, stones, blocks of ice or whatever else they could lay their hands on at the soldiers. A few shots were heard from the direction of the mob, and the troops at first replied with volleys over their heads.

After the second volley fired in the direction of Bagot St., they said: "Come on, you French sons of bitches, we'll trim you!" The soldiers were quite spread out. They were saying: "Go back, you French Cock-suckers" and "Go back, you French Cunt-lickers." And then, during a lull, an officer arrived. He said: "I will fix the machine gun. We will do better work."

Testimony of Wilfrid Dion at the Coroner's inquest,
Quebec, April 12, 1918

So I started the machine gun, and stopped it just like that (the witness snaps his fingers). It ran about three-quarters of the drum: so 36 shots were fired.

Testimony of Major George Rodgers, Quebec, April 10, 1918

There were two more bursts of machine-gun fire. An estimated thirty-five civilians were wounded, and four were killed. One of them was only fourteen years old. It was not exactly the storming of the Bastille, but the authorities feared insurrection in Quebec, and on April 4, 1918, the Governor in Council was given the power to call out the troops whether the civil authorities asked for them or not. In such a situation martial law would be declared; habeas corpus would be suspended and "persons disobedient to such military orders shall be tried and punished by court martial."

———

Bailleulval. May 18, 1918

I got up at 3 o'clock this morning. The rear details of the battalion were ordered to take part in one of the saddest scenes I have ever witnessed, the execution of a soldier, guilty of desertion and cowardice in [the] face of the enemy.

After marching for an hour and a half, we reached a little village whose name I do not know. We entered a big court-yard, surrounded by a stone wall. In a house at one end of the yard were military police. The condemned man appeared suddenly between two policemen. In passing, he cast a glance at us, so hopeless that the tears rose in my eyes. He disappeared behind a screen, erected to conceal him from sight. Behind this screen, the firing squad was in place. All of a sudden, a volley rang out. . . .

Now, we have to march past the body of the executed man, who is still tied to the chair in which he died. Blood has stained his tunic and his head has fallen on his chest. His face reveals complete resignation and on his lips is the trace of a smile.

Arthur Lapointe, *Soldier of Quebec: 1916–1919*

Twenty-five Canadian soldiers were executed in the field during the First World War, all but two of them for desertion or "misbehaviour before the enemy." The executions were a direct measure of the mounting strain on the Canadian army. Until the war was almost two years old, Canadian soldiers convicted of desertion or cowardice all had their sentences commuted to terms of imprisonment, but then, after the Battle of the Somme in July 1916, there were seven executions in seven weeks. Executions "to encourage the others" then continued at a steady pace until the war's end—with one particular group standing out: seven of the twenty-five men executed had French names, and five of them were from the sole French-speaking battalion, the 22nd.

Military machines everywhere were starting to show the strain. In 1917 both the French and the Italian armies had come close to disintegration, and the Russian army had collapsed utterly. The Germans were moving large numbers of troops from the former Eastern Front to the Western Front for a make-or-break offensive, but at home the Allied blockade was causing severe shortages of food and raw material. With British forces worn down by the Passchendaele offensive (which had been launched partly to distract the Germans from noticing the terrible state of the French army), Prime Minister Lloyd George of Britain sent a request to Borden on Easter weekend 1918 for still more Canadian troops. In France General Currie broke his own rule and sent Canadian reinforcements to British units. And in England Lester Pearson, recently commissioned a lieutenant after two years' service in the ranks, was recuperating from an accident that had interrupted his training in the Royal Flying Corps.

I spent much of that sick leave with a Canadian friend, Clifford Hames, who had just finished his abbreviated flying training and was on leave before going to France. We spent hours trying to get some understanding of what we were being asked to do; to bring some reason to the senseless slaughter. For what? King and country? Freedom and democracy? These words sounded hollow now in 1918 and we increasingly rebelled against their hypocrisy. Cliff Hames and I came closer together in that short time than I have ever been with any person since, outside my family. He knew where he was bound within a few days. He could not know it was to his death within the month. I did not know what was to happen to me.

We both assumed that our generation was lost. The war was going badly in France. The great German March offensive was about to begin. The fighting would go on and on and on. We, who were trapped in it, would also go on and on until we joined the others already its victims. All this had to be accepted. It never occurred to us that we could do anything about it. We might as well make the best of it, getting what pleasure we could.

Lester Pearson, Mike: Memoirs, vol. 1

For Germany, the spring of 1918 was the last chance for victory. By March 1918, when the Communists who were fighting to establish their control over Russia signed a peace treaty with Germany at Brest-Litovsk, half a million German troops had already been moved west. For the first time the Germans had something like numerical parity with the Allies on the Western Front, but it would not last long. It was a year since the United States had entered the war on the Allied side in April 1917, and by the summer of 1918 there would be 300,000 American troops arriving in France every month. So the Germans went for broke in the spring, hoping to achieve a breakthrough that would divide the British and imperial troops from the French and drive the British back onto the Channel ports. Then, with a quick peace before American strength built up, maybe Germany could get away with a draw in the west and even keep its conquests in the east.

Colonel Bruchmüller had arrived on the Western Front at the very end of 1917, and in the first couple of months of 1918 hundreds of thousands of Germany's best remaining troops were stripped from their units and retrained as storm-troops who would attack using his new infiltration tactics. At Arras in 1918, 6,608 German guns opened fire on the first day of the offensive without any advance warning—and the German offensive gained more ground in the next two weeks than the Allies had gained in every offensive in the whole war. Further fast-moving offensives followed, and the Allies feared that they were going to lose the war in the spring of 1918.

In Canada, Borden called a secret session of Parliament to explain the peril, and passed an Order in Council effectively cancelling all exemptions for single men, including farmers. In mid-May, five thousand farmers arrived in Ottawa to protest the new policy. Troops prevented them from approaching the Houses of Parliament, but Borden spoke to them and told them bluntly that the government had taken a solemn pledge to reinforce the Canadian Corps. As long as he was prime minister, that pledge would be fulfilled. But long before any further reinforcements reached the Canadian Corps, the Germans' spring offensive ran out of steam.

The Germans lost a million men between March and July 1918, but they never managed to split the Allies apart and roll the British lines up. It was the Canadians and Australians, attacking side by side near Amiens, who made the great breakthrough on August 8, the longest advance that any Allied attack had yet achieved in the war. Ludendorff called it "the black day of the German army." From August on, the Germans were in almost constant retreat—and the Canadian and Australian divisions, whose condition was still far better than most of the British units, were consistently used to spearhead the attacks. Between August 22 and October 11, 1918, the Canadian Corps lost over fifteen hundred officers and thirty thousand casualties in the other ranks.

> I guess you have heard now of the Big Push, of the battle of Amiens, in which the Canadians took a prominent part. . . . It was a terrible battle, our Division winding up the advance and holding the ground gained. Our battalion took the last objective. The Company I am with went into the attack 140 strong, and when the roll was

called, only 32 answered. I am sorry to say I lost two dandy chums—one missing and one killed. I tried to help bandage Aubrey but it was no use, as the bullet had gone through his head. . . .

Corporal Walter Cullen (Paris, Ontario), August 1918

Donald A. Smith, *At the Forks of the Grand*, vol. 2

I got wounded on the Saturday, and the War ended on the Monday morning. I had a rather nice time during the war: I was in the Cycle Corps, we weren't up the line, we weren't in the mud all the time. We were mobile infantry, and they started to use us at the last, so I had a rougher time towards the end than I did earlier on in the war.

I was on a patrol that was trying to get into Mons, and there were four on the patrol. Two were killed, I was wounded, and one got away scot-free—he'd been sent back with a message.

George Turner, Edmonton

The Third Canadian Division, at the price of many sacrifices, penetrated the city at three o'clock in the morning, avenging thus by a brilliant success the retreat of 1914. Glory and gratitude to it.

Proclamation of the Town Council of Mons

On November 11, 1918, Robert Borden was at sea, on his way to England to discuss with Lloyd George and the Imperial War Cabinet what position the British delegates to a peace conference should take after the war was won:

At 12:30 ship's time purser in tremendous excitement came to my room with startling announcement that Germany signed armistice at 5 a.m.; hostilities to cease at 11 a.m. today. . . . This means complete surrender. The Kaiser is reported as seeking refuge in Holland, but the Dutch don't want him. Rumours that several of German princelets and kinglets have abdicated or fled. Revolt has spread all over Germany. The question is whether it will stop there.

Robert Borden, *Memoirs*, vol. 2

————————

We are the Dead. Short days ago
We lived, felt dawn, saw sunset glow,
Loved and were loved, and now we lie
In Flanders fields.
Take up our quarrel with the foe:
To you from failing hands we throw
The torch; be yours to hold it high.
If ye break faith with us who die
We shall not sleep, though poppies grow
In Flanders fields.

John McCrae, Canadian Expeditionary Force (died 1918)

That never-to-be-forgotten day, 11 November 1918, saved the rest of my generation and gave the world not peace, but a reprieve.

1939 was only twenty years away; we did not keep the faith with those who died; the torch was not held high.

Lester Pearson, *Mike: Memoirs*, vol. 1

The First World War remains the most profound trauma in Canada's history, although it all happened long ago and thousands of miles away. The names of our quarter-million dead and wounded are mostly forgotten now, but the effects of that collective act of self-immolation still reverberate in our national life today. However, keeping faith with the dead of the First World War has more often been interpreted by Canadians as an injunction to go and fight the Germans again (or the Russians, or whomever) than in Pearson's sense, as a call for Canadians to play their part in the immense task of abolishing war.

The old international system should have died after the First World War—and there was certainly a determined attempt to kill it. Four years of the most devastating war in European history, over a Balkan quarrel whose protagonists had mostly disappeared by 1918, were enough to convince large numbers of people (and even their governments) that there was something dreadfully wrong with the traditional way of running the world. War had become far too costly a means of settling disputes between the great powers, and so the nations began to cast around for an alternative.

(1)   Open covenants of peace openly arrived at. . . .

(2)   Absolute freedom of the seas. . . .

(4)   General disarmament consistent with domestic safety. . . .

(14) Creation of a general association of nations for the purpose of providing international guarantees of political independence and territorial integrity for all nations.

U.S. President Woodrow Wilson, *The Fourteen Points*,

January 8, 1918

The Lord God had only ten.

French prime minister Georges Clemenceau,

about Wilson's Fourteen Points

Woodrow Wilson's formulation of Allied war aims for the U.S. Congress at the beginning of 1918 was light-years distant from what those aims had been in 1914, but the war had greatly changed the way people saw the world. The international system had staggered on for centuries, periodically producing a general war, but never doing irreparable harm to its major players, so the traditional attitude was: "If it ain't broke, don't fix it." By 1918, however, the system *was* broke: it had delivered all the great powers into a war grotesquely out of proportion to the purposes for which they had entered it (insofar as they had any clear aims at all). They had fought the war to the bitter end because they did not know how to stop it, and dared not admit to their own peoples that it was not about anything worth fighting for.

But at the same time it was quite clear to both the leaders and the led that this must be "the war to end all wars," and that defeating their enemies in this particular war would not suffice to abolish war itself. So many people were prepared to contemplate the radical idea that the international system itself would have to be changed.

The notion of an international organization to prevent war had been floating around for half a century, but it fell to Woodrow Wilson, the rigid and sanctimonious university professor who became president of the United States, to put it on the agenda of the world's governments. His idea for a League of Nations was gravely flawed, but it was an idea that would never go away again. However reluctant governments and peoples might be to change their old ways, there was a general recognition that it had to be tried, because the alternative—a future of ever more destructive technological wars—was even worse.

As far as many English Canadians were concerned, however, the great lesson of the war was that international politics is a crusade of good nations against evil ones. Their consequent willingness to place the country at the disposal of Britain in the great-power struggle (a loyalty subsequently transferred virtually intact to the United States) has been the single most powerful influence on our foreign policy down to the present.

The First World War saw the birth of a distinctive English Canadian national consciousness, but French Canada was not present at the birth. The great irony is that a lot of English Canada wasn't present either, although it later pretended it had been. Even after vigorous and repeated recruiting drives and the ultimate imposition of conscription had dragged many native-born English Canadians into the army, the proportion of native-born in the Canadian forces rose to only 51 percent by the end of 1918. The great bulk of the remainder were drawn from the relatively small fraction of first-generation British immigrants in the population, who volunteered for the war at a rate at least as high as that of the New Zealanders or the British themselves.

In Canada as a whole, the rate of enlistment was lower even than in Australia (with its large Irish population) or in English-speaking South Africa. English-speaking Canadians had, on average, been in their own country longer than the populations of the other "white dominions," and had had the time to get their bearings. Their sentimental attachment to the "Motherland" remained, but they knew that their practical interests were different, so they did not volunteer as readily to fight for Britain. Nevertheless, the fact that so many people fought in Canadian uniform—and suffered so greatly—had a profound effect on English Canadians' subsequent view of themselves and the world. The "British Canadians" who went off to the trenches, whether English-born or native-born, returned simply as Canadians—but they were a very different kind of Canadian from those who spoke French.

> I venture to think that the French Canadians who have fought and died in France and Flanders are more truly representative of the spirit and ambitions of their race than those who, like [Bourassa], have remained in Canada and refused to share in the glory and agony of this our national birth. It was as a Canadian that I appealed to him, not as an Imperialist.
>
> Talbot Papineau, after he had read Bourassa's reply to his
> open letter, August 1916

Talbot Papineau was a gallant figure, but desperately out of step with his compatriots. French Canada's war was waged mostly at home, against the demands that it fight in Britain's war in Europe. The exact figures cannot be determined, but of the more than 600,000 men and women who served in the Canadian forces during the war, only around

35,000 were French Canadians (a proportionate share would have been around 200,000) and fewer than half of the French Canadians who did enlist ever saw the front. Moreover, although Quebec contains about seven-eighths of Canada's French-speaking population, almost half of the 15,000 French Canadian volunteers serving in April 1917 (before conscription began to distort the figures) were from French Canadian communities outside Quebec, which were much more exposed to the influence of English Canadian public opinion.

June 9, 1918

In the trench, wrecked by the bombardment of last night, all is now quiet and peaceful. The gunners are now taking things easily.

Several men are lying in a shelter, thinking probably of the strange vicissitudes of a soldier's life. I recognize some of the conscripted men who joined us yesterday. I am sorry for them from the bottom of my heart. They have been sent out here against their will, while the rest of us have voluntarily assumed our task. A dozen of the conscripts were killed last night, their first night in the line. They lie now in a corner of the trench, waiting until someone moves them to the rear for burial.

Soldier of Quebec: 1916–1919

Conscripts, including a handful of French Canadian conscripts, began to reach the army in France only in the closing months of the war. For all the tumult it caused, the Military Service Act had raised only 83,355 men by November 1918, of whom 7,100 were absent on compassionate leave and 15,333 on agricultural leave. Seventeen months' operation of the conscription law therefore produced only 61,000 soldiers, most of whom never reached France.

The many delays and errors involved in the application of conscription were certainly a blessing, for if the war had lasted long enough for conscripts from Quebec to begin dying in the trenches in large numbers—and the British generals were planning for a war that continued into 1920—then the events of Easter Monday 1918 in Quebec City might have been repeated and magnified a hundredfold. By 1920 the war might really have come to Canada, and Quebec might have been occupied territory. As it was, French Canada's legacy from the war was bitterness at having been isolated and reviled for taking a position that even English Canadians would now concede to have been justifiable. French Canadians owed their loyalty to Canada alone, and would have fought to defend it, but the European war did not threaten Canada.

Although few conscripts from Quebec actually died, the bitterness of that memory has never quite gone away. As for those French Canadians who did volunteer for the war, out of a sense of adventure or a misplaced idealism, they are simply forgotten.

Dear Madam,

In confirmation of my telegram to you of yesterday's date, I regret exceedingly to inform you that an official report has been received to the effect that Captain A/Major T.M. Papineau, M.C., P.P.C.L.l. was killed in action on October 30, 1917.

Yours truly,
J. M. Knowles, Lieut.

WOULD A GERMAN VICTORY HAVE BEEN WORSE?

THE FIRST WORLD WAR INVOLVED FEW FULLY DEMOCRATIC countries on either side. In France all adult males had had the vote since 1792 and in Germany since 1871, while in Britain about 60 percent of adult males also had the vote; but in both Germany and the United Kingdom the actual government was still dominated by the old moneyed elite and (especially in Germany's case) the monarch. Russia and Austria-Hungary were autocracies with only the sketchiest facade of a parliamentary system. Yet even at the time, the war was portrayed in France and the English-speaking countries as a battle in defence of democracy, with the implication that a dark night of tyranny would descend on the world if the other side won. A hundred years later, the same rhetoric is still trotted out every Remembrance Day.

A dark night of tyranny already prevailed over most of the world in 1914, of course, in the sense that almost everybody in the world who was not of European descent was the involuntary subject of some European empire. At the end of the war, some of them got a change of oppressor (the German colonies and the Arabic-speaking parts of the Ottoman empire were all divided up among the victors), but they still had no voice in what happened to them. Different people in some other parts of Africa and Asia might have had a change of rulers if the Central Powers had won, but on the whole it wouldn't have made much difference to them.

As far as the European countries themselves are concerned, however, the question of whether a German victory would have made a lot of difference rarely gets posed. It is taken for granted that the history of the next few decades really would have been a lot worse if the other side had won the First World War, because that was always the victors' story, and it was reinforced when the same alliance won the Second World War as well. But it is not actually a self-evident truth, and there is some value in making a brief excursion into "counter-factual" history. Just how different would the world actually have been if Germany had won the war in 1918?

It's hard to argue that the spring offensives of 1918 could have won the war for Germany even if they had decisively broken through the Allied front and separated the British army from the French. The Allies would have hung on grimly, perhaps with the British army in an enclave on the Channel coast, knowing that the scheduled arrival of more than two million American troops by the end of the year would swing the balance back in their favour. Germany would still have lost in the end: the American declaration of war in 1917 cancelled out the advantage that Germany derived from the Russian exit from the war after the revolution, and Germany was still hugely outmatched both in men and in industrial resources.

It would have been different if Germany had not resumed the campaign of unrestricted U-boat warfare in 1917, knowing full well that the sinking of neutral shipping, including American ships, was almost bound to bring the United States into the war. Admiral Henning von Holzendorff, who wrote the key memorandum in December 1916, claimed that unrestricted submarine warfare would sink 600,000 tons of shipping a month and starve Britain into submission within five months, well before the Americans could act. Holzendorff promised the Kaiser, "not one American will land on the continent." It was an act of desperation, as the German military authorities could see no other chance for a German victory.

At first the submarine campaign was a great success, with fully a quarter of all British-bound shipping being sunk in March 1917, but the campaign began to fail as soon as the Royal Navy brought back the old system of convoys of merchant vessels escorted by warships (which it had previously resisted) in April. And in the same month, the United States declared war on Germany—which meant that by March 1918 its huge new army had been conscripted and trained and was beginning to enter the trenches in France. In that month there were still only 300,000 American troops in France, but they then began to arrive in Europe at the rate of 10,000 a day, and by August there were 1.3 million American soldiers deployed overseas, with another million due by the end of the year. Germany could not really have won the war in 1918, although many on the Allied side, shocked by the success of the first great German offensive in March, were convinced that it might.

On the other hand, only a two-month delay in Germany's fatal decision in January 1917 to launch unrestricted U-boat warfare might have caused the decision to go the other way, for in March the revolution in Petrograd overthrew the Tsar and raised the hope (though not yet the accomplished fact) that Russia might leave the war. And if Germany had not decided to gamble everything on the unrestricted U-boat campaign, then the United States would almost certainly not have declared war in 1917. In that case, Germany just might have won the war.

It would not have been a resounding victory, for the opponents were too evenly matched, but with a bit more luck on the German side and a bit worse generalship on the Allied side the Germans could have made a big breach in the Western Front at the point where the British and French armies met. They might then have rolled up the open

British flank and driven the empire's troops back into an enclave based on the Channel ports, while further south the French army tried to stretch out into a thinly manned new front that reached the sea somewhere near the mouth of the Seine. There would have been no march on Paris: the German troops would have been far too exhausted for that, and the breakthrough would only have been achieved at a huge cost in casualties. But the psychological impact of the defeat might still have been enough to make the Allies ask for an armistice, especially since there would have been no Americans coming and the signature of the Treaty of Brest-Litovsk in March would have just confirmed that the Russians were out of the war for good. So what would the peace treaty between a (barely) victorious Germany and the remaining Allied powers have looked like?

If it looked anything like the Brest-Litovsk treaty, it would have been a dreadful document. The Bolsheviks, who were still struggling to extend their control over Russia, were helpless in the face of the Germans, and so, to gain time to defeat their internal enemies, the new Soviet regime signed away Finland, Estonia, Latvia, Lithuania, Belarus and Ukraine. That effectively moved Russia's old imperial border east by 300 to 400 kilometres everywhere except in Ukraine, where it retreated twice as far. The treaty stated that "Germany and Austria-Hungary intend to determine the future fate of these territories in agreement with their populations," but they were clearly destined to become satellites and client states of Germany and Austria-Hungary.

A 1918 or 1919 peace treaty after a narrow German victory in the west could not have been as severe. Germany's priority in the west would have been a peace that stabilized the situation and gave it time to assimilate its gains in the east. It urgently needed an end to the British naval blockade, for civilians in Germany were starting to die of malnutrition in significant numbers. Having seen Red revolution in Russia, the collapse of the Italian army and the near-collapse of the French army in the previous twelve months, it would have wanted to end the war quickly before there were mutinies in the German army and revolution in the streets at home. And in any case, the strength of the German army, although it was in a temporarily dominant position, would not have been great enough for Berlin to enforce extreme demands on the Allied powers. The peace treaty, as a result, would have been considerably gentler than the one that the Allies actually imposed on Germany at Versailles.

There would have been no reparations and "war guilt" clause imposed on France and Britain; those were luxuries that Germany's precarious military superiority would not have allowed it to indulge in. There would probably have been no border changes in Western Europe; the only region really in dispute was Alsace-Lorraine, and Germany owned that already. There would doubtless have been a requirement for the British army to withdraw from France and never return, and limits would have been placed on the future size of the French army, but Germany would not have been able to impose the kind of limits on the size and composition of Britain's navy that the Treaty of Versailles actually imposed on the German navy. Germany would have got its existing overseas colonies back (they had all been conquered by Britain and France during the war), and perhaps some new ones as compensation for all its trouble. Then everybody would have gone home and lived bitterly ever after.

The bitterness would have been particularly strong in the countries that had "lost" the war. Prime Minister David Lloyd George in Britain, President Georges Clemenceau in France—and, no doubt, Prime Minister Robert Borden in Canada—would have lost power very quickly, but there would have been no collapse of the entire political system of the sort that occurred in Berlin and Vienna in the real 1918.

Two positive things would not have happened in the event of a German victory. There would have been no League of Nations: the idea was almost entirely an American and British one, and only came to fruition because they effectively dominated the peace conference at

Versailles. It didn't succeed, in the end, but it did provide two decades of experience in trying to run an international institution dedicated to the prevention of great-power war that would not have been available in our alternative timeline. And Canada's de facto independence from Britain would have been delayed by a few years, partly because the alternative peace conference would not have provided an opportunity for Canada to insist on being treated as a sovereign state, and partly because we would have been so frightened of German power that we would have clung tightly to Britain's skirts for a little longer.

Austria-Hungary would have come out of the war intact, albeit only by the skin of its teeth, and there would have been no splintering of south-central Europe into half a dozen new countries. However, the contending nationalisms that made the Austrian empire so fractious and fragile would not have evaporated, and it is questionable whether it could have overcome its own divisions in the longer term even in the event that it "won" the war. The Ottoman empire would also have survived the war, recovering its conquered provinces in Iraq and Palestine from Britain and perhaps expanding its borders in the Caucasus. But the Arab revolt that the British had sponsored as part of their strategy against Turkey would not have been forgotten. Both of these ramshackle empires would have provided much raw material for confrontations and crises: there was no risk that the future would be boring.

Germany would have had its hands full getting its various new satellite states in the east up and running, and it might also have got involved in helping the Whites against the Reds in the Russian civil war (as Britain and France did in the real history). That, plus the prestige the German military would have enjoyed for saving the country from a catastrophic defeat, would have ensured a high degree of military influence in the German government for the first few years after the war, but such influence does not usually last in a democracy at peace. There is no particular reason to doubt that German politics would have undergone the same evolution towards greater inclusivity and transparency in

the few decades after a victory in the First World War that British politics did in the real history of 1918–50.

Neither is there any strong reason to believe that the defeated powers, Britain and France, would have descended into fascism and risked
major war again to even the score, as Germany did in the real postwar
history. They could easily have indulged in a witch hunt for those
responsible for losing the war, but their loss would not have been nearly
as traumatic as Germany's was, and democratic traditions were older
and stronger in Britain and France. As for Russia, whether it was the
Whites or the Communists who finally won the civil war, Russia would
probably have been a dictatorship for at least some decades, and as easily
a fascist as a communist one. It would also almost certainly have drifted
into a military confrontation with Germany, which would then have
gone in search of allies elsewhere. Japan, at the other end of Russia,
would have been an obvious candidate if it had not already been allied
to Britain. But that is the sort of difficulty that diplomacy exists to overcome, and it's not inconceivable that Britain, German and Japan could
have ended up allied against a fascist or Communist Russia twenty years
down the line.

The further you get down the timeline of this alternative history
the more difficult it is to stay plausible, because the decision-points multiply and the probabilities get harder to calculate. That doesn't matter,
because the only point of this exercise was to see if the world in which
Germany "won" the war would have been immersed in a dark night of
tyranny. It would appear not. It would have been a complex, combative,
often quite unlovely place, but at worst no worse than the world we
inherited from the Allied victory in 1918. It might also have been a
world in which the next world war was the customary fifty years or so
away, not a mere twenty, as nobody had lost so badly that they would
soon be back seeking vengeance. Of course, all this is true because we
are not really talking about a decisive German victory of the sort that
the Allies finally achieved later in 1918. There was never any possibility

of that sort of victory after the failure of the Schlieffen Plan in 1914, and probably not even then. We are talking about a no-score draw masquerading as a German victory, and that might have been a quite acceptable outcome. Although a no-score draw reached after the Christmas truce in 1914 would have been a much better outcome.

CHAPTER 5

THE FIREPROOF HOUSE

ON NOVEMBER 11, 1918, AS THE ARMISTICE FINALLY DESCENDED ON the Western Front, a group of Canadian gunners were fighting for their lives in northern Russia. Having advanced over a hundred miles up the Dvina River from Archangel on the Arctic coast to the village of Tulgas, they were surprised from the rear by a force of six hundred Soviet infantry. The Bolsheviks ("Bolas," as the Canadians called them) were seen only when they got within two hundred yards of the 67th Battery, and the artillerymen would have been overrun if their drivers and signallers had not managed to slow the attackers down with rifle fire until the gunners could get one of their 18-pounder guns out of its gun-pit, turn it around and fire a quick-bursting shrapnel shell straight into the charging Russians at seventy-five yards' range. In those early days the intervention in Russia generally had a rather impromptu spirit about it.

> The first military operation at Soroka . . . was a dashing reconnais-
> sance carried out by Captain Adams, Canadian Engineers, who
> was sent to Ruguzero in Karelia with a detachment of six Canadian
> sergeants and six Karelian soldiers . . . attached to the Canadian
> Syren Party.

. . . Although they had information that the village was occupied by a Red garrison of at least 150 soldiers, they decided to make an attack. Captain Adams sent Lieutenant Hordliski and the six Karelians with a Lewis gun to the southern end of the village. He and his six Canadian sergeants waited at the other end for zero hour. Then both parties dashed forward, firing and shouting, and the Bolsheviks, thinking they were surrounded and greatly outnumbered, capitulated without a fight. They were all herded into the village square, where they got the surprise of their lives when they discovered that a dozen determined men had killed or captured their whole garrison.

A big celebration was held at Canadian Headquarters when Captain Adams and his party returned with their prisoners, a dozen sleigh-loads of rifles, and all the documents of the Bolshevik headquarters in that district. The patrol had left Soroka on January 14th [1919] and returned on the night of January 17th, having covered 120 miles in horse-drawn sleighs.

John Hundevad, "A Saga of the North," *The Legionary*, 1936

The Allied intervention in northern Russia began in early 1918 with purely military motives. It was aimed at bringing Russia back into the war, which in practice meant trying to overthrow the Bolshevik regime that had signed a separate peace with the Germans. The Canadian soldiers who were sent to northern Russia in March 1918 as part of the "Syren Force," a multinational concoction of British, French, Italian, American and Canadian units, were part of that effort, and nobody in Canada objected to it.

However, the decision to send five hundred Canadian reinforcements to Archangel, the capital city of northern Russia, in September 1918 and, in particular, the decision to dispatch four thousand Canadian troops to Vladivostok in the Russian Far East in October were different from the start. Ottawa was playing its own hand there, for its own political ends.

Intimate relations with that rapidly developing country [Russia] will be a great advantage to Canada in the future. Other nations will make very vigorous and determined efforts to obtain a foothold, and our interposition with a small military force would tend to bring Canada into favourable notice by the strongest elements in that great community.

Sir Robert Borden to Major General Mewburn,
minister of militia and defence,
August 13, 1918

The major Canadian intervention in Russia began when the Germans were on the brink of defeat, and continued well after their surrender. Borden, a nationalist who had come more and more to see Canada as a "principal power" in the war rather than a mere British hanger-on, had observed how the great powers used their military forces to advance their national interests abroad, and was tempted into trying Canada's hand at the game. So, on the assumption that the Bolsheviks would lose the Russian civil war and that the White Russian leaders would be duly grateful to those countries that had helped them win, Borden committed Canadian troops to Russia. He even arranged that a Canadian officer should command the entire five thousand–strong British empire contingent in Vladivostok, which was 80 percent Canadian (largely conscripts).

A considerable number of Canadian airmen also fought for the counter-revolutionary forces in southern Russia in 1918–19. The 47th Squadron, Royal Air Force, which provided air support for General Denikin's White armies, was commanded by Major Raymond Collishaw, Canada's second-highest-scoring ace, and fifty-three of the sixty-two pilots he chose for the squadron were Canadian. The intervention had now turned into an anti-Bolshevik crusade, but almost none of the airmen bothered their heads with political thoughts. They were there to improve their chances of gaining a permanent commission in the postwar Royal Air Force or Canadian Air Force, or just to continue their love affair with the airplane. And they did have some splendid adventures.

> [Captain W. F.] Anderson [of Toronto] and his observer, Lieutenant Mitchell, distinguished themselves on 30 July [1919] while carrying out a photographic reconnaissance along the Volga. When Anderson's fuel tank was punctured by fire from the ground, Mitchell climbed out on the port wing and plugged the leaks with his fingers, while Anderson jettisoned his bomb-load on a gunboat in the Volga. Meanwhile, Anderson's escort, a DH9 flown by Captain William Elliott . . . had been shot down by machine-gun fire; Anderson thereupon landed close by. "Several Squadrons of Cavalry attempted to surround our machine," he reported, "but they were kept clear by our machine-gun fire." Elliott set fire to his aircraft, he and his observer tumbled into the other DH9, and with Mitchell still plugging the holes in the fuel tank with his hand, Anderson flew home.
>
> S.F. Wise, *Canadian Airmen and the First World War*

Eventually, though, the intensely political character of what their troops were doing in the Soviet Union, and the fact that they had no business playing that sort of role in somebody else's country, began to dawn on Canadians. As discontent with the Russian commitment grew at home and the likelihood of a Bolshevik victory in the civil war became clearer, Borden started to backpedal, and by April 1919 he was trying to get the Canadian troops home from Russia as quickly as possible. Not before time, because things were turning increasingly grim in Russia.

On July 7, 1919 there was a major mutiny in one of the new Russian regiments that had been created on the Archangel front: its British and Russian officers were murdered and most of the men went over to the Bolsheviks. Two weeks later all the Russians on the Onega sector of the front mutinied simultaneously, thus isolating the foreign forces based on Archangel from those based on Murmansk. After that, it was just a question of getting the foreign forces out of Russia as quickly as possible, and the last Canadians left Murmansk in August.

> Surely Providence has something better in store for Canada than to become a nasty, quarrelsome little nation.
>
> Professor O.D. Skelton, Queen's University

The First World War was Canada's education in the art of being a sovereign state, and it was a very good time to learn. There is only one way to become a sovereign state: by gaining recognition from the other states in the club and accepting the rules by which they run the international system. By the time Canada joined, however, it was already obvious that the club was becoming a lethal madhouse, and that the rules would have to be changed if the members were to survive.

Prime Minister Borden was in Europe continuously from November 1918 to May 1919. His main preoccupation was to ensure that the wartime recognition of Canada's independent status within the empire, even in questions of defence and foreign policy, should be maintained in peacetime and accepted by the rest of the world as well. The first step was taken at the Imperial War Conference in December 1918: to decide on the form of imperial representation at the Paris Peace Conference. It was a subject about which Borden felt very strongly:

> Canada and the other Dominions would have regarded the situation as intolerable if they, who numbered their dead by the hundred thousands in the fiercest struggle the world had ever known, should stand outside the council chamber of the Conference while nations that had taken no direct or active part in the struggle stood within and determined the conditions of Peace.
>
> Robert Borden, *Memoirs*, vol. 2

Borden, in cooperation with the prime ministers of the other Dominions, managed to get Britain's agreement to separate representation for the Dominions at Paris (plus a place for Canada on the joint imperial delegation). But that was only half the struggle; there remained the task of extracting the same recognition of Canada's new status from the other countries present. The main opposition came from the United States, whose secretary of state, Robert Lansing, was "somewhat arrogant and offensive and desired to know why Canada should be concerned with the settlement of European affairs. . . . Mr Lloyd George replied that [they] believed themselves to have the right because . . . Canada as well as Australia had lost more men than the United States in this war." In the end Canada was permitted to sign the peace treaties in its own right (although its name was indented, as were those of the other Dominions, to reflect its continuing membership in the British empire).

There was a similar clash over the question of separate Canadian membership in the League of Nations, the new international body created by the Treaty of Versailles to keep the peace. Again the main opposition came from the United States, which affected to believe that the Dominions were not free to take an independent stand and that the whole issue was simply a British plot to get six votes (Britain, Canada, Australia, New Zealand, South Africa and India) instead of one. However, American objections were again overridden, and Canada became a founding member of the League. By the middle of 1919 Canada for all practical purposes had received international recognition as a sovereign state, but the achievement of sovereignty came as part of a package that was intended to abolish the most important single aspect of sovereignty: the independent right to make war.

Even if I thought the proposal for a League of Nations absolutely impracticable, and that statesmen a hundred years hence would laugh at it as a vain attempt to accomplish the impossible,

nevertheless, I would support the movement because of its supreme purpose and because it might succeed. . . .
Sir Robert Borden to the Imperial War Cabinet, August 1918

"The psychological and moral conditions are ripe for a great change," General Jan Smuts, soon to become the prime minister of South Africa, wrote in December 1918. "The moment has come for one of the great creative acts of history. . . . The tents have been struck, and the great caravan of humanity is again on the march." But it was not really the "great caravan of humanity" who demanded the creation of the League of Nations. It was mainly people in government, who understood that the war had been an inevitable product of the international system and that the system itself now had to be changed. It had served the victors well enough in the past (and the losers had no vote on how the system was run), but by the time of the First World War, the price of victory in warfare between industrialized countries had begun to race far ahead of any conceivable benefits that victory might bring. A war that was, in its political dimension, scarcely distinguishable from the War of the Austrian Succession in the eighteenth century ended up killing not a couple of hundred thousand regular soldiers but eleven million ordinary citizens.

Perhaps even worse (from the point of view of statesmen and diplomats), the popular passions that were aroused by such mass slaughter had turned the war into a total war, even politically: all the losing great powers in the First World War had their regimes overthrown and their empires entirely dismantled. Indeed, the strain of total war had even destroyed the regime in one of the great powers on the winning side, Russia, and both the French and the Italians had had some anxious moments in 1917. The traditional zero-sum game with limited risks and rewards, and a guaranteed place in the next round for almost all the players, had unexpectedly turned into a no-holds-barred struggle that killed regimes. That was bound to concentrate the minds of those who ran governments quite wonderfully.

The League would never have happened if the sovereign states that created it had not feared for their own future survival; nor, without the experience of the First World War, could any amount of political and historical analysis have persuaded whole populations to accept the decisive break with deeply rooted national reflexes that the League represented. Those who wanted to change the international system had a receptive mass audience for their views in 1918—but they knew they had to move quickly.

> The great force on which we must rely is the hatred of the cruelty and waste of war which now exists. As soon as the war is over the process of oblivion will set in. . . .The chauvinists who believe that all foreigners are barbarians, the bureaucrats who think that whatever is, is right, the militarists who regard perpetual peace as an enervating evil, will . . . say "Can't you leave it alone." It is only, therefore, while the recollection of all we have been through is burningly fresh that we can hope to overcome the inevitable opposition and establish at least the beginning of a new and better organisation of the nations of the world.
>
> Lord Robert Cecil, British War Cabinet, October 5, 1918

In every country there were people who greeted the League of Nations with all the enthusiasm of feudal barons in twelfth-century Britain or France confronted with a proposal to establish a central government and domestic peace. It could never work, they insisted, and perhaps they were right—in which case we are condemned to perpetual war, and perhaps eventually to terminal war. However, people like President Wilson, Lord Cecil and Prime Minister Borden were not naïve idealists trying to create a "world government": they fully recognized the primacy of the sovereign state, the inevitability of conflicting interests and the fact that military force is the final international sanction. What they were trying to do was to *regulate* the ways that force was used and conflicts were settled, in order to break the cycle of great-alliance wars—world wars—that was coming to threaten civilization itself.

The essence of their approach was to replace the competing alliances that had flourished in traditional "balance-of-power" politics with One Big Alliance—the League of Nations—with universal membership. This all-embracing alliance of sovereign states would be bound together by quite new international rules: that no existing borders could be changed by force, and no aspects of the international status quo altered except by negotiation or arbitration. Status quo powers are always the large majority in the international community, so the new rules appealed to the fundamental interests of most nations.

These rules were to be enforced by a principle known as "collective security." Members of the League pledged to "renounce war as an instrument of national policy," and disputes between countries would be submitted to arbitration by the judicial organs of the League. But if any country defied the new rules and attacked another, *all* members of the League were bound to join in repelling the attack—and with this overwhelming preponderance of power at its disposal, the League should be able to deter or pick off aggressive governments one by one as they emerged. The basic purpose of the League was not to abolish sovereign states, but to safeguard every state's independence while averting the world wars that had been the traditional result of that independence: it was really a pragmatic association of poachers turned gamekeepers.

There was a significant political price involved in accepting collective security (and perhaps even a moral price): it meant that no country could legally resort to the unilateral use of force even to rectify what it felt to be a flagrant injustice. In order to gain the cooperation of existing governments, the League had to guarantee all their possessions and borders—and so, in seeking to outlaw war, the League of Nations was automatically committed to slowing down the pace of change to whatever could be achieved by peaceful means. In a world whose borders were largely defined by past acts of military violence, that implied the indefinite perpetuation of a great deal of injustice.

Moreover, the peace treaties of 1918 created a whole host of new injustices by blaming the war entirely on the defeated nations, stripping them of much of their territory and imposing crippling "reparations" payments on them. The League's Covenant meant that all those injustices would have to be defended against violent international challenge—even to the extent of going to war over them if necessary. It couldn't be helped: any attempt to change the international system has to start from existing reality, which will always contain a great deal of injustice. But that is not, in principle, a valid objection to the creation of an international rule of law, especially if the result is an end to war. We have all made a similar compromise within our various national states, where we have outlawed private violence—even at the cost of denying some people "justice" because the rule of law is the price of domestic peace.

Collective security makes a high demand on the capacity of nations to act with enlightened self-interest, even at the cost of some short-term sacrifices. Nevertheless, in the immediate aftermath of the First World War the surviving European governments were so badly frightened by the ultimate consequences of not changing the international system that they were at least determined to try. However, the duty of League members to defend everybody's borders against armed aggression, regardless of where they were or how those borders had originally been achieved, seemed particularly onerous to Canadians.

Canada, after all, had no disputed borders itself, and its geography made it virtually invulnerable to the effects of wars elsewhere if it chose to stay out. Prime Minister Borden supported the League in principle, but he tried hard to water down Article 10 of the Covenant, the clause that obliged all members to take automatic military action against any aggressor. As his adviser in Paris, Justice Minister Charles Doherty, warned him: "A way must be found, said and says Canadian Public Opinion, whereby Canada shall have . . . control over the events that in the future might lead her into war. If this be her view [even about] England's wars, what will be her attitude to [a promise] that France's Wars, Italy's Wars are in future to be hers wherever and whenever such a war is initiated by territorial aggression?"

But if the League's members were not willing to mobilize their forces against any aggressor, even when their own loyalties or interests were not directly involved, then the concept of collective security fell apart. Borden's reservations about accepting this duty for Canada (which were shared by some other governments that also felt relatively safe from potential aggression) were disregarded, and the Covenant of the League was adopted unchanged. By it, Canada was formally bound to defend peace anywhere in the world. But that wasn't very popular in Canada.

Our policy for the next hundred years should be that laid down by . . . Sir Wilfrid Laurier: "freedom from the vortex of European militarism."

C.G. "Chubby" Power, MP for Quebec South, Commons debate
on the League of Nations, September 1919

There are 60,000 [Canadian] graves in France and Flanders, every one of which tells us that, for good or ill, we are in the world and must bear our part in the solution of its troubles.

John W. Dafoe, editor, *Manitoba Free Press*, 1919

In terms of short-term Canadian self-interest, Chubby Power was right in advocating what became known as "isolationism," for it would be at least another generation before technology would end Canada's physical immunity from European wars. (Americans, who enjoyed a similar geographical security, actually erected isolationism into a policy. The United States Senate saw no reason why Americans should make sacrifices to defend peace in areas of no immediate importance to them, and refused to ratify U.S. membership in the League.)

But in the longer term, it was John Dafoe who was right, for the "one world or none" dilemma was already implicit in the military, economic and technological trends of his own time. Dafoe was arguing specifically for a Canadian commitment to the League of Nations, *not* for the kind of reflex loyalty to the British empire that had killed 60,000 Canadians in France and Flanders. It was, however, a new idea in 1919, and a distinction too subtle for many to grasp. A lot of Canadians simply didn't want Canadian troops to serve overseas ever again, whether in support of the British empire or the principles of the League of Nations.

French Canadians were especially unenthusiastic about the League, or indeed any foreign commitments. Their attitude was to have a lasting effect on William Lyon Mackenzie King, who was chosen as Liberal leader on Laurier's death in 1919. King owed his position to the solid support of Quebec, and he knew that it depended as much on his avoidance of foreign military commitments in the future as on his record of opposition to conscription in the past. In 1922, after a brief interval when Arthur Meighen succeeded the ailing Sir Robert Borden as prime minister and leader of the Conservative Party, King and the Liberals came to power.

The fox knows many things; the hedgehog knows one *big* thing.

Archilocus, c. 650 BCE

If Mackenzie King were a cartoon character, he would probably be Mr. Burns from *The Simpsons*. He was a dumpy, fussy bachelor with few close male friends (although power, as Henry Kissinger remarked, is the ultimate aphrodisiac, and King did not suffer from a lack of feminine companionship). He was a product of late-nineteenth-century Ontario, and so was sentimentally attached to the idea of the British empire—but he was also intensely proud of his grandfather, William Lyon Mackenzie, who had led a rebellion against that empire. Politically, he was a manipulator, perpetually balancing the conflicting demands of Britain and Anglo-Canadian imperialists against the instinctive isolationism of

French Canadians. Personally, he was a fruitcake, communing regularly with his dear, dead mother and other denizens of the spirit world. But he knew One Big Thing: Canada must be kept united for the sake of its own future, the Liberal Party's cohesion and his own political prospects—he was not a man to make petty distinctions among the three—and that meant keeping Canada's foreign commitments down.

In September 1922, eight months after he assumed office to begin a prime ministership that would run, with only two interruptions amounting to five years, until 1948, Mackenzie King found the perfect occasion to display his new approach to Canada's international commitments. It came, bizarrely, over Turkey.

STOP THIS NEW WAR!
Cabinet Plan for Great Conflict with the Turks!
France and Italy Against It!
Extraordinary Appeal to the Dominions!
Headlines, *London Daily Mail*, September 18, 1922

I confess [the British government's appeal for military support] annoyed me. It is drafted designedly to play the imperial game, to test out centralization vs. autonomy as regards European wars. . . . I have thought out my plans. . . . No contingent will go without parliament being summoned. . . . The French Canadians will be opposed, I am not so sure of B.C. . . . . I am sure the people of Canada are against participation in this European war.
Mackenzie King's diary, September 1922

The crisis came out of the peace treaty that had been imposed on the defeated Turks after the First World War. Most of Turkey had been handed over to Greece and the European empires, but the Turks, under the leadership of Mustafa Kemal (Ataturk), refused to submit. Withdrawing to the interior of Anatolia, Kemal launched a war of resistance in 1919, and by the autumn of 1922 all that stood between Kemal's army and the reconquest of Istanbul was a small British military force in the dingy town of Chanak, on the Asiatic shore of the Dardanelles.

Prime Minister Lloyd George knew perfectly well that the British public would not tolerate a full-scale war to stop the Turks from reclaiming their homeland, so he decided to run a bluff. His real aim was to force Kemal to accept an international conference on Turkey's future: Kemal would still end up with most of what he wanted, but there would be some restrictions on Turkish sovereignty, and a great deal of face would be saved (much of it Lloyd George's). To force the Turks to accept such a compromise, however, he needed a show of force at Chanak—and his bluff would be a lot more convincing if he seemed to have the whole British empire behind him.

Cabinet today decided to resist Turkish aggression upon Europe. . . . I should be glad to know whether Dominion Governments wish to associate themselves with the action we are taking . . . .

The announcement that all or any of the Dominions were prepared to send contingents even of moderate size . . . might conceivably be a potent factor in preventing actual hostilities.

Lloyd George to Mackenzie King, September 15, 1922

It was not exactly a peremptory imperial summons to war, but it was just the kind of thing King dreaded. The Canadian General Staff, ever eager to be helpful, began making plans for the immediate dispatch of the entire Canadian regular army to Turkey, to be followed within a few months, if necessary, by an expeditionary force of 200,000 Canadian volunteers. However, King simply told Britain that Canada would take no action until Parliament had been consulted—and made no preparations to recall Parliament. It was, perhaps, the most muted declaration of independence any government has ever made, for King had to be careful not to anger English Canadian imperial patriots.

In the end, the crisis was defused and there was no war over Chanak. Lloyd George's government fell, and Turkey regained its territory and its independence. At the Imperial Conference in London the following year, King was openly defiant. If the report of the conference committed the Dominions to the automatic support of British foreign and defence policies, he insisted, he would have to insert a special clause exempting Canada. So the conference closed with a statement that it was not an imperial cabinet but a conference of separate governments, each responsible to its own Parliament. Over the next few years King nailed down Canada's separate and sovereign status by concluding the first foreign treaty that was not also signed by a British representative (the unromantic U.S.-Canadian Halibut Treaty of 1923), and by appointing Canada's first diplomatic legations to foreign capitals (Washington, Paris and Tokyo) in 1927.

By the time the Statute of Westminster formally recognized the independence of all the dominions in 1931, Canada had already had it for years. In 1927, when Canada was elected to the Council of the League of Nations, Senator Raoul Dandurand, the Canadian delegate to Geneva, replied to American criticism that Canada was the puppet of Downing Street by declaring that Canada was "the spokesman of the North American continent's ideals." That was true enough, bearing in mind that the predominant North American ideal at the time was isolationism—for one of the first things King had done with Canada's independence was to undermine the League.

[If the Council of the League should] recommend the application of military measures in consequence of an aggression . . . the Council shall be bound to take account . . . of the geographical situation and of the special conditions of each State. It is for the constitutional authorities of each Member to decide . . . in what

155

degree the Member is bound to assure the execution of this obligation by employment of its military forces.

The "Canadian Resolution" on Article 10,
League of Nations Assembly, September 24, 1923

Article 10 was the heart of the Covenant, committing all members not only to respect "the territorial integrity and existing political independence of all the members of the League," but to defend each member's rights by military force if necessary. That automatic obligation was exactly what King objected to, but he was more subtle than Borden, who had mounted a direct attack on the article and failed. Instead, the "Canadian resolution" appealed to every country's secret desire for a private escape route from the general duty of maintaining the peace, by declaring that each member could decide independently whether it would take part in economic sanctions or offer troops to support any military action decided upon by the League.

After a year-long struggle, King's "interpretation" was accepted, and Article 10 was effectively destroyed. Raoul Dandurand, one of King's few really close associates, was brutally frank about the selfish rationale behind the Canadian resolution. Collective security was like fire insurance, he told the Assembly in 1924, and Canada should not be called upon to pay the heavy premium of military sanctions against a possible aggressor because Canadians faced little risk to their own property: "We live in a fireproof house, far from inflammable materials."

This first attempt to reform the international system and break the cycle of world wars was probably doomed to fail in any event—almost as certainly as a child's first attempt to ride a bicycle—but King's wanton act of sabotage was a premature and unnecessary blow to the League. And it was supported by the Canadian opposition parties as well: wars, most Canadians believed, were caused by wicked governments in Europe, and it was possible for Canada to stay out of them thanks to its fortunate geography. But since no serious crises came along to test the weakened machinery of the League for quite a while, it would be almost a decade before any Canadians began to worry about war again.

———

Lt. Col. Forde and Lt. Col. Hodgins and myself left Ottawa in a motor driven by Colonel Forde about 6:45 a.m. on the 10th July, 1922 . . . and crossed the St. Lawrence by ferry to Ogdensburg, New York at 10 a.m. The American Customs and Emigration Authorities passed us without delay . . .We then took the highway to Canton through a generally rolling country. . . . The country everywhere is passable by infantry.

Extract from *Special Reconnaissance by the director* of
military operations and intelligence, marked "Secret,"
H.Q. C.3487, Ottawa, November 17, 1922.

Colonel J. Sutherland ("Buster") Brown, director of military operations and intelligence of the Canadian army from 1920 to 1927, was convinced, like his ancestors before him, that the main military threat facing Canada was an American invasion—and he had a plan for dealing with it. We should invade them first. If war with the United States seemed likely, his Defence Scheme Number One ordained that the Canadian army would launch pre-emptive attacks deep into the United States. Canadian forces from British Columbia would "advance into and occupy the strategic points including Spokane, Seattle and Portland." Our troops from the Prairie provinces would "converge toward Fargo, North Dakota, and then continue a general advance in the direction of Minneapolis and St. Paul." In the east, the Canadian army would cross the St. Lawrence and the Quebec border to occupy upper New England.

July 12th.

We left Glen Falls at 9 a.m. Near French Mountain we entered the Adirondacks. It is about this point that troops from the North would enter an open rolling country lying between Glen Falls and Albany.

Sutherland Brown, Special Reconnaissance

Sutherland Brown's military strategy was not at fault: his purpose in planning to seize large parts of the northern United States by surprise at the very outbreak of war was to win time for reinforcements from Britain to reach Canada before U.S. troops could pour across the Canadian border and overwhelm us. A similar strategy had been applied, with successful results, in the War of 1812: small contingents of troops from Upper Canada had crossed the frontier as soon as the United States declared war and seized Detroit and the Upper Peninsula of Michigan, thus slowing the main American invasion significantly. The problem lay only in Colonel Brown's grasp of contemporary reality. The British could not have sent reinforcements to Canada even if his strategy had won them the necessary time—and in the 1920s Canada did not have one-tenth the number of trained troops that would have been required to carry out his plan.

What I want to accomplish, if I possibly can, is to have a well organised, snappy defence force that will be a credit to Canada without being too expensive.

Minister of Militia George Graham, 1922

The huge Canadian army of the First World War had been dissolved with great speed. The 350,000 Canadians who were overseas on November 11, 1918, were almost all home and out of uniform by mid-1919 (although not before impatient veterans had turned to violence in the holding camps in Britain; a riot at Kinmel Park in north Wales in March 1919 left five dead and twenty-seven injured). The fifteen militia divisions survived on paper, but with fewer than fifty thousand active members. Nobody was willing to tolerate the idea of conscription in peacetime, and the regular forces wound up with around five thousand men. Most of the numbered battalions of the Canadian Expeditionary Force and their hard-won traditions disappeared in the postwar reorganization of the armed forces, although a few were permitted to convert into militia regiments, with regimental names replacing their old numbers. Only two unique infantry units survived to join the Royal Canadian Regiment as permanent elements of Canada's regular army: Princess Patricia's Canadian Light Infantry and the 22nd Battalion, the only French-speaking battalion in the CEF, which had so distinguished itself that it was even allowed to retain its number, becoming the Royal 22ème Regiment ("Van Doos," in English).

Such courtesies cost very little, but postwar Canadian governments were not willing to spend real money on the armed forces. The Canadian defence budget in 1922 was $12 million—just under a dollar and a half per Canadian—and it did not grow much until the late 1930s. Given the country's remarkably secure strategic situation and the absence of identifiable enemies, this parsimony was not unreasonable. But it was rather demoralizing for the remaining regular soldiers.

When the three-inch mortar came into use . . . there were only three of them in the whole of Canada. Well, I was keen on mortars because I had just been at the Small Arms School and thought I knew something about it.

So we decided to make our own . . . and we had the company pioneer build a wooden mock-up of a three-inch mortar—quite illegally, we paid for it out of the company's sports fund—and we had wooden bombs that we shoved down this black pipe and hoped for the best. At least we learned the drill.

Dan Spry (later General), junior officer,
Royal Canadian Regiment

What would have been even more demoralizing for the soldiers, had they allowed themselves to dwell on it, was their sheer uselessness to the country that paid their wages. The only possible invader of Canada was still the United States, but the American threat was no longer very plausible politically. Moreover, by the Washington Naval Treaty of 1922 London agreed to limit the Royal Navy to the same size as that of the United States, which meant that there was now absolutely no chance that Britain would ever again send troops west across the Atlantic to defend Canada against an American attack. Since Britain had large naval commitments elsewhere, henceforward it would always be inferior to the U.S. Navy in the Western Atlantic. London simply no longer had the ability to get troops west across the Atlantic against American opposition

However, Canada's professional armed forces took no notice whatever of this new strategic reality. The foundation of Canadian military planning continued to be a militia force, which, on mobilization, would amount to eleven infantry divisions and four cavalry divisions (though they were now only planning on having 130,000 men available to man these divisions)—all for fighting the United States. And, according to the calculations of Colonel Brown's Directorate of Military Operations and Intelligence, by the time the "flying columns" of Canadian militia that had been thrown across the American border in a controlled penetration of a few hundred miles had been forced to retreat to Canada's own frontiers, British military operations should be well underway against America's east coast, while Australian and Indian expeditionary forces would be on their way to attack California. The Americans would sure be sorry that they had picked a fight with the British empire.

The real Canadian militia, by contrast only succeeded in giving eight or nine days' training to 38,000 men in 1923. The British reinforcements Brown was counting on would never be sent, and the Australian and Indian contingents were wholly imaginary. "I consider that the most difficult point in the Scheme is the fact that it is drawn up

for forces which are to a certain extent non-existent," the commander of
Military District No. 4 (Montreal) observed drily.

Q. What inspired Sutherland Brown to think that way
in the 1920s—I mean, a war with the United States?
A. Well, I don't know. I think possibly there wasn't any other war
to think about. (laughter)
General E.L.M. Burns, commander of Canadian forces in
Italy, 1944; commander of UN Emergency Force in Suez, 1956

General "Tommy" Burns served with Sutherland Brown in the
1920s, and his observation cuts very close to the bone. A professional
military force needs enemies to justify its existence, and the First World
War's lasting institutional bequest to Canada was a full array of professional armed forces staffed by native-born regular officers who were
paid, quite literally, to identify foreign threats to Canadian national
security. The threats they identified would vary from time to time, as
would the measures they advocated to deal with them, but they were
unlikely ever to declare that there was no threat to Canada. *Of course*
they found threats, whether from the United States or elsewhere, and *of*
course they asked for money to maintain their own profession as a "deterrent" to those threats.

By 1925 the Royal Canadian Navy had only two small destroyers
left, and the Royal Canadian Air Force numbered fewer than a thousand men. The Permanent Force of the army amounted to only 4,125
troops, and the militia organization was somewhat smaller than the one
that had existed before the First World War. Nevertheless, the Canadian
armed forces struggled on, devoting most of their energies to sheer institutional survival, in the hope that they would one day be needed again
by their country. Or if not precisely by their own country, at least by
Britain—and since they were entirely British-oriented in their training,
equipment and strategic thinking, they had no doubt that any British

war would be theirs as well. This had the additional attraction, from the soldiers' point of view, that it allowed them to play a role in the biggest and most professionally interesting military league available: Europe. And the myth that was forged to justify the huge loss of Canadian lives in Europe in the First World War—the pretense that it had somehow been in defence of Canada—made the English Canadian population ready to believe the soldiers when they talked about European "threats" to Canadian security.

The old strategic and psychological equation of dependence on Britain to protect us from American invasion lasted just long enough to deliver us smoothly into our new obsession with playing a role in the European balance of power. Once Sutherland Brown left his post as Canada's senior strategic planner, his Defence Scheme Number One rapidly fell into disrepute. In 1933 every military district in Canada was instructed to burn all documents connected with the plan (which would have caused severe embarrassment if they had somehow fallen into American hands). However, the alternative plans to send Canadian troops to fight in Europe again in case of war did not change.

———

Of all the members of the League, Canada was the first to . . . have torpedoed the organization, or to use another metaphor, to rob it of any teeth it had.

Senator W.A. Griesbach (Conservative, Alberta),
Senate Debates, 1934

The descent into world war again at the end of the 1930s was premature in terms of the normal cycle: only twenty years had elapsed since the last one, rather than the more typical half century. The drastic shortening of the cycle was largely due to the way the First World War ended, but the failure of the League of Nations certainly did its part.

The Treaty of Versailles was a time bomb planted under the League of Nations. It heaped punishments on Germany—loss of territory, a large measure of compulsory disarmament, demilitarized zones, massive reparations and a "war guilt" clause that purported to justify the terms of the treaty by blaming the war exclusively on the Germans—punishments that were neither defensible in terms of justice nor (more important) sustainable over the long term. Britain and France were simply not capable of depriving Germany permanently of great-power status.

However loyally the League's members upheld the principle of collective security—even if they did not take the escape route prepared for them by the Canadian "interpretation" of Article 10 in 1923—the League system was bound to come under severe pressure as a consequence of Germany's resentment at its artificially subordinate status. If the great powers in the League did not move fast enough in removing what the Germans perceived as injustices (and they did not), then they were certain to face an eventual German challenge that could be stopped only by invoking Article 10 and resorting to military force. In fact, however, the challenge that effectively destroyed the collective security system came a little sooner than that, and not from Germany.

On October 2, 1935, Mussolini invaded Ethiopia, and an overwhelming majority of League members promptly declared Italy an aggressor. Mussolini's crime was no worse than what every other great power had done in the late nineteenth century. Ethiopia was one of the last independent bits of Africa, and Italy, only lately arrived on the great-power scene, was belatedly seeking its share of the colonial spoils. But the international rules had been changed by the creation of the League in 1919, and Ethiopia was a member: either the rules had to be enforced or the organization was meaningless. Moreover, this was a crisis the League members could actually deal with. There was plenty of time to organize a response, since ten months elapsed between the first indication of Italy's intention and the actual attack; the Ethiopians themselves were determined to fight; and Italy's sea communications with Africa were highly vulnerable to the stronger British and French navies.

Within a week, the League began to consider economic sanctions against Italy: nobody was talking about military measures yet, but economic sanctions could easily be the first step along that road. And Canada, to everybody's surprise, actually sought and got a seat on the committee that had to decide what those sanctions would be.

> We went into the League, took benefits, must assume responsibilities, or get out, not try to hornswoggle ourselves out.
>
> Prime Minister R.B. Bennett to Dr. O.D. Skelton, permanent
> undersecretary for external affairs, 1935

In 1935 Richard B. Bennett, a former Calgary lawyer "of large displacement" (as they used to say of ocean liners), had been prime minister of Canada for five years. Bombastic in public and autocratic with his colleagues, he was one of those rare Canadian politicians (Pierre Trudeau is the only other one to achieve prime-ministerial rank since) who followed their private convictions quite heedless of popular opinion. In Bennett's case, his intellectual independence was buttressed by considerable wealth and excellent connections in Britain (after he retired from politics he moved to England and acquired a peerage through the help of influential friends), but his support for collective security was quite genuine.

This attitude brought him into permanent conflict with most senior members of his own External Affairs Department, and most notably with Dr. O.D. Skelton, the permanent undersecretary, a gaunt scholar who had had a brilliant academic career before being seduced into government by Mackenzie King ten years before. Skelton had originally supported the idea of the League but had concluded that this particular league was not going to succeed, and he had no confidence whatever in the ability of British diplomacy to avoid another war.

So, in practice, Skelton was an isolationist, convinced that Canada at least might be spared the horrors of the next war if it kept out of overseas commitments.

Skelton did his best to talk Bennett out of having anything to do with League sanctions against Italy, but the prime minister simply wouldn't hear of it. In one bitter discussion in September 1935 he called Skelton and his colleagues at External Affairs "welshers" because of their desire to evade Canada's commitments under the League Covenant, and in October he heatedly overrode External's attempt to have the Canadian delegation in Geneva abstain from the vote condemning Italy for aggression: "No one in Canada is going to deny Italy is guilty or object to our saying so. If they did, [I'm] not going to wriggle out of it if it meant I didn't get one vote," he shouted down the phone to Skelton. But Bennett was deliberately ignoring Skelton's quite plausible reason for wanting Canada to abstain: in early October 1935 Canada was nearing the end of a long federal election campaign and Bennett was almost certain to lose that election to Mackenzie King—who would certainly not want to honour Canada's commitments to the League.

> Do honourable members think it is Canada's role at Geneva to attempt to regulate a European war?
>
> Mackenzie King to the House of Commons, 1935

That was precisely Canada's role (and everybody else's) under the League's Covenant. Only collective security offered any hope of preventing another great war from occurring in Europe sooner or later—but it did involve running the risk of at least a small war to deter aggression. Canadians had paid a high price for their intervention in the last European war, and an isolationist policy was a tempting alternative. The Atlantic was a broad moat, and Canadians could still shelter behind it if they wished.

King instinctively distrusted the League of Nations, in large part because he saw avoiding overseas commitments as a stark political necessity for the Liberals. French Canadian opinion was virtually unanimous in its opposition to foreign military involvement of any kind (not a single French-language newspaper in Quebec supported Canadian participation in League action over Ethiopia).

He needed English Canadian votes too, and he was English Canadian himself. As early as 1923 he had declared: "If a great and clear call of duty comes [to fight by Britain's side], Canada will respond, whether or not the United States responds, as she did in 1914." King was unwilling to risk even the remotest chance of war for the right cause, the League. Yet he was ultimately willing to fight for the wrong one, British imperial interest, if he had to.

With King's overwhelming election victory on October 14, 1935 (the Liberals won 173 seats out of 245), Canada's man on the League sanctions committee at Geneva, Walter Riddell, was put in a very awkward position. Riddell had been Ottawa's permanent representative at Geneva for ten years, and he saw the way things were going: everybody was afraid to ban the export of really vital commodities to Italy for fear of driving Mussolini into a corner and provoking a war. It was one of those situations, not uncommon in diplomacy, where each nation knew what its duty was, but hung back nervously for fear that other countries would not do their duty and it would find itself out front all alone. But mere wrist-slapping would not stop the Italian dictator, so Riddell decided Canada should take a lead.

> By this time I had become thoroughly convinced that this was the last and best chance that the Member States would have of preventing a European collapse and another world war; that it was therefore imperative that the Member States should accept their obligations not only willingly but generously, as any losses they might suffer would be a mere bagatelle in

comparison with the losses in the event of a break-up of the Collective System.

Walter Riddell, *World Security by Conference*

Riddell took a very big chance. He knew perfectly well that Mackenzie King, in full harmony with his old appointee, the isolationist Skelton, would forbid any Canadian initiative that might ultimately involve Canada in the application of military sanctions by the League. Yet he feared that if nobody took a strong line in Geneva, the principle of collective security would slide ignominiously into oblivion amid timid half measures and shabby compromises. So on November 2 he leapt in at the deep end: he formally proposed that League members ban the export of oil, coal, iron and steel to Italy, knowing full well that Mussolini was threatening to go to war with anybody who applied such pressure to Italy.

Riddell's initiative put some spine into the hesitant members of the committee. On November 6 they unanimously recommended the full list of Riddell's sanctions to all League members. If those sanctions had been applied, Italy would have had to stop its attack on Ethiopia or grind to a halt, since it produced no oil itself and had only about two months' reserves. But meanwhile Riddell was having to play a double game, disguising the extent to which he had committed Canada in his telegrams back to Ottawa and pretending to misunderstand the instructions he was getting from there to do nothing conspicuous. It could not last, for newspapers around the world were calling the initiative that had galvanized the committee into action the "Canadian proposal."

Had a few words with Mr King re the Italo-Ethiopian settlement and he spoke with surprising frankness. . . . King complained bitterly about Dr Riddell's gasoline, steel and coal proposal. "I am certainly going to give him a good spanking," was the way he put it. . . . He is very dubious about foreign commitments, and, also, about getting into the League too deeply.

Ottawa correspondent to J.W. Dafoe, editor, *Winnipeg Free Press*, December 1935

King, shocked by his representative's daring action, instinctively ducked for cover. He and Skelton were on vacation together in Sea Island, Georgia, but he sent instructions back to his deputy, Ernest Lapointe, to repudiate Riddell. On December 2, 1935, while the League was still waiting for all the members' replies to the "Canadian proposal" on sanctions, Lapointe issued a press statement: "The suggestion . . . that the Canadian Government has taken the initiative in the extension of the embargo upon exportation of key commodities to Italy . . . is due to a misunderstanding. . . . The opinion which was expressed by the Canadian member of the Committee—and which has led to the reference to the proposals as a Canadian proposal—represented only his personal opinion . . . and not the views of the Canadian Government."

To make a suggestion and then run away is not helpful to the more exposed members of the League.

Sir Robert Vansittart, British undersecretary for foreign affairs, December 1935

It was an act of gross vandalism, motivated by sheer timidity. It cannot be said for certain that King's disavowal of the Riddell proposal was the decisive factor in the League's ultimate failure to impose sanctions on Italy. The British and the French, who would have to do most of the fighting if an oil embargo against Italy had led to war, were wavering in their commitment anyway, especially as they still hoped that Italy might be an ally if they ultimately had to fight Hitler. But King's action was certainly a major factor—and once the impetus given by Riddell's initiative and the apparent (although nervous) unanimity with which it was met had been lost, so was the League of Nations. The question of effective sanctions was repeatedly postponed until Mussolini completed his conquest of Ethiopia in mid-1936 and it became simply irrelevant. The League staggered on for a few more years, but it was only a husk. Collective security had been put to the test, and everybody had run away.

> I went over as a delegate [to the League] in '38. . . . By then it was dying, if not dead. . . . but as a young man I was never prepared to admit that it was that bad. I could hardly accept that the League wasn't going to carry on as Smuts and Wilson and others, Lord Robert Cecil, hoped that it would, but in retrospect one can't conclude anything else.
>
> It didn't invalidate the Covenant and the richness of its contribution, but it certainly was—as the UN is now—an ineffective operation. Not because the idea was wrong, but because of the failure of its members to live up to their obligations. And Canada was one of those that did not.
>
> Paul Martin, MP for Essex East (Windsor, Ontario), later
> secretary of state for external affairs, 1963–68

The attempt to build a new international system had collapsed, and the great powers went back to doing what they had centuries of experience at: building up their armies, giving away bits of other people's territory to buy time or allies and preparing for the next world war. Canadians wondered what they would do when it came—and Mackenzie King, as usual, tried to face in both directions at once.

King wholeheartedly supported the British policy of appeasement. When Germany remilitarized the Rhineland in 1936, he showed not the slightest public inclination to do anything about it: "I believe that Canada's first duty to the League and to the British Empire, with respect to all the great issues that come to us, is, if possible, to keep this country united." His cabinet raised the defence budget by 20 percent, but the rearmament program was not aimed at sending another large Canadian expeditionary force to Europe: "I think that is now wholly out of the question," King noted in his diary.

King's diplomatic statements deliberately left Canada's intentions in case of war obscure, and even in his private dealings with the British government he went out of his way to avoid military cooperation that might imply automatic commitment. He never openly challenged the legal doctrine that Canada, as a member of the British empire, was automatically at war whenever Britain was at war, but in response to all attempts to pin him down, he took refuge in his favourite evasive tactic, saying "Parliament will decide" (as though Parliament would not do whatever he and his cabinet decided). Since he never said publicly what Canada would do if war came, there was no focus around which a destructive national debate could get started.

Two groups in Canada wanted nothing whatever to do with a European war. A large number of Canadian nationalists (including almost all French Canadians) thought solely in terms of Canada's own interests, and were quite content to sit the war out on the sidelines since no vital Canadian interests were involved. There were also those, particularly in English Canadian intellectual circles, who believed that the coming war was simply further proof of the failure of the existing international system. The war would have to run its course, and afterward everybody would have to resume the effort to build some new international institution like the League to prevent future wars. But neither the rationalists nor the nationalists had the final say; King did, and he was infuriatingly reluctant to say anything definite.

[King] saw long before a lot of the rest of us did, who were dubious about getting into a war, that with the composition of our population as it was in 1939, it would have been impossible to stay out; that it would have nothing to do with interests, it had to do with emotions.

Q. English Canada would not have stood for it?

No. Well, enough of English Canada would not have stood for it and, after all, English Canadians as late as 1939 were the dominant element. Much more than their numbers, their influence and their importance were such that it would have been, I think, quite impossible to stay out. I think I recognized that myself in 1939. Very sadly, but I recognized it.

Jack Pickersgill, secretary to Mackenzie King, 1937–48

For all his obfuscations, King was never really in any doubt that Canada would have to go in if war came. He thought it was a bad idea, and he was determined to go in only up to his ankles if he could get away with it, but he understood the nature of Canada at the time too well to imagine that his government could safely remain neutral. Although pro-British sentiments were much weaker in the English-speaking population as a whole than in 1914 (a generation had passed, and the cost of the First World War was graven in everybody's mind), the instinctive British loyalty was still strong in the business and professional elite, and those were the people who mattered.

At their worst, they were the sort of people whom the Conservative opposition leader, Robert J. Manion, described to his son as "the usual crowd of old bachelors and childless parents." They certainly had enough influence to destroy any government that stayed out of the war, but even they would not have been powerful enough on their own to make Canada's entry into the Second World War inevitable. What gave their demands irresistible force was the almost unconscious sense of compulsion in ordinary English Canadians to take part in the war.

If you were to ask any Canadian, "Do you *have* to go to war if England does?" he'd answer at once, "Oh, no." If you then said,

"*Would* you go to war if England does?" he'd answer, "Oh, yes."
And if you asked "Why?" he would say, reflectively, "Well, you
see, we'd *have* to."

Stephen Leacock, *Atlantic Monthly*, June 1939

For most English Canadians, by 1939 the decisive motive was no
longer a helpless tug of loyalty to Britain; at least, not a loyalty strong
enough to die for her. It was more a sense of debt to their own past and
to their dead of the First World War. English Canada is the only part
of the western hemisphere where almost every little town and village
has the kind of haunting war memorial that you find all over Europe,
with a list of the dead that sometimes seems to outnumber those still
living in the place.

The terrible sacrifice of the First World War—a third of all English
Canadian males of military age had served overseas, and one in seven
had actually been killed or wounded—was the very foundation of
English Canada's national identity, and to deny that Canada's duty was
to fight at England's side in the wars of the great powers would have
seemed somehow to devalue that sacrifice. The dead would not necessarily impose that duty on us for all time if they could speak, but that
was the psychology of it. So to justify their past, English Canadians
would feel that they must act in the same way the next time a European
war came along: "Well, you see, we'd *have* to."

The same was not true for French Canadians, however. French
Canada's attitude would *not* shift when the crisis arrived, for it had no
comparable debt to the dead to pull its emotions around. There was
never any doubt that French Canadians would fight to defend *Canada*,
but the issue of conscription for service overseas was as explosive as
ever—and unless that fear was laid to rest, French Canada would resist
the war from the start, the country would split along "racial" lines, and
King's government, heavily dependent on Quebec support, would
probably fall.

Happily for King, English Canadian politicians of all parties were much more conscious of the French Canadian loathing for conscription than they had been in 1917 (and could detect some nervousness about it among their own constituents). It was the opposition leader who took the initiative. In March 1939, when war in Europe had become almost certain, Manion declared that Conservative policy would be "no conscription of Canadians to fight outside our borders in any war." King gratefully associated the government with this formula—and in the spring of 1939 he pulled one last rabbit out of his hat: the Royal Tour.

It is a spontaneous, inspired tribute—a moment of mass and individual exaltation. The tremendous throng is suddenly identified with the spirit of the monument that has just been unveiled. And in the words just spoken by the King, the very soul of the nation is here revealed.

Newsreel commentary on the unveiling of the Cenotaph in
Ottawa by King George VI, May 1939

King George VI and Queen Elizabeth were the first reigning monarchs ever to visit Canada, and in two months they were seen personally by two and a half million Canadians—almost a quarter of the population. The purpose was transparently to revive pro-British sentiment in Canada and that sense of identification with Canada's own past most strikingly displayed in the emotional scenes at the unveiling of the national war memorial in Ottawa. To a considerable extent it worked, even in French Canada. "By the smile of a Queen and the French words of a King, the English have conquered once more the cradle of New France," Omer Héroux noted crossly in *Le Devoir*, and it was largely (if only temporarily) true.

As the "royal recruiting tour" proceeded westward, however, the size and enthusiasm of the crowds dropped off steeply: despite the deeply felt obligation to the dead, English Candians remembered what the last war had done to their families with a depth of emotion that French Canadians could not share. Even in small-town Ontario, although the crowds came out to see the show, many of the people waving the flags felt a deep sense of unease.

> In the bright morning sunshine, at 10:15 Peter and I drove to Paris High School. On our way up the hill, he said hopefully, "Will the King and Queen be wearing a crown?" "No," I said, "they don't always wear them." . . . Obviously disappointed, he gazed up at me.
>
> When the pupils had lined up for their march to the Junction, Miss "X" and Miss "Y" asked me for a ride. On our way along Capron Street I said lightly, "I suppose you two patriots are seething with loyal anticipation."
>
> "Not I," said Miss 'X' coldly. "Mark my words! A war is coming. They want our boys to die for them and the Empire." I was so astonished that I almost ran the car off the road. To me, she had long been a symbol of the ultra-conventional.
>
> "I guess," said Miss 'Y,' "you won't be doing any wild cheering."
>
> "Not much," said Miss 'X.'
>
> Donald A. Smith, *At the Forks of the Grand*, vol. 2, Paris, Ontario, June 7, 1939

In late August war in Europe became inevitable. The Soviet Union, having spent the preceding year in futile attempts to create a joint front with the British and the French to stop Hitler, signed a separate deal with Berlin. In the secret clauses, Hitler gave Stalin a free hand to reannex most of the former territories of the Russian empire that had been lost during the revolutionary turmoil of 1917–20 (Estonia, Latvia, Lithuania, parts of Finland and Romania, and the eastern third of Poland) in return for Soviet acquiescence in whatever Germany wished to do with the rest of Poland. The agreement neatly turned the tables on the Anglo-French ambition to embroil the Russians in a war with Germany from which they could remain aloof; now it would be Britain and France, at least for a while, that would have to stand alone against Hitler (unless they welshed on their guarantee to Poland).

But even after the Nazi-Soviet pact was signed, Mackenzie King kept the British guessing about his government's intentions. The British High Commissioner in Ottawa reported that Dr. Skelton, the undersecretary for external affairs, "like the Prime Minister, felt it unwise to go to war for countries which the United Kingdom could not support effectively. His view was that Poland could be destroyed or overrun in a fortnight, and that Hitler could then sit back and profess his unwillingness to fight the Western powers." And that was exactly what happened.

For the Canadians who actually understood what was happening, especially in the department of external affairs, the choice was enormously difficult. They were honestly appalled at the nature of the fascist regimes, but they knew that the next great-power war would be simply a continuation of the last, and equally devoid of moral content. Most of them had once hoped that the League of Nations could change the dynamics of the international system enough to break this futile cycle of destruction, and almost all of them had now concluded that it had failed. Collective security would certainly have to be tried again eventually, for there seemed no other hope of breaking the cycle, but first there would be a terrible war.

None of them felt that it was Canada's national duty to die in the last ditch to defend the established ranking of the European great powers—nor, indeed, that Canada's military help was especially vital to Britain. The two sides in Europe seemed to be fairly evenly matched, and most people in 1939 expected the war to be a stalemate. But there was still the argument that Canada ought to participate in the war *just a little bit* in order to have a say in the design of the new international institutions whose creation would be the first task when the war ended. More important, there was the domestic political fact that Canada would be less divided by a cautious and limited entry into the war than by staying out entirely. Lester Pearson, still a quarter-century away from the prime ministership, combined the sensibility of the doomed fighter pilot of 1918 with the cynicism of the disillusioned junior diplomat of 1938 in his attitude to the coming war, but his statement can probably stand as representative of the ambivalence felt by most of his colleagues, and by most Canadians who knew what was really going on.

> If [Britain] fights, it will only be in defence of her own imperial interests, defined by herself. Why should she expect any particular world support for that? . . . As a Canadian, having seen the disappearance of all post-war hopes of a new international order based on international cooperation . . . largely because of England's negative . . . policy, I am not going to be impressed if next year I am asked to fight because of Tanganyika or Gibraltar.
>
> . . . But if I am tempted to become completely cynical and isolationist, I think of Hitler screeching into the microphone, Jewish women and children in ditches on the Polish border . . . and then, whatever the British side may represent, the other does indeed stand for savagery and barbarism.
>
> Lester Pearson to O.D. Skelton, November 1938

One week before the war started, he wrote to King: "The first casualty of this war has been Canada's claim to control over her own destinies. If war comes to Poland and we take part, that war came as a consequence of commitments made by the Government of Great Britain, about which we were not in one iota consulted, and about which we were not given the slightest inkling of information in advance."

THE MYTH OF APPEASEMENT

WAR DID NOT COME OUT OF A CLEAR BLUE SKY IN 1939, AS IT HAD seemed to in 1914. People saw it coming years in advance and were preparing for it. In 1933, the year Hitler came to power in Germany, the British foreign secretary, Sir John Simon, told the Cabinet that it must plan for two possibilities if the Nazi regime remained in power: either a preventive war by the French almost right away to strangle the regime in its cradle, or "the success of Hitler, followed . . . by a European war in four or five years time."

British foreign policy in the next six years bore the name of "appeasement," which has subsequently become just about the worst label you can put on a foreign policy. Winston Churchill once defined an appeaser as "one who feeds a crocodile, hoping it will eat him last," and appeasement has subsequently become a one-word argument hurled at anybody who wants to delay an immediate resort to military force. But Churchill was never one to waste fairness on his political rivals. The truth is that British governments of the 1930s, while aware that there would probably be a war against Germany in the end, consciously saw appeasement as a two-way bet. If conceding to Germany various rights and pieces of territory that it had been forced to relinquish in the Treaty of Versailles was enough to satiate Hitler and turn him into a supporter of the international status quo, then appeasement would have avoided a dreadful and unnecessary war. In the far likelier case that it would ultimately take a war to stop Hitler, appeasement would at least buy time for Britain to rearm so as to have a better chance of winning that war.

Britain's preparedness for another European war in 1933 was little more advanced than Canada's. It maintained just enough forces to control its world-spanning empire, but nothing more. This policy was justified by the so-called Ten-Year Rule, first adopted in 1919, which instructed the British armed forces to draft their budget proposals "on the assumption that the British Empire would not be engaged in any great war during the next ten years." In 1919 that was a reasonable assumption, but the Ten-Year Rule was renewed every year until 1932. As a result, British defence expenditure shrank from £766 million in 1919–20 to £102 million in 1932. So the British government simply dared not contemplate fighting another war with Germany until it had time to rearm—and it pressed France (which was better prepared to fight) not to use force against Hitler yet either.

This was particularly the case in 1936, when Hitler marched his soldiers back into the Rhineland, along the French border. The Rhineland had been demilitarized by the Treaty of Versailles precisely because the absence of the German army would leave one of Germany's most important industrial areas, the Ruhr, wide open to French occupation. The French were ready to reoccupy the area militarily in 1936, and there is no doubt that Hitler would have withdrawn his troops if he had been challenged in that way, but British rearmament had barely begun. Besides, from the perspective of a generation in Britain who had already concluded that the Versailles Treaty was extremely unfair to the Germans, it just didn't feel appropriate to deny Germany the right to control a key part of its own territory. So the two-way bet continued: let the Germans recover what really should be theirs, but rearm in case Hitler doesn't intend to stop there. And the British government was not filled with false hope: it strongly suspected that Hitler meant to keep going. As the Cabinet minutes after the Rhineland episode put it: "Our principal aim . . . at the present time was to play for time and for peace. There was some reason to suppose that Germany did not wish to make war on us *now*. Time was vital to the completion of our defensive security."

The "appeasers" in London therefore increased British defence spending from 15 percent of the government's total expenditure in 1935 to 21 percent in 1936, 26 percent in 1937, 38 percent in 1938, and a whopping 48 percent in 1939. They went on re-arming even though Hitler did not move again for two years after the re-occupation of the Rhineland. By the time the war came in 1939, the British army, though smaller than the Reichswehr, was far more mechanized. The Royal Air Force (which had only biplane fighters two years before) had new Hurricanes and Spitfires, and chains of radar stations had been built to give Britain's air defences early warning. Britain's first four-engine heavy bomber flew in 1939, in fulfilment of a Royal Air Force requirement issued in 1936. They did not waste their time.

In Canada, Mackenzie King enthusiastically supported the policy of appeasement, and he also followed Britain's lead in raising Canadian defence spending, which quadrupled from a paltry $14 million in 1933, the year Hitler took power, to $64 million in 1939. However, most of the extra money went to the navy and the air force, whose personnel respectively doubled and tripled in numbers in 1935–39. The army, by contrast, did not grow at all: it stayed around four thousand men right until 1939. King knew there would probably be a war, and that Canada would have to fight at Britain's side, but he had no intention of sending a Canadian army overseas again. All his spending was devoted to the defence of Canada—whether it needed to be defended or not.

Which begs the question: Why did Canada (or even Britain) *have* to fight Germany? Hitler's expressed goals were all about the recovery of German-populated territories in the east that had been severed from

Germany by the Versailles Treaty. His longer-term intention was to attack and destroy the Soviet Union and Bolshevism. (He saw the Communist Party of the Soviet Union as a Jewish-controlled plot against "civilization.") In support of that latter goal, he also clearly had an interest in extending his control, either diplomatically or militarily, over much of Eastern Europe. In early 1939 he even offered Poland a military alliance, clearly directed against their common enemy, the Soviet Union, if only the Poles would return the "Free City of Danzig" (95 percent German in population) and allow the construction of a German-controlled road and railway across the Polish Corridor to join up the two parts of Germany. Poland might have agreed to a German alliance, too, if Britain and France had not issued their unconditional guarantee of Polish sovereignty at just that moment.

Hitler never expressed any interest in expanding westward. Indeed, as a veteran of the First World War who had spent four years in the trenches, he had a horror of seeing Germany end up in another two-front war. As for the notion that Hitler was dreaming of "world conquest," that is as ridiculous an accusation as it was when Kaiser Wilhelm II was accused of the same thing by Allied propaganda in the First World War. Germany was no bigger than it had been last time around, and Britain's naval supremacy still denied the German navy any safe access to the sea. Hitler was an ambitious and ruthless man, but there is no evidence whatever that he indulged in such fantasies. Indeed, he was quite explicit about the need to preserve the British empire.

In his book *The Other Side of the Hill,* based on postwar interviews with German commanders, British strategist Sir Basil Liddell Hart includes a conversation that Hitler had with General Gerd von Rundstedt and two of his staff just after the trapped British army had been successfully evacuated from the port of Dunkirk in 1940. Hitler had ordered Rundstedt's tanks to stop, allowing the British troops to escape, and the general wanted to know why.

He [Hitler] then astonished us by speaking with admiration of the British empire, of the necessity for its existence and of the civilisation that Britain had brought to the world. . . . He compared the British empire with the Catholic Church, saying they were both essential elements of stability in the world. He said that all he wanted from Britain was that she should acknowledge Germany's position on the continent. The return of Germany's lost colonies would be desirable but not essential, and he would even offer to support Britain with troops if she should be involved in any difficulties anywhere.

The problem with Germany was not that it wanted to conquer Britain; Hitler's ambitions lay in the east. But if he were to achieve them all, then Germany would be by far the strongest power in Europe. That, more than the fate of small countries in Eastern Europe or the wickedness of Hitler's regime, was the main reason that Britain was preparing to fight the Führer. It was the old great-power game again, and the rise of Germany made war inevitable.

CHAPTER 6

THE "NO-GROUND-TROOPS" WAR, 1939–41

The crisis is scheduled for about early September, very shortly before the one of last year. I suspect that it will be war this time. It has ceased to have any connection with democracy or any other ideological considerations and it's just a naked question of interest. If I were English or French I'd feel like cutting Chamberlain's throat, but as a Canadian I feel more like sneering cynically this season.

There aren't any more issues that matter a damn in it, except incidentally. Not that we won't be all dragged in too. . . .

Frank Pickersgill, Warsaw, July 27, 1939

FRANK PICKERSGILL WAS TWENTY-FOUR IN 1939, AND HIS VIEWS were not unusual for well-educated young English Canadians (though he was more privileged than most). Brought up in Winnipeg, he had degrees in history and classics from the University of Manitoba and the University of Toronto, and he had arrived in Europe in 1938 for a year of travel and study before heading home to Canada. Prospects were

183

bright for him there because his elder brother, Jack, had become the private secretary to Prime Minister Mackenzie King. But Frank stayed in France, supported by money from his brother and the occasional piece of freelance journalism. He was fascinated but appalled by what was happening, and he couldn't drag himself away.

> I never dreamed that the day would come when . . . it should be my lot to be the one to lead this Dominion of Canada into a great war.
> [. . .] The present Government believe that conscription of men for overseas service will not be a necessary or an effective step. No such measure will be introduced by the present Administration. We have full faith in the readiness of Canadian men and women to put forth every effort in their power to preserve and to defend free institutions. . . .
>
> Prime Minister Mackenzie King, September 8, 1939

Finally, the war upon which "parliament would decide" had come—but in practical political terms, Mackenzie King had no choice but to take the country in. For years his main effort had gone into ensuring that if war came, Canada would at least enter it united, and at the special session of Parliament in September 1939, his patient strategy was rewarded with almost complete success: only J.S. Woodsworth, the leader of the socialist CCF party, resisted participation to the bitter end.

The foundation of King's strategy was his promise that no compulsion would be used to enlist men for overseas service. It was, in effect, a promise that no French Canadian would have to fight in the war unless he really wanted to—and on the basis of that guarantee, King and his Quebec lieutenant, Ernest Lapointe, convinced the Quebec members to accept the declaration of war. Two Quebec MPs, Liguori Lacombe and Wilfrid Lacroix, wanted an amendment explicitly stating that Canada should not become actively involved in war overseas, but only Woodsworth supported them. Most Quebec Liberals were ruled by their fear that divisions within the Liberal party would lead either to a Conservative government or to a coalition between Conservatives and rebel Liberals like the configuration that had imposed conscription in 1917, and in the end even Lacombe and Lacroix dropped their amendment: English Canada's emotions could not be ignored entirely.

This was very much an act of faith in King on the part of most French Canadians, who had a stereotyped image of English Canadians as gullible "blockheads" with an instinctive British loyalty that they were incapable of resisting. But in fact the mood of English Canadians in 1939 was very different from that of 1914.

> As the *Paris Star* reported on September 7, "Parisians greeted the British declaration of war on September 3 with gloomy quiet."...Not only were there no celebrations, but also there were no official send-offs for volunteers—no band music, parades, speeches or crisp $10.00 bills.
>
> Indeed, when the first high-school boy enlisted, there was no ceremony at the school, and a number of fellow-pupils expressed their lack of enthusiasm by saying things like, "He must be nuts," and "He'll be sorry." He was killed while taking part in the Dieppe raid . . . .
>
> Donald A. Smith, *At the Forks of the Grand*, vol. 2

Even among the shrinking majority of English speakers who were of British descent, there was a good deal of isolationist sentiment to serve as a brake on the pro-British enthusiasms of the English Canadian establishment. It was the very subdued mood of places like Paris, Ontario, that gave King reason to hope that his strategy of waging only a limited war might succeed—and there were still enough Canadians eager to volunteer for the war that commitments on a limited scale could probably be met without conscription. The Royal Canadian Naval Volunteer Reserve divisions across the country were a case in point:

I was a bank clerk and I joined the Naval Reserve in Vancouver in '37 as a midshipman . . .I was "called up" on the 31st of August '39. I remember I was in the bank and a lieutenant by the name of Brock telephoned me (he became an admiral incidentally, Jeffry Brock). He said: "Campbell, come down immediately in uniform. There's going to be a war on."

So I locked my cash drawer, walked past the accountant, went to the Manager's office and said: "Sir, there's going to be a war on and I have to go." And I've never been back to the bank other than to cash a cheque.

Craig Campbell

The Royal Canadian Navy was long on enthusiasm but short of just about everything else. In 1939 there were only seven destroyers in the RCN, and although a large construction program was started immediately, no new Canadian ships would be completed in at least a year. Fishing boats were requisitioned, and a secret scheme was set up to buy yachts on the American market and convert them into naval patrol boats. Halifax was the scene of colossal confusion as the dockyard was transformed into a more or less modern naval base. Hundreds of ships were marshalled there to sail under escort to Britain, for convoy rules were imposed at once. On September 3 a U-boat sank the passenger liner *Athenia*, causing the first Canadian war casualties, and by the end of September forty ships had been sunk approaching Britain.

However, in 1939 the U-boats could not sail more than five hundred miles west into the Atlantic, so the Canadian navy had no dealings with them yet. Canadian ships escorted the convoys only as far as St. John's, Newfoundland: from there they were escorted by British battleships and armed merchant cruisers until they came within range of U-boat attack, at which point Royal Navy destroyers and flying boats took up the task of protecting them. And no other Canadian forces were anywhere near the enemy.

That was reassuring to French Canadians, as was King's promise that the war would be a voluntary effort, but a large majority of French Canadians opposed Canada's entry into the war anyway, and many suspected that King would not be able to maintain his anti-conscription guarantee indefinitely. So Premier Maurice Duplessis's Union Nationale government in Quebec immediately called a provincial election, hoping to capitalize on French Canadians' fears.

What Wilfrid Laurier, in opposition, could not do, King and Laporte, in power, have accomplished. In 1917 Laurier fought against conscription (in vain, but) in 1939 King, Lapointe, Cardin, Power and Dandurand save us from conscription.

Liberal newspaper advertisement, Quebec provincial

election, October 1939

Touring Quebec along with the provincial Liberal leader, Adélard Godbout, the Quebec ministers in King's cabinet—Ernest Lapointe, P.J.A. Cardin and "Chubby" Power—reassured Quebec voters that the Liberal government in Ottawa was the best possible defence against conscription. If Duplessis won the election in Quebec, they threatened, then all the federal cabinet ministers from Quebec would resign. Some people called it election by blackmail, and others warned that Quebec would eventually be betrayed anyway, but Godbout won an upset victory, taking 55 percent of the vote to a mere 36 percent for Duplessis's Union Nationale. Imperialist English Canadian newspapers utterly misinterpreted the result and rejoiced at Quebec's loyalty to Britain: Canada could now "fight the war to the finish." But fighting the war to the finish was not King's intention at all—and indeed, as O.J. Skelton had predicted, there was not much war to fight for the moment anyway. A bit in the air, and a bit at sea, and that was it. The most dangerous seas were around Britain, where the U-boats were operating within range of German land-based aircraft.

That was where most of the Royal Canadian Navy's pre-war destroyers were operating in the early days.

Most of the U-boats were manned by old-style naval officers. Many of them in the Navy were not Nazis at all—certainly not in the early days—and they were a pretty decent bunch. . . . It was rather a clean way to fight a war, in many ways, at sea, because . . .you can't see who's in the submarine, so there wasn't anything very personal about it. But I did get very angry on one occasion.

Four great merchant ships carrying passengers were torpedoed in convoy in the space of about forty or fifty seconds. And curiously enough—an unusual thing to happen—all four broke their backs and fell into two halves. One half of one sank quite rapidly, so we had seven halves of ships floating around quite close to one another. And the lights were burning, so that you could see a cross-section of the ships: seven, eight, nine decks.

It was horrid to watch the passengers, who didn't know any better, struggling out of their staterooms and pushing along the corridors towards a precipitous descent into the sea. Those behind not seeing what the trouble was and those in front wanting to push back, and they just tumbled over the edges by the hundreds.

Dawn eventually came, and we were being shadowed by aircraft all the time, of course, to keep the U-boats in touch with the convoy. During rescue operations, when it was clearly evident that we were stopped in the water to do nothing but pick up boats full of people, we were machine-gunned—some harum-scarum young fellow out to take back a head-count or something to the Fuhrer, I don't know. Well, after that night of horror, to have this happen the following day. . . . You can get pretty mad.

Lieutenant Jeffrey Brock (later admiral)

Having overrun Poland in three weeks, Germany made no move to attack the Western powers, and the period of the "Phoney War" began. The Second World War took a lot longer to get properly underway than the First because neither side was ready: Hitler's rearmament plans had envisaged being fully prepared for war only in 1944, and the British and French were even further behind. The premature onset of the war was due to Hitler's impatient gamble that he could get Poland without triggering a war with the Anglo-French alliance, and a belief in London and Paris that it would be better to fight now, before Germany's acquisitions of further allies and territories in Eastern Europe added to the Reich's strength. But neither side was ready for a real war on the Western Front, so through the winter of 1939–40 they just sat on the frontiers and mulled things over.

Nor was it really a world war yet in the winter of 1940: only three of the seven great powers were involved. If it went on long enough, however, it was almost bound to expand into a world war, because any war involving some of the great powers tends to drag in all the others eventually. And from Germany's point of view—from that of all three Axis powers, Germany, Italy and Japan—a world war would be a very bad idea. The other four great powers (Britain, France, the Soviet Union and the United States, plus all their allies and dependencies) had an effective superiority in wealth and population of at least three-to-one over the Axis powers. There was, in fact, very little chance that the challengers could win a world war—so their only options were to achieve a quick win with their existing forces before the relative weight of resources began to tell, or to avoid war entirely. In Germany's case, it was a bit late for that, but well into 1940 Hitler hoped that a change of government in London would make possible a negotiated peace that recognized Germany's gains in Eastern Europe.

The "Phoney War" suited Mackenzie King right down to the ground. He agreed to send one army division across the Atlantic, to satisfy the English Canadian feeling that there should be at least some Canadian troops in Europe, but he didn't want to see them in combat—and even King's generals weren't thinking of the kind of mass army that Canada had sent to Europe in the First World War. In fact, if King could have got away with it, he would have sent no troops to Europe at all—and just too late to be of any use to him, the British prime minister, Neville Chamberlain, asked for Canada's help in a huge military training scheme that might have given him an excuse to keep Canadian troops at home.

> Actually, [King] was very distressed when Chamberlain proposed the Air Training Plan (September 26) that the proposal hadn't been made earlier, because he felt that if it had been made earlier he could have reduced the army component, or at any rate delayed it. And it was the army that he recognised as the threat to the country itself.
>
> I mean, no one objected to the Air Force, and nobody thought you'd ever conscript for the Air Force—nor for the Navy, for that matter. But every time the army was expanded, the first question he asked was: "Can this be maintained without conscription?"
>
> Jack Pickersgill

The Commonwealth Air Training Plan was a proposal for tens of thousands of Canadian, Australian, New Zealand and British airmen to be trained in Canada, where the skies were safe and there was lots of space. The plan was to set up sixty-seven training schools in Canada for pilots and other aircrew, all administered by the RCAF. The flood of trainees began to arrive almost immediately.

There was a wonderful and tremendous mixture of people here at that time. You had the Aussies, you had the English who trained here. . . . I've no idea of the actual numbers, but they came in their thousands. . . .They simply didn't know what they had struck.

That was a very cold winter. And the Aussies, whose winter uniforms hadn't followed them—there they were walking around in tropical outfits at maybe 35 below, and a northern wind. They thought they had come to the end of the world.

Naomi Radford, Edmonton

This was exactly the kind of war King wanted to fight: one waged almost exclusively on the home front, with no casualties. In his speech announcing the Commonwealth Air Training Plan on December 17, 1939, he stressed that this was also the approach the British themselves favoured: "The United Kingdom Government . . . feels that . . . the Air Training Scheme would provide for more effective assistance towards ultimate victory than any other form of military cooperation which Canada can give."

King had gone to some trouble to get the British to agree to this wording, but he couldn't really conceal the fact that this was not all the British government expected from Canada. There were, moreover, plenty of influential English Canadians who expected more commitment to the war from their government. On the day of King's speech, the first Canadian troops landed in Britain—and a month later the Ontario Legislature passed a resolution condemning the federal government's half-hearted war effort. King was worried that his Ontario critics would call a provincial election and use the campaign to demand a "National" (coalition) government in Ottawa, so he decided to pre-empt them by holding a federal election first.

It caught everybody off guard, and the Liberal victory in the March 1940 election was massive (181 out of a total of 245 seats). King's strategy of avoiding a major role in a shooting war was still working, but it depended heavily on the fact that there wasn't much shooting going on. Hitler could not afford to wait too long before attacking, however, for his enemies' resources were greater than his own: Germany's strategic position would deteriorate as time went on.

Contrary to expectation, the real fighting began not on the German-French border but in Northern Europe, where the neutrals were picked off one by one. The Soviet Union went first, in the winter of 1940, annexing the three Baltic republics and seizing a large amount of Finland's territory (in accord with the treaty it had signed with Nazi Germany the previous fall). The next target was Norway, which was important because most of the iron ore that Germany imported from Sweden was taken by train to the Norwegian coast and thence by ship to Germany. The British moved first, in April, mining Norway's coastal waters in violation of its neutrality—just in time to catch the German ships that arrived off the coast the following day carrying an invasion force.

The Norwegians fought back and appealed to Winston Churchill (who had just replaced Chamberlain as prime minister) for help. Churchill agreed, but noted: "The whole of Northern Norway was covered with snow to depths which none of our soldiers had ever seen, felt or imagined. There were neither snowshoes nor skis—still less skiers. We must do our best. Thus began this ramshackle campaign." In fact, the only troops in Britain who had seen such conditions were the Canadians, but they never made it to Norway. Thirteen hundred troops from the Edmonton Regiment and Princess Patricia's Canadian Light Infantry were sent to Scotland en route to Trondheim, but the Germans had driven the British forces out of northern Norway before the Canadians embarked. The following month, British and Canadian troops completed the subjugation of the North by occupying Iceland (allegedly to pre-empt a German invasion, but that was not actually a strategic possibility). Only Sweden's neutrality was still unviolated. Then, with scarcely a pause, the focus of the war shifted south.

One of my best friends is a fellow who fought [in the French army] in the last war and has just been mobilised again—he knows what it's like—and after the failure of the last twenty years he goes back into uniform in the firm conviction that the last war, and this one too, are just put-up jobs arranged by high finance and the armaments manufacturers to sell their products and reduce employment by killing off a few million solders. You couldn't persuade him otherwise—and it's a pretty common opinion among re-mobilised war veterans.

Frank Pickersgill, April 1940

Pickersgill's own opinions were a trifle more sophisticated than those of his French soldier friend, but not much: "The war is one between rival systems of oppression—the only thing in favor of the Allies is that the Anglo-Franco-American system of oppression is less odious in its results than the Italo-Russo-German one." But they were both driven to such crude formulas by their perfectly understandable conviction that none of what was happening made sense in terms of the interests of those whose lives were being disrupted by it—not even the Germans. It would be tempting to argue that these attitudes, which were widespread throughout the Allied countries, had a lot to do with the sudden collapse of France when the Germans attacked in May 1940—but actually, the collapse was military, not moral.

The German attack on France and the Low Countries cut through the Allied defences with dismaying speed, but not because the latter were unwilling to fight. Although the British and French were as strong numerically as the Germans—they even had more tanks—the Allies simply had no answer to the new *Blitzkrieg* tactics the Germans were using. Soon the British army in France was isolated near the Channel coast and in danger of being cut off from it. As part of a desperate plan to keep a toehold on the continent, the Canadian troops in Britain were ordered to embark at Dover to sail across and hold the Channel ports—but their commander, General Andy MacNaughton, made a personal reconnaissance of the shambles near Dunkirk and decided that they could accomplish nothing useful there. The order was cancelled, and one week later, at the end of May, 338,000 British, French and Belgian troops had to be evacuated from Dunkirk.

One week after that, Italy entered the war on Germany's side and invaded southern France. Just before France capitulated on June 16, a further British attempt to save their allies saw the First Canadian Division ordered to land near Brest in Brittany as part of the "Second British Expeditionary Force." The intention was to reestablish a British military presence on French territory not yet occupied by the Germans, and keep the French government in the war.

> The First Brigade was the only brigade that really got there, and we got on troop trains—cattle cars, actually—and moved into France. In the middle of the night we were given an order to turn around and get back to Brest and get on the ships and get out.
>
> We scrambled back, and came back to England having had to burn all our vehicles and ammunition supplies and so on, and came out with just what we were standing in. I lost everything I owned that side of the Atlantic except for my small pack, as did everybody.
>
> Dan Spry

> We overestimated the strength of the French army and underestimated the strength of the German army. It was not until France fell in June 1940 that I became convinced that Canada had to participate fully in the war.
>
> Escott Reid, *On Duty* (External Affairs, 1941–62)

For Escott Reid, it was still true that the war was essentially just one more round in the perennial great-power struggle, but that did not mean that it made no difference who won. In the long run, there would have to be another attempt to abolish war as the main currency of international relations, for the level of destruction wrought by modern military technology was becoming unbearable. But first Hitler and his allies had to be stopped, and that now seemed to require Canada's help.

With the fall of France, Canada became Britain's largest remaining ally in the war—and the British were expecting an invasion during the summer. The Imperial General Staff calculated the odds as sixty-forty in favour of invasion, and the entire country was mobilized to repel it—but the British army had left most of its weapons behind on the Dunkirk beaches. The First Canadian Division was one of the few army units in England still equipped to fight (apart from its First Brigade), and the pressure on King to contribute more to the British war effort rose dramatically. Four Canadian destroyers were sent across the Atlantic to help hold the Channel, and the 2nd and 3rd Canadian Divisions were authorized for overseas service as soon as they could be made ready.

> I think the Germans were far more experienced than we were, and we took tremendous losses. In 401 Squadron we had losses, at first, that were phenomenal. . . . For any aircraft we ever shot down, we lost two or three aircraft.
>
> Omer Lévesque, Ottawa, RCAF fighter pilot

401 Squadron was one of the first RCAF fighter squadrons to be sent overseas. Like the many others that followed, its casualties were at first far higher than those of the Germans it was flying against, many of whom had previous combat experience in the Spanish Civil War, Poland and France. The "learning curve" for fighter pilots is quite short and steep: it took a pilot about ten missions to get good at the game, but a great many never got beyond the first or second mission. However, the total numbers of Canadian airmen lost were not large by the standards

of land warfare, and by the summer of 1940 King was in the welcome position of having the Canadian Expeditionary Force safe in England, where it was suffering no casualties, while a relative handful of Canadian fighter pilots showed that Canada was "doing its part" by fighting in the Battle of Britain.

When the Germans lost that battle and cancelled their hastily prepared plans for the invasion of England, that politically happy situation was perpetuated, for Britain had no immediate ability to carry the ground battle back to the continent. With the exception of the disastrous raid at Dieppe in August 1942, in which over nine hundred Canadians died, Canadian ground troops would not see battle in Europe for another three years. In fact, after the danger of a German cross-Channel invasion passed, something akin to the Phoney War returned to the west of Europe. Hitler turned east to the Balkans and then, in June 1941, invaded Russia. British and German ground troops were in contact only in North Africa (where there were no Canadian soldiers), so King shouldn't have been under any pressure on the subject that worried him most: conscription. But he was.

The pro- and anti-conscriptionists were already staking out their positions within King's cabinet. Some were even talking about a "Union" government, and King was particularly upset by a "desire to have Meighen brought into Government. Said I would not countenance anything of kind in regard to a man who had been responsible for Wartime Elections Act, and for conscription in the last war."

The Conservative opposition demanded the same draconian measures that had just been introduced in Britain, which had given the government total control over the nation's manpower, industry and resources in order to wage a total war. Conscription for military service was only a part of that package, but it was a part especially dear to the Tory opposition and the Liberal conscriptionists in Canada—and what they meant, of course, was conscription for service overseas to defend Britain. In fact, military manpower was just about the only defence requirement that

Britain wasn't short of at the time, but that was irrelevant: the purpose of conscription was to make imperial patriots in Canada feel better.

King's response was a brilliant example of diversionary tactics in politics: he began worrying aloud about "the possibility of an invasion of our shores. [If Britain falls], an effort will be made to seize this country as a prize of war. We have, therefore, changed to the stage where defence of this land becomes our most important duty. It will involve far-reaching measures. . . ."

King's grasp of military strategy was erratic at best, but he probably never actually believed that the fall of Britain could lead to an invasion of Canada. It was strategic nonsense: the Atlantic is three thousand kilometres wide, and the Germans did not even have much by way of a surface navy. However, King certainly knew that conscription *for home defence only* would ease the English Canadian pressure on him to do more without angering French Canadians too much—so in June 1940 the new defence minister, Colonel J.L. Ralston, introduced the National Resources Mobilization Act (NRMA). Parliament passed it with scarcely a murmur of protest. As the marching song went:

Why don't you join up?
Why don't you join up?
Why don't you join old Ralston's army?
Two bucks a week; all you want to eat;
Great big boots and blisters on your feet.
Why don't you join up?

The NRMA gave Ottawa total control over the property and services of Canadians for war purposes—with one exception. The government could conscript men into the army, but the conscripts were to serve only on Canadian soil or in Canadian waters—and technically, King was still not breaking his earlier promise: "Once again I wish to repeat my undertaking . . . that no measure for the conscription of men for overseas service will be introduced by the present administration," he told the House of Commons one month after the fall of France.

This halfway conscription bill was an elegant solution to a political problem. It helped King fend off the Tories and his critics within the Liberal party. On the whole, French Canadians recognized King's strategy for what it was, and went along with it in the hope that it would keep English Canadian imperial patriots from escalating their demands. Recruiting for the regular army was still satisfactory: enough idealists, adventurers and unemployed were volunteering to fill the new units as quickly as equipment became available for them—and the NRMA conscripts would defend Canada if the Nazis invaded (or the Martians). But it wasn't much fun for the "Zombies," as they were called.

> In the winter of 1941 we got a bunch of Zombies in to train. Some French Canadians, but a lot of Ukrainians and what-have-you from towns and places in Manitoba and Saskatchewan. Our C.O. at Brandon, he told us to run the asses off them if we wanted. . . .
>
> We decided these Zombies better start the day right. . . . Except, Christ Almighty, when I think of it, there was no gymnasium, no drill hangar, and here's these Zombies running through the streets of this town at 6.30 in the morning and it would often be 20 below. Hell, even colder. And in gymwear, too! . . . Anyway they knew they were in the army, and they knew they were NRMA crud because the regular troops didn't get this treatment . . .
>
> Barry Broadfoot, *Six War Years*

Few isolationists, French- or English-speaking, had worried much about who would win in 1939, since they anticipated a repetition of the long stalemate of the First World War. But most of them recognized that the Nazi regime in Germany was a profoundly evil phenomenon, and by late 1940 it had, by clever military tactics and much good luck, reached a point where it looked as though it might succeed in establishing permanent domination over much of Europe. To a certain extent, that could affect practical North American interests—and to a far greater extent, it affected North American attitudes.

> The fall of France completely changed my views, as it did the views of a great many Canadians, even a great many French Canadians. I think the fall of France probably affected me the most of all public events in my whole life. . . .
>
> You didn't need to tell me after that that we were vitally concerned about the outcome of the war. So when Ogdensburg happened it just seemed to me to make good sense; anything we could do to get the Americans more involved was a good thing.
>
> Jack Pickersgill, secretary to Prime Minister Mackenzie
> King, 1937–48

In the summer of 1940 the United States was still officially neutral, and a majority of the American public was still isolationist, but President Franklin D. Roosevelt was not. Both his political sympathies and his concern for the balance of power drove him to work patiently to bring the United States into the war on Britain's side. From Roosevelt's point of view, the fall of France and the subsequent rapid extension of German U-boat activities into the western Atlantic were useful pretexts for bringing his country a little closer to commitment to the war, but the mythical military threat to Canada that Mackenzie King had evoked was even better. If Canada faced attack, after all, he could invoke the Monroe Doctrine to come to its defence.

As early as 1938, in a speech at Queen's University in Kingston, Ontario, Roosevelt had promised that the United States would "not stand idly by if domination of Canadian soil is threatened by any other empire." Mackenzie King, recognizing the American strategic interest in Canadian territory, had replied realistically: "We too have obligations as a good and friendly neighbour, and one of these is to see that . . . our country is made as immune from attack or possible invasion as we can reasonably be expected to make it."

Now, in the summer of 1940, it could plausibly (though inaccurately) be argued that Canada could no longer fulfill that guarantee unaided. That gave Roosevelt an excuse to start negotiating directly with the British for U.S. air bases in Newfoundland, Bermuda and the British West Indies, and a deal was nearing completion for the supply of fifty over-age American destroyers to Britain. But it was still politically easier for Roosevelt to provide military support to the British empire through Canada, since that could be said to fall under the heading of continental defence.

Shortly before two o'clock the 'phone rang, and the girl at the switchboard said it was the President of the United States who wished to speak to me. The President said: "Hello, is that you, Mackenzie?" . . . I replied: Yes. He then said: "I am going tomorrow night in my train to Ogdensburg. If you are free I would like to have you come and have dinner with me there. I would like to talk with you about the matter of the destroyers, and they [the British] are arranging to let us have bases on some of their Atlantic colonial possessions for our naval and air forces.

"I gave an interview, this morning, to the press in which I said that I was in direct communication with Great Britain with regard to these matters in the Atlantic. That I was taking up with you direct the matter of mutual defence of our coasts on the Atlantic. I thought it was better to keep the two things distinct. . . . I have told the press that we will be meeting together. Are you free tomorrow night?"

I said: Yes.

"Mackenzie" King, August 16, 1940

It is strange that the man who became furious if he thought he was being pushed (he would have said "railroaded") by the British, was so acquiescent when Roosevelt did the same thing. Probably it had a lot to do with the fact that King had spent a number of years in the United States and was more at ease with American manners than British. "Mackenzie" (whose old friends actually called him "Rex") recognized Roosevelt's power, but he was so charmed by the President's easy informality that he didn't always notice that the decision had already been made for him.

At Ogdensburg the two men talked about the destroyers and the bases, but the really significant development for Canada was not the promise that it would get half a dozen of the ancient American destroyers. It was the creation of the "Canada–United States Permanent Joint Board on Defence." King fretted about the significance of the word "Permanent," but Roosevelt felt the board should be designed not "to meet this particular situation alone but to help secure the continent for the future," and King gave in. He also consented to joint military exercises, and to the movement of American troops through Canada. Ralston, the minister of defence, was delighted, and so was Skelton at External Affairs: Canada was finally "escaping from the embraces of mother England ," he said. Churchill noticed this too, and was "querulous" about the Permanent Joint Board. The dominion had found a new protector.

Mackenzie King would later grow quite nervous about the closeness of Canada's developing relationship with the United States, but at this point he gloried in his role as a vital intermediary between Churchill and Roosevelt.

———

Right down through 1941, the war went splendidly well for Mackenzie King. The political situation at home had stabilized, and very few Canadians were getting hurt in the war. In fact, only the air force was taking significant casualties, and even that could be turned to political advantage.

The main killing ground was over northern France and Belgium, where the British and Canadian air forces continually "harrassed the enemy" by bombing railway lines, bridges, airfields and other military targets. The raids had no real strategic purpose, since the British and Canadian armies were nowhere near ready for an attack on France at that time; they were mainly a morale-boosting activity to demonstrate that the fight wasn't over. It was a very expensive way to accomplish very little.

> There was a raid and a fighter sweep in October or November of '41 where seven of our aircraft were shot down out of nine that wound up in combat. It was over France. In other words two pilots came back and the rest were killed or prisoners of war, so that would be the equivalent of seventy percent of the squadron being disabled.
>
> Omer Lévesque

Omer Lévesque survived that disaster, and a few weeks later his squadron got four confirmed kills, including the first Focke-Wulf 190 shot down in combat (which was downed by Lévesque himself). However, even good fighter pilots have short careers.

One of the prime targets for the raids over France had been three large German warships, the *Scharnhorst*, *Gneisenau* and *Prinz Eugen*, which had been tied up at Brest since May 1941, when the *Bismarck* was sunk in the North Atlantic. By the end of the year Hitler was insisting that they be moved north to Norway, from where they could attack the convoys to Russia—and to get there, they had to run the English Channel. On February 11, 1942 the three ships slipped out of Brest in the middle of the night, and by the time they were spotted by an RAF patrol at eleven the following morning they were already approaching the Straits of Dover. They had been given all the air cover that the Luftwaffe could spare:

We went over the area, but we didn't see the bombers we were supposed to escort. We just saw aircraft in absolute combat, and in the middle of it the German ships shooting at anything that came close. So there were aircraft from twenty feet above the water to about twelve hundred feet. I was leading a section, and while I was firing at a 109 I remember my number two just about sawed my wing off on my left side. I looked up and this propellor was just about touching my wing, and that took me off that 109 I was aiming for. . . .

Then I got into real dogfights with 109s and 190s, until I was hit myself. I was too low to parachute. . . .There was smoke on the side of the aircraft, there were some ships shooting at me, and I settled over the water. . . .

And I remember waking up under water thirty, forty feet, like a dark green bottle colour, and I remember my canopy had been back. I hadn't closed it, because it would have entombed me. I had my hand on the canopy so it wouldn't close on me. You could never open it under water, I'm pretty sure. . . .

I saw little bubbles of air, and little bubbles of light—you know, when you go deep—and then I said I must be alive, I must be okay. I eventually got myself loose by grabbing the antenna of the Spitfire, and then swam to the surface. I couldn't inflate my Mae West, but the kapok kept me just above the water, though each wave would go in my face. After about three-quarters of an hour of that I saw a net coming to pick me up.

Then I really woke up, lying on a bed, bleeding and being bandaged. And pictures of Hitler and listening to Beethoven music, I'll never forget that. I said I must be with the Germans, all right. But the Captain gave me some cognac. He didn't ask me any questions. He knew what was going on.

Lévesque, one kill short of being an ace, spent the rest of the war as a prisoner, but the feats of Canadian fighter pilots were heavily exploited by King's government. Since Canada's losses in the air would never raise the issue of conscription, it went down well even in French Canada.

> When Leo Robillard of Ottawa, who recently was decorated by the King, blew two planes in a day out of the sky over France, when Jean-Paul Sabourin took down three in as many hours in Libya, were they not destroying planes which might some day be attacking Canada—yes, even the city of Quebec? Auger, Morin, Lecavalier, Desloges, St. Pierre, they destroyed enemy planes in every part of Europe. For every bomber our men destroy away from here, there is that much less risk of one of them coming here. . . .
>
> C.G. "Chubby" Power, minister of national defence for air,
> Quebec, 1942

It wasn't true, of course: it would be another decade before any "enemy" bomber had the range to reach Canada. But it sounded well— and meanwhile Canada got on with what it saw as its real contribution to the war effort: the production of weapons.

––––––––

> Before the war we had a very high level of unemployment in Canada, and in Windsor particularly, and we used to say if there was a war we would find the money to provide work. . . . It took some months after 1939 for unemployment to be mitigated, but it wasn't very long before the Ford Motor Company received contracts to build trucks and other military vehicles, and by the middle of 1940 we were experiencing almost full employment.
>
> Paul Martin, parliamentary assistant for labour, 1943

At the outbreak of war, there was virtually no armaments manufacturing industry in Canada: the Inglis (washing machine) Company was producing Bren guns, but they made hardly enough to meet Canada's needs, let alone Britain's. For the first few months of the war the government floundered, uncertain of what the requirements would be, but on the day that the Germans invaded Norway C.D. Howe, a powerful Ontario Liberal, was appointed minister of munitions and supply. It was an inspired choice.

> Howe was one of my great ministers. He was . . . a most satisfactory man to work for, because his method was to say: "Okay, you're my man. You go and do the job. If you fail, I'll fire you; if you succeed, I'll do what you say."
>
> He didn't have policies. He had men. . . . And it was a very effective way of getting things done. He wasn't a man who had papers all over his desk. He just had people who came to see him and talked to him about the problems.
>
> Mitchell Sharp, Department of Finance, 1942–51

Howe recruited a small cadre of brilliant and ruthless managers to create and run a Canadian war economy. They were the "dollar a year" men, who came to work for the government for free. (Well, sort of—their companies carried on paying their salaries.) "Howe's boys" included men like R.A.C. Henry, an engineer who had been general manager of the Beauharnois Light, Heat and Power Company, E.P. Taylor, a financier from Toronto, and Henry Borden (nephew of Sir Robert Borden), a Toronto corporate lawyer. They nominally constituted a departmental executive committee—but in reality they were the wheeler-dealers who enabled Howe to work miracles. When C.D. Howe became minister of munitions and supply, Canada lacked almost everything: money, skills and tools. But demand was unlimited, thanks to the insatiable British and American requirements for weapons and raw materials, and credit to fuel the expansion was effectively unlimited too. In just two years, Canada's gross national product grew by 47 percent: over 1,200,000 men and women were involved in industrial production for war by 1943, turning out everything from synthetic rubber to radar sets and binoculars.

At the Malton aircraft factory north of Toronto (originally National Steel Car, until Howe took it over and reorganized it as Victory Aircraft), they built long-range Lancaster bombers:

Q. When did you come to work here, Faye?
I started in 1943.
Q. How old were you then?
I was 17.
Q. What was it like there then?
It was very nice. We had mostly female employees. We did have the odd disabled person, but they were very fine workers. We didn't have a coffee break; we had canteens every second little corner. And we had a dance-hall at lunchtime upstairs.
Q. Did you go dancing there at lunch-hour?
Every lunchtime. I also had two sisters working here. I worked in the heat treatment and my sisters were "Rosie the riveters," you know, and they were only about 5 feet tall and the guns were as big as they were. But the job I had, I'd get the [hot] rivets out of the bath and run them on the floor. I can tell you every corner of this building.
Q. You'd actually run with the rivets?
I would run, yeah. At seventeen you had a little more speed.
Q. What were you paid in the war?
Oh, I think I got about $53 a week—but that was big money in those days.

Faye Denton (worked at Victory Aircraft, 1944–45)

Canada was going to have to produce everything: trucks, tanks, rifles, ammunition, artillery, warships, bombs and aircraft. Everything was needed right now, and only the government had the resources to bulldoze its way through the obstacles. By the middle of 1940 Howe had brought Canadian industry firmly under government supervision. Factories produced what the government told them to, with raw materials that were controlled by the government (and often bought by special crown corporations), and, under the NRMA, labour was directed into critical areas by the government.

> We received a cable from England asking for information on the manufacture of hundreds of items of equipment. You see, they had lost everything at Dunkirk, and they wanted to know how much it would cost, and what the unit prices would be. . . . We met in Howe's office . . . and here's what he said: "We have no idea of the cost, but before the war is over everything will be needed, so let's go ahead anyway. If we lose the war, nothing will matter. If we win the war, the cost will still have been of no consequence and will be forgotten."
>
> Henry Borden

Howe's greatest difficulty, in fact, was in deciding what to produce, for the British requirements kept changing. Facing invasion in 1940, they had wanted the weapons to repel it, but by the following year they were starting to think in offensive terms, which required rather different weapons. Frustrated by second-hand information, Howe decided to sail to London to find out for himself, accompanied by three leading Canadian businessmen: Gordon Scott of Montreal, E.P. Taylor of Toronto and W.C. Woodward of Vancouver. "I pray he . . . will get through all right and return in safety," King wrote in his diary—but on December 14, 1941, Angus Macdonald, the navy minister, called to say that Howe's ship had been torpedoed. There was no further news.

But December 1941 was when it became obvious to anyone with eyes to see that the Allies were bound to win the war. It should have been clear six months before, when Hitler invaded Russia, for in the end it was the Red Army that destroyed the German army: about 85 percent of German casualties were suffered on the Eastern Front. But that wasn't yet obvious, for in late 1941 the Russians were still mounting a last desperate defence in front of Moscow, deep in the Soviet Union. But the Japanese attack on Pearl Harbor on December 7, 1941 brought the United States into the war on the Allied side, and after that it was settled: the Allies were bound to win. As for Mackenzie King, his strategy had been a brilliant success: Canada's casualties in two and a half years of war had been under 5,000 dead—and almost none of them had been ground troops.

I am far from despairing for his life, though I believe, if [he is] spared, it will be as a result of rescue at sea—a perfectly terrible experience . . .There is a certain irony in the situation in that Howe, himself, usually prefers to travel by plane and was taking this method to rest.

Mackenzie King Record, December 14, 1941

In fact, C.D. Howe was rescued off Iceland after a short time in the water (although one of his party, Gordon Scott, was drowned). The Canadian delegation arrived in London to a hero's welcome. In the talks that ensued over the next few weeks with the British ministries of supply and aircraft production, it turned out that what London now wanted above all was long-range bombers to carry the war to Germany. Canadians were not the only ones who were reluctant to get into a big ground war. But whichever strategy the Allies ultimately adopted against Germany, most of the troops and equipment would have to come across the Atlantic first.

By 1941, with the whole western coastline of Europe in German hands and longer-range submarines coming into service, the U-boat war had spread west to within sight of the Canadian coast. It became necessary to give convoys continuous anti-submarine escort all the way across the Atlantic, and the British navy was already stretched to the limit. So the Canadian Navy was asked to establish the Newfoundland Escort Force, and in June 1941 Commodore L.W. Murray set up headquarters in St. John's. At that point the Canadian Navy's strength was about nineteen thousand men—of whom twelve thousand had been in for less than a year. What training they got tended to be done on the job—at sea.

By now the Canadian Navy was building up toward its eventual astonishing strength of six hundred ships. It remained predominantly a small-ship navy down to the end: corvettes were the classic Canadian warships of the Second World War. They were small, overcrowded ships with a wicked motion: they would "roll even on wet grass," as the sailors put it. Every available space was crammed with equipment or weapons—not that they had much in the way of that either. Most of them, until quite late in the war, had no radar, only the most primitive versions of ASDIC (an early form of sonar), and no High-Frequency Direction-Finders (HF/DF) for radio-locating submarines that were shadowing the convoys. For attacking submerged submarines they had only depth charges: large drums of high explosive that were rolled off the ship's stern and exploded at a pre-set depth.

If the submarines were attacking on the surface at night, as they often did, the corvettes could try to hit them with their single 4-inch gun—or resort to the ancient tactic of ramming. To try to avoid the German submarines the convoys regularly sailed very far north, and even in summer the North Atlantic weather was a constant enemy. The corvettes were perpetually wet inside and out—except when it froze, and their superstructure became encased in a thick sheath of ice whose weight would eventually capsize the ship if it were not continuously chipped off. Below deck the cramped crew quarters stank of diesel fumes, stale food, unwashed bodies and vomit. The crews had little chance of survival if they were torpedoed in mid-Atlantic: for most of the year, thirty minutes in the frigid water was enough to kill a man.

The convoy battles were non-stop, for no sooner would a Canadian escort group hand over an eastbound convoy to the British navy somewhere in mid-Atlantic than it would pick up a westbound convoy for the trip home. The U-boats operated in packs, with one or more submarines trailing a convoy and radioing its position ahead to others, which would gather in its path. The British Admiralty was able to intercept and decipher some of the radio messages and reroute the convoys out of danger, but if the messages took too long to decode, the slaughter would begin.

Convoys made up of faster merchant ships could sometimes simply outrun the U-boats, but the slow convoys that sailed from Sydney, Nova Scotia, were a nightmare. One of the worst experiences for the Canadian Navy was convoy SC42 in September 1941. It was known that a group of U-boats were gathering at the southeastern tip of Greenland and ten other convoys, westbound and eastbound, were diverted to the south. But SC42 could not be rerouted as the escorts were short of fuel. The conditions were ideal for the U-boats: the heavy seas and gale-force winds had died down, and several of the aged freighters were leaving a trail of black smoke. The convoy was out of range of the air patrols that flew out of Newfoundland, and the escort consisted of only one destroyer, HMCS *Skeena*, and three corvettes. *Skeena* had no radar, no HF/DF and no experience of anti-submarine warfare.

Eight U-boats were lying in wait for the 64-ship convoy south of Greenland, and shortly after midnight on September 10 the first ship was sunk. The entire convoy then made an emergency forty-five-degree turn, but failed to shake the submarines, one of which passed right down through the middle of the convoy on the surface. By the time dawn arrived, the toll was seven ships sunk and an eighth badly damaged.

During the day another ship was torpedoed, and as night fell the wolf pack closed in again, sinking two ships almost at once. At that point two more Canadian corvettes arrived on the scene—*Moose Jaw* and *Chambly*—and promptly got an ASDIC contact. Their depth charges forced the U-boat to the surface, and *Moose Jaw* rammed it. The U-boat's captain abandoned ship by leaping from his conning tower onto the corvette's deck, but the boarding party sent aboard by *Chambly* to retrieve *U-501*'s secret papers had to abandon the rapidly sinking submarine in a hurry, and one Canadian stoker was trapped inside and drowned.

It was the first confirmed "kill" ever achieved by the Royal Canadian Navy (after two years of war), but it hardly evened the score: before the night was over another five ships were lost, bringing the total to fifteen in two days. Before the hapless convoy reached its final destination, another ship was sunk: the casualty rate was 25 percent for the merchant ships on a single crossing. No organization could have withstood these sorts of losses for long, but SC42's ordeal took place in the "Black Pit," the mid-Atlantic gap where no land-based air cover was available. Few convoys took so bad a beating after continuous air cover across the Atlantic became available by long-range aircraft operating out of Britain, Iceland and Newfoundland.

Canada's navy was the third-largest in the world by 1945, and it was fighting exactly the kind of capital-intensive war that both Mackenzie King and C.D. Howe felt most comfortable with. It allowed Canada to exploit and develop its industrial resources, and it would never kill so many people that the government would face political difficulties at home. In terms of sheer nervous strain and sustained physical misery, nobody had a harder war than the Royal Canadian Navy, but it only lost two thousand dead during the entire war.

BLITZKRIEG

IT TOOK THE GERMAN WEHRMACHT SIX WEEKS IN THE SPRING OF 1940 to conquer France and the Low Countries and drive the British army out of Europe. Germany's total losses were 45,000 dead and missing and 110,000 wounded, fewer than in any one of twenty major battles of the First World War. Yet the Germans enjoyed no significant superiority over the French and British forces either in numbers or in equipment. How did they do it?

There was a brief period after the fall of France when *Blitzkrieg* (lightning war) was seen as an unstoppable, almost magical technique, but it was nothing of the sort. Military theorists in every great power were well aware of the techniques of surprise and rapid penetration that had achieved the breakthroughs of 1918, and in the two decades between the wars they had worked hard to refine them. If you could make everything mobile—tanks, of course, but also self-propelled artillery and infantry in armoured personnel carriers—then the breakthroughs would happen faster and go deeper. Provide lots of close air support from ground-attack aircraft that were in radio contact with the ground forces, and they would go faster still. Maybe fast enough that you could break right through into open country and collapse the enemy's defences entirely.

The German theorists were not cleverer than the others; they were just better or luckier in getting their senior officers to listen to them. And even then, the German High Command might not have bet the farm on a flat-out blitzkrieg attack in 1940 if an earlier plan for a more conventional offensive that was virtually a replay of the Schlieffen Plan had not been captured by the Allies in January 1940. With that plan compromised, it was much easier for General Gerd von Manstein to sell a radical alternative proposal that was fully supported by his subordinate, General Heinz Guderian, the leading German expert on armoured warfare. By all means go ahead and send the bulk of the German army marching in a great sweeping curve west and then south through Holland and Belgium as the British and French expect, said Manstein, and the Allies will move their armies up into Belgium to meet it. But then the real attack will come as an armoured spearhead advancing straight west from Germany through the Ardennnes, hilly country that is not generally thought suitable for tanks. Move fast enough and you'll come out into open country before the French can react and get anybody there to stop you—and then just keep going.

Guderian's tanks took three days to get through the narrow, twisting roads of the Ardennes, using Stuka dive-bombers to crack any French resistance. After that it was practically a free run straight across northern France to the English Channel—and now the Germans were *behind* all the French and British troops that had advanced into Belgium. They might all have been captured, but Hitler let most of them get away at Dunkirk.

The French didn't lose because they were demoralized. They became demoralized because they were losing badly, and simply could not react fast enough to this new blitzkrieg technique. But tactical innovation of this kind never remains a surprise for long, and the counter-move was obvious: make your defences even deeper. Many miles deep, with successive belts of trenches, minefields, bunkers, gun positions and tank traps to slow down the armoured spearheads and eventually wear them away. And even if there is a breakthrough, you will have had time to get your reserves in place. You may have to retreat—the whole front may have to roll back dozens or even hundreds of miles—but the front will not collapse completely. And that was the problem, in a way.

Pure blitzkrieg only lasted about eighteen months. What the new technique actually did was to set the continuous front in motion. During the First World War, between the end of 1914 and the end of 1918, the Western Front barely moved fifty miles. There were just as many soldiers available in the Second World War, and even more firepower, so the continuous front was still a fact, but now it moved a lot. And as it did it would roll over towns and villages and crush them—in some cases not just once, but several times, back and forth. It was a war of attrition, but on an even larger scale. The Soviet Union, for example, built at least 100,000 tanks, 100,000 aircraft and 175,000 artillery pieces during the war, of which at least two-thirds were destroyed in the fighting. Twice as many soldiers were killed as in the First World War—and almost twice as many civilians were killed as soldiers. They were killed almost incidentally, as a by-product of the fighting. They didn't have to go to the front; it came to them. Most countries in Europe from Germany eastward saw around 10 percent of their population killed.

It was really a very good war in which to avoid ground combat—and for most of the time, the English-speaking countries did.

THE DAY AFTER THE BATTLE

Field Hospital at Paardeberg Drift on 19th Feby 1900. This little farmhouse is on the bluff overhanging the drifts. Close by it I was given breakfast by R. Thiele at 8 a.m on the 18th Just before we forded the drift. The space in front is a courtyard, bounded in front, to the spectator's left, by a low semi-circular mud wall. Clear the end of the house was a stable. The river is in the same direction. The house and stable were crammed with wounded. The row of seated men are on the stoop or low verandah. From the mud wall to the tree a tarpaulin was stretched so as to make a rude tent, and many wounded were under it. Among Corps represented were Royal Canadians (lying on ground) Black Watch, Gordons, Argyle and Suther- land Shropshires, etc. To the left were tents also filled. Major Arnold died in one of these tents. Capt. Mason was kept in one until the Convoy moved.

photo by R. Thiele

Wounded Canadians after Paardeberg. "Leavitt is not expected to live. Boers surrendered to the Canadians. Roberts said we did fine work. . . . Men are horribly shot." Albert Perkins, February 27, 1900.

Soldiers leave for war, 1915.

B Company, Newfoundland Regiment, in front line, Suvla Bay, 1915. Capt. Alexander (left) and Capt. Nunns (right).

The enthusiasm of the early days was long gone, but in its place was an inflexible determination to win the war and to make sure that the suffering was shared by all.

Talbot M. Papineau,
April 1916.

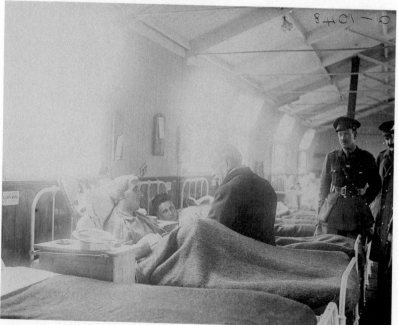

Sir Robert Borden chats with a wounded man at Base Hospital,
March 1917.

How did people in the West feel about conscription? "Well, I think they were all for it. Because after all, the flower of the flock had already been taken." Naomi Radford, Edmonton.

Lester B. Pearson, spring 1918. "Mike" was the invention of Pearson's Royal Flying Corps squadron commander who thought "Lester" an inappropriate name for a fighter pilot.

Members of 5th Canadian Mounted Rifles return from the Battle of Amiens on a tank.

Mackenzie King was a dumpy, fussy bachelor, communing regularly with his dear, dead mother and other denizens of the spirit world.

Sutherland Brown, Special Reconnaissance. In the Upper Ausable Valley, east of Lake Placid, planning to invade the United States.

Mackenzie King inspecting guard of honour from the Régiment de la Chaudière: "I never dreamed that the day would come when ... it should be my lot to be the one to lead this Dominion of Canada into a great war."

The Malton aircraft factory in Toronto (originally the National Steel Car Company, until C.D. Howe took it over and reorganized it as Victory Aircraft), which built Avro Lancaster bombers.

"I've been in a permanent state of exhilaration since March 8.... I don't know where it's going to land me, but it's damned good while it lasts." Frank Pickersgill, January 1943.

Survivors of the HMCS *Clayoquot*, torpedoed Christmas Eve 1944.

Carriers in soft, flooded ground, Breskens Pocket: "So it was a slow, painful, bloody, muddy battle, and it wasn't helped by the fact we were short of reinforcements." Major-General Dan Spry, October 1944.

HMCS *Summerside* in heavy seas.

Sherman tanks of Lord Strathcona's Horse make their way north from the Pintail Bridge over the Imjin River, Korea.

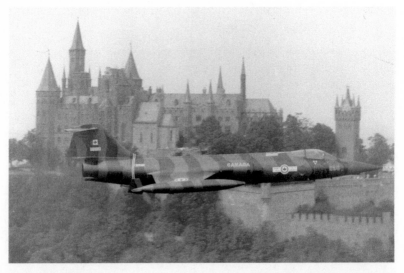

CF-101 Starfighter in 1977 with Hohenzollern Castle in the background. In July 1959 the government announced that the RCAF in Europe would be re-equipped with CF-104 Starfighters, whose sole mission would be nuclear strikes into Eastern Europe.

President Dwight Eisenhower meets Prime Minister Diefenbaker and Minister of Foreign Affairs Howard Green, 1960.

By the end of 1962 the Bomarcs were all fully operational in their Canadian launching sites—except, of course, for the nuclear warheads without which they were about as useful as the tail fins on a '62 Chevy.

Canadian soldiers on NATO manoeuvres, 1984: at least 90 percent of Canada's soldiers and an even higher proportion of its military spending were always devoted to the purposes of its Cold War alliances, NATO and NORAD.

CHAPTER 7

THE REAL WAR, 1942–45

"YOU BASTARDS ARE GOING WITH ME RIGHT TO THE TOP AND WE'LL kill every one of those bloody Japs," Sergeant Major John Robert Osborn told his sixty-five men, all that were left of 'B' Company, Winnipeg Grenadiers by December 19, 1941. They were the first Canadian soldiers to see ground combat in the war, and the people who sent them should have known they were doomed. It was clear that war was coming with Japan. It was clear that the British colony of Hong Kong could not be defended successfully. And there is a lingering suspicion that the Canadian troops were deliberately sent there to get killed.

When two Canadian battalions arrived in Hong Kong in November 1941, Mackenzie King gave a statement to the press saying that their dispatch had been necessary because "we regarded as a part of the defence of Canada and of freedom, any attack which might be made by the Japanese against British territory or forces in the Orient." The inhabitants of Hong Kong might well prefer British imperial rule to Japanese imperial rule, but it was hardly "freedom" the Canadian troops were being sent to defend. They were there as sacrificial pawns in King's rearguard action against British pressure for greater Canadian participation in the war and pro-conscription pressure from his own cabinet and armed forces

There was obviously no need for conscription in Canada in the winter of 1941–42, as there was no steady drain of army casualties that would require large-scale replacements. But army recruiting was slowing down because jobs were plentiful, wages were high and, with the army not yet involved in any fighting, volunteers who were eager to get into the war tended to avoid signing up. So some members of King's own cabinet were urging him to get the army committed to combat somewhere—anywhere, in fact.

> Ralston brought forward a suggestion from the Defence officials that we should ask the British authorities to have our men put into action somewhere at once . . . even if it involved some being killed. . . . The fact that our men were not in action was causing very few to enlist.
>
> *Mackenzie King Record*, May 20, 1941

The pressures for conscription for overseas service were also mounting steadily in English Canada. Already in 1941 *Saturday Night* magazine was writing: "There is among English-speaking Canadians a widespread feeling that the real motive of the French Canadian attitude toward conscription is the desire to improve the numerical strength of that element of the population, by avoiding its full proportionate share of the casualties." Paranoia has never been a Quebec monopoly.

At the same time Arthur Meighen, regarded by King as his nemesis, became the leader of the Conservative Party in November 1941, and immediately declared himself in favour of compulsory selective service over the whole field of war. It soon became obvious that Meighen's strategy was to try to engineer a "National" government along the lines of Borden's Union government of 1917 (which had also been created largely by Meighen), by fostering a split in the Liberal Party over conscription. And Meighen was quite willing to appeal to the old Upper-Canadian desire to compel French Canadians to sacrifice to English

Canada's gods: "A trembling servitude to a sinister tradition," he pro-
claimed, "has gone far to benumb the striking power of Canada."

King recognized the danger: if the pro-conscription movement
gained much more steam, many English-speaking Liberals would
come under irresistible pressure to conform, and the government's
majority might well drain away into a Meighen-led Union government. Except that it would have nothing to do with unity: it would
split the country as badly as in 1917, and Canada might not survive a
second round of that. Faced with this dual threat—from across the
aisle and also from within his own cabinet—King took two radical
decisions. The first was to send Canadian troops into combat somewhere, partly to encourage army recruiting (although whether it would
actually have that effect was much to be doubted), and partly just to
placate his own English Canadian ministers. The other, to fend off the
challenge from Meighen's Conservatives, was to steal their thunder by
holding a plebiscite asking Canadians to release him from his promise
not to send conscripts into combat abroad—without actually promising to send them. "Conscription if necessary, but not necessarily conscription," as he later put it.

At just that time the British were seeking reinforcements for their
Hong Kong garrison (where they would be sure to see fighting soon), so
in October 1941 the Royal Rifles of Canada (a Quebec regiment) and
the Winnipeg Grenadiers were sent to Hong Kong. The two Canadian
battalions, about two thousand men, arrived in Hong Kong in November
1941, and three weeks later, on the morning after Pearl Harbor, the
Japanese launched their attack. The Canadian soldiers (some of whom
had been hastily drafted to the battalions to bring them up to strength)
fought desperately, but eventually the garrison was split in two and
pinned down in the peninsulas south and west of the island.

In the early morning of the 21st the Japs stormed the house using
hand grenades and a small portable type of machine gun. The

wounded men were literally murdered in cold blood. Our white flag was torn down and our interpreter was bayoneted and pinned to a door to die.

They tied us up together and made us march back down to the road. Eventually we were made to crawl in a ditch and we knew the end had arrived for us. We said goodbye to each other and the staff sergeant said a prayer for us. Then the noise started. It seemed to me that the rifles and revolvers used were placed at my ears, the noise was so great.

I was first to be hit. It got me in the left shoulder and sent me over on my face where I lay very quiet waiting and hoping that the next one would be a clean shot and have it finished. I heard the "death rattle" three times that day as my comrades died miserable deaths.

Canadian soldier (quoted in *A Terrible Beauty*)

Three hundred Canadian troops were killed in the fighting, and another five hundred were wounded. Sergeant Major John Osborn won Canada's first Victoria Cross of the Second World War; it was awarded posthumously. Those who survived to be taken prisoner probably had the worst war of all: 260 died in Japanese prison camps. In Canada a Royal Commission was appointed to investigate the Hong Kong tragedy, but nobody was ever found at fault. And all that can be said in King's defence is that he had no idea the Japanese army was so good in battle, or so cruel in victory.

His strategy for dealing with the threat from Meighen and the Conservatives worked rather better. By January 1942 P.J.A. Cardin, now the senior Quebec minister, was persuaded that a plebiscite was better than a Union government under Meighen, although most Québécois felt very uneasy about the question: "Are you in favour of releasing the Government from any obligations arising out of any past commitments restricting the methods of raising men for military service?" A hastily formed group, La Ligue pour la défense du Canada, campaigned for a "no" vote in Quebec on the grounds that nobody would ask to be released from commitments if they did not intend to break them, and Mackenzie King found himself opposing Henri Bourassa, most of the Catholic church and a variety of young French Canadian politicians like Jean Drapeau and Andre Laurendeau (and the then-unknown Pierre Elliott Trudeau).

Despite the mistrust his policy aroused among French Canadians, King was taking the only possible course that might avert conscription in fact. He just couldn't say that out loud without alienating the English Canadian voters he was seeking to mollify. He was not actually promising to bring in conscription, but his apparent change of front on the principle of the thing completely took the wind out of Meighen's sails.

The campaign was nevertheless emotional and occasionally violent in Montreal—the remnants of a pro-fascist group, Adrien Arcand's Blackshirts, attacked Jewish shops on St. Lawrence Boulevard, and windows were broken and trams attacked after political meetings. The provincial Liberals tried to avoid the issue of conscription entirely: Premier Godbout's position on the plebiscite was described as "noui" (neither *oui* nor *non*).

The results of the plebiscite in April 1942 almost exactly parallelled the outcome of the 1917 election. In Quebec four out of five people voted "no"; in English Canada four out of five people voted "yes." Nevertheless, King was happy with the outcome. On the morning after the plebiscite, he told the Cabinet that "the Government appeared to be safe." He was quite clear in his own mind that he had been fighting a delaying action on conscription from the start, and he had just won another year or two before a crisis on the issue really drove the country apart. He even took the time afterward to feel a little bit bad about Hong Kong.

The Hong Kong business has been the most distressing thing next to conscription of the whole situation. The two have been so interwoven that each made the other a more difficult subject to deal with.

`Mackenzie King Record, April 28, 1942

———

I've seen and done some things which have rather radically changed my outlook. After seeing a French soldier clubbed to death by German cops at Quimper, after starving in a gravel-pit at Montreuil-Bellay and getting blood poisoning through being made to put up barbed-wire entanglements without any gloves on, and after sawing my way out of St. Denis through a barred window-well, I'm afraid I'd find it pretty difficult to settle down to pushing a pen in an Ottawa office for the duration of the war.

Frank Pickersgill, October 1942

Frank Pickersgill, the young Canadian who had felt like "sneering" at the war in 1939, was a different person by 1942. He was just a bit too slow in trying to get out of France when the Germans arrived in June 1940, and had been captured and interned as an enemy civilian. It wasn't an awful existence, but he saw a good deal of brutality meted out to other people by his German jailers, and in March 1942 he broke out of the former barracks in Paris where he was being held. It was a classic movie scene, with a hacksaw and three blades smuggled into the prison in a loaf of bread, and then an escape made good by sawing through the bars on a window and dropping into the street below.

Pickersgill managed to make his way from Paris to Vichy France, the part of the country run by a collaborationist regime but free of German soldiers, and it took him another four months to make his way to neutral Portugal and from there to England. But he arrived in London a changed man. He was angry about what he had seen in France: "I'm feeling too belligerent to be happy 4,000 miles away from the Nazis," he wrote to a friend in Winnipeg. He was too sophisticated an observer to be taken in by the war propaganda about a crusade for freedom, but he may also have shared Escott Reid's belief that the balance of power was now in danger of shifting seriously to Canada's disadvantage. Finally (and perhaps decisively), he was swept up in the excitement of great events.

> I've been in a permanent state of exhilaration since March 8 last (the date when I made my get-away) on the crest of a wave which kept getting higher and higher as each frontier was crossed, and which now, instead of subsiding, seems to be going on up. I don't know where it's going to land me, but it's damned good while it lasts.
>
> Frank Pickersgill, January 1943

Frank Pickersgill's brother Jack, Prime Minister King's private secretary, telegraphed for him to come home, but he refused. On arrival in England, Pickersgill enlisted in the Canadian army, and immediately volunteered for service in the British "Special Operations Executive," which controlled a network of undercover agents in France. "I'm afraid I'm in the war up to my neck," he said. "There are certain jobs I can do better than others." The wave broke in June 1943: Pickersgill was arrested almost immediately after he parachuted into France.

———

At the time when Frank Pickersgill finally got into the war, the Canadian army was still mostly sitting in England or at home. Only a few thousand Canadian soldiers had seen any fighting, and only for a few days, in the disaster at Hong Kong in early 1942 and on the Dieppe raid in August of the same year. But the Royal Canadian Air Force was in battle every day, and by now most of its pilots were flying bombers over Germany.

When you first join a squadron, nobody talks to you because they don't expect you to be around very long. If you got through your first five trips then you became more or less an accepted fact. There was a bit of hope for you, so somebody would begin to take you on—not with close friendship, but at least they would talk to you. And then after a month or so you would get into the mess with a group that had probably ten trips in, and you stayed with these people and they're the only ones you remember. You never knew the new guys coming in, because it wasn't worth your effort to get to know them. And then as you got up to the end of your tour you became known to all those new fellows, but you didn't know them.

It was a peculiar society: mess life went on around them, rather than with them. You never bought one a beer. The odd guy coming back on a second tour that you had known, the boys would buy him a beer and then guess how many trips he'd do before he went down, just to see how he'd take it. But it was a rather sad society.

George Laing, RCAF bomber pilot

Beginning in 1942 the British committed themselves fully to a campaign of mass bomber raids whose purpose was to destroy the German economy. It was known as "strategic" bombing, and it was the quintessential weapon of total war. If a country's industrial strength was now the main source of its military strength, then it was also the logical target of a war-winning strategy. Both the British and American air forces had believed in this strategy for many years, and Canadian airmen (insofar as they dabbled in strategic doctrine) followed suit. Initially, the idea was to hit factories, railway yards and the like: civilians would obviously be killed in the process, but they were not the primary target. However, the bombers had to fly at night in order to have any chance of survival at all, and analysis of photographs eventually showed that most bombs were not falling within miles of their targets.

So Sir Arthur Harris, known as "Bomber" Harris to civilians and as "Butch" (short for "butcher") to the aircrew, changed the policy. Instead of trying to hit pinpoint targets they could not find, the aircrew would mass-bomb large areas—working-class suburbs, mostly—in an attempt to kill the people who worked in the factories. The heavy bombers were typically loaded with one 4,000-lb high-explosive bomb and hundreds of large and small incendiary bombs. The high explosives smashed water mains and blew in doors and windows over a wide area, creating suitable conditions for the spread of the thousands of fires set by the incendiaries. The ideal result was a firestorm, where all the separate fires joined together into an inferno that incinerated a huge area of the city and almost everybody in it:

> Most of the times it didn't work, but it was supposed to work as it did in Darmstadt and in Dresden and in Hamburg—burn them down.
>
> We were not after the town of Darmstadt, we were after the chemical works between Darmstadt and Frankfurt, and they smoked us out, so we marked Darmstadt, and I don't think that was incorrect. That was the RAF's opinion: if you can't get the factory, get the people. But that was a terrible night. I watched that place and it. . . . There weren't too many burners, you know.
>
> George Laing

Moral considerations aside, the strategy made sense in principle: the main objective in total war is the enemy's economy, and an economy is mostly people. It just wasn't very cost-effective in practice, because the bombers couldn't do enough damage to justify the terrible loss rate they suffered. On average, each sortie by a seven-man bomber crew produced (if that's the right word) three dead Germans, of whom maybe one was a production worker—the rest being mainly women and children. And after an average of only fourteen sorties, the crew themselves were dead or prisoners-of-war.

By 1943 fully one-third of British war production was being devoted to the bomber offensive against Germany—and around a fifth of all the aircrew in Bomber Command were Canadians. The Commonwealth Air Training Plan turned them out, and Bomber Command ate them up: out of one group of fifty navigators who trained together, five completed their first tour (about thirty missions), ten were shot down and taken prisoner, and the rest were killed.

Q. What's it actually feel like when you're getting flak?
Rather a lonely feeling. You wish someone else would come over and share it with you—and if you could get someone else to get it, then you'd get away from it. The same with searchlights: somebody would get caught in the cone, and then you'd go in beside him. He's in big, deep trouble, so you get in beside him and try not to share it, try and get through. It worked quite successfully, especially in searchlights, because [after the bomber the searchlights were tracking was shot down] they'd move back and try to pick someone up a bit further back in the target area.

Preferably if you could drag back a little or speed up a little, and use the other chap. I wasn't above doing that: get to the target, get your picture and get out. . . . Just survival.
Q. Nasty business.
It was. And frightening.

George Laing

It was a nasty business—and making it more efficient would just make it nastier. (There was already a group of physicists working secretly in the New Mexico desert to find a way to destroy a whole city with only one plane carrying one bomb.) But the bomber crews couldn't be blamed for the strategy, and in 1943 their odds of dying were still far higher than those faced by the civilians they were trying to kill. Two-thirds of Canada's dead in the war up to 1943 were from the air force.

They say ten percent got through their first tour, and ten percent through their second.

Q. That makes you one in a hundred.

Yeah, there's not too many two-tour guys kicking around.

Q. You knew those figures, didn't you?

Not really. We didn't play. . . . I had a friend from Saskatchewan, Yellow Grass, and he played with numbers. He said it was impossible to do a tour. But he was shot down on his first trip—they proved him right.

George Laing

On the whole, Mackenzie King's strategy of limiting Canada's commitments and casualties had been a brilliant success: in the first four years of the Second World War, Canada lost only eleven thousand men killed—less than a fifth of its losses in the same period in the First World War. The army's turn was coming, though, and when it finally did, it would destroy King's strategy. He had got away with it for so long principally because the Allies had not been involved in major ground combat on the continent since mid-1940. When armies fight, however, they use up men in huge numbers, and by 1943 the Canadian army in England was getting itchy. So were its generals in Ottawa: as General Ken Stuart, the chief of the general staff, told the prime minister, they felt they had a good army now, but it wasn't being used.

Q. What did you think about the attitude that simply wanted to get some troops "blooded," to be crude about it?

Well, "blooded" makes it rather crude, but the troops that were in England had to have experience of actual warfare. There was the feeling that we hadn't really been taking part in the war. I wasn't going around taking a poll of the opinions of the rank and file, but I think they all felt: "Well, we're here. We were told we were coming to the war, let's go and get some fighting. And we should not be subject to the jeers of the Americans who said, "Well, you've been over here for four years now. Instead of telling us what to do, why don't you go and do something yourself?"

General "Tommy" Burns, Canadian commander in Italy

General McNaughton, the commander of the Canadian forces in England, had resisted all proposals to commit his divisions piecemeal to various peripheral theatres of the war. His policy was that the Canadian army should fight as a national unit, as it had in the First World War. Morale would be better, supply problems would be eased, and there would be less chance of Canadian divisions being sacrificed by non-Canadian commanders. But the long-awaited invasion of northwest Europe was still many months away, and the Allied armies, having cleared the Germans and Italians out of North Africa, were scheduled to attack Italy in July 1943. A lot of Canadian soldiers wanted to be in on it. McNaughton lost what was essentially a political battle to the eagerness of his subordinates and to the enthusiasm of the minister of national defence, and resigned at the end of the year.

Mackenzie King finally accepted the plan to send a Canadian Army Corps to Italy because General Stuart convinced him that battle experience in Italy would help to reduce Canadian casualties when the main assault against the Germans took place. If King had ever been a soldier, he would have known the only appropriate response: "There's no need to practice bleeding."

Even in Sicily the Canadians suffered 2,310 casualties—over five hundred of them fatal. The rest of the Italian campaign was arduous and bloody: so much for the "soft underbelly of Europe." It was also acrimonious, for General "Tommy" Burns, who had lost all his illusions about glory in the trenches of the First World War, took a cautious, methodical approach to the fighting that concentrated on keeping as many Canadian soldiers alive as possible. This did not sit well with his British superiors, who saw themselves as being in some sort of race with the Americans to enter Rome first, or with some of his more fiery subordinates.

> We were going forward pretty well all the time, even if not very fast, or as fast as some of the British Command thought that we ought to. But we were winning operations and not suffering too great casualties, compared to what the previous experience [First World War] had been. . . .
>
> General "Tommy" Burns

Burns was ultimately relieved of his command in late 1944 for being insufficiently "aggressive," but even in later life, he was totally unrepentant:

> When I went out there with some other generals and Canadian officers after the war, I counted up through the cemeteries we visited, and during the period I was out there, there were three thousand fatal casualties in the Canadian forces out of seventy-eight thousand total numbers. Better they should come home alive than have a monument in Italy.
>
> General "Tommy" Burns

The Italian campaign went on until the end of the war, and included the brutal battle in the small city of Ortona in December 1943, where 1,345 Canadian troops died in eight days. But the high point of the campaign was the liberation of Rome on June 4, 1944. Two days later the Allied armies finally landed in northern France, and everybody forgot about Italy.

———

By the latter part of 1944, the public was starting to forget about the Battle of the Atlantic, too, but it was still taking its toll. It was relatively quiet on the western side of the Atlantic, however, and there were few mines around Halifax, so the RCN's Bangor-class minesweepers doubled as "understudy" corvettes, escorting ships on the "milk run" between St. John's, Halifax, Boston and New York. Occasionally, though, they were asked to do some minesweeping.

> I was in Chester and Captain (D) phoned and said: "Get here immediately. There's a flap on." And I took a cab and went to Halifax and two-thirds of the ship's company were on Christmas leave. So I phoned the Peregrine, the base with all the poor miserable sailors that hadn't been to sea, and they sent me a bunch of sailors, and we got to sea about three in the morning.
>
> We had to go across the harbour and get all this minesweeping gear which we knew nothing about, and I found a manual in the confidential books and we went minesweeping. I remember having a manual on the bridge.
>
> Craig Campbell

Two-thirds of the sailors who boarded HMCS *Clayoquot* that evening had never been to sea before, so perhaps they did not notice the captain hurriedly mugging up on minesweeping. It turned out not to be necessary. Campbell's ship had been sent out because a merchant vessel had run aground off Halifax the previous day after an explosion thought to have been caused by a mine. But it was soon realized that it had been torpedoed: there was a submarine in the vicinity. So *Clayoquot* and two other escorts were ordered to conduct an anti-submarine sweep fifteen miles ahead of a troopship that was passing through the area. It was a purely routine operation: Campbell didn't know, as he waited for the executive order to take up his position on the screen, that in turning onto that course he would be heading straight for *U-806*.

As a matter of fact I was in my cabin reading an "interesting" book, and I told the Officer of the Watch: "When you get the executive signal, give me a shout." I had a voice-pipe above my bunk, and he called me and said:

"Sir, we've got the executive signal." I said: "Well, away you go, full ahead both, I'll be up in a moment."

So I finished, you know, the paragraph—it was a rather exciting part—jumped into my sea-boots, went up to the bridge and took over the watch. And the next thing I knew, the ship disintegrated.

Craig Campbell

The German submarine (whose officers Campbell met after the war) had been attempting to get into position to sink one of the merchant ships in the area, but suddenly *Clayoquot* was heading straight for it. Convinced that he was under attack, the U-boat's captain turned his stern toward the ship and fired an acoustic homing torpedo, then dove to fifty metres to escape his own weapon. The powerful Gnat torpedo homed in on the noise from *Clayoquot*'s screws, and sixty-nine seconds later the submariners heard it strike.

If you're going sixteen knots and the stern's blown off, you're dead in your tracks, flat on your back. . . .

Everything is flying in all directions. I remember a depth charge landed alongside me on the bridge, and half the minesweeping winch went over the mast and landed on the fo'c'sle. There was a terrible racket because all the steam was escaping, and you couldn't hear very much.

Then she started to list to starboard rather rapidly—and this is all in a matter of seconds—so I thought of my drill. You're not allowed to say "abandon ship," so I said in a loud voice: "Stand by boats and floats." Nobody could hear me anyway—but they were busily cutting floats away.

> Then the ship capsized. I was sitting on the bilge-keel, actually, on the bottom, and then I reckoned it was time to leave: I was in no rush, it was cold. The sailors were waving at me, and I swam for it.
>
> Craig Campbell

When Kapitänleutnant Klaus Hornbostel brought *U-806* to periscope depth, all he saw was "a corvette sinking quickly with only the aft superstructure towering out of the water. . . . But *Clayoquot* was actually fairly lucky: most of the crew had mustered up forward for the forenoon rum issue, and only the eight who had been aft when the torpedo struck were killed. The twenty-seven-year-old captain, Craig Campbell, was the last to leave the ship. As he swam across to the rafts and debris the rest of the crew were clinging to—remembering to roll over on his back when the ship went down, so as to avoid serious internal injuries from the shock waves when the depth charges went off at their pre-set depth—a sailor shouted out an imaginary news bulletin: "Flash! Canadian Minesweeper Destroys German Torpedo!" They were all picked up by HMCS *Fennel* soon after, and so did not have to endure the cold Atlantic for very long. More than one hundred depth charges were dropped in the subsequent hunt for *U-508*, which lay on the bottom of the main shipping channel off Halifax Harbour for almost twelve hours before creeping away, but it survived unscathed.

> Pick and Mac [Lieutenant Ken Macalister, Pickersgill's radio operator] were given the usual beating up, rubber truncheons, electric shocks, kicks in the genitals and what have you. They were in possession of names, addresses and codes that the Germans badly wanted, but neither of them squealed.
>
> Wing Commander Yeo-Thomas
(also captured by the Gestapo)

Pickersgill, canadian army officer   26-6-43

trial and condemnation   7-7-43

not yet [?executed. Wait] and see   8-7-43

fragmentary inscription scratched on the wall

of Fresnes Prison, Paris

It was Gestapo policy to keep captured agents barely alive for some time in case they might eventually come in useful. Frank Pickersgill was sent to a concentration camp in Poland, but when the Allies finally began to suspect that the Germans were operating his radio and codes to foist a fake network of agents on London, the Gestapo extracted him from the emaciated mass of "subhumans" at Rawicz and brought him back to Paris. They promised that he could spend the rest of the war in comfortable detention if he cooperated with them in continuing the deception. Instead, Pickersgill seized a bottle from his interrogator's desk, slashed one SS guard to death with it, knocked another out and leapt into the courtyard from an upstairs window.

> He was exhausted from such a long period of inactivity and imprisonment; he was unable to run very fast. The SS opened fire from the windows with their sub-machine guns; he was hit four times, fell, tried to run again, but stopped from exhaustion and lost consciousness.
>
> Bertrand Gilbert (another agent then being held at
>
> Gestapo HQ in Paris).

Frank Pickersgill spent the last weeks of his life at Buchenwald, in permanent agony from his wounds, but still defiant down to the moment when he was hanged from a hook and died by strangulation on September 10, 1944.

The Normandy landing. . . . Well, I was in the artillery. We were fired at from 10,000 yards all the way in. And then we were to do a ninety-minute circle, to let the infantry clear the beach, and then come in.

We did a somewhat shorter circle than that, and when we came in the rudder of the craft was hit, and we floated around for several hours, until we drifted in.

George Freeman, 19th Army Field Regt.,
Royal Canadian Artillery

Before dawn on June 6, 1944 two Allied airborne divisions dropped behind the German defences on the Normandy coast. As the skies lightened, five further divisions—two American, two British and one Canadian—began landing along fifty miles of beach. Facing them was a rather debilitated German army: most of its fit and experienced soldiers had been sent to the Russian front, leaving the Atlantic Wall in the hands of inexperienced eighteen-year-olds (one German general referred to them as "babes in arms"), men over thirty-five, those who had suffered third-degree frostbite in the Russian campaign, and ex-prisoners of war from the Caucusus and Turkestan (the Ost Battalion).

But an assault landing on a fortified coast is never easy, and although the German army had been unable to reinforce the Atlantic Wall as much as General Erwin Rommel would have liked, it had spread mines and underwater obstructions lavishly along the beaches, and backed them up with huge concrete pillboxes, artillery and anti-tank weapons, plus entrenched infantry with mortars and machineguns. The Canadian Third Division and the 2nd Canadian Armoured Brigade had been picked to land on D-Day, with the rest of the First Canadian Army to follow later. For most Canadian soldiers, this was their first experience in battle.

Others had survived on the battlefield, and I thought I could, with all the training we were getting. . . . I got a little bit of a shock when I was committed to my first action, of course.

On the way from If to attack Beauvoir, I had to cross a little hedgerow . . . and then an aircraft came right at me. It was one of our own. I had a pipe in my hand, and I lit a cigarette at the same time, and I had a pipe and a cigarette, and there was a lot of noise and a lot of shelling. It was the first time I was under actual shelling, and you don't realise that the shells are coming that hard at you for about two, three minutes, then you realise what's happening.

Anyway, my company and I went through that night. The Germans shelled us, and I lost about 80 percent of my company there.

Major Jacques Dextraze, (later General), Fusiliers Mont
Royal

Other companies were also suffering very heavy casualties, far heavier than General Stuart and his staff had expected and warned the government to expect. The Germans poured in reinforcements, knowing that they had to defeat the invasion near the beachhead or find themselves in a two-front war (the Russians were already advancing into Poland). The fighting in Normandy raged for over two months, and between D-Day and August 23 the Canadian army in France had 18,444 casualties, including over five thousand dead. It found out a lot about the realities of war.

At a certain place, I'm in battle. I have a unit that is advancing. I have a tank knocked out by the Germans. The four men inside get out, not wounded but stunned. Instead of coming back toward my lines, they head off toward the German line. The Germans there, who aimed—b-r-r-r—they killed them, right there.

Some of my men see that and say: "They killed them without giving them a chance. That's wrong." OK. The battle continues and we take some prisoners. I pick someone to take the prisoners to the rear.

When the man in charge of the prisoners comes to a bridge— he had made them run almost three miles—he says: "No, you lot blew up the bridges, you are going to swim." Well, you can well imagine that a man who has run three miles and then tries to swim. . . . Most of them drowned.

And me, passing near there in my jeep, when I see thirty, forty, fifty bodies of drowned men . . . I wonder what happened, but I don't ask too many questions. . . . I took internal action within the unit, but I didn't put out any press release about what I did.

So I said to myself when I saw the Nuremberg trials: "Listen, you're lucky that we won." Because I would be there: it's me who is responsible for what my subordinates do.

Jacques Dextraze

It was after the Canadians landed in France that Mackenzie King's carefully managed "limited" war began to fall apart. Much to Mackenzie King's anguish, the army began to have trouble finding replacements for its infantry units. On August 9 General Guy Simonds reported that the 2nd Canadian Infantry Division, which had only been ashore for a month, was nineteen hundred men short.

When we crossed the Seine, we had thirteen men left in our rifle company, out of one hundred and twenty.

Serres Sadler, Calgary Highlanders

Having fought their way through France, the Canadians would now have to make their way through Belgium and Holland. In only a couple of months the Canadian army had lost almost half as many men as the armed forces' total casualities in the first four years of the war—and it was facing a reinforcement crisis. It was not that the Canadian army was actually short of men. It was just short of men with the right kind of training: infantry training. For all the talk about mechanized war, it was still the infantry who had to go in and take the ground in the end—and it was the infantry who were taking the majority of the casualties.

The lack of trained infantry reinforcements in Europe was the result of two earlier decisions. One was to send Canadian troops to Italy in 1943, which tied up huge numbers of men in two separate administrative and supply "tails," one for the forces in Italy and one for the troops in France. The other was a mistaken forecast of the "wastage" rates in the various combat trades: too few soldiers in the existing pool of reinforcements had been trained as infantry.

> Most units were down, well, maybe half-strength is over-dramatizing it, but they didn't have enough men to do the job they were sent in to do. And that really brought on the crisis here at home, with McNaughton and Ralston and the great turmoil politically, about reinforcements and conscription and overseas service.
>
> Ross Munro, war correspondent

From the soldiers' perspective, the shortage of trained infantry reinforcements had a cruel consequence: higher casualties among the men who were already bearing the brunt of the losses. Under-strength units still got the same jobs to do, because the jobs had to be done—but their weakness meant they were likely to lose more people than if they had been at full strength. The survivors of the Normandy battles were being used up at an appalling rate. Even wounds might mean only a temporary reprieve, for the desperate shortage of trained infantrymen meant that wounded men were often sent back to the front as soon as they recovered. Alas for Mackenzie King, it was hard for the army, faced with this problem, to ignore the fact that there were large numbers of allegedly trained infantry sitting in Canada: the NRMA conscripts whom King had once promised would never be sent overseas.

In reality, very few of the "home defence only" conscripts had enough practical infantry training to be useful as reinforcements, at least in the immediate crisis. Nevertheless, by late 1944 the army's resentment at the government's refusal to send conscripts into battle was close to boiling over. At home, feelings in English Canada were running equally high, though the emotional logic was even cruder:

> A large section of English Canadians, especially the well-to-do ones and also a good many of those who had relatives overseas, really were not primarily concerned about the military aspects of the question. They believed that most of the conscripts who were in Canada were French Canadians and they just wanted to make the French do their share.
>
> Jack Pickersgill,
> secretary to Prime Minister King, 1937–48

> It was delusion and a snare to make the dependents of men now at the front think that their boys would be any safer by sending the zombies over. . . .Their boys would be sent back to the line anyway. . . . The fact is that unless you have two or three lines, as they do in hockey, which is tactically and physically impossible in war, the burden and the risk will continue to be borne by the experienced men.
>
> Commanders will still continue to use them—even when they have fresh troops.
>
> "Chubby" Power

"Chubby" Power, the ex-infantryman and ultimate realist, was speaking the truth: it is monstrously unfair, but there is never really any escape for trained infantrymen in war, no matter how worn down they are. But the pressures on King to do something about the reinforcement crisis were so great that in October 1944 he sent Colonel

Ralston, the defence minister, over to Europe to find out the real extent of the problem.

> After leaving Monty's Tactical HQ, Ralston proceeded to Canadian
> Army HQ at Antwerp. There was a small mess dinner for him that
> night. . . . I have seldom seen him so preoccupied as during the
> dinner. He hardly noticed what he was eating, and at times com-
> pletely lost touch with the conversation that went on around him.
>
> [After dinner he] caught my arm and suggested I come over
> to his caravan in the park for a short talk before leaving. . . . It was
> after three in the morning before I got on the road. The Colonel
> was terribly despondent and lonely. His mind was completely
> made up. . . . He would either force the government to bring in
> full conscription on his return or he would resign.
>
> Richard Malone, *A World in Flames, 1944–45*

Ralston had arrived in the middle of the worst battle the Canadians had yet encountered: the struggle to clear the Germans out of the Scheldt Estuary, the region between Antwerp and the sea. Antwerp, the second-largest seaport in Europe, was the key port which the Allies hoped to utilize for their drive eastward into Germany (all the French Channel ports were either destroyed or still in German hands).

The British had managed to liberate the city of Antwerp virtually undamaged in the early autumn with the help of Belgian resistance fighters, but the Germans still controlled the Scheldt Estuary and, as long as they did, Antwerp would be useless to the Allies. The German troops holding Walcheren Island on the north side of the estuary and the Breskens Pocket on the southern side were ordered to fight to the death—and in case any of them changed their minds, they were told that their families in Germany would suffer if any of them surren-dered. The Canadian army was ordered to clear the Scheldt Estuary of Germans, and Major General Charles Foulkes, temporarily in command of the Second Canadian Corps, committed his forces on October 2, 1944. Dan Spry commanded the Third Canadian Division:

> It was a dreadful battle because the Germans had flooded large parts of the so-called Pocket. They were fighting desperately with their backs to the sea. They had nowhere to go . . . and they fought very well, very professionally. And the trouble was that the weather was against us.
>
> There were many days when we couldn't get air support because of cloud and rain. It seemed to me it was raining all the time, which added to the flooding, and the result was that the dyke roads were all sitting up anything from a foot to ten feet above water, and the fighting had to take place along these exposed roads. That was a dangerous place to be, and the poor infantry had one hell of a time.
>
> It was a dreadful, dreadful battle, and it was a slow battle because you could only commit so many people at a time down one road. We found it useless trying to fight across these polders, because the troops would just sink in to their armpits in mud and, in fact, drown in some cases.
>
> So it was a slow, painful, bloody, muddy battle, and it wasn't helped by the fact we were short of reinforcements, and in many cases the reinforcements we were getting were not adequately trained.
>
> Brigadier General Dan Spry

The Canadian infantry were fighting in conditions that resembled those of the First World War, as far as mud and sheer misery were concerned. But there were no trenches: the Germans were dug in along canals, or in bunkers in farmyards and villages, or embedded in the suburbs of Antwerp, Ghent and Bruges. So not only was it confused, vicious fighting, but civilians were often mixed up in it.

The Breskens Pocket, like much of the area around the Scheldt

Estuary, is land reclaimed from the sea. Even now it is flat from horizon to horizon, the only features being the built-up dykes, most of them with tree-lined roads running along the top. The "polders" that the soldiers had to cross are now fields, but in 1944 they were swamps or lakes. There was little cover, and much of the fighting was at very close quarters: there was virtually no possibility of using tanks in the flooded terrain. Even the battle-hardened veterans of Normandy found it hard to cope.

How we ever got through the war, I don't know, because it's impossible to hide in Holland, especially on the flats. . . . We ran through water one day when I was wounded, with some of my friends, till it was up to my shoulders. If they couldn't shoot you, they tried to drown you—one way or the other.

Private "Hap" Hawken, Highland Light Infantry

When the reinforcements came in, there was a kind of reluctance to get to know them right away. You make 'em do as they're told, you put them with someone, and you tell them: "you do exactly what that person tells you. If he tells you go to the bathroom, you go to the bathroom. If he tells you to load that rifle, you load that rifle. You do everything he tells you, and with a little bit of luck you'll make it through. Now, if you don't, just don't blame him, or me. Blame yourself, because it's a war of survival."

Specially through this area, because you were so close, and it was mean. It could have been a lot easier, had you had more space to work in, but in this area you were confined, so your casualties were greater in a very short period of time.

Sergeant Al Clavette, Canadian Scottish Regiment

I was on the flame-throwers. Up in Holland we ran into a bunch of Germans, a couple of hundred Germans one night. We were out on a recce, and I used a flame-thrower on them, and that made me sick. I was crying like a baby when I came back afterwards. I used a flame-thrower on these Germans in the open, in an open field at night. And that was too much. . . .

Serres Sadler, Calgary Highlanders

When you think back about some of the things you did, and they did to you, it was totally frightening. You were petrified every day. Every time you could find some cognac or something, you drank it, because you didn't know if tomorrow would ever come or not. You were just petrified. We were only kids.

Private "Hap" Hawken, Highland Light Infantry

The kids were dying off by the day: both the kids who had become veterans in the three or four months since Normandy, and the greener kids who trickled up the reinforcement pipeline (many of them not trained infantry at all, but hastily "converted" gunners, supply clerks and cooks). It was clear to them that there was little hope of reprieve, even if the Canadian government started sending reinforcements over from Canada at once: either they would be dead before their replacements arrived, or the war would have ended. There was some bitterness toward Mackenzie King and his government, but it was curiously muted: they were not living in the same world.

The reinforcement situation was pretty grim and we were putting up young officers who really didn't know how to handle themselves in those circumstances. I'd sit around the mess at night with the older guys trying to buoy the spirits of the new recruits. It was a very touching period, because these were kids of nineteen and twenty. And they'd go out the next day and probably get killed.

Ross Munro, war correspondent

242

We were volunteers. We were the only volunteer army there was in Europe. It's something to be proud of, in a way. And we had a job to do—and children in Canada whom we didn't know. We were in a hurry to finish the war. And when our commander told us "Go there" we said "On our way."

I was in the Sluis sector and he said: "Clausson, take your platoon, go to such-and-such a place, and dig the Germans out right away." I said: "But Colonel, I have only nine soldiers left in my platoon." "Well then," he said, "take your section and go get the Germans." So off we went.

Gilles Clausson, Régiment de la Chaudière

Finally, after over a month of painfully winkling the Germans out of their positions, the Canadians cleared the Scheldt Estuary. On November 1, General Knut Eberding, the commander of the German forces in the Breskens Pocket, surrendered to the North Nova Scotia Highlanders. On that date, the government in Ottawa had still not decided on conscription.

Well, the scheme worked, but not as quickly as I'd been told it was going to work. I remember General Foulkes had told me that there were only a handful of Germans over there—you know, five or six thousand—you should be able to clean it up in four, five or six days.

Well, of course, it took us a month, and a lot of casualties. But when it was all over, and I went to report personally that that piece of battle was over, I said to General Foulkes: "Remember those five or six thousand Germans you said were on the other side of the Canal?"

He said: "Yes, what about it?" I said: "Well, we've just taken twelve thousand of them prisoner." And he said: "Don't you talk to me like that." He didn't think it was funny.

Major General Dan Spry

It wasn't actually very funny, and Colonel Ralston, the defence minister, having talked to the generals and visited the troops and the hospitals, returned to Canada in very much the same frame of mind as Prime Minister Borden in 1917. He wanted conscription for overseas service to be applied immediately. Mackenzie King could hardly believe what he was hearing. For five years he had managed to avoid conscription, and now the war was clearly nearing its end. (The German surrender came only six months later.) And now, of all times, his soldiers and his defence minister were telling him he had to do what he most feared and bring in conscription for overseas service. It would "undo much of the good which our war effort up to the present time had effected." There would be "a repetition of what occurred after the last war when Borden returned and demanded conscription, only the situation will be worse."

> Finally I said to Ralston that it seemed to me that what we had to consider was . . . the probability, if not the certainty of civil war . . . in consequence of any attempt at conscription. That I could understand, for reasons of pride, the desire of the army to be kept up to full strength to the last.
>
> MacKenzie King Record, vol. 2

King was understandably furious with his generals. There were plenty of volunteers in the military who could have been filling the gaps in the infantry's ranks, but they were all in the wrong places: in the two parallel administrative and supply chains serving the Canadian armies in Italy and in France; in the hypertrophied air force, which had a superabundance of aircrew; in the army's non-infantry trades, because the military planners, making their decisions back in the days when the German air force could still attack the rear areas of the Allied armies, had trained too many men as replacements for casualties among the artillery, engineers and cooks. But the only (allegedly) trained infantrymen available as replacements were the NRMA conscripts still sitting in Canada.

Every time the army had expanded or taken on a new role, King had asked his generals if this commitment could be maintained without resorting to conscription; they had always said yes. Nevertheless, it was clear to King that if he now refused to send NRMA men overseas his cabinet would split, and that before long he would be forced into an election which the Liberals would lose. Moreover, if recent by-elections were any guide, it was quite possible that the winner in such an election would be the CCF. (It was only a few months later that British voters threw Churchill out and elected a Labour government.) Clutching at straws, King made one last effort to wriggle off the hook of conscription: in November 1944 he forced Ralston to resign, and appointed General Andrew McNaughton as defence minister in his place.

McNaughton, who had also always opposed conscription, spent the next three weeks trying to convince NRMA men to *volunteer* for overseas service. He was wasting his breath.

[King] thought use could be made of the great popularity that McNaughton had achieved as Commander of Canadian forces and that this would do the trick. Well, it didn't do the trick at all, of course . . . and during that three weeks the resistance in the Department of Defence . . . developed.

The senior officers were going to resign. They weren't going to try to establish a military government or a coup d'état or anything of that sort, but the fact of the matter is that the government could not have survived . . . a vote in parliament on maintaining the opposition to conscription.

The night of November 22, when he was having the Cabinet at eight to announce (his decision) to the Ministers, most of them didn't know up to that time that he had changed his mind at all.

Jack Pickersgill

245

By November 22, 1944 McNaughton had been told by the chiefs of staff that voluntary enlistment would not get them enough men. The commanding officer in Winnipeg had already resigned, and it looked as if others might follow him. McNaughton was worried that the whole military machine might disintegrate. The Army Council believed conscription was the only solution, and told McNaughton they would resign as a group if their recommendation was not implemented. King, the great political survivor, announced that NRMA conscripts would be sent overseas at once. There was an outcry in French Canada and among the sections of English-speaking Canada traditionally most opposed to conscription: the farmers and the central and Eastern European communities in the Prairie provinces. There were even a few outbreaks of resistance in NRMA camps when Zombies were ordered overseas. But on the whole, conscription, when it finally came, caused far less uproar than it had in the First World War.

> I feel, in a way, that we had bored the country with it. It had been delayed long enough, and it had been evident enough that Mackenzie King was doing everything he could to minimise it, that the resistance didn't develop really.
>
> Jack Pickersgill, secretary to Prime Minister King,
> 1937–48

King was lucky to the end. There was not time for the resentment in French Canada to build up to an explosion as it had in 1918; the war was over less than six months after conscription was brought in. Fewer than 2,500 Zombies ever got to the front, and only sixty-nine were killed, so there were hardly any unwilling French Canadian "martyrs of British imperialism" to serve as the kindling for an eventual open rift in the country, let alone the civil war King feared.

Just at the very end of the war we had a few zombies come in as reinforcements. They didn't see much action, but I'm afraid they got pretty bad treatment from the soldiers that had been fighting. I was really ashamed of the way the cooks treated them.

Serres Sadler

Canada lost 42,000 dead in the Second World War—only half its loss ratio in the First World War, allowing for the intervening growth in its population—and by 1945 it was a fully industrialized country. King was a devious and deeply unlovable man, but he brought the country through the war more or less united. A week before the German surrender on May 8, 1945, preparing to depart for San Francisco where the leaders and diplomats of fifty nations would discuss what was to become the Charter of the United Nations, King indulged in a little gloating in his diary. He had outlasted almost all the other leaders.

Apart from Stalin, I would be the only original left on either side. I have, of course, led my party longer than Stalin has his.

Mackenzie King Record, April 30, 1945

General Dan Spry was one of the last Canadian soldiers to return from Europe after the war, having supervised the rather chaotic business of getting all the troops embarked on homeward-bound ships. Hitler was gone—but the sovereign state was still a thriving reality:

My wife and two very small children and I were the lone Canadians on the *Queen Mary* with 17,000 American paratroopers. The paratroopers thought I was an odd bod, with a funny uniform and a red band on my cap. I think they thought I was Salvation Army, but they were very good to the kids.

But as we were getting ready to disembark, I was given a form to fill out for the U.S. Immigration Authorities. One question,

247

I think question 31 or 32, asked me whether I was entering the
United States to overthrow the government by force, or to assassinate the President. I said that I didn't think so really because I was
in transit to Canada and I wouldn't have time.

Well, you should never try to be funny with a foreign immigration authority. They separated me from my family, and put me
in a wire cage, like a monkey, on Pier 90. And my wife and two
kids and fourteen pieces of baggage were stacked up outside, and
here were the kids saying, "Mommy, why is Daddy locked up in
the cage?" I thought that was really quite a way to come home.
The conquering hero, and I end up in a wire cage on Pier 90.

WHAT IF WE HAD NOT FOUGHT HITLER?

ANOTHER "COUNTER-FACTUAL" SPECULATION? YES, BECAUSE there's no better way to examine whether the choices that were made were the only or the best ones. What would have happened if Britain and France had not extended the unconditional guarantee to Poland in March 1939 that subsequently triggered their declaration of war on Germany in September? After all, it was both rash and dishonest to promise to protect Poland when they had no conceivable means of getting military help to the Poles, and no intention of mounting an offensive against Germany's western frontier to draw the Wehrmacht away from Poland. A little more thought, and perhaps a little more honesty, might have persuaded the British and French governments that they should not make a promise they couldn't keep.

Without that Anglo-French guarantee, there probably wouldn't have been a war in September 1939 at all. Knowing that no help was coming, the Poles would probably have given the Germans what they wanted—the city of Danzig, and a sovereign road and rail route across the "Polish Corridor" to connect East Prussia to the rest of Germany— and then they would have concluded an anti-Soviet alliance with

Germany. That was Hitler's original plan for Poland, whose 35 million people would be useful in his planned anti-Soviet crusade. True, they were "racially inferior" Slavs according to Nazi ideology, but Hitler was prepared to be flexible on such matters, and official Poland, at least, shared his own anti-Semitism.

There would not have been a cynical and temporary Nazi-Soviet pact in this history either, for that was a direct response by both countries to the Anglo-French guarantee to Poland. There would certainly have been a war between Nazi Germany and the Soviet Union eventually, for Hitler saw Communism as a "Jewish-Bolshevik conspiracy" and truly believed that the Soviet Union had to be destroyed. The war might have come a bit earlier than June 1941, when he invaded the Soviet Union in the real history, or it might even have come a bit later, but it would probably have unfolded in much the same way.

It's very unlikely that Britain and France would have gone to war at that stage in the game to save the Communists, so the Russians would have been on their own. Hitler would have enjoyed a few more advantages in this counter-factual version of his attack on the Soviet Union, as Poland would have been his ally and the start line for the invasion would have been several hundred kilometres closer to Moscow. He would also have been spared the distraction of an unresolved war with Britain at his back—but he might have found the need to keep up his guard against a hostile Britain and an unconquered France even more burdensome.

Could Hitler have won his war in our alternative history? Probably not, for in the real history the outcome of the German-Soviet war, the greatest land battle in the history of the world, was not heavily influenced by events on other fronts of the Second World War. The Allied bombing offensive, for all its casualties, did not significantly reduce German industrial production before late 1944; nor did the Atlantic Wall tie up more German troops than, in the alternative history, would need to have been kept in the West to protect Germany from an Anglo-French declaration of war. Germany lost the war on the Eastern Front because it was outnumbered two-to-one, outproduced by Soviet industry and decisively beaten on the battlefield, and those same factors would have led to a Soviet victory over Germany even if Britain and France had stayed out of the war.

Britain and France would have gone to war with Germany in the end, of course, because they would not have wanted victorious Soviet troops to occupy all of Germany up to the French border. Indeed, they would probably have attacked Germany around the time when the advancing Soviet army entered Poland: that is to say, at around the same time as the Allied landings in Normandy reopened the main ground war in the West with Germany in the real history. And the United States would almost certainly have been part of that anti-Nazi alliance.

Even by the rather flexible rules of writing counter-factual history, we are obliged to leave events beyond the specific area where we are making an alteration (no Anglo-French guarantee to Poland) unchanged. And in truth we may safely assume that Japan would have launched its campaign of conquest in South-East Asia and the Pacific around the time (late 1941 in the real history) when it looked as if Hitler's invasion of the Soviet Union was going to succeed. That would have made Britain, France and the United States allies in the war against Japan, and they would no doubt have remained allies when the time came to enter the war against Germany. Their motive would have been to prevent an overwhelming Soviet dominance in the centre of Europe—but in practice, they would have been countering it by introducing an overwhelming American military presence into the west of the continent, because the United States was the only potential counterbalance available.

This alternative Second World War would still have ended, therefore, with American, British and French troops sharing a divided Germany with Soviet troops—and in all likelihood falling into serious disaccord quite quickly. No matter how you fiddled with the details of the history, you would still get a Communized Eastern Europe and a divided Germany out of this alternative scenario.

Some details would have been different, of course. The Jews of France and the Low Countries would have survived. So perhaps might the Italian Jews, for Mussolini might not have taken Italy all the way into a war with the Soviet Union, which offered him no territory or other advantages. Instead, he might have limited himself to sending "volunteers" to the Eastern Front as Spain's fascist dictator, Francisco Franco, did—and perhaps stayed in power after Germany's defeat as Franco did. But the details do not really matter, because the object of this exercise was simply to see how inevitable the outcome of the war was. And at the end of the exercise, it looks pretty inevitable.

This does not prove that Britain and France *should* have stayed out almost until the end of the war. We can moralize or strategize about that until the cows come home. But it does suggest that the war was really just another great-power struggle, driven by the same calculations as all the others. Even though it certainly didn't feel that way to Sergeant Al Clavette, who fought in the Breskens Pocket with the Canadian Scottish Regiment.

> I think that the boys themselves felt that we were making a contribution to rid a menace to the world, and I think they're right as proved out. Because if Germany had, for example, got the atomic bomb, I don't think [Hitler] would have hesitated two seconds to use it.
>
> Al Clavette, Canadian Scottish Regiment

The trouble is that our side would have used it too. In fact, it did.

CHAPTER 8

A DREADFUL MISTAKE

THE FIRST ATTEMPT TO CREATE AN INSTITUTION THAT WOULD PREVENT another great-power war, in 1919, was made in the same place, at the same time, by the same people who wrote the vengeful peace treaty that had virtually guaranteed exactly such a war. In 1945 the problem was different. The losers were punished even more severely than in 1919: their countries were occupied militarily for a decade, their wartime leaders were executed, some of their territory was handed over to their neighbours, and (in Germany's case) a country was physically divided in two. But none of that was a great threat to future peace, because both Germany and Japan fell out of the ranks of the great powers after 1945. The real danger this time was that the victorious great powers would fall apart and become enemies, and everybody was aware of it. Especially the Canadians.

It was hard for Western governments to ignore the Soviet Union's constant indulgence in the crudest invective, predicting inevitable conflict with the "imperialist states" and their eventual bloody demise. It created the impression that the Russians would attack if only they could. The Marxist-Leninist mode of thought, 1940s vintage—with its simple-minded Social-Darwinian belief in a final, inescapable world cataclysm from which "socialism," the higher form of social organization, would emerge victorious—has a lot to answer for. However, it is almost always a mistake to take the statements of ideological true-believers too literally. Most of them manage to find ways of incorporating a realistic assessment of the world within their ideology, and make decisions remarkably similar to those that would be made by a non-ideologue on the grounds of rational self-interest.

> Now, one of the myths of San Francisco is that the people who framed the Charter assumed that there was going to be close co-operation. I can't believe they did. . . . Our custom was, when each of us came back from the committee meeting we would go to [Undersecretary of State for External Affairs] Norman Robertson's room to report on what had happened at that committee that day. One time I had started to report and he said, "I wish to God somebody would come into this room and not start his report by saying 'those bloody Russians.'"
>
> Escott Reid , External Affairs 1941–62

> The Soviet delegates . . . use aggressive tactics about every question large or small. They remind people of Nazi diplomatic methods and create, sometimes needlessly, suspicions and resentment. They enjoy equally making fools of their opponents and their supporters. Slyness, bullying and bad manners are other features of their Conference behaviour. . . . It is unfortunate from our point of view as well as theirs that they should have made such a bad showing, for I think they are proposing to make a serious effort to use the organisation and are not out to wreck it.
>
> Charles Ritchie, External Affairs, 1934–71,
> *The Siren Years*

In April 1945, less than two weeks before Germany's surrender, the four Allied great powers and fifty other nations came together in San

Francisco to draw up the charter for the new "United Nations Organization." President Roosevelt had died, but not his vision of world peace enforced by continuing cooperation among the victorious great powers: the "four policemen," as he called them (two sergeants and two constables, in practice, since the United States and the Soviet Union far outweighed Britain and China in power).

This cooperation would take place within the framework of the United Nations, which was actually a second attempt to make the League of Nations work, with somewhat tougher rules but the same basic concept of collective security. Everybody at San Francisco was determined that the enterprise should succeed this time, for there had never been a war as bad as the one just ending. Forty-five million people had been killed, and every traditional standard of civilized behaviour had been repeatedly violated. (Newsreels showing the horrors of the concentration camps were just being released.)

The Americans, who were acting as hosts, were disorganized. The War Memorial Opera House building was still being converted for the conference when the delegates arrived and nobody had been given office space. In his diary Charles Ritchie, a Canadian diplomat, mocked the theatricality of the plenary sessions.

> The session is declared open by [U.S. secretary of state Edward] Stettinius, who comes onto the dais chewing (whether gum or the remains of his lunch is a subject of speculation). . . . He makes the worst impression on the delegates. He reads his speech in a lay-preacher's voice husky with corny emotion. . . .
>
> After him Molotov mounts the tribune in an atmosphere of intense curiosity and some nervousness. He looks like an employee in any *hôtel de ville*—one of those individuals who sits behind a wire grille entering figures in a ledger, and when you ask them anything always say "no." You forgive their rudeness because you know they are underpaid and that someone bullies them, and they

must, in accordance with Nature's unsavoury laws, "take it out on" someone else.

The Siren Years

The great powers were in constant disagreement at San Francisco, but the main problem for the Canadian diplomats was that they all cooperated in trying to exclude the lesser powers from the discussion. In their determination to avoid the paralysis that had destroyed the League, the great powers were concentrating most of the United Nations' powers in the Security Council (of which they would be permanent members). And although Canada was almost a great military power itself in 1945—it had the fourth-largest armed forces among the victorious Allies—"almost" was not good enough for a seat on the board of directors.

> We wanted to be a middle power which would be a kind of semi-permanent member of the Security Council. We said important military countries like ourselves ought to have this special position. Well, the trouble with that argument was that we had to demobilize. You know, our boys had been away longer than anybody else's. You had to get them home. Everyone wanted to reduce the defence expenditure, and if we'd got some kind of semi-permanent seat in the Security Council on those grounds we would have had to maintain an army of several hundred thousand men or so. So I don't think we really wanted to be a great military power.
>
> John Holmes, External Affairs, 1943–60

Although Canada's relative economic and military power in the world was greater in 1945 than it ever had been (or ever would be again), the country still lacked the instincts of a great power. However, it had lost its isolationist reflexes: Prime Minister Mackenzie King was only a very reluctant convert to collective security, but the younger generation of Canadian politicians and diplomats who had matured in the war desperately wanted the United Nations to succeed. Lester Pearson, for example, was suggesting a two-hundred-thousand-man United Nations standing army to which Canada would contribute (exactly the sort of idea that made King nervous about Pearson). But the question of who would control the army was crucial.

If the United Nations actually ended up as the world's policeman, then it would presumably have to enforce the rules of collective security against aggressors by armed force from time to time, and Canada might find itself being ordered by the great powers to contribute troops to impose Security Council decisions in which it had no voice. So the Canadians fought hard for better representation for all the middle and smaller powers, especially on the Security Council. Norman Robertson argued, "We are confident that no workable international system can be based on the concentration of influence and authority wholly in bodies composed of a few great powers to the exclusion of all the rest."

Yet even while trying to keep the United Nations from turning into a great-power directorate, the Canadians were of a generation who had learned that the world runs on power. They were quite realistic about the difficulty of persuading jealous great powers to surrender any of their sovereignty to an international organization, and about the gulf of suspicion and incomprehension between the "Anglo-Saxon" and Russian great powers (who were the only great powers still on their feet in 1945). If the price of getting them to support the United Nations wholeheartedly was giving them control of it, then they were willing to pay it.

It was the Russians, above all, who insisted on the great-power veto and the primacy of the Security Council—but then, the Soviet Union could expect very little support in the General Assembly, where all the Latin American countries and a lot of the other Western countries would automatically support the United States. (Most of the rest of the world was still under European colonial rule.) It was finally agreed that the smaller nations in the General Assembly would have the right to raise issues and make recommendations to the Security Council. But the Big Five (France joined the original "four policemen" after May 9, 1945) retained permanent seats in the Security Council and had the veto over decisions taken by that body.

It could not be avoided: the great powers, and especially the Soviet Union, simply would not allow themselves to be put in a position where the United Nations had the legal right to take military action against them. So in the end the Canadian representatives, like everyone else, bowed to the inevitable: they decided that a United Nations dominated by the great powers was better than no United Nations at all.

Finally, after two months of tedious haggling, the exhausted delegates managed to agree on a charter (though some issues, like how to choose the secretary-general, were postponed). But the length and difficulty of the negotiations were actually good signs: it meant that the nations were taking the new organization seriously—as did President Harry Truman, the small-time politician who had suddenly been catapulted into the most powerful job on earth by Roosevelt's death, when he flew in for the signing of the Charter.

> If we had had this Charter a few years ago—and above all the will to use it—millions now dead would be alive. If we falter in the future in our will to use it, millions now living will surely die. . . . We all have to recognize—no matter how great our strength—that we must deny ourselves the license to do always as we please. Unless we are willing to pay that price, no organization for world peace can accomplish its purpose. And what a reasonable price that is!
>
> U.S. president Harry S. Truman,
> Address at final session

It could have been Sir Robert Borden or General Jan Smuts talking about the League of Nations in 1919. But the resolve to change the way the international system worked had been great at the end of that war, too. The question was: Would it last this time?

———

PERSONAL AND MOST SECRET.

In December 1938 and January 1939 in France and Germany discovery was made that certain elements, chiefly uranium, could be made to "burst" (scientific term "fission").

Since 1941 active research in the U.K., and the U.S., and Canada has been carried out and it is now certain a bomb can and will be made that will be, if not a million times, at least hundreds of times more powerful than anything yet known. . . .

C.J. Mackenzie, National Research Council,

to C.D. Howe, April 10, 1944

The Potsdam Conference, held just outside the ruins of the German capital in July 1945, was the last of the wartime meetings at which the United States, Britain and the Soviet Union decided the basic shape of the postwar world. It was the old world of power politics, but that was the reality the new United Nations had to deal with: the Americans and the British argued with the Russians over the Polish border and the future of Germany (whose division was implicit in the Potsdam agreement), and all three powers sent an ultimatum to Japan. When no reply came, the United States dropped the first atomic bomb on Hiroshima on August 6, 1945.

The Russians scrambled to declare war on Japan before it surrendered, so as to get their agreed share of the spoils, but the destructive power of the atomic bomb shocked them. Atomic weapons threatened to change all the traditional calculations about the balance of power, which had been moving strongly in the Soviet Union's favour in Europe. In 1945 most of Europe was in ruins, France was just emerging from more than four years of German occupation, Germany was now occupied by Allied troops, and Britain, though nominally a great power, was bankrupt. The Russians had paid the price (twenty million dead) and they intended to collect the reward: a predominant influence in European affairs.

This did not mean that the Russians intended to station tanks in Italy or to direct the traffic in Paris, but Moscow did expect to have the largest voice in the shaping of the European peace settlement. It also looked forward to having no rivals on the continent capable of threatening its security—especially if the Americans went home again, as they had done after the First World War. But the power of the Soviet Union was of a familiar, quite conventional kind: it relied on large armed forces, ideological allies and diplomatic manoeuvre to exert its influence. Atomic weapons might cancel all that out.

The United States had huge armies too in 1945, but even after they had been demobilized it would still have an awesome new kind of power. Atomic power was secret and invisible, and it had changed everything (except, as Einstein said, the way people think).

> Norman Robertson . . . is obsessed with the problems of the atomic bomb. He is afraid that one day they will start going off and that the statesmen of the world will say, in surprise, like the clumsy maid, "It just came to pieces in my hands."
>
> Escott Reid, External Affairs, 1941–62
> Letter to his mother, November 1945

For the generation of 1945 nuclear weapons were profoundly unsettling and corrupting. Those who possessed what seemed like absolute power could not ultimately resist the temptation to arrogance, while those who did not possess it felt terribly vulnerable and struggled to catch up. The Bomb at once cast a shadow over the new United Nations, even as it made it more urgent to find a way to end great-power war.

In spite of the great secrecy that surrounded it, the Russians knew long before Hiroshima that the Americans were far ahead in the development of the new weapon. They knew it because they had a very efficient organization spying on the American atomic weapons programme—until it sprang a leak in Ottawa. Only a month after the first atomic bombs fell on Hiroshima and Nagasaki, a cipher clerk in the Russian embassy in Ottawa called Igor Gouzenko defected, bringing evidence of the spy ring with him.

In September 1944 Gouzenko had been told he was going to be recalled to Moscow. He managed to have his stay extended for another year, but by then he and his wife, Anna, were determined not to return to Stalin's Russia. During the next year he secretly marked the most incriminating documents that the Soviet spy ring in Canada was collecting. The ring had been operating for years, and in the course of the war its focus had changed from radar and high explosives to the research on uranium and atomic energy that was being carried out in Montreal. One of its chief informants was Allan Nunn May, an English physicist working with the National Research Council. In spite of the extreme security precautions protecting the project, Nunn May (code name "Alek") was able to send the Russians detailed information about the work, and even samples:

Facts given by Alek: (1) The test of the atomic bomb was conducted at New Mexico. The bomb dropped on Japan was made of uranium 235. It is known that the output of uranium 235 amounts to 400 grams daily at the magnetic separation plant at Clinton. . . . (2) Alek handed over to us a platinum leaf with 162 micrograms of uranium 235 in the form of oxide in a thin lamina.

Telegram from Nikolai Zabotin, Soviet Military Attaché in Ottawa, August 9, 1945

In early September 1945 Gouzenko gathered up all his marked documents, made a run for it and asked the Canadian government for asylum. He was instructed to return to the Soviet embassy with his documents, even though he was threatening to kill himself rather than go back. Prime Minister King wanted nothing to do with him. He didn't want to believe Gouzenko, because the information he brought, if true, would utterly poison relations between the Western powers and the Russians.

> We learned later that the Russian man had left saying . . . that there was nothing but suicide ahead of him. I suggested that a Secret Service man in plain clothes watch the premises. If suicide took place let the city police take charge and . . . secure what there was in the way of documents, but on no account for us to take the initiative.
>
> My own feeling is that the individual has incurred the displeasure of the Embassy and is really seeking to shield himself. I do not believe his story about their avowed treachery.
>
> *The Mackenzie King Record*, September 6, 1945

The Soviet embassy sent a team to break into Gouzenko's apartment, but he and his wife and two-year-old son survived by hiding with the neighbours in the apartment next door until the Ottawa police arrived. Meanwhile Sir William Stephenson, a Canadian who headed British intelligence operations in the western hemisphere, dropped by Norman Robertson's apartment for a late drink and learned what was happening. The two men decided that the potential implications of the case were serious enough to override the prime minister's instructions, and arranged for Gouzenko to make a statement to the RCMP early the next morning. Late on the seventh Robertson came to see the prime minister with details:

He said he had got particulars of what the police had and that everything was much worse than we would have believed. . . . They disclose an espionage system on a large scale. . . . Not only had [U.S. secretary of state] Stettinius been surrounded by spies, etc. [Alger Hiss], and the Russian Government been kept informed of all that was being done from that source, but things came right into our own country to a degree we could not have believed possible. . . .

In our Research Laboratories here at Ottawa, where we have been working on the atomic bomb, there is a scientist who is a Russian agent [Raymond Boyer]. In the Research Laboratories in Montreal where most of the work was done there is an English scientist who is pro-Russian [Nunn May] and acting as a Russian agent.

The Mackenzie King Record, September 7, 1945

Eleven Canadians were eventually convicted of spying for the Soviet Union, and the "Gouzenko Affair" was widely used as evidence that Moscow was planning to attack Western countries. But the Soviet espionage effort proved nothing except the ancient truth that no great power will willingly accept strategic inferiority to a potential rival. If the American atomic-bomb project had been a number of years behind the Russian, no American president would have refrained from mounting a comparable espionage operation against the Soviet atomic-weapons programme. But this sort of comparison almost always eludes harried decision-makers in the moment.

On September 30 Mackenzie King visited President Truman in Washington (it was their first meeting) to brief him about the Gouzenko Affair, and then went on to London to meet Prime Minister Clement Attlee and his foreign secretary, Ernest Bevin. By now Allan Nunn May was in London and being shadowed, but King found the British curiously relaxed about the whole business of Soviet espionage.

[Bevin] was inclined to think that an arrest or two or three might be made here and he assumed that we would adopt a similar course. I told him that I had seen the President on the way through and that Truman was strongly of the view that all three countries should meet together and decide the course they should take. . . .

I begin to feel that what Russia perhaps is aiming at is to get outside of the United Nations altogether just as Germany and Japan and Italy did in the League of Nations in the years preceding the last war. They are determined to let the rest of the world know that what they are capable of doing is to go back into power politics and with greater vengeance than ever.

The Mackenzie King Record, vol. 3

Stalin was a monster, but he was not a lunatic. The Soviet Union's industrial resources were vastly inferior to those of its American, British and Canadian allies. Much of the Soviet Union had been occupied during the war and dozens of its cities destroyed, while in the West only Britain had suffered even moderate damage. At least twenty million Soviet citizens had been killed in the war, while no more than a million British, Canadians and Americans had died. At the end of the war, the Americans had nuclear weapons, while the Soviet Union was still years away from possessing them. The Soviet Union could not possibly win a war with the West, so it was most unlikely to start one.

Yet King, like others in the West, was moving toward the view that the gravely crippled Soviet Union was about to embark on a career of military expansion. Moreover, in the absence of effective international controls, the Soviet Union would be bound to build and test its own nuclear weapons eventually. For Canada, this raised the frightening prospect of a future in which it would be the no man's land between two nuclear-armed giants who were rapidly turning hostile: the "fireproof house" was becoming a tinderbox.

> Russia was very near to Canada. Could bomb us from across
> the North Pole. . . . Her route to the States would be through
> Canada, and if the Americans felt security required it, [they]
> would take peaceful possession of part of Canada with a wel-
> come of the people of B.C., Alta., and Saskatchewan who would
> become terrified.
>
> *The Mackenzie King Record*, vol. 3

Mackenzie King had no more faith in Americans than he did in Russians or Western Canadians. He expected them all to behave badly— or rather, he expected them to conform to the steps of the traditional dance. The United States and the Soviet Union, as the most powerful states surviving amidst the wreckage in 1945, were almost bound to identify each other as potential enemies. It wasn't really about ideology at all: as John Starnes, a young diplomat who later became under-secretary of state for external affairs and then director general of the Security and Intelligence Directorate of the RCMP, wrote in January 1948, "If the United States and the U.S.S.R. were both Communist states . . . the degree of conflict would be unabated and [perhaps] even be more sharply drawn."

Great powers automatically fear and mistrust each other—a point U.S. secretary of commerce (and former vice-president) Henry Wallace made forcibly to President Truman in March 1946, writing to him that "the events of the past few months have thrown the Soviets back to their pre-1939 fears of 'capitalist encirclement.'" In a subsequent letter, Wallace warned Truman that the large peacetime U.S. defence budget, American atomic bomb tests in the Pacific, the production of long-range bombers and American attempts to get overseas bases "must make it look to the rest of the world as if we are only paying lip-service to peace at the conference table. These facts rather make it appear either (1) that we are preparing ourselves to win the war which we regard as inevitable or (2) that we are trying hard to build up a preponderance of force to intimidate the rest of mankind." But when Wallace made the same remarks in public later in the year, Truman fired him: "I was afraid that, knowingly or not, he would lend himself to the more sinister ends of the Reds and those who served them," he said. Truman's own attitude had already been defined in instructions to his secretary of state on January 5, 1946, only four months after the war's end.

> Unless Russia is faced with an iron fist and strong language another war is in the making. Only one language do they understand: "How many divisions have you?" I do not think we should play compromise any longer. . . . I'm tired of babying the Soviets.

It actually didn't take as long after San Francisco as it did after Versailles before normal service was resumed.

———

> The Cold War was an accumulation of misperceptions on both sides. There's no doubt about it. We were unduly afraid of their intentions, and they were paranoid about ours, and these worked on each other. It was a dreadful mistake.
>
> John Holmes, Canadian Embassy, Moscow, 1947–48

In later years, when the Cold War had set as hard as ice, a comment like that would have attracted the charge of "moral equivalence": that the speaker was wilfully ignoring the titanic moral struggle that underlay the military confrontation, and justified even the risk of nuclear war. Western ideologues would have added that the Soviet Union's behaviour was inherently aggressive because it was driven by Marxist ideology, which sought, as an ultimate goal, the conquest (or at least the conversion) of the entire world, and that all Soviet actions past and present must be seen in the light of that interpretation. But that was later. In the early days, even Canadian generals could see that this was nonsense.

> I have never yet heard a convincing argument to prove that the USSR harbours aggressive designs, that is to say, the use of physical force in Western Europe.
>
> General Maurice Pope, Canadian Military Mission,
> Berlin, September 1947

There was a time, it is true, when the Soviet Union was ruled by revolutionaries who really expected Communism to conquer the whole world. "What? Are we going to have foreign relations?" Lenin reputedly exclaimed in 1917 when it was proposed that he appoint a commissar for foreign affairs. Why do that if, as he expected, the rest of Europe was going to fall to the same revolution within a few weeks or months? And even after the Bolsheviks had faced up to the fact that the revolution was not going to spread, they denied that the Soviet state was any more than a transitional phenomenon. But that was before Stalin virtually annihilated the old revolutionaries in the great purges of 1935–39, and made the state bureaucracy the dominant force in the land.

By the late 1930s, the Soviet Union was behaving just like other great states in its foreign relations, making alliances with Nazis or "imperialists" as the state's interests dictated, and showing no interest whatever in the fate of the Communist parties in other countries if they did not serve Soviet state interests. Soviet foreign policy had become so utterly traditional and non-ideological that Moscow vigorously pursued its claims to all the lost territories that had once belonged to the Russian empire but had been lost at the time of the revolution. Latvia, Lithuania, Estonia and the former Russian shares of Poland and Romania were recovered at the time of the alliance with Hitler in 1940. When the Soviet Union declared war on Japan in August 1945, with the intention of recovering the territories lost to Japan at the end of the

Russo-Japanese War of 1904–05, Stalin's Order of the Day urged the troops to "efface the shame of forty years before."

Soviet behaviour in the countries that had been liberated by its armies fitted the same pattern of duplicating (but not exceeding) tsarist ambitions. The war aims that had been discussed by the tsar's diplomats with his Western allies in the First World War—a Russian-dominated Eastern Europe, a Western Europe essentially run by Britain and France, with a weak and divided Germany in between—were also the Soviet war aims in the Second World War. And, except that Western Europe became American-dominated instead, it all came to pass.

This was hard on Eastern Europe, but at Yalta, the conference between Churchill, Roosevelt and Stalin in February 1945 where the main lines of postwar policy in Europe were laid down, the Western powers had signalled (quite sensibly) that they would not do anything practical to dispute Soviet domination there. Stalin wanted a ring of client states in Eastern Europe for all the usual reasons that great powers like to have that sort of thing: military buffer zones, areas for economic exploitation, sheer prestige. He reckoned the Soviet Union's sacrifices in the war entitled him to demand it, and he would have interpreted any Western attempt to frustrate it as an attack on the vital interests of the Soviet state.

> The Soviet occupation of Eastern Europe was much more brutal than I think anybody had expected—perhaps we should have expected it, but it was extremely brutal. . . . We could just feel the alliance with the Soviet Union eroding away under our feet.
>
> Escott Reid, External Affairs, 1941–62

It is still difficult to explain what caused so much Western alarm about Soviet intentions after the war. It cannot have been the actual division of Europe into Soviet and Anglo-American spheres of influence: that had effectively been agreed at Yalta. Nor should the fact that all the "liberated" lands received political systems similar to those of their respective liberators have caused any astonishment. Thus Romania, where you could have counted the number of genuine native Communists in 1945 without taking your shoes off, duly had a "Communist revolution" in 1947, while France and Italy, where the Communists were the most powerful and credible political force at the end of the war thanks to their leading role in the resistance movement, nevertheless wound up with liberal-democratic political systems and capitalist economic systems.

Stalin's Communization of the Eastern European states had nothing to do with ideological fervour. He did it because the Eastern European countries, if they were not confined within a system that shackled them to the Soviet Union and cut them off from the West, would have drifted into the orbit of the richer and culturally more attractive Western European states sooner or later. But Stalin's first step after the Communists came to power in Eastern European countries was to instigate purges (like his own in the Soviet Union in the late 1930s) in which all the dangerous revolutionaries and "real" Communists were killed off, leaving conservative, state-oriented bureaucrats like himself in command.

Stalin never showed the slightest ambition to extend the Soviet domain in Europe beyond the territories allocated to the Soviet Union at Yalta. There was a good deal of violence involved in the process of imposing an alien Communist system on the countries of Eastern Europe, but that was an implicit part of the deal that had been struck in 1945. The other half of the deal, also implicit, was that the Soviet Union would not seek to boost the powerful Communist parties of Western Europe into power, and it did not. Even in the Italian election of 1948, when the Communist Party stood a real chance of winning and huge amounts of American money were being spread around to stop it, the Soviet Union sent no money to help the Italian Communists.

So how did the Soviet Union's ruthless actions in nailing down the empire it had acquired in Eastern Europe (by agreement with the

Western allies) get reinterpreted as proof that it was an irresistibly expansionist state embarking on an ideological crusade aimed at world conquest? That is a good question.

———

Czechoslovakia definitely fell within the Soviet sphere of influence by the terms of the Yalta agreement, but it was the only Eastern European country that had been a genuine democracy before the Second World War, and it weighed heavily on Western European consciences as the country they had sold down the river in 1938 to win another year of peace. Moreover, the Czechs had managed to resurrect their democracy after the end of the German occupation in 1945, and by 1948 the country was not occupied by Soviet troops. So the Communist coup in Prague in February 1948, and the subsequent "defenestration of Prague"—the death of Foreign Minister Jan Masaryk in a fall from a second-storey window at the Foreign Office on March 10, 1948—came as a profound shock to the countries of the West. It was not an overt Soviet military move, but the Prague coup was just the kind of subversive internal action that most people had been predicting in Western Europe, and it had a profound effect on Mackenzie King.

> He had really become a kind of anti-Communist by this time, as well as fearing Russian military power, but . . . he wanted us to follow and never to lead (and not to follow too soon). I think that was quite true until the defenestration of Prague.
>
> Mackenzie King had known Masaryk and liked him, and he was really quite horrified. There was a kind of real conversion that day. I watched the whole thing, and of course the whole Cabinet went down to listen to Truman's speech on the radio, and that's when the Western alliance was really founded. You know, it took

months to get the treaty made, but that's when it was really founded, that day, and it was a sudden conversion.

Jack Pickersgill, secretary to Prime Minister Mackenzie
King, 1937–48

Mackenzie King was still profoundly opposed to any peacetime alliances for Canada, but he was deeply shaken by Masaryk's fate. "Time may tell whether this was a suicide or whether that means was taken by the Communists to destroy his life," King wrote. "One thing is certain. It has proven there can be no collaboration with Communists." And on March 11, 1948, the day after Masaryk's death, King received an urgent letter from the British prime minister, Clement Attlee:

[It] pointed out the need for a united front on the part of free nations. The importance of assistance from the United States. Necessity to organize collective security groups—one now being worked out in the Benelux group [nations associated under the Treaty of Brussels signed on March 17]. The other one to be worked out for the French–U.K.–U.S. and Canada in particular. Another, a Mediterranean group.

This message stated they . . . wanted to know if I would be agreeable to having the situation regarding Atlantic regional security group explored by British officials, United States and ourselves.

The Mackenzie King Record, vol. 4

The prime minister was still nervous, but Attlee's letter was just the opening the activists in the Department of External Affairs were looking for. King was persuaded to send Pearson to Washington, and in early 1948 Canada and Britain set about seducing the United States into joining a formal alliance with Western Europe.

Mr Pearson's cover story for his absence from Ottawa was that he was going to New York for a few days to help out General McNaughton, the Canadian representative on the Security Council, who was under the weather. General Charles Foulkes, the chairman of the Canadian Chiefs of Staff Committee, came in civilian clothes. . . .

The meetings were held in the War Room of the United States Joint Chiefs of Staff in the bowels of the Pentagon, and staff cars were sent to pick up the participants and to deliver them directly to a secret entrance in the basement of the Pentagon. The entrance was so secret that one Pentagon chauffeur got lost trying to find it.

Escott Reid

As far as the Russians were concerned, all the secrecy was a bit superfluous, since the second secretary at the British embassy in Washington, Donald Maclean, was a Soviet spy, and was providing Moscow with a "fairly full record" of the talks. But in the first couple of months this would not have occasioned much alarm in Moscow, for the negotiations did not go smoothly.

It was a miraculous birth. . . . Most informed observers at the beginning of 1948 would have said that a North Atlantic treaty was impossible. . . .

I can't believe that one could have had the treaty if there hadn't been two people at the State Department, not at the very top, who were enthusiasts for it—Jack Hickerson and Ted Achilles. Even though their superiors were opposed: George Kennan and Chip Bohlen and Robert Lovett.

Escott Reid

For a long time we were afraid to admit we were really negotiating a treaty. We were saying we were discussing common security problems. As a matter of fact we didn't even admit that we were talking privately with the Canadians and the British about it. There had been indications in Canada, by St. Laurent, by Mike Pearson and Norman Robertson, of interest in some Western defence agreement supplementing the United Nations. We knew they were thinking along these lines—as the British were. We thought that the three of us had a basically common approach. . . . We felt that anyone else might be approaching it from a national-istic point of view.

Ted Achilles, director, Western European Affairs, U.S.
State Department, 1947

It was, to begin with, very much the old Anglo-Saxon alliance of the war years revived: those excitable Europeans were too nationalistic, and they might have spies in their midst. But even this cozy English-speaking club might not have reached agreement if the first of the Berlin crises had not spurred them on. Only a couple of months after the secret talks began, the Western powers introduced a new currency in Germany, which meant, in effect, that the three-quarters of Germany that they occupied would henceforth be linked to the capitalist world economy.

Very few people in what was to become West Germany objected to this measure (which rapidly rescued the economy from the utter collapse in which it had been mired), and the Western powers had only done it after despairing of getting any agreement with the Soviets on a joint programme for German economic recovery. But Moscow inter-preted it as a Western decision to divide Germany—which it was, in effect. The Russians struck back two days later, on June 24, 1948, by cutting off electricity to the Western-occupied sectors of the German capital, Berlin (which was located deep in the Soviet zone of Germany), and blockading the land access routes by which West Berlin's food and fuel supplies arrived from the West. The U.S. Army briefly considered sending a convoy to fight its way down the autobahn to Berlin, but in the end the Western occupying powers decided to circumvent the Soviet blockade by an airlift.

The blockade (which lasted almost a year, until the Russians finally agreed to reopen the land routes to West Berlin) was just what the secret NATO negotiations needed. It lent added strength to the view that the Russians were an unreasoning power that could only be dealt with by the threat of force. It was also a powerful propaganda tool—all those planes carrying food and supplies to a besieged population—to prepare Western public opinion for the alliance being secretly hatched in Washington. However, the increasingly militarized context of the secret discussions in Washington was disturbing to people like Pearson:

> There is, I think, real danger of old-fashioned alliance policies dictated by purely military considerations. . . . [Ideally, NATO] would set forth the principles of Western society which we were trying not only to defend but to make the basis of an eventually united world, and not simply make us part of an American war machine against the Russians.
>
> Lester Pearson, *"Mike": Memoirs*, vol. 2

Pearson eventually managed to get Article 2 (the "Canadian article") included in the NATO treaty, calling for economic collaboration, and social and cultural cooperation among the members as well as military guarantees. But Article 2 was mainly a sop to the fastidious and faint-hearted who didn't want to admit to themselves that they were creating a military alliance. For the more robust and single-minded, the events of the past couple of years were ample proof that the Soviet Union was an inherently aggressive "outlaw state" that could only be stopped by force.

The Soviet Union was not on an expansionist rampage in the late 1940s, but it was behaving in a ruthlessly opportunistic fashion in what it considered its sphere of influence. This greatly facilitated the general round-up of stray nations that took place in 1948. As the secret tripartite talks progressed in Washington, the idea gradually expanded to a "North Atlantic" security pact that would embrace all the countries of Europe that weren't under Communist domination. And even though the Russians knew all about the secret talks, the secrecy paid off in the end, for it allowed the stage to be thoroughly set before the Europeans and the U.S. Congress and public were invited in to contemplate the manifold virtues of a North Atlantic treaty.

> It enabled the United States administration to pretend to Congress that the second stage of the negotiations, which began in July 1948 with France, the Netherlands and Belgium added to the original three [the U.S., Canada and Britain], grew out of the resolution of [Senator] Vandenberg's which had been adopted by the Senate authorizing that kind of negotiation. Whereas, in fact, the State Department when it drafted the Vandenberg resolution was securing a legitimation of the results of the tripartite talks. The secrecy about the first stage of discussions also enabled the United States and Britain and Canada to pretend to France and the Benelux countries that they had participated in the discussions from the outset.
> Q. *You didn't tell them that there had been talks?*
> No, we pretended there hadn't been. I've seen no indication that the French realised the talks had been taking place, or the Belgians or the Dutch. It's hard to believe that they didn't, but apparently the preservation of secrecy may have worked.
>
> Escott Reid

The British and Canadian scheme was a brilliant success. By the time the talks concluded in early 1949, Americans generally believed that NATO had been their own idea, and the Italians, the Portuguese, the Danes, the Norwegians and the Icelanders had also agreed to join. "It was a reversion to alliances and away from some of the universal aspirations we'd had," fretted John Holmes, but for many people the pain of failure was eased by the rationalization that they were trying to stop another Hitler. This analogy was reinforced by the striking post-1945 linguistic fashion in the West to use the word "totalitarian" to describe both Nazis and Communists, implicitly putting them in the same category. (In the Soviet Union, the same political goal was accomplished by referring to both Nazis and Moscow's current Western opponents as "imperialists.")

> Now we are faced with exactly the same situation with which Britain and France were faced in 1938–39 with Hitler. A totalitarian state is no different whether you call it Nazi, Fascist, Communist or Franco Spain. . . . The oligarchy in Russia is no different from the Czars, Louis XIV, Napoleon, Charles I and Cromwell. It is a Frankenstein dictatorship worse than any of the others, Hitler included.
>
> I hope it will end in peace. Be a nice girl and don't worry about your Dad's worries.
>
> U.S. president Truman, letter to his daughter Margaret
> (then aged 24), March 1948

The Canadians who helped to create NATO in 1948–49 had no intention of dividing the world permanently: they saw the organization as a temporary measure designed to stabilize Western Europe politically while the Marshall Plan restored it economically—and in 1949 it was still possible to believe (with just a little effort) that we were not re-creating the alliance system. Although the NATO countries promised to consult politically in the event of any threat, and to come to the aid of any member under attack, NATO as created in 1949 involved no military command structure and no vast scheme of rearmament.

NATO was an alliance founded to stop an attack that wasn't coming, by people who knew it wasn't coming and were creating it for purposes of political morale-building among their own friends. That didn't seem such an inexcusable crime to those who had to deal with the problems of the time, especially since one could hardly say that the Soviet Union was behaving in a more responsible manner. By the time the NATO treaty was ready to be signed, Louis St. Laurent had become prime minister. In 1947 he had publicly admitted that the proposal that eventually grew into NATO was "most undesirable," but now both he and his new secretary of state for external affairs, Lester Pearson, believed it was a vital necessity.

> I was present at the signing of the treaty. I remember Mr. Pearson stating the Canadian position, which was that this should not be just a military alliance, and that this required a consultation system which would try and align our policies as far as possible. At the time when the signature was taking place and Mr. Pearson had just made this speech, it happened that the Marine Band that was deployed by Mr. Truman for the occasion struck up "It Ain't Necessarily So." (laughter).
>
> It seemed an appropriate comment.
>
> George Ignatieff, External Affairs, 1940–62

The treaty was signed on April 4, 1949. Less than six months later, the Soviets tested their first atomic bomb. Eight months after that, war broke out in Korea.

————

> It was quite a quantum leap for the United States to go against the last will of Washington to keep out of European entangling alliances, as it was for Canada. But Korea was the explosive charge

which really exploded the world of uncommitment that Mr. King
had depended on.

George Ignatieff

NATO remained a paper alliance of mutual guarantees from April 1949
until June 1950. Then the coming of the Korean War stampeded its
members into crash rearmament and the creation of a joint military
command in Europe—with, naturally, an American as supreme commander. The arms race got underway in earnest, the Cold War entered
its coldest phase and the anti-Communist witch hunt went into high
gear in the United States. That was quite a list of repercussions for a war
in a place that most Canadians would have had a hard time finding on
a map in 1950.

Korea had been a Japanese colony since 1910, and after the
Japanese surrender in 1945, it was occupied by both American and
Soviet troops. The Soviets, arriving by land, took over the northern part
of the peninsula, while the Americans, coming by sea, assumed control
of the southern part. At a meeting of foreign ministers in Moscow in
1945, a joint commission of the United States and the USSR was set up
to organize a "trustee" government for a period of five years. Once a
freely elected Korean government had been established, the arbitrary
border at the 38th Parallel would disappear and a unified Korea would
re-emerge. Predictably, however, Washington and Moscow could not
agree on how to run the elections.

The resistance against the Japanese had been largely Communist,
which gave Kim Il-sung's former guerrilla group a degree of legiti-
macy, and the Soviets helped him to entrench himself in the North.
The Americans tried to help their own candidate, an American-
educated politician called Syngman Rhee, by getting the United
Nations to create the United Nations Temporary Commission on
Korea (UNTCOK) to supervise elections throughout the peninsula. If
the Soviets agreed to this commission, Rhee would likely win the

election, as the U.S.-controlled zone had twice the population of the Soviet zone. If they refused, then Rhee could at least be put in charge of the south.

In November 1947, St. Laurent, then still secretary of state for external affairs, agreed to Canadian participation in UNTCOK, but Prime Minister Mackenzie King refused. He believed, quite correctly, that the Russians would bar UNTCOK from the North, and he also suspected that the Americans had already decided to hold elections only in South Korea and wanted Canada in UNTCOK merely to help legitimize the decision. King sent Under-Secretary of State for External Affairs Lester Pearson to Washington to explain his concerns to President Truman. Pearson was hardly reassured by Truman's response: "Don't worry, you won't get into any trouble over there, and if you do we are behind you." Moreover, the president kept emphasizing that Canada was the most respectable member on the commission—and "that was exactly what worried Mr. King."

> Mr. King, as you know, was a spiritualist and one of the messages he had received from the Beyond [from the late President Roosevelt] was that World War Three was going to break out over the division of Korea. As soon as he had received this message he really reverted instinctively to his former isolationism and said: "Canada must not be involved in this in any way." St. Laurent went to him and said: "If you want me in this government, you have to support this kind of intervention. It's the only way of the future."
>
> Dale Thomson, secretary to Prime Minister
> Louis St. Laurent, 1953–58

St. Laurent's resignation threat worked: King agreed that a Canadian member could be appointed to UNTCOK, although the representative was instructed to withdraw if it became clear that Russian cooperation was not forthcoming. He was to have nothing to do with organizing an election in South Korea alone, which would merely freeze the division of the country. But Roosevelt had given King better advice than St. Laurent, despite the considerable handicap of being dead.

The Russians predictably refused to admit the UNTCOK commissioners to their zone of Korea, and the United States used its huge majority in the United Nations to ram through a motion resolving that elections be held "in those parts of Korea accessible to the Commission." (Canada was one of two countries to vote against it.) And in February 1948, while Canada's representative in Korea, Dr. George Patterson, "happened" to be away in Japan, the other members of the commission decided to hold elections in South Korea only. Patterson had left instructions that he should be contacted if anything important came up while he was away, but this was evidently not considered an important matter.

The May 1948 elections duly produced a Republic of Korea in the American-occupied part of the peninsula, run by Syngman Rhee with ample assistance from the army and the secret police. Canada made it clear that it would regard any government of South Korea resulting from the 1948 elections as the creation of the U.S. occupation authorities and not of the United Nations, but the Americans had achieved their aim. Two and a half months later, the Soviets retaliated by recognizing Kim Il-sung as the leader of the "People's Democratic Republic of Korea" in the North—and less than two years after that, we all got the Korean War.

> They always attacked at night because of our air superiority. They
> would rush through the minefield, blow it up, and lay on the wire.
> Then the next wave would come through with grenades, throw
> the grenades and go to ground. The next wave with burp-guns
> and so on, and just keep coming in waves. . . . You couldn't fire
> fast enough to stop them, so the only way to stop them was massed
> artillery fire, often on your own position. The infantry would call
> down fire on their own position with VT fuses—a little radar set

in the nose of the fuse would explode it [about 20 metres] above the ground and the shrapnel would all go down.

So the night of 2/3 May [1953] on Hill 187, the 1ˢᵗ Battalion Royal Canadian Regiment, who our battery supported, were over-run, and the first order we got was "DFSOS. Drop 200. Fire till you're told to stop." DFSOS was as close as you could get for safety. So we questioned the order and we were told "Bloody well fire it." So we kept getting drops—"Drop 200." "Drop 400." "Drop 800."—until we were right on the RCR position. We kept firing all night. In my troop alone, with four guns, we fired at least 1,200 rounds. . . . The barrels got red hot and we were throwing water on them to try and cool them down. We fired right through till dawn, till the Chinese withdrew. The Chinese were bundling up their dead and rolling them down the hill. They wrapped them in wire and rolled them down the hill. . . . Two of my very good friends were killed that night.

Francis Bayne, 81ˢᵗ Field Regiment (RCHA)

EXCURSION 8

WHY WAR IS HARD TO STOP

THEY WERE BACK DOING WHAT THEY HAD ALWAYS DONE. Governments knew what needed to be done, but they still couldn't bring themselves to do it. They understood that war is a systems problem, yet they allowed themselves to be swept back into an alliance, a great-power military confrontation and an actual shooting war practically before the ink was dry on the UN Charter. Why is it so hard for human beings to break out of the war system?

Prior to the twentieth century, most people did not see war as a problem in need of a solution. *Losing* a war could be a very big problem, but the solution to that was to be good at war. It was the First World War, with its unprecedented level of destruction, that changed all that, and for the first time a number of serious people in positions of power addressed the problem directly. As people who lived and worked within the institutions of the state, they naturally emphasized the need to change the rules by which states operated, and in operational terms they were quite right. But they were not aware of how deep the roots of the problem go.

The creators of the League of Nations knew that it would be very hard to put an end to war, as it has played a big role in civilized societies from the earliest times. At a rough guess, 95 percent of the civilized states that have ever existed were ultimately destroyed by war. As the great-great-grandchildren of the Enlightenment, however, most of these people would have shared Jean-Jacques Rousseau's belief that before the rise of civilization, when human beings lived in the "state of nature," they lived in peace with one another. The problem was the behaviour of states, and it could be solved (if only very slowly and against great resistance) by changing the rules.

Then along came the archaeologists and anthropologists of the next half century, who discovered that warfare had been even more prominent in the lives of the thousands of generations before civilization. The hunter-gatherers and horticulturalists, who lived in groups of a hundred or less, whose attitudes and values evolved over hundreds of thousands of years, were fundamental to shaping what we now call human nature. They matched Rousseau's description of "noble savages" in the sense that they were deeply egalitarian—but they were also extremely warlike. Indeed, the cumulative toll of deaths from war in these little societies was far higher than anything seen in civilized warfare. It took a long time for this fact to inform public debate about war and peace, for it was most unwelcome news and strongly denied by many. But however disheartening, it could not be ignored: in every place and time, human beings have almost always fought wars.

And after that, from the 1970s on, came the primatologists, with the further bad news that our closest relatives among the higher primates (and almost certainly our own pre-human ancestors) also fought wars. If this behaviour is not actually inscribed in our DNA, it is at the least deeply ingrained in our culture all the way back to *Homo erectus*.

One year later, a gang from Kasekela found their third victim. This time their target was Goliath, now well past his prime, with a bald head, very worn teeth, protruding ribs and spine. . . .

It began as a border patrol. At one point . . . they spotted

Goliath, apparently hiding only 25 metres away. The raiders rushed madly down the slope to their target. While Goliath screamed and the patrol hooted and displayed, he was held and beaten and kicked and lifted and dropped and bitten and jumped on. At first he tried to protect his head, but soon he gave up and lay stretched out and still. . . . They kept up the attack for 18 minutes, then turned for home. . . . Bleeding freely from his head, gashed on his back, Goliath tried to sit up but fell back shivering. He too was never seen again.

The death of a Gombe chimpanzee,
from Richard Wrangham and Dale Peterson, <i>Demonic Males:
Apes and the Origins of Human Violence</i>

Jane Goodall's discovery in 1973 that the chimpanzee troop she was observing in Tanzania's Gombe National Park actually waged a kind of war against neighbouring bands came as a great surprise at the time, but subsequent studies by a number of primatologists—some chimpanzee bands have been observed for forty years now, with each member named and his or her behaviour recorded over lengthy periods of time—confirmed that fighting between rival groups of chimps is widespread, chronic and very serious. How relevant is this to human beings?

Our line of descent separated from that of the chimpanzees five or six million years ago, but about 98 percent of our genetic material is still common to the two species. Until ten or twelve thousand years ago, all our human ancestors made their living in essentially the same way as chimps, by foraging for food in small bands. Both humans and chimpanzees were hunters as well as gatherers—chimps hunt monkeys regularly, and do so in coordinated groups using clearly conscious strategies—but chimpanzee "warfare" is hampered by the fact that they lack weapons, and it is very difficult for chimps to kill each other with their bare hands. As a result, most successful raids involve a number of male chimps from one band attacking a lone chimp from another, with some holding him down while others pummel and bite him—and even then the victim is often still alive when the attackers leave, although he generally dies afterward. But it *is* warfare, in the sense that it is purposeful and calculated.

According to primatologist Richard Wrangham, who did his earliest work with Goodall's team in Gombe in the early 1970s, chimpanzees conduct deliberate raids and make considerable use of surprise. Nor is it just blind aggression, triggered by the proximity of a chimp from another band: these raiding parties wait and count the calls of other troops to see if they are outnumbered, and almost always withdraw rather than attack unless they can catch a single chimp from a rival band on his own. Moreover, although the great majority of killings involve the ambush of single chimps separated from their groups, a campaign may be waged over a period of months or years until all the males of the rival band have been annihilated. Once that is done, the territory of the defeated group may be taken over and the surviving females incorporated into the victorious group—but the infants will be killed.

Two more things, both with worrisome echoes in human behaviour. One is that chimpanzee bands typically have a territory of about 35 square kilometres, but spend almost all their time in only the central 15 square kilometres. The rest is equally rich in resources but they treat it as a no man's land, presumably because of the danger of ambush and death at the hands of a neighbouring troop. The other thing is that this endemic chimpanzee warfare, according to long-term studies of several troops, eventually causes the death of about 30 percent of males and a much lower but still significant proportion of females.

Similar studies of human hunter-gatherers who still lived in intact societies were almost never made by direct observation. In the 1930s, however, anthropologist Lloyd Warner conducted extensive interviews among the Murngin people of Arnhem Land in northern Australia, who had only recently come into regular contact with Europeans. Trusting the strong oral history tradition among preliterate peoples, he reconstructed as best he could from interviews the scale of warfare among the Murngin in the late 1800s. The Murngin numbered about three thousand people and lived in many separate bands of the classic hunter-gatherer type. Out of a fighting-age population of about eight hundred adult males, Warner estimated that around two hundred died in warfare over a two-decade period at the end of the nineteenth century. Twenty years is roughly the length of time that any individual male would have been regarded as an active warrior, so these figures translate into a 25 percent death rate from warfare among males.

The Murngin rarely fought pitched battles. The great majority of clashes followed the usual hunter-gatherer pattern of raids on sleeping camps or ambushes of severely outnumbered opponents. In most of these events, only a few individuals, or one, or most frequently none at all, were killed, but the clashes were so constant that over a lifetime Murngin men stood as great a chance of dying in war as the conscript soldiers of Napoleon's France or Hitler's Germany. The same pattern of constant low-level warfare was reported by other anthropologists studying the Eskimos of northwestern Alaska, the Mae Enga horticulturalists in highland New Guinea and the Yanomamo in the Amazon forest. Indeed, the latter two groups were both losing about the same proportion of their populations to war—25 percent of males and 5 percent of females—and their territories consisted of a relatively safe central area and a bigger buffer zone that they only entered in large groups.

Civilized people did not invent warfare. They inherited it from their hunter-gatherer ancestors, who in turn almost certainly inherited it from their pre-human ancestors. Some of the fossilized remains of *Homo erectus* found in Europe show signs of violence that might well have been inflicted by human-style weapons 750,000 years ago, particularly depression fractures in skulls that could be the result of blows from clubs. Neanderthal fossils found on several continents and ranging from forty to a hundred thousand years ago show stronger evidence of death inflicted by human weapons—spear wounds, a stone blade lodged between the ribs—and the evidence for chronic warfare among pre-civilized *Homo sapiens* is pretty conclusive. Why did they all behave like this?

In most cases, of course, they were simply born into a world where that was the way things worked, but there was a good reason why it worked that way. The world was never empty, and food was always limited. Human hunter-gatherers, like other predators, lived at very low population densities compared to their prey animals, but they invariably bred up to the local carrying capacity or even a bit beyond it. Then sooner or later, the normal food supply would be interrupted by changing weather patterns, alterations in animal migration routes, or other unpredictable factors. In a matter of weeks or months everybody in the band would be hungry all the time, and since human beings are gifted with foresight, they would know what lay ahead for the group if this continued. They would also know that other groups in the vicinity were facing the same problems. So it's us or the neighbours, and we're not both going to make it.

If this happens just once a century, then there will be ten times a millennium when some groups don't make it, and more aggressive groups do. This sort of winnowing, extended over tens of thousands of years, would produce the kind of warfare between hunter-gatherer groups that the anthropologists discovered, including the phenomenon of apparently pointless aggression even in times of plenty. Whether this is just a deeply entrenched cultural phenomenon or to some extent genetic as well, it won't be the sort of thing you can turn off in good times and switch back on when the going gets tough. Besides, every enemy you eliminate now is one you won't have to deal with in a crisis.

This pattern of behaviour probably emerged not long after the first proto-humans became full-time group-living predators. After that, it was just passed down in the human lineage (and presumably the chimpanzee lineage as well) because it was the best strategy for long-term group survival. It probably still made sense right down to the time when human beings invented agriculture around eleven thousand years ago, although the cost in adult male lives was quite high.

If the goal is to tame the institution of warfare because it has become too destructive to tolerate any more—and that was what the founders of the League of Nations intended—then this is all very bad news. War is a much older and more deeply entrenched social institution than they realized. But there is also some good news at this point in history: as soon as people started farming, the population began to multiply and the first mass societies came into existence. At that point, the death rate from war dropped dramatically.

Wars did not stop, but even the early mass civilizations were so large that most people no longer lived an hour's walk (or even a day's) from the potentially hostile society next door, so most people were no longer so exposed to raiding. Moreover, when these societies did fight, they simply could not bring everybody to the battle. The relatively small proportion of the adult male population that ended up on the battlefield might have a very bad day, for battles undoubtedly got bloodier, but most people were not there and anyway battles only happened once or twice a year. Terrible things would still happen from time to time (for example, when cities were conquered and their entire populations enslaved or killed), but over the long run far fewer people died in war than in the hunter-gatherer societies. In fact, there have not been many generations of human beings since the rise of civilization in which the direct loss of life from war has exceeded 2 or 3 percent of the population—which is why nobody really saw war as a grave problem until recently.

The generation that fought the First World War was an exception to that rule, and the generation that fought the Second World War was another: the twentieth century saw the invention of weapons that briefly drove war back up almost to hunter-gatherer casualty rates. The last six decades have seen a return to "normal" casualty rates for civilized states, but the technologies now exist to make another great-power war (with nuclear weapons) a global holocaust, so the enterprise launched at

Versailles by the survivors of the First World War and relaunched in San Francisco in 1945 is still highly relevant.

How much of our war-related behaviour is written in our genes? The fear and mistrust of strangers is probably innate, but our identities are fluid: we now live quite comfortably in mass societies that are descended from hundreds of different hunter-gatherer groups that once lived in a state of permanent warfare. It is much less likely that the actual institution of warfare has any genetic component. It is a cultural institution with very deep and ancient roots, but it is too complex and calculated to be purely instinctive. Nor are we trapped in the Malthusian dilemma of the hunter-gatherers: when the reasons to fight fade away, people don't mind at all.

The little village societies of highland New Guinea, for example, went on fighting their vicious local wars even as the Second World War raged around them. But afterward, when the Australian police went around telling people that they couldn't fight any more, the New Guineans thought that was wonderful. They were glad to have the excuse to stop.

CHAPTER 9

ALLIANCES AND PEACEKEEPING

I don't think, to begin with, that the Russians had very much to do with the outbreak of the Korean War. It's very hard to tell. . . . I don't know this for certain, but I strongly suspect that the North Koreans had been pretty badly aggravated by attacks by the South Koreans before they ever invaded South Korea.

Admiral Jeffry Brock, Commander of Canadian Destroyers,

Far East, 1950–51

The North Koreans wanted to prod South Korea with the point of a bayonet. Kim Il-sung said the first poke would touch off an internal explosion in South Korea and that the power of the people would prevail. . . .

Stalin persuaded Kim Il-sung that he should think it over, make some calculations, and then come back with a concrete plan. Kim went home and then returned to Moscow when he had worked everything out. He told Stalin he was absolutely certain of success. I remember Stalin had his doubts. He was worried that the Americans would jump in. . . . The war wasn't Stalin's idea, but Kim Il-sung's.

Nikita Khrushchev, *Khrushchev Remembers*

INITIALLY, NEITHER OF THE TWO MAJOR POWERS INTENDED TO become embroiled in a war over Korea. By the beginning of 1950, Rhee, the South Korean strongman, had built up an army of 98,000 men, commanded mainly by Korean officers who had served in the Japanese imperial forces, but his political methods caused such distaste that President Truman was having difficulty getting aid for South Korea approved in Congress. It is entirely plausible, therefore, as Admiral Brock suggests, that Rhee's army was making attacks along the 38th Parallel with the aim of creating a crisis to increase the flow of American aid.

In Moscow, Stalin certainly knew of Kim's decision to try to reunify the country by a surprise attack on the South, and did not try to talk him out of it. On the other hand, Stalin himself wanted nothing to do with the scheme, which might draw him into a military confrontation with the vastly more powerful forces of the West: he made sure that all Soviet advisers were withdrawn from the country before the North Koreans attacked. (These two explanations for the Korean War—that the South Koreans were trying to provoke the North into a large-scale retaliation along the border, and that Kim was planning an invasion anyway—are *not* mutually exclusive.)

In June 1950 the North Korean army struck in force all along the 38th Parallel, and had almost complete success. The South Korean army crumbled, Seoul fell, and the North Koreans were soon driving south toward the bottom of the peninsula. Even though General Douglas MacArthur had not thought that Korea was vital to American security, President Truman declared that Korea was "an ideological battleground upon which our entire success in Asia may depend," and MacArthur, also the allied supreme commander in occupied Japan, immediately began air strikes from Japan against the North Korean tank columns. Troops from the U.S. occupation forces in Japan followed within days. As for consulting with its NATO partners before taking this momentous step. . . .

> We were all summoned to the State Department, and I remember that one of the NATO allies said, "Is this a consultation or information?" and I think it was George Kennan who was holding the meeting on behalf of Dean Acheson, or it may have been Dean Acheson himself, who said, "The President of the United States has informed Congress of the decision of the United States to take military action already, so you can draw your conclusions, gentlemen. It is for you to decide."
>
> George Ignatieff, External Affairs, 1940–62

Lester Pearson, who had become external affairs minister in the St. Laurent government in September 1948, felt that Canada "had to keep the U.S. action within the framework of the UN." He needn't have worried: the Americans were happy to oblige. By the time Truman and all his key advisers had assembled in Washington, they had decided that their response should be characterized as a UN operation. In those days the United Nations still had a positive image in the United States, being largely American-controlled apart from the Soviet veto, and associating the American action with the United Nations would help justify the war to the American people. In addition, the UN label would help in getting other countries more actively involved in the worldwide American crusade against "Communism."

Truman also knew that the West would not be thwarted at the United Nations by a Soviet veto, since the Soviet Union's representative, Yakov Malik, had walked out of the Security Council early in the year over a fight about the recognition of China. Moscow wanted the People's Republic of China (Mao Tse-tung's Communists, who had won the civil war in 1949) to have China's seat in the Security Council, but the Americans insisted that Nationalist China keep it, even though the Nationalist forces now controlled nothing except the island of Taiwan. So the Soviet Union was not present to use its veto when the Security Council declared that there had been a breach of the peace and requested aid for South Korea. Ten days later the United Nations Unified Command was created, making the Korean war a UN operation at least in theory, and General MacArthur, who had taken command of U.S. military operations in South Korea on the war's outbreak, became the UN commander as well.

I considered this to be a very important event; the first time in history, so far as I know, an assembly of nations had formally condemned and voted against an aggressor and, unlike the League of Nations in 1935 and 1936, had followed through. . . . I have always felt since that, however it worked out in practice, it was a most valuable precedent for the future of the United Nations.

Lester Pearson, *"Mike": Memoirs*, vol. 2

"However it worked out in practice. . . ." There was still, in most Western countries, a conviction that the United Nations *had* to be made to work, and therefore those countries were psychologically prepared to participate even in a sham collective security operation. But it was a sham. By 1950 the Western majority in the United Nations had, in effect, defined the Soviet Union as an aggressive state against which collective security measures had to be applied, and all other Communist states as mere extensions of Soviet policy. That was not truly the case, but it can be argued that the West needed to create some sort of political structure like NATO in the late 1940s to reassure the beleaguered democratic governments in Europe, even if everybody knew that the Russian tanks were not going to roll. If it had gone no further than that, NATO might have fulfilled the limited tasks that Escott Reid had envisaged for it: containing the Russians and the Americans until things settled down and they both grew up a bit. Then everybody could have got back to the serious business of making the United Nations work. But Korea put paid to all that.

> We were always looking for Soviets in Korea, but they didn't seem to turn up. But the fact was that Korea was regarded as a prime example of the threat of a monolithic Communist movement in the world, and was so represented in Washington.
>
> George Ignatieff

The flagrant aggression of Kim Il-sung was precisely the sort of thing that collective security had to stop if there was to be any hope of a more stable and peaceful world, but the war in Korea was not really a UN operation at all. From start to finish it was an American war fought for U.S. strategic objectives, with some assistance from other NATO members and a few other American allies. The war was waged not against the North Korean aggressor regime but against the "world Communist conspiracy," and the UN force was actually NATO-in-Asia.

Even worse, the United States exploited the Korean War to do what should never have been done at all: to convert NATO from a political association into a real military alliance, with a joint command, a formal strategic doctrine and heaps of weapons. The Russians *still* weren't coming, but by the end of the Korean War NATO had been thoroughly militarized—and it was a very deliberate business on the part of the United States. Within a week of the Korean invasion, U.S. forces were fully committed in Korea and armed with UN credentials to boot. Now, the Truman administration wanted America's allies to send troops. Before the Canadian government committed itself (some members of cabinet were distinctly reluctant), Pearson made a secret visit to Washington to see Secretary of State Dean Acheson. It was an enlightening trip.

To Mr Acheson the fighting in Korea was only an incident—though politically an incident of great importance—in a very dangerous international situation. This incident had . . . made it politically possible for the United States to secure Congressional and public support for a quick and great increase in defence expenditures [and] for the imposition of needed controls, higher taxes, the diversion of manpower to the armed forces and defence industries, etc. This will amount to a partial mobilization and will prepare the way for a rapid and complete mobilization in the event of war.

"Mike": Memoirs, vol. 2

In short, the U.S. State Department was going to use Korea as the excuse and the goad for general rearmament, both in the United States and among its NATO allies. While he would be happy to have a detachment of trained Canadian soldiers in Korea for military reasons, Acheson concluded, he was even more interested in their political value.

———

The Korean War resembles the Boer War more than any of Canada's other wars. It was fought far from Canada's traditional areas of interest, and as Britain had used the South African war to set a precedent for the participation of its overseas dominions in imperial defence, so the United States was using the war in Asia to transform its purely political alliance into a militarily useful organization.

Following Pearson's interview with Acheson, Ottawa agreed to send some destroyers to the Korean War and to airlift arms and supplies to the South Koreans. The Canadian government hoped that this would satisfy the Americans, for Pearson was already having to deny that Canada was merely following "the orders of a single member of the United Nations which has particular interests to safeguard in Korea." Besides, despite Canada's commitment to collective security, the country did not have troops available to send to Korea (or anywhere else for that matter).

> We had this illusion that collective security was a scheme by which if you say you're all going to unite against an aggressor, nobody will aggress. You don't actually have to have forces. We didn't realize that as members of a UN dedicated to collective security, even as members of NATO, we had to have troops, and we didn't have them, so it was a very embarrassing month in New York.
>
> John Holmes, Canadian Mission to the United Nations,
> 1950–51

The request for Canadian ground troops in Korea formally came via UN Secretary-General Trygve Lie, but in fact it came from the United States, whose UN representative, Warren Austin, had told the secretary-general that American support for the United Nations "would be put in jeopardy" if he didn't make the appeal. The Unified Command being set up in Korea was really just the American command with a few bangles and beads hung on it, but for those Canadians who recalled that a crusading anti-Communist alliance was not what we had been seeking to create in 1945 (or even 1949), there was a soothing source of confusion: the growing tendency to talk about NATO and the United Nations as though they were the same thing.

This grew out of the mental juggling act by which the founders of NATO had reconciled it with their earlier commitment to collective security, but by 1950 it had gone a step further. When Prime Minister St. Laurent announced on August 4 that Canada would raise a "special force" of troops for UN service in Korea, he told the public that they would also be available for "carrying out Canada's obligations . . . under the North Atlantic Pact." The distinction between NATO and the United Nations had vanished utterly.

This was precisely the result Dean Acheson had intended: his primary purpose in getting the NATO allies to send troops to Korea was to make them rearm in Europe, and it worked wonderfully well. In Ottawa, Lieutenant-General Guy Simonds, the Chief of the General Staff, was more than half convinced by the interpretation, popular in U.S. military circles, that the attack in Korea was a feint by a monolithic "world Communist conspiracy" to draw Western troops off into Asia before the Russians launched the main onslaught in Europe. And so Canada agreed to send troops not just to Korea but also to Europe, and commenced a wholesale rearmament programme. Nor, it turned out, was there any difficulty in raising the extra troops that were needed, even though the urgency of getting a brigade to Korea meant that the government was looking for trained men.

> When it was suggested, after the outbreak of the war, that Canada should send a brigade to Korea and a brigade to Western Europe, I remember having a talk about it with Charles Foulkes, who was then Chairman of the Chiefs of Staff Committee, and Charles said to me, "You know, the politicians think it would be difficult to recruit enough men to form two brigades. I told them there would be no difficulty at all. It's now four years since the end of the war and there are plenty of men who've now decided after four years that they've had enough of their wives and children. They'd jump at a chance to enlist."
>
> Escott Reid, External Affairs, 1941–62

By August 26, 1950 eight thousand experienced men, regular soldiers or veterans of the Second World War, had volunteered. The Korean War never appealed strongly to Canadian patriotism or idealism, but it did not require more manpower than was available in that limited reservoir of "natural soldiers" which exists in every country. In these circumstances it is not surprising that Quebec provided its full 30 percent share of the force. But for a time, it looked as if they would all get there too late for the war.

———

When Canada first agreed to send forces to Korea, the Americans and their South Korean protégés were barely clinging to the bottom of the peninsula around Pusan, and nine-tenths of South Korea had been occupied. But on September 15, 1950 General MacArthur opened his counter-offensive with an amphibious assault on Inchon, the port for Seoul. By September 27 Seoul itself had been recaptured and most of the North Korean army destroyed. South Korea was liberated, and the pre-war situation could have been re-established without much further bloodshed.

> I used to quarrel quite frequently with General MacArthur out in the Far East because of his determination to go and dip his feet in the Yalu River [on the border between North Korea and China], in my view quite unnecessarily. At one stage of the war we had reached a position just north of the 38th Parallel—a defensible position on land.
>
> We had accomplished what we had set out to do: that is, to send the North Koreans back where they came from, and to rescue the South Koreans. We should have stopped there. Indeed, that is where we are stopped today. But that only came after we had embarked upon further ventures, going further and further north.
>
> Rear Admiral Jeffry Brock, commander of Canadian
> Destroyers Far East, 1950–51

With the North Korean army in ruins, the United States could not resist a little expansionism of its own. As U.S. ambassador Austin put it at the United Nations: "A living social, political and spiritual monument to the achievement of the first enforcement of the United Nations peace-keeping function must be erected." Freely translated, that meant that the United States got the UN General Assembly to agree, on October 7, to the conquest of North Korea and the unification of the country under the American-backed regime in the South.

The Canadian government, having failed to persuade the Americans to stop at the 38th Parallel, tried to get their consent to what Pearson ironically called "the inevitable Canadian compromise." Meeting with the American ambassador to the United Nations in New York the night before the crucial General Assembly meeting, he suggested that the United Nations should give the North Koreans a period of grace, three or four days, in which to agree to a ceasefire and armistice negotiations before the UN forces crossed the old border. If it did prove necessary to cross the 38th Parallel, then the UN troops should at least go no farther north than the narrow "neck" of the peninsula between the 39th and 40th parallels, far enough away from the Chinese border that Peking would not feel threatened. Senator Austin agreed to put forward these proposals himself the following morning—or so Pearson was led to believe.

> When the meeting opened, to my amazement and disgust, the United States representative got up and, in effect, asked support for an immediate pursuit of the North Koreans beyond the 38th Parallel and for their destruction—for a follow-through to the Chinese boundary, if necessary, to destroy the aggressor.
>
> *"Mike": Memoirs*, vol. 2

The UN forces plunged north across the 38th Parallel the following day on a "Home-by-Christmas" offensive, while General MacArthur sent his air forces ranging all the way north to the Chinese border along the Yalu River. His ground forces were still almost entirely American, but a few of his pilots were Canadian airmen attached to American squadrons. Omer Lévesque, shot down over France in 1941 with four kills to his credit, became an ace while serving as an exchange officer with the U.S. Air Force in Korea.

> We went 250 miles through enemy territory and flew along the Yalu River, and the [Chinese MiG-15s] would come up when they felt like it. You could see the sand kicked up from the air-base right below you, and yet you weren't supposed to go across, and most of the time we would stay well south of that [line]. . . .
>
> This time they were already there waiting for us in the sun, high above us, about three to five thousand feet. The lead aircraft was attacked so I shouted for [the others] to break. And then I started following that MiG down, that's how I got closer in to him and fired. . . . I think I must have hit his hydraulics or something, and then the aircraft started spiralling to the right. I followed it right down to pretty close [to the ground] and he crashed. It took me everything to pull out. . . .
>
> Squadron Leader Omer Lévesque, RCAF

As American troops approached the Yalu River, the nervous Chinese government, only one year in power after a long civil war against an American-backed opponent, sent a steady stream of warnings through the Indian ambassador in Peking, K.M. Panikkar, that it would intervene in the war if the Americans came too close to the frontier. American diplomats at the United Nations flippantly remarked, "Pannikar is panicking." Ottawa, however, had serious doubts about the advisability of trying to establish a U.S.-supported government by military force on the borders of Manchuria, China's major industrial area.

> China proved to be as willing to admit such a plan for Korea as the United States might have been if UN forces, mostly Chinese, had been about to arrange for a people's democracy in Mexico.
>
> Escott Reid, *The Conscience of the Diplomat*

The American dream of reuniting Korea by force lasted less than two months. At the end of October 1950, as American and South Korean forces closed up to the Chinese frontier, the first Chinese units were reported across the Yalu—and in late November the roof fell in. Two hundred thousand Chinese "volunteers" struck the UN front, and the American forces, desperately trying to avoid being cut off, began a rapid retreat back down the peninsula: the "Big Bug-out," as the G.I.s called it.

> Had we been wise enough we would have learned some very important lessons from the Chinese, the most important being that they required no air cover, no tanks, no sea power. They just put a handful of rice in one pocket and a handful of bullets in the other, and they marched straight forward knocking off the enemy ahead of them. . . .
>
> They gave us a damn good thrashing with just really sticks and stones and the courage to go and win. And all our tanks and our air power and our sea power, and the Coca-Cola machines and the typewriters and the barbers' chairs that we landed at Inchon and had to take off a few months later, were of no help whatsoever.
>
> Rear Admiral Jeffry Brock

As the UN forces retreated south through the endless Korean hills in bitter winter weather, stumbling into ambush after ambush, anxiety grew among America's allies that Washington would try to turn the tables by sharply escalating the war, either by attacking China directly, or by using nuclear weapons, or both. Britain's prime minister, Clement Attlee, consulted with the Canadian government and then flew to Washington for talks with Truman. He got an American promise to confine operations to the Korean theatre itself—but in return for American restraint in Asia, both Canada and Britain promised to beef up NATO's defences in Europe (just as Acheson had intended).

By the time the first Canadian ground troops actually entered the line in Korea later that month, the front was forty miles south of Seoul, which was once again in enemy hands. The war of rapid movement was over, and the UN forces (which eventually included contingents from seventeen countries, but were always at least 90 percent American) were gradually clawing their way back up to the 38th Parallel in fighting marked by extraordinarily lavish artillery fire and bombing. But General MacArthur was growing increasingly restive under the constraints placed on him by President Truman, and was demanding that the Chinese be forced to the negotiating table by the aerial bombardment and naval blockade of China itself. By February 1951 he had also prepared a plan to block all further Chinese access to Korea by sowing a "defensive field of radioactive wastes" that would make the south bank of the Yalu impassable, to be followed by large airborne and amphibious landings at the upper end of both coasts of North Korea, perhaps using Nationalist Chinese troops from Taiwan to supplement his own forces. MacArthur's idea was to close a "gigantic trap" on all the Chinese and North Korean troops in the peninsula, and he was prepared to risk almost anything to win his local war.

But that was not the point of the exercise for the U.S. government, which despite its momentary enthusiasm for reuniting Korea the previous autumn was really concerned mainly with building up NATO's strength in Europe. It was ironic, therefore, that in the incident that finally got MacArthur fired—a letter to the minority leader in the House of Representatives that was read into the *Congressional Record* on April 5, 1951—the general got it so precisely backward. The Truman administration, MacArthur insisted in the letter, failed to realize that "here in Asia is where the Communist conspirators have elected to make their play for global conquest. . . . Here we fight Europe's wars with arms while the diplomats there still fight it with words. . . . If we lose this war to Communism in Asia the fall of Europe is inevitable; win it and Europe most probably would avoid war and still preserve freedom. . . . There is no substitute for victory."

> I fired him because he wouldn't respect the authority of the President. . . . I didn't fire him because he was a dumb son of a bitch, although he was, but that's not against the law for generals. If it was, half to three-quarters of them would be in jail.
>
> Harry S. Truman, Plain Speaking

President Truman and the Joint Chiefs of Staff in Washington also believed in the Communist conspiracy, but *they* believed that Korea was probably a feint to distract attention from Europe. Moreover, the war had now served its purpose in terms of galvanizing the American public and America's allies into accepting large-scale rearmament programmes. With the front line now back around the 38th Parallel, armistice talks began in July 1951. They lasted for fully two years, while bitter, futile trench battles took a steady toll of men all up and down the line. It was in these two years that the Canadian troops took the bulk of their casualties—but Korea was a half-forgotten war by then, and nobody at home much cared.

> I had an order in my unit that we don't walk at night. At last light you get into your slit trench, your foxhole, whatever, you don't walk. Anything that walks is enemy.
>
> There was quite an attack put in by the Chinese on Hill 355. Americans held it, and it was on Thanksgiving Day that year, they were knocked off it. So the Americans were pulling out and coming back through my lines, and finally the Brigade Commander, John Rockingham, wanted me to pull out. I said, "I can't pull out. I've got to stay in until first light." And we were all right, but we had Chinese penetrating all over our lines, some killed ten and fifteen yards away from me. Of course, I was safe; I was very well protected by my people. The next morning we stuck out like a sore finger on battle maps, you know, but we did stick to it.
>
> General Jacques Dextrase, Royal 22e Régiment

At one point the Vancouver *Sun* ran the same Korean War story
on its front page for three days running, then gleefully announced
that not a single reader had noticed this fact.

Blair Fraser, *Search for Identity*

The Korean armistice was finally signed in July 1953, after
President Truman had been succeeded by General Eisenhower and the
new secretary of state, John Foster Dulles, began to drop not very subtle
hints that the United States was considering the use of nuclear weapons.
The ceasefire line closely parallelled the pre-war border. The first
United Nations attempt at enforcing the concept of collective security
came to an end, leaving the concept itself discredited in many people's
minds. But in terms of turning NATO from a paper pact into a real military alliance, the Korean War unquestionably did the job very well.
Three hundred and twelve Canadians were killed in combat in Korea,
a few score more than in the Boer War, and it cost only about $200 mil-
lion. But like the Boer War, it fundamentally changed Canada's attitude
toward international affairs.

I think a lot of Canadians took quite a lot of pride in what was done
in Korea, and having sent troops to a country much further away
than Europe, and a place that we much less understood, it was a lot
easier to send our troops and our air force into Europe. . . . It was a
great achievement, and I don't think we would have done either of
those things if we hadn't had a French-speaking prime minister.

Jack Pickersgill, secretary to Prime Minister Louis St.
Laurent, 1948–52

St. Laurent was able to do what Sir Wilfrid Laurier could not: take a
united Canada into foreign wars that really had nothing to do with the
defence of Canada itself. The difference was that now there were only two
empires left in the world, and in the fifties anti-Communism came as

naturally to French Canadians (for whom Communism was the enemy of the Catholic Church) as to English Canadians. Between 1950 and 1953 Canadian defence budgets doubled, and then doubled again. Our armed forces tripled in size, and Canada sent ten thousand troops to Europe. What's more, we sent them there, for the first time, in peacetime.

> There was no acceptance of the idea that [Canadian troops would be in Europe] permanently. . . . First of all we hoped that NATO itself, as a military alliance, would be temporary until you could get back to a universal system. Secondly, we were doing this because our European allies were still flat on their backs, but as soon as they were able to take the load then we withdraw.
>
> I think there was this continuing assumption. I know Mr. Pearson always had this view that we wouldn't have to keep these troops there all the time.
>
> John Holmes, External Affairs, 1943–60

When the Canadian troops arrived in Europe in late 1951, to a rousing welcome speech by the new Supreme Allied Commander Europe, General Dwight D. Eisenhower (who had been brought back to fill his wartime role again in a deliberately symbolic act), there was indeed no intention in Ottawa to create a permanent presence of Canadian armed forces in Europe. As time passed, however, the European allies who had been "flat on their backs" grew to be as rich and industrially powerful as the North American allies whose troops were allegedly there to defend them—and vastly wealthier than the Soviets and Eastern Europeans from whom they were allegedly being defended. Yet the Canadian troops stayed there for forty-two years. Some of the American troops are still there today. Why?

Why, to be precise, did 300 million Western Europeans need the help of 265 million North Americans to hold off 280 million Soviets (who, after the Sino-Soviet split of the 1960s, also had a billion angry

Chinese at their backs)? The answer is that they didn't *need* them. They were happy to have the help, since it meant that Western Europe had to take less responsibility for its own defence, but the Western Europeans were perfectly capable of looking after themselves militarily by the mid-1950s at the latest. There were no Soviet hordes and, as historian A.J.P. Taylor pointed out in 1951, there was no huge and unprecedented lurch in the balance of power among the European countries after the Second World War. Rather there was a reversion to a familiar and quite manageable pattern: "The one new thing between 1917 and 1941, which made it a freak period, was that Russia ceased to count as a Great Power [because of the revolution and its aftermath]; now the situation is more normal and more old-fashioned."

Russia has been a major factor in the European balance of power for centuries: it was only the suddenness of its reappearance in 1945, after a quarter-century's absence, that caused a level of panic sufficient to make the Western Europeans seek American help in peacetime. But the help was not free: that sort of arrangement is always a bargain with costs and advantages for both sides. By assuming the ultimate responsibility for the defence of Western Europe, the United States acquired the role and responsibilities of a "superpower," the position of "leader of the Free World," and various other titles, responsibilities and benefits, which, although mostly intangible, were very dear to a wide variety of people and interests in the U.S. government and society. And although the original NATO defence arrangements were not intended to be permanent, they lasted for over four decades because the continued U.S. military commitment allowed the Western Europeans to avoid the scale of military effort they might otherwise have had to put forth to balance Soviet power.

However, the American guarantee to Europe did not really depend on the presence of a mere third of a million U.S. troops on the continent; they were there mainly to reassure Western Europeans that the United States really could not avoid fighting in their defence if the Soviet Union ever attacked. The real military guarantee was the U.S.

Air Force's Strategic Air Command, which would destroy the Soviet Union with nuclear weapons. When Lester Pearson had asked U.S. secretary of state Dean Acheson during the Korean War what would happen if the "Communists" launched a major offensive in Europe, he replied: "The free countries [in Europe] would have to do what they could to defend themselves from Russia while American air power was brought to bear on Russian cities and industries."

As time wore on and the Soviet Union gradually acquired the ability to strike the United States with nuclear weapons too, that simple, iron-clad U.S. guarantee became suspect: would the Americans really attack the Soviet Union with nuclear weapons and expose their own homeland to Soviet retaliation in order to "save" Europe in a crisis? To reassure the Europeans that yes, indeed, they would do that implausible thing, the Americans consistently tried to stay far ahead of the Soviet Union in the number and variety of their nuclear weapons.

But nuclear weapons cannot be counted like spears. Once the Soviet Union had acquired the ability to deliver a couple of hundred large nuclear warheads on American cities (which it had by 1965, in the form of unstoppable Intercontinental Ballistic Missiles), then the number of nuclear weapons the United States possessed became quite irrelevant. It could have them by the million and it still wouldn't be able to save the American population, no matter how thoroughly it could annihilate the Soviet Union. At that point, the American nuclear guarantee that lay at the heart of NATO strategy became logically inconsistent and, in the strictly technical sense of the word, incredible. In a rational world, this development should have led to the withdrawal of the U.S. nuclear guarantee from Western Europe, since it could only be fulfilled at the cost of seeing American society utterly destroyed. Alternatively, it could have been replaced by an enormous buildup of U.S. and allied conventional military forces in Europe, which would have freed NATO from its need to rely on nuclear weapons at every level.

But neither of those things occurred. The alliance continued to rely on a fundamentally incredible nuclear threat to compensate for its deliberate and self-imposed weakness in conventional forces, maintaining only enough American troops in Europe to ensure that the United States would be irrevocably involved in any war there. Indeed, the fact that NATO blithely carried on for a quarter-century with a strategy that no longer made military sense, and that the Soviet Union was never tempted for a moment to call the bluff, demonstrated the fundamental and quite awesome stability of the post-1945 settlement in Europe. The partition of Europe between the superpowers was never seriously challenged by either side, and there was probably never a single day between 1945 and 1991 when either side seriously contemplated initiating a war there.

Indeed, the superpowers showed a good deal of tacit complicity, in Europe as elsewhere, in pursuing policies designed to reinforce the deeply entrenched bipolar character of international politics that gave each of them such a dominant position in their respective blocs. And although it was nonsense to claim, as people often did, that NATO (or the Warsaw Pact, for that matter) "kept the peace" in Europe for forty years, it was certainly true that neither superpower had the slightest incentive to break it, for they were the greatest beneficiaries of the status quo.

At one level, therefore, the NATO and Warsaw Pact alliances were simply the means by which the superpowers preserved and perpetuated the very agreeable division of power in the world that had come about as a consequence of the Second World War. But at another level, these familiar old alliances were not at all harmless. Although the confrontation between them was heavily ritualized, large numbers of people on both sides took their own propaganda seriously, and the fifty thousand nuclear weapons were quite real. Moreover, the fact that the industrialized world had been corralled into hostile military blocs provided the military-industrial complex on each side with an inexhaustible supply of "threat" images. And if the long period of relative stability in great-power politics had ever broken down, the alliances ensured that the ensuing crises would be faced by an extremely over-armed and hair-trigger world.

Canada would have been involved from the start, for the main purpose of stationing Canadian forces in Europe was exactly the same as it was in the American case: to guarantee to the Europeans that Canada would be in the next world war from the opening shot. Our country had no direct role in the central relationship of nuclear dependency between the United States and Western Europe, but we were certainly complicit in it, and the presence of Canadian troops in Europe, by making the presence of American troops there seem less of an anomaly than it really was, helped to blur the otherwise stark outline of that central relationship.

The alliance that the West created in the late 1940s and the early 1950s was indeed a "dreadful mistake," but it never actually tumbled into a nuclear war, and the fact that the Soviet Union never attacked Western Europe was frequently offered as proof that NATO was necessary. It was an inherently unanswerable argument, but reminiscent of the story about a man who was sitting in a train, tearing up little bits of paper and throwing them out of the window. Somebody asked him: "What are you doing that for?"

"To keep the elephants away," he replied, tearing off another piece of paper.

"But that's crazy, there are no elephants around here."

"Of course not," he explained patiently. "I'm keeping them away."

For the Canadian forces—and especially for the army, given the unlikelihood that anyone would ever invade Canada's own territory—NATO was a godsend. Being part of the alliance gave meaning and interest to our soldiers' careers: their spiritual home was Europe, where they could be competitive and well-respected professionals playing in the military big league. They got to play there for two whole generations, and most of them never questioned the politics or the strategy of it. And, of course, they would have died bravely and uncomplainingly if that was the ultimate price of being able to practise the profession they loved in the service of the country they loved.

> I don't think anyone has illusions that we're going to live all the way through the next war. Everyone's going to try their best and do it as long as possible; however, in any war someone's got to die, and that's just what we're here for, I would imagine. . . . I don't think we're going to have a war in the next few years. But if we did, and I've been getting paid for the last ten or fifteen years now without a war, then it's my duty to go and fight the good fight.
>
> Major Jim Calvin, Princess Patricia's Canadian Light
> Infantry, West Germany, 1986

The great expansion of the Canadian forces in the 1950s, which carried them from 35,000 men in 1948 to 120,000 in 1960, virtually smothered the old militia spirit, for the new armed forces were entirely professional. They were, of course, motivated by patriotism as well as by the attraction of practising their profession at the highest level, but they were never asked to choose between the two: after 1950, the defence of Canada was fully equated with membership in the alliances that gave our forces access to the military big league. They would no more have volunteered the argument that Canada's defence could be separated from the NATO alliance than they would have suggested before 1939 that it was separable from the British imperial context. Asking our soldiers if NATO was a good thing was like asking the barber if you need a haircut.

There is no deliberate deception or conscious self-interest in it, but no other section of Canadian society subscribed with such near-unanimity as our armed forces to the view that having heavily armed alliances is the best and indeed the only way to prevent the "other side" (defined by the alliance system) from starting a war. Like many theological propositions, this was neither provable nor disprovable by logic, nor was it desirable to settle the argument by experiment. But by the mid-fifties, as the panic engendered by the Korean War wore off, for people like Lester Pearson the alliance case was starting to lose its glitter.

Late in 1955 Pearson was the first Western foreign minister to visit Moscow since the Cold War had begun. On the last day of his visit he was flown down to the Crimea to meet Nikita Khrushchev, the man who was already clearly emerging as "first among equals" in the post-Stalin collective leadership. Khrushchev, whom Pearson described in his report to Ottawa as being "as blunt and volatile as only a Ukrainian peasant turned into one of the most powerful figures in the world can be," came straight to the point: why didn't Canada leave NATO, which was "an aggressive alliance and a direct threat to Russia and to peace"? The usual futile argument ensued, but after things had mellowed a bit Khrushchev returned to the subject in a subtler way, referring to the repeated Soviet efforts to embarrass the West by pretending to take the NATO treaty literally. If it was really a regional collective security organization authorized under Article 51 of the UN Charter, Moscow kept asking, then could the Soviet Union please join too?

I was about to explain why NATO should be [regarded as a purely defensive organization] when Khrushchev broke in with the remark, "You should let us into NATO—we have been knocking at the door two years." I replied that if the world situation were such as to permit entry of the U.S.S.R. into NATO it would also presumably permit proper functioning of the United Nations in the security field. . . . I also pointed out that if the Soviets were in NATO they would have to accept an integrated defence system and unified command. If they were prepared to accept that why not make the United Nations security system work?

"Mike": Memoirs, vol. 2

And besides, Pearson added, the Soviet Union might be worse off without NATO, since it would then face "the United States 'going it alone' and Germany freewheeling in the centre of Europe, without the cautious and restraining influence of countries like the United Kingdom, Belgium, France and Canada." It is not recorded whether Khrushchev expressed his gratitude for Canada's restraining influence.

———

Like most of the generation who had helped to create the NATO alliance, Pearson had a sense of parental pride that would never allow him to renounce it entirely, however disillusioned he might become with its practical shortcomings. But although most Canadians still considered NATO to be necessary, it was quite clear to them by the mid-fifties that the alliance was *not* in any practical sense a part of the UN process. In fact, it was mostly a rival to it, and many Canadians still believed in the United Nations too. Moreover, many Canadians were feeling stifled within the alliance, where Canadian compliance was increasingly taken for granted, and—although this was mostly just the result of the relative decline in Canada's power as the rest of the world recovered economically from the war—it chafed at the national pride. So peacekeeping, the great Canadian invention of 1956, was a cause for much national self-congratulation.

> It is one of those cases where the Canadians felt good, because here we were, the very virtuous people who had no colonial past and a good reputation throughout the world. We were the mediators, we were the peacekeepers, that was our self-image at the time.
> Dale Thomson, secretary to Prime Minister St. Laurent,
> 1953–58

Peacekeeping was a last-ditch invention by the disillusioned idealists of the 1940s when their dream of a world made safe by collective security had collapsed under the weight of postwar rivalry and suspicion.

It was a pale facsimile of what the United Nations was supposed to do by way of keeping the peace, done on a voluntary rather than an obligatory basis, with forces that could only cajole, not compel. It operated only in places where peacekeeping forces had been invited by the local government, and never on the territory of a great power. But peacekeeping was the only vestige of the original vision of a more orderly world that became a kind of reality—and it came into existence during the week that saw the most concentrated outburst of international stupidity and bloody-mindedness since the 1945 war.

In the same crowded week in late 1956, the Soviet Union invaded Hungary to crush a revolt against Communist rule, and Britain and France invaded Egypt (in collusion with Israel) in order to force it to submit to European interests. Both were attempts to reimpose imperial discipline on restive subject peoples, the only significant distinction being that Hungary was in thrall to one of the new informal empires cloaked by ideology and military alliances, while Egypt had only recently emerged from one of the old colonial empires that were based on naked power.

But that was a very important distinction in practice, for the new-style empires had a basis in the realities of power, and a credibility in terms of the prevailing psychology of the time, which allowed them to rebuff any outside interference from the United Nations or anywhere else. The crumbling European colonial empires, on the other hand, lacked both power and credibility. The United Nations was no more able to prevent the Soviet suppression of the Hungarian revolt in 1956 than it could have stopped the U.S.-backed "rebel army" in CIA pay that had invaded Guatemala and overthrown the elected left-wing government of that country two years before. But Egypt was different.

The "Suez crisis" was a quarrel between Britain and France on one side and Egypt on the other over the control and profits of the Suez Canal. Britain reflexively saw the canal as a "lifeline of empire" even though its remaining imperial interests "east of Suez" were already in the process of liquidation; the Suez Canal Company, which owned and operated the canal, was a private French company with many influential shareholders. Moreover, both European powers were then critically dependent on oil imports from the Gulf. A group of nationalist, pan-Arab officers led by Colonel Gamal Abdel Nasser had seized power in Egypt in 1952, and both the British and their French allies were concerned that Nasser might close the canal to them in a crisis.

Meanwhile Israel was angry at Nasser for allowing Palestinian guerrillas to operate out of the Gaza Strip and Sinai Peninsula, and U.S. secretary of state John Foster Dulles was corralling various countries of the region, including Iraq, Iran and Pakistan, into the Baghdad Pact, yet another alliance to "contain" the Soviet Union. (Pearson described it as his "passion for surrounding the Communist bloc with a ring of mini-NATOs.") What triggered the Suez crisis, in fact, was American displeasure with Nasser's attitude toward the Soviet Union:

> Dulles had begun to think of Egypt as a threat to his policy of containment of Soviet Russia, rather than as a people struggling to be free from British imperialism. The matter came to a head over the issue of help to build the Aswan high dam.
>
> *"Mike": Memoirs, vol. 2*

Washington, afraid that the Egyptians would seek aid from the Soviet Union for their ambitious plan to dam the Nile at Aswan, offered to help finance the project. Nasser accepted the offer but remained friendly with Moscow, recognized Red China and kept up a stream of propaganda insisting that the Arabs ought to be creating an alliance against Israel, not the Russians—so Dulles suddenly announced in July of 1956 that the United States would withdraw its support of the dam. The Soviet Union, seizing the opportunity that the West had created, said it would give "favourable and friendly consideration" to any economic aid that Egypt might ask for. The Aswan High Dam was eventually built with Soviet aid (and Egypt did not catch Marxism or join the Warsaw Pact as a result), but President Nasser was furious: "Let [the Americans] choke with rage," he said, and nationalized the Suez Canal. He promised to compensate the shareholders, but his aim was to finance the dam with the tolls from the canal, which meant that they would probably have a long wait for their money.

Britain, under the Conservative government of Sir Anthony Eden, was incensed. "We believe that we should seize this opportunity of putting the Canal under proper international control," said Eden—and in a cretinous outburst of late-imperial machismo, Britain began conspiring secretly with France and Israel for a surprise attack on Egypt. Lester Pearson, anxious to stop Britain from doing something criminally foolish, tried to have the Suez crisis discussed at NATO meetings without much success, and he also tried directly to talk the British down off their high horse. It seemed as if they were listening, but while London was sending reassuring telegrams to Ottawa and the other Dominion capitals, the secret talks with the French and the Israelis about a surprise attack on Egypt were continuing at a "safe house" outside Paris.

Israel's tanks invaded the Sinai Peninsula on October 29, while its air force destroyed the Egyptian air force on the ground. As prearranged with the Israelis, the British and the French issued an ultimatum the next day calling for a ceasefire: both sides, they demanded, should withdraw ten miles from the canal. If the ultimatum was not accepted within twelve hours, Anglo-French forces would land in Egypt, ostensibly to keep the canal traffic moving. Since the canal was 193 kilometres from the Israeli frontier, this would effectively leave the entire Sinai Peninsula under Israeli occupation (which was to be Israel's reward for giving Britain and France a pretext to invade Egypt).

Not surprisingly, the Egyptian government rejected the ultimatum. (The Israelis accepted it, of course, on condition that the Egyptians also accept.) On October 31 the British and the French began to bomb selected targets along the canal, and Canada received a secret message from Anthony Eden asking for Canada's diplomatic support. Prime Minister St. Laurent's reaction was sheer outrage. "I had never before seen him in such a state of controlled anger," Pearson wrote afterward. "I had never seen him in a state of any kind of anger. He threw me the telegram and said 'What do you think of this?'"

Although St. Laurent had no proof at this point that Britain and France had actually plotted the war in secret alliance with the Israelis, he replied at once to Eden saying that the Canadian government did not believe that the Israeli action was justified, and that neither was the Anglo-French decision to send troops to the Canal Zone. The Canadian government also stopped the shipment of arms (including Sabre Jets) to Israel immediately. All the usual suspects promptly emitted the statutory cries of outrage. The Liberal government's decision not to say "Ready, aye, ready" when Britain was at war caused a great deal of fulmination in certain English Canadian circles, while others saw Pearson's reluctance to brand Britain and France as aggressors as weakness. And the Americans were so furious at having been deceived by Britain and France that President Eisenhower was refusing even to speak to Eden on the phone.

At the United Nations, the Security Council was deadlocked both over Suez (British and French vetoes) and the carnage in Hungary (a Soviet veto). But the Anglo-French military arrangements were almost as arthritic as the thinking behind them: their naval task force had still not got their troops ashore on the canal. "It was an amazing miscalculation of forces and circumstances," said Pearson; "the landings hardly seemed much of an improvement over Gallipoli." In fact the British were getting cold feet: Ottawa learned that Eden was planning to ask the United Nations to take over the task of separating Israel and Egypt, in whose war, according to the cover story, Britain and France were intervening to protect the Suez Canal. "If the UN were willing to take over the physical task of maintaining peace, no one would be better pleased than we," Eden told the British House of Commons. Pearson saw his opportunity, and grabbed it with both hands.

I was with Mr. Pearson at the time in New York. What was on his mind was how on earth to get our dear British and French friends out of a mess, and in particular how to prevent the war from spreading, so that the real purpose of peacekeeping was not the fulfilment of a Canadian ambition.

At the same time it did suit us. . . . It came at a time when we were wondering about our place in the world, more and more concerned about being part of an alliance run largely by the major power, and it was comfortable and comforting to feel that there was something we could do. . . . Something, of course, that the Americans were quite happy for us to do, but they couldn't do themselves.

John Holmes, External Affairs, 1943–60

What Pearson had to do was get enough UN members to agree to his idea for interposing a UN peacekeeping force between the Egyptians and the Israelis (instead of an uninvited Anglo-French force with ulterior motives) before Britain and France were condemned as aggressors. He also had to present it in a way that allowed Britain and France to save face, for otherwise they would block any attempts at intervention by the United Nations. By November 2 Pearson had Canadian cabinet support for his proposal, including the idea of contributing a Canadian contingent to the UN force. Drumming up support within the United Nations took a lot of effort, however, and there were ominous signs of dissension within the Commonwealth: Australia and New Zealand had already come out in support of Britain while India, Pakistan and Ceylon were attacking Britain violently. The Commonwealth was about to divide on racial lines, and Canada was also splitting: the Conservatives felt that Canada should side with Britain.

By now it was also becoming clear that if the war escalated, Britain and France would be outgunned. The Soviet Union was threatening to use nuclear weapons to stop the invasion if necessary, and the United States had not promised to support Britain and France against any such action unless it occurred on NATO territory—which meant, in effect, that Israel and the Anglo-French forces on the canal were fair game for Soviet nuclear weapons. On the night of November 4, while the United Nations was still discussing Pearson's resolution, British infantry began landing at Port Said behind a curtain of naval shellfire, while French paratroops landed at the northern entrance to the canal. During the attack, Egyptian blockships were sunk in the canal, closing it for many months.

Soon afterward the Canadian resolution was adopted by the UN General Assembly, but there remained the practical problems of finding troops for the UN force and sending them there. It soon became obvious that none of the great powers was acceptable. The ideal solution might have been to include only troops from the non-aligned nations in the "UN Emergency Force," but too few of the non-aligned countries had appropriate forces available and the means to transport them to the Middle East quickly. Besides, Canada had earned itself a place on the team: it had been a Canadian idea. Indeed, UN secretary-general Dag Hammarskjöld felt that a Canadian, General E.L.M. "Tommy" Burns, would make a good commander for the force. "I'd been out there [in Palestine] as Chairman of the Truce Supervision outfit," Burns later explained, "and as I hadn't done anything very wrong Mr Hammarskjold apparently recommended me to go ahead. Nobody else was competing for it: one man who'd been in the job before had been assassinated [Count Bernadotte of Sweden was murdered by Israeli terrorists while acting as UN mediator in the Arab-Israeli war of 1948], so it wasn't really a top desirability."

Unfortunately for Pearson, the Canadian contingent was not welcome in Egypt. The regiment Canada planned to send was the Queen's Own Rifles from Calgary. As if the name weren't bad enough (the Egyptians had just been fighting the other Queen's Own Rifles, a British regiment in the invading force), the Canadian uniforms looked very British, and President Nasser objected that this would be confusing for

Egyptian soldiers. So General Burns had to tell Ottawa that Canadian infantry were not acceptable to Egypt, although Canadian communications specialists and other technical personnel would be welcome.

"What we needed was the First East Kootenay Anti-Imperialistic Rifles," Pearson mused, but although he could see the humour of the situation it was this Egyptian "insult" to Canada and to its British traditions that caught the public's imagination. It was much more exciting than interminable UN wranglings in language that nobody understood: Pearson, in the view of the Tories and many other Canadians, had let down the Commonwealth and embarrassed the military. It turned out in the end that the highly trained Canadian communications specialists were exactly what General Burns needed: he had lots of infantry, but desperately needed efficient administration and communications. But national honour demanded something more than a "typewriter army," or so the opposition said.

During the debate in Parliament on November 26, 1956 John Diefenbaker, the leader of the opposition, bitterly condemned the government for failing to support Britain. St. Laurent forthrightly replied that he agreed with the UN resolution that blamed the Israelis, the French and the British for "having taken the law into their own hands. . . . The era when the supermen of Europe could govern the whole world . . . is coming pretty close to an end." The prime minister was quite right, but this statement merely added fuel to the Conservative fire. The fact that the United States was also condemning the British only made matters worse, and the Egyptian rejection of the Queen's Own Rifles was intolerable.

It was a final curtain call for the old pro-British instinct in English Canadians: to the next generation the sentiment would be largely meaningless. But it was also the first sign of hope that Canada and the rest of the world had not completely forgotten what they'd invented the United Nations for. It couldn't stop the great powers when they ran amok, or even the lesser powers—but the United Nations could provide the great powers with a face-saving way out when they got frightened of the consequences of their actions, and it could actually make the smaller countries stop fighting if it had the backing of the great powers. The peacekeeping force that was sent to Egypt bore no resemblance to the 200,000-man UN standing army Pearson had envisaged ten years before, but it was a more credible sign of life and promise than the League of Nations had ever shown.

Trying to create an international rule of law, and persuading states steeped in a tradition of international anarchy dozens of centuries old to accept the restraints of that law voluntarily, are tasks that will take a very long time to accomplish. But there has been progress: the principle is now universally accepted that invasion is an illegal act, and that any territory or advantages gained by it are inadmissible. And ever since Pearson's brilliant piece of legerdemain in 1956, there have always been multinational UN peacekeeping forces in various of the world's trouble spots. They rarely solve basic problems, but they save some lives and win some time, and they are a tangible down payment on the promise that the world's governments will one day accept their collective responsibility for its future. Although Canadians felt virtuous about peacekeeping, however, they had had enough of the Liberals after more than twenty years of them: in June 1957 they voted in John Diefenbaker. Six months later, Lester Pearson was awarded the Nobel Peace Prize.

All my adult life has been spent . . . in an atmosphere of international conflict, of fear and insecurity. As a soldier I survived World War I when most of my comrades did not. As a civilian during the Second War, I was exposed to danger in circumstances which removed any distinction between man in and out of uniform [the London blitz]. And I have lived since—as you have—in a period of cold war, during which we have ensured, by our achievements in the science and technology of destruction, that a third act in this tragedy of war will result in the peace of extinction. I have, therefore, had compelling reason, and some opportunity, to think about peace, to ponder over our failures since 1914 to establish it, and to shudder at the possible consequences if we fail.

Lester B. Pearson accepting the Nobel Peace Prize, Oslo,

December 11, 1957

By 1957 the alliance system was virtually complete: even the two Germanys were included in it. The Soviet suppression of the Hungarian revolt had shown that the scope for reform in Eastern Europe did not extend, at least in the strategically important countries, to any kind of non-alignment, and also that the blocs now recognized each other's borders as permanent: NATO did not lift a finger to help the Hungarians. The industrialized world was frozen in the pattern of 1956 for the next three decades, trapped in a time warp, waiting for the next world war to arrive. And while a succession of peacekeeping missions—in the Congo, in the Middle East, in Cyprus—allowed Canadians to feel they had a distinctive and somehow more "peaceful" role in the world, at least 90 percent of Canada's soldiers and an even higher proportion of its military spending were always devoted to the purposes of its Cold War alliances, NATO and NORAD.

THE THEORY AND PRACTICE
OF NUCLEAR DETERRENCE

Thus far the chief purpose of our military establishment has been
to win wars. From now on its chief purpose must be to avert them.
It can have almost no other useful purpose.

Bernard Brodie, 1946

The Absolute Weapon

THE ONLY SANE STRATEGY FOR DEALING WITH THE IMMENSE AND
irreversible change wrought in warfare by the invention of nuclear
weapons was "deterrence," and that strategy was defined and elaborated
by a small group of American civilian academics within six months of
the destruction of Hiroshima and Nagasaki by U.S. atomic bombs in
August 1945. The leading figure was a young scholar who had just
joined the Institute for International Studies at Yale University, Bernard
Brodie. He brought two key insights to the table. One, fairly obvious,
was that there could be no defence against these terrible weapons,
because at least a few bombers would always get through, and a few
would be too many. British defences against the German V-1 cruise

missiles that had been aimed at London in the previous year had managed to shoot down 97 out of 101 V-1's on their single best day, but if the four that made it through had carried atomic bombs, London survivors would not have considered the record good.

Brodie's other insight was that there was a limited number of targets in any country that were worth using a nuclear weapon on: mainly cities and military bases of various kinds. Once those had been destroyed, additional nuclear weapons conferred no additional advantage. "If 2,000 bombs in the hands of either party is enough to destroy entirely the economy of the other, the fact that one side has 6,000 and the other 2,000 will be of relatively small significance."

In two conferences in September and November 1945 and in many private discussions and arguments, Brodie and a small group of like-minded colleagues built on these two concepts and arrived at the necessary conclusion: that military victory in total war was no longer possible, and that the only sensible policy was deterrence. Actually attacking an enemy with nuclear weapons would be pointless, since each side "must fear retaliation, [and] the fact that it destroys the opponent's cities some hours or even days before its own are destroyed may avail it little." The only condition required to guarantee stable mutual deterrence and the avoidance of a nuclear war was that each country disperse its nuclear-capable bombers in such a way (perhaps even storing them underground) that they could not be destroyed in a surprise attack. (Much later, in a world of "hardened" missile silos and missiles made mobile and invisible by putting them in submarines, this became known as a "secure second-strike capability.")

And there it was: nuclear strategy, complete and irrefutable. Bernard Brodie and his colleagues published their conclusions in 1946 as *The Absolute Weapon: Atomic Power and World Order*, and after that there was not much left to say about how a nuclear-armed world would have to work. By 1985 it was the way the nuclear-armed world actually did work. But in practice it took quite a while to get there, because the world of the late 1940s was not a nuclear-armed world. It was a conventionally-armed world with one nuclear-weapons power in it: the United States. In such a world, nuclear weapons were eminently usable, as Hiroshima had just demonstrated.

As the sole possessor of nuclear weapons on the planet, the United States was free to adopt a strategy of "massive retaliation" rather than match the Soviet Union in conventional weapons, and the Western Europeans were free to depend on the U.S. nuclear monopoly for their defence as well. Even after a great war in which the indiscriminate bombing of civilians had played a large part in the Allied strategy, there was something horrific about this doctrine, but it was undeniably cheaper than maintaining mass armies (including a huge American army) in Western Europe.

> The theory was that as soon as the other side established beyond a
> doubt that they were invading, you then let loose the American stra-
> tegic arm and blasted, incinerated, irradiated enough of the people
> on the other side to make them stop doing what they were doing,
> whatever it was. Well, that was the raving of a feverish child, but I
> lost a lot of friends by saying this, particularly among the airmen.
>
> General Sir John Hackett, former commander,
> NATO Northern Army Group

In theory, the United States should have had to abandon massive retaliation soon after the Soviet Union tested its own atomic weapon in 1949, but in fact the heyday of the strategy still lay ahead of it. Partly this was just because of the greater wealth and bigger production facilities for nuclear weapons of the United States, which allowed it to maintain a huge numerical superiority in the things. In 1949, when the Soviet Union had precisely one bomb, the United States had 235. In 1955, when the United States had 3,200 bombs, the Soviet Union had perhaps 300. By 1962, the year of the Cuban crisis, the United States had a preposterous 30,000 nuclear weapons (most of them only useful for "bouncing the rubble," as one critic put it)—but the Soviet Union had at least a couple of thousand, which met Brodie's criterion for being sufficient to destroy the opposing country. So at this point, at last, Brodie's theory of mutual deterrence should have been fully applicable, and any thought of using nuclear weapons as an instrument of policy should have been abandoned by both sides. But there was one further hurdle to cross: could the things be reliably delivered on the enemy targets.

For Strategic Air Command, it was never a problem. From the very beginning of the Cold War, its bomber bases encircled the Soviet Union in Western and Southern Europe, the Middle East and Asia, only a few hours' flight time from Soviet cities and bases. But the Soviet Union had no overseas bases, and its bombers at first did not have the range to reach the United States at all. By the mid-1950s it did have some planes that could attack the United States by flying across the Arctic Ocean— but the U.S. Strategic Air Command reckoned it had a solution for that threat that would keep the massive retaliation strategy alive.

> I have heard this thought [of the U.S. never launching a pre-emp-tive nuclear attack] stated many times, and it sounds very fine. However, it is not in keeping with United States history. Just look and note who started the Revolutionary War, the War of 1812, the Indian Wars and the Spanish-American War. I want to make it clear that I am not advocating a preventive war; however, I believe that if the U.S. is pushed into the corner far enough we would not hesitate to strike first.
>
> General Curtis LeMay, commander,
> U.S. Strategic Air Command, 1954

Curtis LeMay, as commander of SAC and later head of the Air Staff, controlled virtually all aspects of U.S. planning for nuclear war from the late 1940s to the early 1960s. He never wavered in his convic-tion that the United States should and would strike first in a nuclear war.

In fact, as he once told a group of SAC pilots, he "could not imagine a circumstance under which the United States would go second." The technical phrase is "first strike"—and in practice the United States Air Force was always and exclusively committed to first strike during the first fifteen years of the American-Soviet confrontation.

It all followed perfectly logically from the doctrine of massive retaliation. By 1955 SAC had almost two thousand nuclear weapons—the rest of the U.S. armed forces had to make do with a mere thousand—and its war plan (it only had one) involved destroying at least three-quarters of the population in 118 Soviet cities. It estimated Soviet casualties at around sixty million. And it was so confident of its ability to crush the Soviet Union that it did not worry at all about the possibility of a Soviet nuclear attack on North America. The public were pumped full of stories about the threat of a Soviet surprise attack in order to maintain their support for the enormous defence budgets of the time, but nobody in the know really believed in the possibility of a nuclear "Pearl Harbor."

General Curtis LeMay certainly didn't. In 1955, for example, an academic strategist called Albert Wohlstetter tried to persuade the SAC commander that his bombers could be destroyed on the ground in a Soviet surprise attack unless he developed policies for dispersing them and built shelters for them. General LeMay was profoundly unimpressed, and gently confided to one of Wohlstetter's young assistants that SAC already had a policy on shelters. "Really?" the eager young man asked. "What is it?" "Piss on shelters," replied General LeMay.

LeMay wasn't worried because he knew that if anybody's bombers were going to be caught on the ground, it would be the Soviets'. And that was the unspoken context in which the whole saga of North American air defence developed and Canada got dragged into the world of nuclear strategies: NORAD was designed not to cope with a Soviet surprise attack but to deal with a ragged retaliation by the relatively few Soviet bombers that survived an American first strike.

CHAPTER 10

THE SPACE BETWEEN

If you look at our position on a global projection, you will see that
we are the land, or rather the sky, where the exchange will take
place . . . where the battle that consists of an exchange of inter–
continental missiles carrying nuclear warheads will be fought,
and we are obliged to foresee that we would be the victims whether
we were involved or not.

Hon. Léo Cadieux, minister of
national defence, 1967–70

CANADA WAS NEVER STRATEGIC TERRITORY THAT MATTERED IN
the great-power game before 1945—and it isn't now—but for a brief
period, from the late 1950s to the late 1960s, we really did matter, because
Canada lay on the shortest air route between the Soviet Union and the
United States. Indeed, in terms of aircraft ranges at the time, Canadian
airspace was the only non-stop route between the two countries.

You'd look up and you'd see a plane of some sort going overhead
with a red star on it. The Americans would bring the planes up as

far as Edmonton, and the Russians would come, I presume, over the Pole practically, and the planes would be handed over to them.

A large proportion of the Russian planes were piloted by women. It was quite a sight to see them on the street in their uniforms—of course they were tremendously bulky uniforms, because they would be going back over the Pole. And an awful lot of vodka suddenly appeared in the town.

Naomi Radford, Edmonton

The United States and the Soviet Union were allies during the Second World War, and the planes flying over Edmonton with Soviet markings were American-built fighters and bombers on their way to serve in the Soviet Air Force. But it was already clear that something was happening to Canada's strategic geography. As early as April 1944 Major-General Maurice Pope of the Canadian Joint Staff Mission in Washington was warning Ottawa:

> Sometime in the future the United States, from their (ideological) dislike of Russia, may find their relations with that country somewhat strained. . . . In such circumstances our position would be a difficult one. To the Americans the defence of the United States is continental defence, and nothing that I can think of will ever drive that idea out of their heads. Should, then, the United States go to war with Russia they would look to us to make common cause with them and, as I judge their public opinion, they would brook no delay.

A month later Mackenzie King's government set up a "Working Committee on Post-Hostilities Problems." Its initial assumption was that there would be at least ten years of peace between the United States and the Soviet Union, but General Pope warned urgently from Washington that the U.S. armed forces did not share that assumption.

The Pentagon had plans for a very large postwar military establishment, Pope pointed out, and it would need congressional support to get it. That meant that the Pentagon needed an external threat big enough to justify such a huge force—and although the Soviet Union was still an American ally in 1944, it was the only plausible candidate for a future enemy that filled the bill.

If the Canadian government rejected the view that a Soviet-American confrontation was imminent, General Pope warned, the U.S. armed forces would be extremely unhappy, for if a persuasive Canadian counter-argument "ever reached the ears of Congress, the hopes [the Pentagon] now cherished and planned to achieve would be dashed against the rocks." The report on "Post-War Canadian Defence Relations with the United States" concluded:

> Canada, lying across the shortest air routes from either Europe or Asia, has now become of more direct strategic significance to the United States. . . . In the circumstances, the United States may be expected to take an active interest in Canadian defence preparations in the future. Moreover, that interest may be expressed with an absence of the tact and restraint customarily employed by the United Kingdom in putting forward defence proposals . . . . [and] the pressure on Canada to maintain defences at a higher level than might seem necessary from the point of view of purely Canadian interests might be very strong.
>
> Department of External Affairs, January 23, 1945

First impressions are often best, and External Affairs' view of Canada's new strategic situation before everybody there had been marinated in Cold War assumptions for a decade or so are probably more reliable than the views held by the same people in the 1960s. Canada's real strategic situation in 1960 was just about what had been forecast in 1945—but by then all sorts of nuances of justification and rationalization had been added to the basic description of Canada's strategic dilemma, in a perfectly human attempt to demonstrate that what had happened was also what should have happened or at least what had to happen.

By 1946 Mackenzie King was warning his cabinet that the American bases and facilities in the north must be bought out by the Canadian government as soon as possible because "the long-range policy of the Americans was to absorb Canada." It was duly done, but it made no difference to what was really happening: King was barking up the wrong tree. The time of the homesteaders was long past, and the postwar generation of Americans was no longer interested in the physical possession of Canada's territory. What they wanted now was the free use of Canada for strategic purposes—in a nuclear war.

Canada "Another Belgium" in U.S. Air Bases Proposal
Washington Insists Dominion's Northern Frontier be Fortified
"Atomic Age Maginot Line" is Feared

Financial Post headlines, June 29, 1946

In November 1945, only three months after the war's end—long before there was an open split between the United States and the Soviet Union—the American military representatives on the Permanent Joint Board on Defence (PJBD) brought up the question of a war with Russia. What they wanted was a Canadian agreement on continental air defence. The American air force experts reckoned that by 1950 the "enemy" (the Soviet Union) would be in a position to launch an air attack on North America, and therefore the two countries must cooperate in creating a network of early-warning radar stations and fighter bases in Canada, as far north as possible from populated areas. However, it turned out in the end that the American airmen on the PJBD were not actually expressing U.S. government policy. They had just been overstating the case for continental air defence in the hope of getting a Canadian commitment, which they could then use ("our allies demand it") in order to further the U.S. Air Force's interests in the perennial inter-service battle for resources in the Pentagon.

In fact, Canada's awkward geographical position as "the space between" the Soviet Union and the United States took time to mature into a real strategic concern. In the 1940s neither the Americans nor the Russians had bombers capable of flying literally over the Pole. For the moment all the Americans wanted was staging bases through which their nuclear bombers could pass on their way to their forward deployment bases in Europe, the Middle East or the Far East, from which they would then fly onward to obliterate the Soviet Union. In that context, the only foreign base in North America that really inter-ested the Pentagon was Goose Bay in Labrador, which a U.S. Air Force spokesman described to a top secret meeting in Ottawa in late 1946 as "the most important all-round strategic air base in the Western Hemisphere."

However, Newfoundland did not become a Canadian province until 1949. So far as Canada's own territory was involved, Canadian governments faced with regular American requests for the use of Canadian airspace by Strategic Air Command (SAC) bombers carrying nuclear weapons continued to insist on a meticulous respect for Canadian sovereignty. Even after the increased range of the new American B-52 bombers made it possible, by the early 1950s, for Strategic Air Command to fly from its bases in the United States directly to targets in the Soviet Union, Washington felt no need for anything more than "Meetings of Consultation" so far as SAC was concerned. If war ever came, either the Canadians would instantly give SAC's bombers permission to fly north across Canada on their way to bomb the Soviet Union—or they would go anyway, and Washington would sort out the diplomatic niceties afterward.

But in 1949 the Soviets tested their first nuclear weapon, and by the early fifties they were starting to build bombers that could cross Canadian territory and hit the United States. If the Americans wanted to create a defence against them, they would have to coordinate it with the Canadians in advance, which meant negotiating some sort of formal agreement between the two countries. They did not, however, want to explain the strategic context of North American air defence too bluntly to civilians—especially foreign civilians—for fear of offending their delicate sensibilities.

———

I went to Air Defence Command in 1951, and by then the early [Canadian-U.S.] talks had taken place—the general structure of the warning system, the utilization [of Canadian airspace] by American aircraft, all those items were discussed and agreements reached. From then on it was really refining those agreements: knowing what could be done from a given base and that sort of thing. After that it was not a matter of principle; it was a matter of mechanics.

Air Vice Marshal Claire Annis, RCAF

It may have been only a matter of mechanics for the RCAF, which was finding an exciting new role for itself in North American air defence, and powerful new friends in the air defence establishment of the U.S. Air Force. But as far as the Canadian government was concerned, no questions of principle had been decided; there had not even been any discussions about the subject at the political level. However, after the newly elected Republican administration of President Dwight D. Eisenhower took office in early 1953, a series of sensational leaks about the alleged inadequacies of North American air defence began to appear in the American press. Canada's defence minister, Brooke Claxton, suspected the worst.

The reason for this flood of propaganda is not so much the increased fear of attack by Russia as growing fear of the hostility of the electors when it becomes apparent that the Republican Party's promises to balance the budget and cut taxes while strengthening their defences has not got the slightest chance in the world of being carried out. . . . Apparently the Administration has it in mind that the anger of the electorate may be flooded out in a wave of fear of atomic attack.

Brooke Claxton to Prime Minister St. Laurent,
September 23, 1953

But there was more behind the growing interest in North American air defence than just domestic American politics. In both the United States and Canada, the air forces were becoming the politically dominant services, and they cooperated closely in the task of extracting money from their respective governments.

The 1950s was the golden decade of the Royal Canadian Air Force. In 1951 fewer than a third of Canada's servicemen wore light blue, and the RCAF got around 42 percent of the money allocated to the armed forces. By 1955 Canada had become the only country in the world where the air force had more people than the army, and as the spending on new fighter aircraft soared, the air force budget overtook those of the other two services combined. All this gave Canada's airmen a predominant voice in the Department of National Defence in Ottawa, and the issue where it counted most was the emerging American plan for a unified command that ignored the U.S.-Canadian border and put all air defences in North America under U.S. control: NORAD.

The talks leading to the creation of NORAD took place mostly on the inter-service network, and the fact that it was to be a purely bilateral alliance didn't bother the Canadian Chiefs of Staff: they saw only the operational and career benefits of being integrated into the U.S. defence structure. However, the evolving shape of NORAD started alarm bells ringing at External Affairs.

> My reaction as a NATO desk officer [at External] was to see dangers in this for Canada. . . . I mean a NORAD outside NATO meant that . . . we were dealing perforce with only one partner, and that in a framework of disparity of power that could not in any way be modified. I raised the question of associating NORAD in some way with NATO, if not bringing it within NATO, but that did not prove possible.
>
> John Halstead, External Affairs, 1946–82

In February 1956 the U.S. Joint Chiefs of Staff asked Canada its views on the integration of all air defences in North America. The RCAF then swung into action, providing favourable reports to the Canadian Chiefs of Staff Committee, which approved the proposal in February 1957. All they needed now was political approval.

It is easy enough to see why the Canadian airmen wanted a joint air defence command: access to better equipment, deeper military secrets and lots of jobs in the command structure of a major league organization. But the Strategic Air Command was the dominant branch of the U.S. Air Force; it was wholly offensive in its outlook, and it jealously guarded its position against rival branches of the air force. Why did it let continental air defence grow so important that it required a joint air defence command and a bilateral alliance with the Canadians? There was a perfectly good strategic reason, but it was a bit too embarrassing to discuss in public. North American air defence was originally sold to the American public, and later to the Canadian government, as a necessary measure to protect North American cities from a Soviet surprise attack. In fact, however, NORAD in the fifties was inextricably linked to American nuclear first-strike doctrines.

———

In December 1949, only months after the first Soviet nuclear test, the Pentagon informed Ottawa that the Soviet Union would probably have 150 atomic bombs available for delivery on North America within five years. By the time the mid-fifties actually rolled around, the U.S. Joint Chiefs of Staff were predicting that a Soviet attack on North America in 1960 would dispose of 750 heavy bombers, followed by 700 medium bombers. It was quite obvious that no air defence system could cope with such numbers in the nuclear age, so why bother? But the air force did bother, because the planners didn't really expect to face an attack on that scale at all.

> Nobody saw a thousand-bomber raid coming against North America, but it could be big enough that some of them would get through unless it was an air-tight defence.
>
> Air Chief Marshal Frank Miller, RCAF,
> vice-chief of the Air Staff, 1953

All air defence works by attrition: it is not like a castle wall that keeps out all intruders until it is breached. There is no wall, but merely a system that must seek out and shoot down the attackers one by one. In practice that means that some proportion of the attackers, however small, will almost always get through: the best interception rate that anybody ever achieved in practice against mass bomber raids during the Second World War was around 10 percent. The air defence planners of the early fifties were promising a breathtaking 70 percent kill rate, but that would still not have counted as a success now that each bomber was carrying nuclear weapons. Even against the 1949 U.S. estimate of 150 Soviet bombers, a 70 percent kill rate would have meant that forty or fifty bombers would have got through in a surprise attack, and even if they carried only one bomb each, the results would have devastated the United States.

337

However, it would be quite a different matter if an American first strike destroyed most of the Soviet bomber force on the ground, and if there was a comprehensive radar network and hundreds of fighters in North America to deal with the Soviet bombers that survived. The real problem was not how to deal with a Soviet surprise attack, which was utterly improbable, given the balance of forces. It was how to stop an attempted "revenge from the grave" by a dozen or so Soviet bombers that had escaped destruction on the ground.

Even if the United States did not launch a deliberate first strike against the Soviet Union, SAC was totally confident of being able to pre-empt a Soviet attack. As General LeMay privately told a senior American official early in 1957, the U.S. had aircraft flying secret missions over the Soviet Union every hour of the day, collecting radio intelligence that would give him ample warning of any Soviet preparations for a surprise attack. "If I see that the Russians are amassing their planes for an attack, I'm going to knock the shit out of them before they take off the ground," he explained.

"But General LeMay," the official protested, "that's not national policy." "I don't care," said LeMay. "It's my policy. That's what I'm going to do."

The undeniable arithmetic of air defence kill ratios should have made it obvious that NORAD was a total waste of money unless the number of Soviet attackers was small—and it would only be small enough if most Soviet bombers had already been eliminated by an American first strike. Moreover, the inflated U.S. Air Force intelligence estimates of Soviet bomber strength, concocted to justify an ever-expanding American bomber force, ignored the fact that the Soviets had decided to skip the stage of building up a large bomber force and move straight on to the next technological stage: intercontinental ballistic missiles (ICBMs).

Our potential enemy—our principal, our most powerful, our most dangerous enemy—was so far away from us that we couldn't have reached him with our air force. Only by building up a nuclear missile force could we keep the enemy from unleashing war.

Nikita Khrushchev,
Khrushchev Remembers

The Russians built only enough long-range bombers to have some sort of strategic insurance policy if their missile programme failed utterly: their "Long-Range Aviation" amounted to 145 bombers in 1960, and peaked at 195 in 1965. Meanwhile, most of their resources went into developing missiles—against which NORAD provided no defence whatever. Although the actual numbers of strategic weapons and aircraft in the superpower arsenals were closely guarded secrets in the 1950s, it would not have been beyond the wit of a moderately competent Canadian intelligence officer to draw the appropriate conclusions about U.S. strategy simply from the facts that were available to him—including the conclusion that NORAD would soon become redundant.

> Traditionally, no strategic thinking was done in Canada. We were doers but not thinkers. In the Second World War we provided the fourth biggest force on the Allied side, yet we had no influence whatsoever in the conduct of the war because we did not think independently, strategically. And here again we simply took over something which was worked out elsewhere.
>
> John Gellner, Canadian defence analyst

The secret of NORAD was that it just might have succeeded in protecting the United States from Soviet nuclear weapons between about 1957 (when it went into operation) and 1963 (when enough Soviet ICBMs became operational to make anti-bomber defences quite pointless). But it would only have worked during that period if the United States had struck first and destroyed most Soviet bombers on the ground. The darker secret was that it would have been Canada that paid the price for this success, which would be measured by how many of the surviving Soviet bombers were shot down over Canada before they reached the United States—and the defending planes would use nuclear missiles to destroy the attacking bombers (which would all be carrying nuclear weapons themselves).

Few if any Canadian military officers or politicians living in the 1950s would have described the situation in these terms. The categories of thought, the justifying myths and the unmentionable topics were different then: the past is a foreign country. Yet just beneath the surface, many Canadians did suspect the truth about the role Canada was being asked to play: that of a nuclear battlefield whose sacrifice might save the United States. That was why NORAD caused a crisis that eventually toppled a Canadian government.

There is no evidence that the Canadian Chiefs of Staff ever passed such an analysis on to the government. Knowing what NORAD was really about might not have enabled the Canadian government to resist U.S. pressure to join, but it would at least have given Ottawa some ammunition to argue with. Instead, the government was left in ignorance—while the armed forces enthusiastically clamoured to be allowed to join NORAD.

Even army officers like General Charles Foulkes, the chairman of the Chiefs of Staff Committee, were thoroughly seduced by their access to American secrets. The price they had to pay was an almost uncritical adoption of American views on defence policy and priorities, and many of them paid it gladly. But this made it hard for the government to exercise proper control over Canadian defence policy, because mere civilians did not have access to the same secrets. For example, when External Affairs officer George Ignatieff was told to put together an analysis of Canada's new strategic dilemmas for the prime minister that could be made available to parliament and the public, he went to General Foulkes for information—and encountered a stone wall.

He said he wasn't going to be told by eggheads from External Affairs how to plan joint defence, nor could he satisfy the Pentagon that the release of this kind of information would be without peril. And so we were absolutely stalled.. . . .

The difficulties I was encountering, of course, were reported to the Prime Minister and the Secretary of State, and the clerk of the Privy Council, Bob Bryce, called a meeting at which he hoped to resolve the difficulties, but General Foulkes was absolutely adamant. What he said, in fact, was that the real security of Canada depended on his personal relation with "Rad and Brad"—that was Admiral Radford, who was Chairman of the Joint Chiefs of Staff in Washington, and General Omar Bradley, who was Chief of the General Staff and an old friend of Foulkes from the war.

He said that the information which he derived through that channel personally was what was required for the security of Canada.. . . . And that was the end of that particular effort. Soon after that I was sent off to Yugoslavia, out of the way.

George Ignatieff, External Affairs
ambassador to Yugoslavia, 1956–58

So the discussions continued between the military professionals, delineating a joint command in which an American officer in Colorado Springs (with a Canadian deputy) would exercise operational control over all air defence activities in both the United States and Canada. By the time the NORAD agreement was ready to be passed over to the politicians for signature, however, the St. Laurent government was planning an early election—which, to its considerable surprise, it lost. So the NORAD treaty was lying in wait in July 1957 when the new Conservative government took office, led by John Diefenbaker.

It was almost a generation since the Conservatives had last been in office. John Diefenbaker had never sat in a cabinet, and he had no experience whatever of foreign affairs. However, he temporarily took over the role of secretary of state for external affairs in addition to his prime-ministerial duties, mainly because he felt a need to master the department in which the new leader of the opposition, Lester Pearson, had had such a distinguished career. But Diefenbaker didn't trust his diplomatic advisers in External Affairs, whom he suspected of being pro-Liberal (if only because they had spent their entire careers working for Liberal governments). And on defence matters, he depended entirely on his defence minister, General George Pearkes.

> General Foulkes had served under General Pearkes, and on the old boy network had intimated to General Pearkes that, you know, this had been under discussion for a long time, that it had gone to the previous [St. Laurent] Cabinet, and that all that was really required was the Prime Minister's signature on something that was regarded as acceptable. He didn't explain that there was some hesitation on the part of the preceding government. I mean it had been to Cabinet, yes, but it had been postponed. But he intimated that it was simply a matter of they were too busy or whatever it was. Anyway, the full implication was not explained.
>
> George Ignatieff, External Affairs, 1940–60

> From the moment I took over, [Foulkes] pressed the urgency of getting a decision. He certainly gave me the impression that it was all tied up by the Liberal government, and promises had been made that it would be signed immediately after the election. . . . I do know that they [the Canadian military] were under almost daily pressure from the military in the United States.
>
> General George Pearkes, VC, minister of national defence, 1957–60

Diefenbaker signed the NORAD agreement on July 24, 1957, only weeks after taking office, apparently without the slightest idea of what it entailed. Foulkes had passed along only just enough information about it to get his agreement, and had done an end run around all the people at External Affairs and elsewhere who might have pointed out its draw-backs and defects to him. Diefenbaker, presumably, thought he was being efficient and decisive.

> Oh hell, I don't even know if he read it. It came out of there so . . . signed so suddenly. We were prepared to make a presentation to cabinet and so on.
> Q. *It just came back signed, sealed and delivered?*
> Yeah.

Air Chief Marshal Frank Miller,
deputy minister of national defence, 1957

There have been a few attempts to turn Prime Minister Diefenbaker into the tragic hero of Canada's lost independence, but that is ludicrous. For one thing, the country's independence was certainly compromised, but it was not really lost. For another, Diefenbaker is nobody's hero: he was a bombastic prairie politico who combined a crude but saleable version of English Canadian nationalism with an unwavering commitment to a Cold War view of the world.

"Dief" never admitted a mistake, had no particular attachment to the truth and suffered from chronic indecisiveness and low-grade paranoia. The image that lingers from his latter days is that of an old-fashioned and rigidly self-righteous man shaking his wattles in muddled indignation. But even though he was dedicated to the struggle against "the Communist evil," he gradually came to doubt both the methods and the motives of his American allies in pursuing this objective, and to regret his early and unconditional surrender of Canadian freedom of action in signing the NORAD agreement. If he cannot be a tragic hero, he can at least serve as a cautionary tale.

Not only did the NORAD agreement commit Diefenbaker's government to a joint command that put the air defence of Canada under American control, with little by way of effective guarantees on consultation. It also effectively committed Canada to follow the United States in putting nuclear weapons onto practically everything that could float, crawl or fly—and, most particularly, onto all the air defence fighters and anti-aircraft missiles that would be used to intercept Soviet bombers over Canada. It took some time for it to sink in, but by 1959 Diefenbaker was beginning to realize that he had been had.

———

It was very traumatic. All of us were fired on a loudspeaker on February the 20th, 1959 at eleven o'clock. The shock of it within the plant was very great.
Q. *Could there ever be another Canadian fighter?*
I would hope that there could never be another.
Syd Young, chief engineer, McDonnell Douglas of Canada Ltd.
(formerly A.V. Roe Canada)

The cancellation of the Avro Arrow in early 1959, with the loss of fourteen thousand Canadian jobs, was the toughest decision that the Diefenbaker government ever took. The all-Canadian fighter project had turned into a monumental problem for the government due to performance difficulties and huge cost overruns, so Diefenbaker was grateful to have an alternative at hand: the pilotless missiles known as Bomarc-Bs that NORAD was planning to deploy in the interceptor role. Diefenbaker was able to point out that Canada had recently agreed to deploy two squadrons of Bomarcs at North Bay, Ontario, and La Macaza, Quebec, which would help to fill the gap left by the cancelled Arrow fighters. And to his dying day he insisted that he didn't know those Bomarcs would be carrying nuclear warheads.

Diefenbaker must have been told, probably a number of times, that the Bomarc-B would only be available with nuclear warheads. (Sometimes, when he didn't want to hear something, he just didn't listen.) But he certainly didn't comprehend what that implied. The warhead intended for use on the Bomarc-B was variously reported to have been five hundred kilotons or one megaton—between twenty-five and fifty times the size of the Hiroshima weapon—and Bomarc was intended to intercept low-flying bombers over Canadian soil. Even a 500-kiloton warhead, exploded at an altitude of a thousand feet, would cause deaths and injuries over an area of 1,200 square miles. In a war, dozens of these huge warheads would have been exploded over the more northerly populated regions of Ontario and Quebec. In the likely event that not every incoming bomber was destroyed in the northern sector of the Bomarcs' 150-mile radius of action, these warheads would probably have been exploded over the more southerly parts of Quebec and Ontario too—and what was true of the Bomarcs was true also of all NORAD's other weapons.

The performance forecasts for radars and interceptors that had been made in the early fifties, when the North American air defence system was planned, had turned out to be overoptimistic. In practice, the only way to ensure a worthwhile kill rate against incoming bombers was to use nuclear warheads that would destroy them even if they missed by a mile or two. The Bomarc-B was strictly nuclear because the Bomarc-A, with a conventional warhead, simply couldn't do the job. American air defence fighters were also being equipped with nuclear-tipped missiles, even though many of the U.S.-based squadrons, charged with the task of intercepting Soviet bombers as far north as possible from American population centres, could barely reach the heavily populated southern fringes of Canada with their limited range of two to four hundred miles. And NORAD expected Canada to equip its own interceptors with nuclear weapons too.

The same process was going on all over the Western alliance: nuclear weapons had become plentiful, and they were being adopted as the solution to every tactical problem. In Europe the Americans were equipping their forces (and those of some of their allies) with "tactical nuclear weapons": bombs for dropping from fighter-bombers, short-range nuclear rockets and nuclear artillery. There were even portable nuclear land mines and a hand-held nuclear bazooka (known, of course, as the "Davy Crockett"). The U.S. Navy was getting nuclear depth-charges and working on nuclear missile-firing submarines, and SAC was getting still more and bigger bombs for its bombers, plus the prospect of ICBMs with nuclear warheads in the near future.

It was the last hurrah of the confident, one-way nuclear "deterrence" of the early postwar era, which was being rapidly undermined by the growth of a real Soviet capability to inflict comparable damage in response. The United States expected Canada to play its full role in nuclearization of the Western alliance both in North America in Europe, and it heard nothing from the Canadian armed forces to suggest that there would be any political difficulties. Nor were there, at first.

In January 1958 the Canadian government opened "exploratory talks" on U.S. requests to arm its fighters at air bases in Newfoundland and Labrador with nuclear-tipped MB-1 missiles, and to store large numbers of high-yield nuclear bombs at Goose Bay for "reflex strikes." (SAC wanted a place to reload American strategic bombers that had already dumped their first cargo of nuclear bombs on the Soviet Union so they could go back immediately and do it again, and Goose Bay was the nearest point in North America to the Soviet targets.) In September 1958 came Ottawa's decision to acquire the Bomarc-Bs (and, by implication, their nuclear warheads). In December that was followed by an agreement to provide the Canadian navy with nuclear depth charges and to equip whatever Canadian interceptor the cancelled Arrow (the USAF eventually sold Canada 66 obsolescent F-101 Voodoos) with MB-1 nuclear missiles.

It was also decided to equip the Canadian army in Europe with "Honest John" short-range nuclear missiles, and in July 1959 the government announced that the RCAF in Europe would be re-equipped with CF-104 Starfighters, whose sole mission would be nuclear strikes into Eastern Europe. They were intended to fit into the evolving strategy of fighting a "limited" nuclear war in Europe instead of (or at least as a prelude to) a full-scale strategic nuclear war.

There was no discussion whatsoever, as I recall, about changing the role of the overseas forces to atomic carriers, because that wasn't in Canada, it wasn't at home here. It didn't pollute Canada with this nasty business—although it put us right in the middle of the bombing business.

Air Chief Marshal Frank Miller, chairman,
Chiefs of Staff Committee, 1960–64

General Foulkes was an excellent man, but. . . . It must have been in 1957. I was on the Directing Staff of the RCAF Staff College here in Toronto and he came and gave a lecture and he said: "We are going along because we want to be in the Big League." The Big League! That's why we got the nuclear weapons.

John Gellner

By mid-1959 there were no fewer than nine different proposals for placing nuclear weapons on Canadian soil or in the hands of the Canadian forces, and half of them had been approved (in principle, at least) by the Canadian government. Everything was proceeding smoothly—and then the tide began to turn.

Should Canadian forces be armed with nuclear weapons? Our own answer is a flat unqualified no. . . . Nothing can justify nuclear war. . . . The first step towards preventing it is to stop planning to wage it.

Maclean's, September 10, 1960

Canada . . . can play a noteworthy role in the efforts for peace and disarmament, but this role would be reduced practically to zero if we were a nuclear satellite of Washington.

Le Devoir, September 23, 1961

In June 1959, the same month Canada made the Starfighter deal, Norman Robertson, just back from two years in Washington as ambassador and now once again undersecretary of state for external affairs, sent Prime Minister Diefenbaker a clipping from the previous month's copy of the British magazine the *Spectator*. The author of the article, Christopher Hollis, argued that the thermonuclear weapons had changed the nature of war: destruction would now be so great that even if the West emerged from a nuclear war as the nominal victor "there is no chance that the pattern of our own national life . . . would still survive when we emerge from it."

Hollis's article went on to argue for nuclear disarmament and a buildup of NATO's conventional forces: in effect, a reversal of the Western decision to rely on cheap nuclear firepower rather than expensive soldiers that had been taken at a time when the West had a near-monopoly of nuclear weapons. There was, after all, no objective reason why the West could not rely on its superior numbers, wealth and technology to deter the Soviet Union with non-nuclear weapons, if it were willing to pay the cost. However, Hollis didn't only want the West to stop threatening to use nuclear weapons against a Soviet conventional attack. He advocated unilateral Western nuclear disarmament—no matter what the Soviets did. And attached to Hollis's article was a memo to Prime Minister Diefenbaker from the undersecretary: "Mr Robertson wishes you to know that his views coincide with those of the author of the article."

Norman Robertson had hitherto held quite orthodox views on the question of nuclear weapons for Canada, but recently they had begun to change. In March 1959, having just been briefed by some External Affairs officers who had visited SAC and NORAD headquarters, he remarked that "the whole philosophy of [nuclear] deterrence had been developed at a time when conditions were vastly different from those existing today. . . . Our minds should be turned instead to the tremendous political effort that needed to be undertaken to avoid the awesome consequences of nuclear warfare."

The Soviet Union, of course, had already been living with the grim prospect of those "awesome consequences" for over a decade. What caused numbers of Canadians to begin questioning the West's nuclear-oriented strategies was the growing probability that the West itself would suffer those same consequences. A policy that had been seen as a regrettable strategic necessity when it implied immolating tens of millions of Soviet citizens became a great deal less acceptable when it also involved the prospect of unstoppable Soviet ICBMs aimed at North America, and millions of Canadians dead. And in June 1959 Robertson got a new minister who shared his thinking: Howard Green.

This was the time when the frozen silence between the two great alliances was hesitantly starting to give way to semi-permanent (if glacially slow) arms control talks—and Howard Green devoted a great deal of time and effort to promoting various proposals to lessen the danger of nuclear war. He insisted that Canada's ability to take a lead on these issues would be undermined if at the same time it was equipping its own forces with nuclear weapons.

> Mr Green was passionately committed to two things. One is that he was against war: he had been a veteran who was wounded in the First World War, and like most people who have seen the horrors of war at first hand he was not a great enthusiast about repeating it for other generations.
>
> The other thing was that he was a tremendous believer in the United Nations. . . . He was not a great enthusiast about NATO, and an essential part of security as he saw it was arms control and disarmament.
>
> George Ignatieff

The great issue during Green's time in office was a nuclear test ban, which was universally seen as the indispensable condition for any other arms control or disarmament measures. And things were falling apart: the moratorium on nuclear tests that had been agreed by the United States, the Soviet Union and Britain in 1958 had not led to a treaty on account of differences about "verification," and the Soviet Union had finally denounced it. In October 1961 the Soviets tested the biggest bomb ever, the "Tsar Bomb"—fifty megatons—and in early 1962 the Americans also began testing again in the atmosphere. But Green never lost heart.

Green felt it necessary to keep up a public facade of optimism which led many to call him naïve, but in fact he was an adroit operator who knew how to exploit Canada's prestige, especially among the non-aligned states, to get proposals on the agenda that could break the logjam. In October 1962, for example, his close ally General E.L M. Burns, Canada's representative on the UN Disarmament Committee, put forward (much against the wishes of the United States) the amendment that finally made a limited test-ban treaty possible: it separated underground tests from all the others, and proposed banning all the rest. And it was Green himself who first brought up, at the eighteen-nation Geneva Disarmament Conference, the idea of a ban on all weapons of mass destruction in outer space. That annoyed the Americans even more, but it too produced a treaty in the end.

The Limited Test Ban Treaty of 1963 and the ban on nuclear weapons in outer space in 1966 are monuments to Howard Green's persistence, and it was quite true that Canada's influence among the neutral countries was very important to these results. But Green's constant argument that Canada should shun nuclear weapons in order to retain its influence among the non-aligned nations was probably deliberately overstated: the Indians and the Egyptians weren't really worried about nuclear warheads on Bomarcs in North Bay, or even slung beneath Starfighters in Germany.

The truth is that Green thought the whole nuclear game was insane, and used any argument he could find to keep Canada out of it. From 1959 on, Canadian defence policy was a battleground in which

External Affairs, under Howard Green and Norman Robertson, fought against the Department of National Defence to win Diefenbaker's support for radically divergent policies, with the nuclear weapons to be acquired from the Americans as the main focus of the argument. Most people in Ottawa still subscribed to the orthodox credo about Western defence policy, but there were a couple of wild cards operating in Green's and Robertson's favour. One was that Diefenbaker, unlike most politicians, had no faith in opinion polls. Instead, he read his mail—and Canadians active in the peace movement wrote him a lot of letters. Diefenbaker became persuaded that an anti-nuclear stance was popular with the Canadian public.

> Dogs know best what to do with polls.
>
> John Diefenbaker, November 1, 1971

The other wild card was Diefenbaker's nationalism. He was not reflexively anti-American, but there were signs of strain even when President Eisenhower was still in office.

> In spite of all the flowery exchanges between "Ike" and Mr. Diefen-baker, he was already brewing up for trouble with the United States because he thought they were getting above themselves: "They think they can lead the world and shove us all around."
>
> Q. *Was there a reason for Mr. Diefenbaker's feelings?*
>
> Well, yes, of course. It was the great moment of American imperi-alism at its height, when they really felt they had the answers to everything in the world, and had dozens of alliances, and were willing to move into any cabbage patch anywhere in the world and fight against Communism or feudalism or anything which didn't go with the American way of life. It was rather overpowering.
>
> Charles Ritchie, ambassador to Washington, 1962–66

It was this coincidental combination of things—Diefenbaker's conviction that there was a powerful groundswell of anti-nuclear feeling in the Canadian public, his growing inclination to resist American pressures on every subject, and a small band of determined partisans of nuclear disarmament at External Affairs headed by Green and Robertson—that inexorably led the Conservative government into confrontation with the Americans over nuclear weapons. And Diefenbaker's legendary capacity for dither, delay and indecision defined Green's and Robertson's tactics for them.

By the time Green became secretary of state for external affairs, it was too late for the government to make a principled rejection of the whole idea of nuclear weapons for Canada: the basic agreements to acquire nuclear weapons systems for the Canadian forces both in Canada and in Europe had almost all been signed. So Green simply produced innumerable objections to the terms of the agreements that had to be negotiated with the Americans for the custody of the nuclear warheads.

> I was given the task of negotiating these agreements. So, working with the people in National Defence and others, we worked out a draft agreement and sent it up to Mr Green and it sat there for six weeks and nothing happened. Finally General Pearkes, who was the Minister of Defence, got hold of Mr. Green and said: "We've got to get moving on this, Howard." And so Mr. Green called me in and said: "This is not tough enough. Go back to the drawing board."
>
> And over the loud objections of National Defence, we went back to the drawing board, and the same performance was repeated at least three times. By then I had drawn the conclusion that Mr. Green had no intention of having such an agreement concluded. At that point I decided this was no place for me, so I succeeded in negotiating my way to another assignment .
>
> Q. *Were the armed forces very upset by all this?*
> I think they just sort of despaired, you know . . . . They eventually

reached the sort of numbed stage where they felt they would do anything they had to to get the agreement.

Bill Barton, External Affairs, 1952–70

Diefenbaker dealt with this guerrilla warfare between his ministers and advisers by simply stalling on the nuclear warheads—for years. The acquisition of various nuclear-weapons carriers went ahead as planned, Canadian servicemen were sent to the United States for courses on how to handle and use nuclear warheads, and Diefenbaker never said he wouldn't accept them in the end. But he didn't actually do anything about arranging to take them, either, and after John F. Kennedy became the president of the United States in early 1961 U.S.-Canadian relations went from bad to worse. It was loathing at first sight.

Kennedy thought that Dief was a mischievous old man who was a nuisance, and I think Dief thought Kennedy was, as he used to say, an arrogant young pup. And then their styles were completely different: that sort of Harvard veneer on top of the Irish politician, and the social mix, and the Camelot bit—it was completely antipathetic to Dief, who was a real populist. He had no use for any of that sort of thing.

And I think that Kennedy wrongly saw Dief as someone from the sticks, and so they were temperamentally . . . it was very unfortunate.

Charles Ritchie

But despite fraying tempers and an ever-lengthening delay on the outstanding question of accepting nuclear warheads for all of Canada's new weapons, relations between Ottawa and Washington staggered along without an open break until the Cuban Missile Crisis of October 1962. Then they fell apart.

I knew that President Kennedy was still smarting over the 1961 Bay of Pigs fiasco. . . . I also knew that the President thought he had something to prove in his personal dealings with Khrushchev after their unpleasant Vienna meeting, where Khrushchev had treated him like a child, referring to him as "the boy." I considered that he was perfectly capable of taking the world to the brink of thermonuclear destruction to prove himself the man for our times, a courageous champion of Western democracy.

John Diefenbaker, *One Canada*, vol. 3

The Cuban crisis came in the last year when the United States still had a sufficient margin of nuclear advantage for its strategy of "massive retaliation" to be practicable. The ability to carry out a first strike against the Soviet Union and survive the retaliation with relatively little damage, which had been the foundation of American strategy for fifteen years, was eroding rapidly, but in 1962 the United States still had a decisive nuclear superiority.

During the Berlin crisis of 1961, the U.S. Air Force had advised President Kennedy that American civilian losses in a nuclear war would probably not exceed ten million dead and injured, provided the United States struck first. "That ten million estimate," remarked Daniel Ellsberg, a strategic analyst serving in the Kennedy administration, "reflected to me that the Joint Chiefs all knew—including SAC—that what [the Russians] had was four missiles." In the same year the basic American war plan, the SIOP (Single Integrated Operational Plan), called for almost 2,500 American nuclear strikes against Soviet, Eastern European and Chinese military and civilian targets, destroying the Soviet bomber fleet on the ground and killing an estimated 350 million people in less than a day. It would probably still have succeeded when the Cuban Missile Crisis occurred just one year later.

If we installed the missiles [in Cuba] secretly, and then if the United States discovered the missiles were there after they were already poised and ready to strike, the Americans would think twice before trying to liquidate our installations by military means.

I knew that the United States could knock out some of our installations, but not all of them. If a quarter or even a tenth of our missiles survived—even if only one or two big ones were left—we could still hit New York, and there wouldn't be much of New York left. I don't mean to say that everybody in New York would be killed—not everyone, of course, but an awful lot of people would be wiped out.

The main thing was that the installation of our missiles in Cuba would, I thought, restrain the United States from precipitate action against Castro's government. In addition to protecting Cuba, our missiles would have equalized what the West likes to call the "balance of power." The Americans had surrounded our country with military bases and threatened us with nuclear weapons, and now they would learn just what it feels like to have enemy missiles pointing at you.

Khrushchev Remembers

Khrushchev's decision to extend a Soviet military guarantee to Fidel Castro's regime in Cuba, taken soon after the defeat of the American-backed rebel landing at the Bay of Pigs, was mainly meant to deter further invasion attempts by the United States or its surrogates, but the fact that the Soviet guarantee to Cuba took the form of nuclear missiles simultaneously made it a confrontation about the whole strategic balance.

At the time the Cuban crisis occurred, the Soviet Union still did not have a reliable force of ICBMs capable of hitting the United States from its own territory. The emplacement of shorter-range missiles in Cuba was a Soviet attempt to leapfrog to strategic parity with the United States by "forward basing": from Cuba, those missiles could hit most U.S. cities. True, it would be only another year or so before the Soviet Union had enough home-based ICBMs for a guaranteed "second-strike capability"—the ability to retaliate massively against the United States even after an American first strike. But even a week is sometimes a long time in politics.

If a nuclear war occurred over Cuba before the Soviet missiles there became operational, the results would resemble those predicted for the Berlin crisis the previous year: 350 million dead "Communists," and total American casualties of perhaps ten million. But if war broke out after the Soviet missiles in Cuba became operational, then the United States would probably lose most of its big cities in the subsequent exchange. However, once U.S. reconnaissance planes discovered the Soviet missile sites in Cuba prematurely, the game was up for Moscow.

It shall be the policy of this nation to regard any nuclear missile launched from Cuba against any nation in the Western Hemisphere as an attack by the Soviet Union on the United States requiring a full retaliatory response upon the Soviet Union.

U.S. president John F. Kennedy,
October 22, 1962

The U.S. Air Force had an inflexible commitment to destroying the Soviet missiles in Cuba before they became operational, and for the Soviet Union to risk a nuclear war without those missiles would be a unilateral act of national suicide. The Cuban crisis was therefore never really as dangerous as it seemed. But the Americans did expect prompt and unquestioning support from their allies in this crisis—and from one ally, it was not forthcoming.

President Kennedy requested that we immediately and publicly place the Canadian NORAD component on maximum alert. I considered it unacceptable that every agreed requirement for consultation between our two countries should be ignored. We were not a satellite state at the beck and call of an imperial master.

I telephoned the President . . . [and told him] that I did not believe that Mr. Khrushchev would allow things to reach that stage. While I hated the Communist system and its philosophy . . . I knew something about politicians, whatever their stripe.

I saw Nikita Khrushchev as essentially a cautious man, well aware of the strategic superiority of the United States. He could have no interest in a major confrontation with the United States except where the vital security interests of the USSR were at stake. He had been caught fishing in American waters, and the President had seized the opportunity to erase the memory of the Bay of Pigs fiasco.

One Canada, vol. 3

As soon as Kennedy's speech ended, NORAD declared a DEFCON 3 alert (the third-highest alert status). NORAD headquarters at Colorado Springs naturally expected that Diefenbaker would instruct the Canadian forces to go to the same level of alert at once—but he didn't.

I think that one of the reasons why he delayed . . . was because he saw this as the first test of consultation under NORAD. He didn't feel that what had been said and done by the President . . . amounted to the degree of consultation that Canada had a right to expect under the agreement.

Basil Robinson, External Affairs liaison officer
to the Prime Minister's Office, 1957–62

Such Canadian foot-dragging, especially in a crisis, was bound to irritate the Americans. That was no reason to act otherwise, if enthusiastic compliance was not the appropriate response to an American request. But Diefenbaker never realized the degree to which his own Department of National Defence had lost its ability to distinguish a separate Canadian perspective in matters of national security.

My response immediately was that we had to go to the same stage of alert. I went to see Mr Diefenbaker and told him that this was the situation. He insisted on holding a cabinet meeting [the following day]. . . .

So following that I went back to my headquarters and called the Chiefs of Staff together—that would be in the evening, well on in the evening as a matter of fact—and told them that this was the situation; that we'd go on the alert anyway but say nothing about it. They put those orders out immediately, starting, I should think, about midnight.

> Hon. Douglas Harkness, minister of national defence,
> 1960–63

Harkness's act of disobedience to the prime minister was merely a ratification of what had already occurred. The Canadian armed forces had gone on alert even before their minister secretly authorized their action.

I suppose that I bore the ultimate responsibility for that. It was just too abhorrent to me that Canadians should be put in the position, the whole of Canada, of dishonouring its solemn pledge and word. How wrong it would have been for us to have been caught unaware, with neither ships in position, nor ammunition, nor fuel. Somebody had to do it so I said: "Go ahead, do it."

> Rear Admiral Jeffry Brock, DSO DSC,
> vice-chief of Naval Staff

The American government was far too busy deciding whether or not to blow up the world to worry very much about Diefenbaker's recalcitrance during the crisis, and in any case Washington knew that its allies at the Department of National Defence in Ottawa had taken all the military measures it desired. The cabinet meeting on October 23 accepted Diefenbaker's decision not to go on alert for the moment (unaware that the Canadian forces were already on alert for all practical purposes). But when the Americans actually began their naval blockade of Cuba on October 24, NORAD bumped its alert state up to DEFCON 2, and Harkness finally got the prime minister's reluctant assent to formally place the Canadian forces on the same alert status.

> As to the popular notion that Canada's Minister of National Defence, Mr. Harkness, under the influence of the Canadian military and the United States Pentagon, engaged in a clandestine authorization of a full alert on 22 October, I do not believe it to be true.
>
> John Diefenbaker, *One Canada*, vol. 3

> I never did tell Diefenbaker that I'd done it, but no doubt he learned of it later. . . . So far as the American armed forces were concerned, particularly through NORAD, they were aware of the fact that we were on the same stage of alert as they were although it hadn't been announced.
>
> Hon. Douglas Harkness

———

Torn between obedience to their own national authority and a "higher'" alliance loyalty during the Cuban crisis, the Canadian armed forces chose the latter. They rationalized their disobedience by making the same distinction between the orders of the present government and the "true interests of the state" which has served as the justification for every coup from Chile to Thailand, but the Canadian forces are not coup-prone.

In 1962, at the end of a decade of headlong expansion and deeply immersed in the self-righteous rhetoric of the Cold War, the Canadian military followed their instincts (and their interests), and aligned themselves with the great English-speaking allies whose strategic interests had always provided them with their reason for being in the past. In the far humbler circumstances the armed forces find themselves in today, even this degree of military disloyalty is difficult to imagine: the Canadian forces can probably be relied upon to obey the decisions of the Canadian government in almost any circumstances.

As for the Cuban crisis, it ended more or less in a draw: the Soviet Union withdrew its missiles in return for a U.S. pledge not to invade Cuba (and the United States withdrew its own comparable Jupiter missiles from Italy and Turkey after a face-saving interval of a couple of months). In the longer term, the much-chastened governments in both Washington and Moscow would begin to approach the problem of managing their nuclear-armed confrontation in a somewhat more cooperative spirit. As for Diefenbaker, what got him, in the end, was Canadian nuclear weapons.

By the end of 1962 the Bomarcs were all fully operational in their Canadian launching sites—except, of course, for the nuclear warheads without which they were about as useful as the tail fins on a '62 Chevy. But then, they wouldn't be very useful *with* their nuclear warheads either: the bomber threat was fading rapidly in U.S. strategic calculations as intercontinental ballistic missiles became the main strategic weapon. However, there was still the question of alliance discipline. As Diefenbaker observed: "What the Kennedy administration actually wanted was Canadian acceptance of nuclear weapons in NORAD and NATO. It did not matter that the Bomarc was useless, or that the threat was now from the ICBMs; we were to take the warheads because the President said we must."

Canada's growing "nuclear allergy" was becoming a problem for the United States. The Americans were concerned that the Canadian reluctance to take nuclear weapons might spread to infect other members of the alliance unless checked—there was already an active "Campaign for Nuclear Disarmament" in Britain—and that could have serious effects on American strategy.

I think they took the nuclear issue seriously, not so much in terms of relations with Canada but as an exemplary issue. They were frightened, or they alleged that they were frightened, that things would come unstuck in other countries, and that the whole thing would begin to erode. . . . And on top of that, there was a desire for a change in the terms of general Canadian-American relations—there were the two things.

Charles Ritchie, Canadian ambassador
to Washington, 1962–66

The simple strategic bargain that had underpinned NATO in the fifties—by which the Western European countries gave their political loyalty to the United States in return for an American promise to exterminate the Russians with nuclear weapons if they dared to attack—was getting much more complicated. As the American ability to keep that promise without suffering unacceptable Soviet retaliation on their own homeland declined, U.S. strategists tried to shore up its credibility by inserting an intermediate phase of "limited" nuclear war in Europe.

The notion of a limited nuclear war allegedly "reinforced deterrence." The American threat to blow up the Soviet Union in response to a Soviet attack on Western Europe got hard to believe once the Soviet Union could also blow up the United States, but it seemed plausible that the Americans would start using nuclear weapons in Europe. But since that would probably start an uncontrollable pattern of rapid nuclear escalation, you would still get your nuclear war between the superpowers out of it in the end. So the basic American threat to blow up the Soviet Union if they laid a finger on Western Europe was still effective after all.

I apologize for the baroque logical processes on display here, but that, stripped of the jargon, is what the strategists of the time said the doctrine of limited nuclear war in Europe was actually for. Governments can believe this sort of thing, but you can hardly expect ordinary people to swallow it, so the move to a limited nuclear war strategy caused serious political problems in Europe. It required basing U.S. nuclear weapons on European soil, getting many of the European allies to accept them for their own armed forces and getting everybody to accept the probability that those weapons might end up being used on their own territory in a war. So the whole business of spreading nuclear weapons through most of NATO's armed forces and preparing for a limited nuclear war in Europe was almost comically furtive.

Most NATO countries quietly bought the appropriate equipment for delivering "tactical" nuclear weapons, and the appropriate agreements were signed to make American nuclear warheads available. In theory the Americans remained responsible because these weapons could only be armed by an American soldier (plus a soldier from the country where the weapons were located—the so-called "dual-key" system), and this enabled the European governments to pretend that it was a purely technical matter best left to the soldiers. However, Canada's increasingly obvious refusal to accept its quota of nuclear weapons was not helping at all. In the aftermath of the Cuban crisis, Washington was determined to shift its reluctant ally on the nuclear weapons issue, and the pro-nuclear faction within the Conservative cabinet, led by Defence Minister Douglas Harkness, was equally determined to push Diefenbaker to a decision:

> Howard Green and the External Affairs people followed a policy of delay, constantly saying: "Well, we can't do this; agree to this; now let's do something else; and so on and so forth." And kept delaying it and delaying it and delaying it until finally it got to the point that it was quite apparent that no action was going to be taken. I finally brought the matter to a crux by [stating] that I would resign if this wasn't done.
>
> Hon. Douglas Harkness

General Norstad, retiring as supreme commander of NATO in Europe, was invited to call at Ottawa on January 3, 1963, on his way home to the United States. It was widely assumed that he would be a presidential candidate in the next election, so anything he said in public would carry considerable weight in Canada. He had lunch with Harkness and the Canadian Armed Forces Chiefs of Staff—and at the end of it they told him about the press conference.

> So I remember saying: "What press conference?" We went down and the room was full. I've never seen so many cameras. . . . The questions started flying . . . and it started boring down on this: Was Canada meeting its commitments? Well, it got to a point where I thought it deserved an answer. So when they asked the question whether Canada had met the [nuclear] commitment, I just said "No." And you've never seen so many people leave a room so fast. (Chuckles.) They were all running for the phone and the cameras were dismantled and people ran away.
>
> General Lauris Norstad

The impact of Norstad's remarks in Canada was enormous: for the first time, a senior American official had implied in public that Canada was not a reliable ally. The effect was even greater because his visit came only ten weeks after the Cuban crisis, which had scared Canadians half to death. A widespread initial reaction to that experience in Canada had been to conclude that American nuclear weapons were, after all, good for you. In effect, a great many Canadians followed their armed forces' example and defected from the government to the Americans: by December 1962, 54 percent of Canadians believed that the country should accept U.S. nuclear weapons. The landslide that would sweep Diefenbaker away was beginning to move: just a week after Norstad's visit, Lester Pearson announced that the Liberals now favoured accepting the nuclear warheads.

On January 25, 1963 Diefenbaker claimed in a speech in Parliament that it would be inappropriate for Canada to accept nuclear weapons at that time. Among other things, he said that the United States and Britain had recently discussed moving the whole NATO alliance's strategy away from nuclear weapons at a summit meeting in Nassau. This was not even a half-truth, and on January 30 the U.S. State Department issued a press release correcting what Diefenbaker had said about the Nassau summit and all but calling him a liar. It added tartly that "the Canadian government has not as yet proposed any arrangement sufficiently practical to contribute effectively to North American air defence." Diefenbaker replied by recalling the Canadian ambassador from Washington—the only time that has ever been done.

By the time that I was recalled to Ottawa to "mark our displeasure," Dief and the government were dead-set for an election with anti-American overtones and they thought they could win it.

I, rather naively—the way diplomats are very naive, compared to anybody else—thought that we could sort of patch up the difficulty that had arisen over this very arrogant and hamhanded operation of the press release. I thought that we could get, you know, apologies, "misunderstandings," denials. But of course when I arrived here I found I was barking up the wrong tree entirely.

That was the last thing they wanted: to patch it up, paper over the cracks. Because they had got their eyes set on an election in which anti-American overtones would play a very important and perhaps victorious part. So there you were.

Charles Ritchie

Diefenbaker soon got his election: the cabinet was torn almost daily by chaotic disputes as Harkness pressed his demand that the government accept nuclear weapons. On February 3, 1963 Harkness resigned, and the following day he read out his resignation letter on national radio and television, explaining that it had been explicitly over the nuclear issue. The government lost a vote of confidence in the Commons on February 5, and Parliament was dissolved the next day.

> Q. *When you submitted your resignation, did you know it would bring the government down?*
> Well, I was pretty sure it would, yes.
> Q. *And at that point you reckoned this was necessary?*
> Yes.
> Q. *Do you still think so?*
> I still think so.
>
> Hon. Douglas Harkness, 1984

If Harkness really believed it was worth resigning to get nuclear warheads onto Canada's Bomarcs, he was desperately out of touch with military realities. The day after Diefenbaker's government fell, U.S. secretary of defense Robert McNamara was testifying about air defence to a subcommittee of the Committee on Appropriations of the House of Representatives. He was not having an easy time of it: the whole concept of North American air defence had been taking a beating over the previous few years in the United States, as American strategists slowly came to terms with the looming reality of unstoppable ICBMs. In due course the congressmen got around to their favourite topic.

> REPRESENTATIVE MINSHALL: No hearings of this subcommittee would be complete unless I at least mentioned in passing the word "Bomarc."
> REP. FLOOD: You are speaking of the woman I love.
> REP. MINSHALL: . . . If I remember correctly . . . we put somewhere between $3 billions and $4 billions into this program. I just wonder . . . why we even put any money into the operational cost of this weapon when it is so useless.

SECRETARY McNAMARA: For the protection we get, I do not believe it is an unreasonable amount.

REP. MINSHALL: The protection is practically nil, Mr. Secretary, as you said here in your statement. . . .

SECRETARY McNAMARA: At the very least, they would cause the Soviets to target missiles against them and thereby . . . draw missiles onto these Bomarc targets that would otherwise be available for other targets.

REP. MINSHALL: In view of the statement you just made, Mr. Secretary, why do we not leave the Jupiter missiles in Italy and Turkey? If we have to draw enemy fire, that is a good place to draw it. . . .

SECRETARY McNAMARA: As they are deployed, [the Bomarcs in Canada] draw more fire than those Jupiter missiles will.

Edited transcript of House Committee on
Appropriations hearing, February 6, 1963

On March 29, 1963, in the last week of the Canadian election campaign, this testimony was released in the United States, and Diefenbaker leaped on it with glad cries. Conveniently forgetting that his own government had installed the Bomarcs in the first place, he told an enthusiastic crowd in Maple Leaf Gardens in Toronto that "the Canadian people would not approve of useless Bomarcs being used as missile bait in Canada." In the days that followed he accused Pearson of making Canada into a "decoy duck in a nuclear war" by agreeing to arm the Bomarcs, and asked if it was Liberal policy to "make Canada into a burnt sacrifice."

Pearson was clearly unhappy about his U-turn on nuclear weapons, but he stuck it out and promised the voters that a Liberal government would take and keep the nuclear weapons Canada had signed up for "as long as they are useful for defence." The fact that some of these nuclear weapons, at least, were manifestly not useful for defence, and had just been so described by no less an authority than the U.S. secretary of defense, didn't matter, because the electorate wasn't interested in details.

If the election had really been about NORAD and the nuclear weapons that came with it, Diefenbaker could hardly have lost, for NORAD was a strategic irrelevance almost from the day it was created. The first successful Soviet intercontinental ballistic missile (ICBM) test took place only one month after Diefenbaker agreed to join in mid-1957, and by early 1963 the U.S. Department of Defense had been reduced to justifying the Bomarcs as targets to soak up Russian firepower. But Diefenbaker was constrained from discussing the full and brutal truth about NORAD in public by the rules of secrecy covering strategic information obtained from the Americans, and also by the fact that he himself had signed the NORAD treaty. So the election campaign rapidly moved on from a muddled argument about nuclear warheads to a straightforward loyalty call: Diefenbaker's vision of Canada (whatever that might be) versus loyalty to the alliance, and especially to the Americans. But he got the wrong answer from the Canadian people.

Canada has voted American.

Headline, *Paris-Presse*, April 9, 1963

Canadians, it turned out, trusted and admired the U.S. president, John F. Kennedy, more than they did their own prime minister. The Liberals won the election in April 1963, forming a minority government that inaugurated another twenty-one-year run of Liberal rule with only one brief interruption. Five months later, Prime Minister Pearson signed the agreement with the United States, accepting nuclear warheads for Canada's forces at home and in Europe. And within another few years, Canada's short and hectic ride as strategically important territory was at an end.

ALL PASSION SPENT

MORE THAN HALF A CENTURY AFTER IT WAS CREATED, NORAD still soldiers on, picking up what work it can, but its survival owes much more to institutional interests than strategic logic. By the mid-1960s, as intercontinental ballistic missiles (ICBMs) and submarine-launched ballistic missiles (SLBMs) took over the main deterrent task, bombers were demoted to the third leg of the "triad" of strategic nuclear weapons systems. The bombers probably wouldn't even retain that status if air forces were not run by pilots, and they certainly pose no measurable threat to North America.

More to the point, since ICBMs and SLBMs really could not be stopped, or successfully eliminated in a surprise attack, the mutual deterrence first envisaged by Bernard Brodie almost two decades earlier really began to operate for the first time. The United States formally abandoned its doctrine of "massive retaliation" under Secretary of Defense Robert McNamara in the early years of the Kennedy administration, replacing it with a strategy of "flexible response" that emphasized conventional weapons and proportional (rather than "massive") responses to provocations. Nuclear weapons were still there in large numbers, but the new strategy was straight out of Brodie's playbook: the most important part of deterrence was ensuring that one's own weapons would survive a first strike and be able to retaliate—and so long as that was true for both sides, first strikes were suicidal and to be avoided at all costs. McNamara even introduced into the thinking about deterrence strategy the further subtlety that it was important not to confuse or frighten the opponent too much, for fear of driving him into irrational behaviour.

This strategic shift not only made the world a good deal safer, but it also drained the passion and the sheer terror out of the American-Soviet relationship, and that had the further effect of allowing a new era of negotiations over the very weapons that had previously poisoned the relationship. Nuclear test ban treaties, negotiated limits on nuclear warheads and delivery vehicles, non-proliferation agreements and a variety of other arms control measures calmed matters further. Rivalries persisted between the superpowers and there were strong reactions to events like the Soviet invasion of Afghanistan in 1979 and Ronald Reagan's "Star Wars" project in 1983, but on the whole the relations between the superpowers were civil. All of which made it difficult to understand why the forces and commands that had been built up in the panic-stricken early years of the Cold War persisted virtually unchanged down through the placid final two decades of the confrontation. But they did.

CHAPTER 11

GOING WITH THE FLOW

PRIME MINSTER LESTER PEARSON'S ARRIVAL AT THE HEAD OF
a minority Liberal government in April 1963 put an end to the confrontation with the United States over nuclear weapons that had
blighted the relationship between the two countries under John
Diefenbaker. Pearson accepted all sorts of nuclear weapons for
Canada's air force and army under the agreement that Diefenbaker
had signed in ignorance, all under "dual-key" arrangements that
allowed Ottawa to maintain the fiction that they weren't really
Canadian nuclear weapons since an American officer also had to
turn a key to arm them.

> The warheads will remain in United States custody, and for this
> purpose small units of United States custodial personnel will be
> stationed at the Canadian storage sites, at bases which will of
> course remain under Canadian command and control. . . . The
> arrangement does not add to the numbers of governments having
> nuclear weapons at their independent disposal.
>
> Prime Minister's Office, press release, August 16, 1963

I think [there was] sort of a feeling that this was a super-power business, and that we had no business being involved in it. Some of us felt, "well, that's fine as long as we're not hypocritical about it." I mean after all, it was our uranium that armed the western world to a very large extent. We were very pleased to have those dollars in our country, especially in Mr. Pearson's riding [Algoma East]. And so, you can make a case for us not being in this business (and a good case), but let's not say it's due to superior righteousness. Let's just admit that it's because we're a small power and we can do other things that are more useful and more effective, and spend our dollars more wisely than getting into a game that leads nowhere but to destruction.

Paul Hellyer, minister of national defence, 1963–67

Canadian public opinion had never really been very excited by the nuclear weapons controversy, and when the weapons finally arrived over the next few years there was no outcry—even though the ones with our NATO forces in Germany were clearly destined to be used in densely populated parts of Western Europe. And then, as the vehicles that carried them (Bomarcs, Voodoos, Starfighters and Honest John missiles) became obsolete and were scrapped, their nuclear warheads were quietly handed back to the Americans. Canada became a born-again nuclear virgin, and nobody in Washington minded all that much; by then twenty years had passed, and nuclear fashions had changed.

What really did bother Canadians was the U.S. war in Vietnam. President John F. Kennedy's early commitment of U.S. forces to South Vietnam went virtually unnoticed in Canada, where he was liked and trusted, but the rapid escalation of the U.S. military commitment by the more abrasive President Lyndon Johnson after Kennedy's assassination in 1963 quickly created a vocal opposition to the war in Canada that tracked the rapid growth of the anti-war movement in the United States itself.

Canada was never under serious pressure from the United States to send Canadian troops to Vietnam; no other NATO member sent troops either. (The Australians and New Zealanders did, of course, but they were a great deal closer to the scene, and their defence policy at the time consisted solely of a determination to send troops to help in every American war, however needless or futile, in the hope that such loyalty would guarantee U.S. military intervention to defend them if it ever became necessary.) The pressure on the Canadian government came from the radicalization of the youth in both countries, the steady flow of draft dodgers/war resisters across the border from the United States, and the growing demand that Canada should "take a stand" against the war. Since official Ottawa also thought that the Vietnam War was a great folly, it was willing to oblige—but at first it was all done through diplomatic channels. Mustn't cause a fuss.

> We said to the Americans . . . "We are against the war. We think you have made a mistake. I think it's going to cause you a whole lot of trouble. We don't intend to get into it." And then [U.S. secretary of state Dean] Rusk said, "Oh well, it isn't going to last as long as you think." And I said, "How long is it going to last?" and [U.S. secretary of defense Robert] McNamara said, "If necessary, a thousand years."
>
> Paul Martin, secretary of state for external affairs,
> 1963–68

It was a particularly frustrating business for Charles Ritchie, the Canadian ambassador in Washington. "It was all very well to say, 'you just trust the diplomatic channels' and so on, but I would go down and see Rusk, and he'd be like this sort of Buddha, you know, nodding his head about Canadian views and suggestions and hesitations and so on. He would sort of take note of them. He would never discuss them, or refute them." Nevertheless, Ritchie warned Pearson: "Don't move into public criticism on the war in Vietnam. Try to influence through diplomatic channels, and through contacts between the Prime Minister and the President, but don't make speeches about it."

From Pearson's point of view, however, the "softly, softly" approach had two major defects. Not only was it not working, but the fact that he was trying to get the Americans to see reason about Vietnam was not visible to the Canadian public. Safely back in office with a four-year mandate, President Johnson went for broke in 1965, increasing the number of U.S. ground troops in South Vietnam eightfold and plastering North Vietnam with bombs in "Operation Rolling Thunder." The Americans had completely lost their sense of proportion. Pearson felt compelled to say something in public—and to say it in the United States.

In April 1965 Pearson was going to Temple University in Philadelphia to accept a World Peace Award, and he decided to address the Vietnam War directly. His speech was ultra-cautious, full of praise for the American decision to help the South Vietnamese government and warning that "no newly independent nation could ever feel secure if capitulation in Vietnam led to the sanctification of aggression through subversion and spurious 'wars of national liberation.'" He was humble, he was tentative, he was polite almost to the point of sycophancy—but he suggested a partial ceasefire. "There are many factors which I am not in a position to weigh," Pearson said. "But there does appear to be at least a possibility that a suspension of air strikes against North Vietnam, at the right time, might provide the Hanoi authorities with an opportunity, if they wish to take it, to inject some flexibility into their policy without appearing to do so as the direct result of military pressure."

Immediately after the speech, Pearson was invited to Camp David by President Johnson, and as usual a helicopter was sent to pick him up. Charles Ritchie, who was still Canadian ambassador in Washington, accompanied Pearson to the mountain retreat, where they were greeted by Lady Bird Johnson and the president. As far as Ritchie was concerned, things started off badly: the president only had one Bloody

Mary before lunch. Then he spent the entire time on the phone, often discussing Vietnam, while "Mike" and Lady Bird made polite small talk about their mutual interest in the Civil War, trying desperately to pretend that everything was fine.

Then after lunch, Mike sort of led by saying something like, "What did you think of my speech?" And then the President said, "I thought it was awful, awful." After that I ceased to be part of the meeting because they went out onto the terrace, and I was taken for a walk by [national security adviser McGeorge] "Mac" Bundy, who kept needling and needling me about this whole thing. You know, how could I?, and hadn't I taken it on board that he had said that this would be the result, and it was counter-productive, and it was so sad, and regrettable, and all the rest of it. And I got very fed up with this in the end and said that if they couldn't get on with Mike Pearson they couldn't get on with anybody.

Then there was this story that the President picked up Mike by the collar and swung him in the air or something. He didn't do anything of the kind. In the first place, Mike was quite a solid person, besides he would have been intolerably insulted, it didn't happen. What he did, he grasped hold of Mike by the lapel of his coat, and he was anguished, you know, shaking Mike, and sounding and resounding and appealing and recriminating and exhorting. And Mike was sort of, you know, leaning against the terrace getting further and further back, while this great man moved in on him, getting closer and closer. It was a close encounter. Then it sort of quieted down. Mike wasn't as shaken as I was. He was very India-rubbery.

Charles Ritchie, Canadian ambassador to Washington, 1962–66

If there had not been a kind of "et tu, Brute" feeling about the assault, without any personal unpleasantness of any kind, I would

have felt almost like Schuschnigg [the Austrian chancellor] before
Hitler at Berchtesgaden.

"Mike": Memoirs, vol 3

It was, nevertheless, Canada's muted declaration of independence from the ideologically driven Cold War policies of its giant ally, and when Pierre Elliott Trudeau succeeded Pearson as prime minister in 1969 he was able to go a good deal further. The Canadian public's uncritical admiration of the United States, which had been Diefenbaker's undoing, had pretty much dissipated by the end of the 1960s. The growing nightmare of the Vietnam War was sabotaging America's reputation as an effective operator abroad just as the wave of urban violence was destroying its image as a bastion of justice and democracy at home, and the United States was coming to be seen in Canada as just another muscle-bound great power stumbling around without a clue. At the same time (and somewhat in contradiction to the above), the rise of détente, with frequent negotiations between the rival superpowers over various questions of arms control and nuclear security, created the space for a more detailed and leisurely examination of just what the panic of the early postwar years had got us into. So Trudeau launched a defence and foreign policy review that left no stone unturned.

> Mr. Trudeau, for example, said we're going to look at neutrality, we're going to look at non-alignment, we're going to look at just having a defence alliance with the United States—we're going to look at them all. We start from zero and we examine every possible alternative. . . . He asked the question that nobody else dared to ask: "Are we on the right track?"
>
> Mitchell Sharp, secretary of state for external affairs,
1968–74

It was a time when almost everybody was overwrought if not downright hysterical, and Trudeau was, as Pearson said, "the man to match the times." Speaking at Queen's University in November 1968, Trudeau declared: "Civilization and culture in North America are more menaced, more strongly threatened, by internal disorders than by external pressure. And this is the background of these reviews [of foreign and defence policy] in which we are embarked. I am not predicting what the outcome will be, but I am saying that in my scale of values I am perhaps less worried now about what might happen over the Berlin Wall than what might happen in Chicago, New York, and perhaps our own great cities in Canada." And to be fair to Trudeau, the October Crisis in Montreal was less than two years away.

In the meantime, everybody who was anybody in Ottawa got stuck into the defence and foreign policy reviews. NORAD got next to no attention, having been reduced to near irrelevance by the collapse of the "bomber threat," and the option of neutrality got only a cursory examination (although a group of Canadian parliamentarians got a nice trip to Sweden out of it). All the attention focused on NATO and Canada's role in it, which seemed more than ripe for reconsideration. Canadian troops had been sent to Europe in the early 1950s during the panic caused by the Korean War; why were they still there twenty years later? There was a group of powerful ministers in the cabinet—Eric Kierans, Gérard Pelletier, Jean Marchand and Donald MacDonald—who favoured a military withdrawal from NATO, and possibly quitting the alliance altogether, but in the end they settled for a good old Canadian compromise. Canada stayed in NATO and the European commitment was kept, but half the Canadian troops in Europe were brought home.

Trudeau managed to pull this off without facing severe recriminations from the European NATO members because by then they had figured out that the presence of the Canadian brigade and air division in Germany was very important politically, but not so much so militarily. The Canadian troops were really there so that they would be involved in a war with the Warsaw Pact from the first shot, thereby guaranteeing that Canada would be fully committed to the ensuing war regardless of the (nuclear) risks to the Canadian homeland. For those purposes, five thousand Canadian soldiers were just as good as ten thousand, so the rest came home. And that was pretty much it for serious debates about Canadian defence policy for the next fifteen years. The one lasting defence-related achievement of the Trudeau years was the transformation of the Canadian Forces into a genuinely bilingual institution in which francophones were present in numbers that corresponded to their share of the national population and enjoyed the same promotion prospects as anglophones even at the highest ranks.

There was some excitement in 1970, when Trudeau deployed troops in the streets of Montreal during the confrontation with Front de libération du Québec terrorists at that time, but in general the Canadian Forces (as they were now officially known thanks to the "unification" of the three services under Defence Minister Paul Hellyer in the 1960s) entered a prolonged period of neglect and genteel decline. Indeed, this could be seen as the real consequence of the defence and foreign policy reviews, which concluded in essence that the Canadian Forces were still politically important as part of Canada's foreign policy, but militarily almost irrelevant. Even peacekeeping, which had allowed Canadians to luxuriate in the belief that their army was actually an instrument of love, was losing popularity by the late 1960s, and was downgraded to the lowest level of priority in Trudeau's defence review. The strength of the Canadian armed forces was cut from 120,000 in 1963 to just over 80,000 by the end of the decade, and new equipment purchases were few and far between during the next fifteen years: 128 used Leopard I tanks from Germany and 18 maritime reconnaissance aircraft from the United States in 1978, 137 new F-18 fighters in 1983, and six "patrol frigates" for the navy, for delivery in the late 1980s.

And the consequence of all these cuts and neglect was . . . nothing. They had no more effect on how the rest of the world unfolded during these years than cuts to the summer camp training budget for the Canadian militia would have had on the world in the 1880s. They wouldn't have made any difference if we had all tumbled into World War Three, either. A few more fisheries surveillance vessels would have come in handy, but Canada's maritime sovereignty was never at risk despite the alleged shortage of ships to enforce it. It was a perfect illustration of the extreme "elasticity" of Canada's military requirements in the circumstances that prevailed then (and are even more pronounced in the current era).

The size and composition of the Canadian armed forces, to a far greater extent than those of most other countries, are not determined by the "threats" that face the country, and that might be deterred or defeated by military means. Broad oceans and Arctic ice protect us from the rest of the planet, and our one vulnerable border, to the south, is guaranteed not by force but by our commercial and treaty relations with the United States. So our options in national security are very wide. We could have very small armed forces and a minimal capacity for territorial and maritime surveillance—say, twenty thousand service personnel—and we'd still be all right. Since 1939 we have always been far above that level, but those choices are driven by the ideological fashions of the moment, by the expectations of our neighbours, allies and commercial partners (and how much we choose to give in to them) and by the needs and wishes of our own military-industrial complex. For almost half a century now, with the single exception of the Mulroney years, that level has never risen far above eighty thousand or fallen far below sixty thousand. That is, you might say, what the market will bear—and the fluctuations in the numbers occur almost independently of any external reality. As in the case of the great defence mini-buildup of the late 1980s.

———

Here's my strategy on the Cold War: we win, they lose.

Ronald Reagan, Moscow summit, May 1988

379

There is an American political myth, cherished by the right, that President Ronald Reagan "won" the Cold War by forcing the Soviet Union to spend itself into bankruptcy. He did this, it is alleged, by raising American defence spending to an unprecedented level and devoting it to various projects, like the "Star Wars" anti-ballistic missile programme, that forced Moscow to spend comparable amounts to keep up. Since the Soviet economy was much smaller than that of America, the Russians eventually went broke, Communism collapsed and the Cold War ended.

It is an agreeable story, especially if you happen to be in charge of the U.S. defence budget, but it is simply false. It's true that excessive defence spending forced the Soviet Union to try to make fundamental reforms in the economy, and that the political repercussions of that effort destroyed the entire system, but the dates are wrong. Ronald Reagan inherited a defence budget of $440 billion in current (2013) dollars when he took office at the beginning of 1981. His own first defence budget, for 1982/83, was $488 billion. It then continued to rise until 1985/86, peaking at $580 billion—but the Soviet attempt at reform actually began in 1982, after the death of the long-ruling Leonid Brezhnev.

The first reformer in Moscow, Yuri Andropov, unexpectedly died in 1984, and was briefly succeeded by a conservative, Konstantin Chernenko, before Mikhail Gorbachev came to power in 1985 and resumed the reform effort. Even in 1985, given the ponderous nature of the Soviet planning and budgetary processes, there had scarcely been time for Soviet defence spending to rise in response to Reagan's higher budgets. Excessive defence spending did play a large part in bringing down the Soviet system, but Reagan was too late on the scene to have any appreciable impact. It was the relatively modest defence budgets of Eisenhower, Kennedy, Nixon and Carter that brought the Soviet Union down.

Does this mean that the Soviet Union might have survived for at least another decade or two if it had not tried so hard to match American defence spending? Impossible to say, of course. But it is clear that by the time Brian Mulroney's Conservative government took power in Canada in 1984, after a generation of Liberal rule, Soviet power—and in particular Soviet military power—was in irreversible decline. Gorbachev's assigned (but hopeless) task was to save the Communist system politically by re-basing it on consent rather than compulsion, and to rescue it economically by breaking the stranglehold of the "metal-eaters' alliance" (the Soviet version of the military-industrial complex), which was consuming an estimated one-third of the country's gross domestic product. And it was precisely at this point that the Mulroney government decided it needed to build up the Canadian armed forces to counter the "growing Soviet threat."

First, however, there was the peculiar episode of Defence Minister Erik Nielsen's attempt to pull all the Canadian troops out of Germany. Nielsen was actually deputy prime minister, but he was parachuted into the Defence job as well when Mulroney's first appointment, Robert Coates, was forced to resign after an ill-advised visit to a West German strip club while visiting the Canadian troops in Europe. By chance Nielsen, who had been a bomber pilot in the Second World War and had a healthy disdain for the defence orthodoxy of the time, inherited a chief of defence staff, General Gérard Thériault, who was also something of an iconoclast—and together they came up with the most radical proposal for a new Canadian defence policy of the entire Cold War era. (It may have had something to do with the fact that they both had air force backgrounds, for the proposal would have eliminated the Canadian army's main justification for staying in the "big leagues," while leaving the air force's roles more or less intact.)

Nielsen and Thériault began with the belief, never adequately documented but widely accepted, that Canada's Mechanized Brigade Group and the Canadian Air Group in Germany, which accounted for only about 8 percent of Canadian Forces' personnel, were consuming about half of the defence budget in one way or another. Yet in fact (as Thériault later said in public), "Our forces in Central Europe mean next to nothing in military terms." They were purely symbolic, a token of Canada's intent to stand by its NATO allies in the event of war. So Nielsen and Thériault began concocting a plan to maintain a token Canadian commitment somewhere else in Europe, while bringing the great majority of Canada's troops home. The device they hit upon was the Canadian Air Sea Transportable (CAST) Brigade, a commitment dating from 1968 to send Canadian troops in an emergency to reinforce Norway's northern frontier with Russia.

It was a paper commitment only: the notion that a Canadian brigade and its equipment could be rapidly moved from Canada to Norway in the midst of a NATO-wide panic about an imminent war in Europe was risible. But it gave Nielsen and Thériault something to work with, and in consultation with a selected group of National Defence officials (who were ordered not to report their work to their superiors) they came up with a plan. The Mechanized Brigade Group would come home from Germany, but all its heavy equipment would be moved to northern Norway. The Canadian Air Group would return home too, but in an emergency three squadrons of CF-18s would fly over to Norway, as would the Canadian soldiers who would man the pre-positioned equipment. In normal times, however, there would be no significant number of Canadian troops left in Europe.

It was a bold but quite rational plan, although there was bound to be hell to pay when the Canadian army and the External Affairs Department found out about it. Nielsen even got initial approval from U.S. secretary of defense Caspar Weinberger, although he must later have realized that he was simply being sent out to draw fire. When Nielsen travelled on to London and Bonn, however, he ran into a wall of panic and outrage: British defence secretary Michael Heseltine refused even to discuss the proposal, and West German defence minister Manfred Woerner "just went crazy." They didn't care about the Canadian forces as such, but they saw the plan as setting a precedent for an American withdrawal from Europe.

Nielsen came home with his tail between his legs, to meet a

comparable barrage of condemnation from the defenders of NATO ortho-doxy at home. Weinberger, of course, disavowed Nielsen, who was sub-sequently forced to resign all his government offices and soon afterward left politics entirely. During House of Commons hearings Thériault's successor as chief of defence staff, General Paul Manson, denied ever having heard of or seen a paper on the "Thériault plan"; it had been consigned to the memory hole. And it was perhaps a minor by-product of the incident that the second broadcast of the television series that the original draft of this book was based on was cancelled by the CBC.

By 1986 a new defence minister, Perrin Beatty, was laying plans for a major expansion of the Canadian Forces, including an upgrade of its NATO contribution in Central Europe: he argued that Ottawa should station a full mechanized division in Germany, with another fully equipped mechanized division to be held in Canada as a backup. The reserves would be expanded to forty thousand and integrated more closely with the regulars, and extra maritime reconnaissance aircraft, more CF-18s and patrol frigates, and new EH-101 anti-submarine heli-copters were ordered. He even promised the navy a dozen nuclear-pow-ered submarines. The price tag was forecast to be $8 billion ($14 billion in today's money), but cost overruns would inevitably have pushed that even higher. Assuming that Beatty was not a Soviet agent tasked with turning the "Reagan strategy" against Canada and spending the coun-try into bankruptcy, how could he have got it so wrong?

The answer probably goes like this. During two decades of almost continuous Liberal rule, one of the Conservatives' main criticisms against the government, regardless of the state of the international envi-ronment, was its neglect of the armed forces, so it was hard for the Conservatives to walk away from all their promises to build up the forces even if the Soviet Union was in steep decline by the time they actually got back in power. Moreover, they really didn't understand just how rapid and terminal the decline was. It should have been obvious to them—I went back to the Soviet Union for a week in 1987 after five years' absence, and immediately went home and made a deal with the CBC to visit the place every three months and interview all the major players, in order to deliver them a radio series as soon as the crash actually happened—but the Canadian government's main source of information was, as usual, American intelligence assessments. In those intelligence reports, the Soviet "threat" was always "growing": in all four decades of the Cold War, the American intelligence services never once issued a report that said the Soviet threat was shrinking. So the apparently sudden collapse of Soviet power in 1989 actually took both the U.S. and the Canadian governments by surprise.

That put paid to Beatty's grand plans, of course. The personnel strength of the forces continued to grow for a time, peaking at ninety thousand in 1990 before falling back to seventy-one thousand in 1995, but the nuclear submarines vanished at once and the new aircraft were also cancelled. The first of the promised new helicopters (now Sikorsky H-92s, to be known as CH-124s in Canadian service) may be delivered as soon as 2015.

In 1993, after forty years in Europe, the Canadian forces in Germany all came home, and some wondered whether the Canadian armed forces could avoid serious shrinkage now that the only plausible enemy had retired from the confrontation. The NATO alliance that had been created to "contain" the Soviet Union had worked itself out of a job, and many thought it would just fade away. But they all underestimated the resourcefulness and staying power of a very large and experienced bureaucratic organization with powerful allies in the military forces of every member country.

NATO did not fade away; it expanded right up to the borders of the former Soviet Union, taking in former Warsaw Pact members (Poland, the Czech Republic, Slovakia, Hungary, Romania and Bulgaria) and even territories that had been part of the Soviet Union itself (Estonia, Latvia and Lithuania). By the early twenty-first century its easternmost border was only 120 kilometres from Russia's second city, St Petersburg.

This was all in direct contradiction to the promise made by U.S. president George H.W. Bush to the last Soviet president, Mikhail Gorbachev, that if Moscow were to withdraw its garrisons peacefully from Eastern Europe and accept the reunification of Germany, NATO would not recruit these former Warsaw Pact members to its ranks. But Russia under the leadership of the drunken Boris Yeltsin did not object very loudly in the 1990s, and even when Vladimir Putin took over at the beginning of the twenty-first century he grudgingly accepted the situation. One of the reasons he did so, no doubt, was that NATO had at least been tactful enough not to station foreign troops (i.e., Americans or Germans) on the soil of any of the new members of the alliance who directly bordered on Russian territory.

This brings us to the serious question, first raised in Excursion 1, of whether we are still living in a tightly coupled "critical system" that could pitch us almost randomly into a great war at any time. We and the Soviets certainly began to construct such a system again in the early years of the Cold War, but from the mid-1960s a great deal of effort was expended to move in the other direction: "hot lines" that permitted instant, direct communications between national leaders in a crisis, arms control agreements, early notification of missile launches and military exercises and a variety of "confidence-building" measures whose real purpose was to catch that random pebble before it started the avalanche. It was still an extremely dangerous system, but not a fully-fledged Doomsday Machine. And the post–Cold War relations between the former adversaries have been marked by the same desire to avoid unnecessary escalation and limit confrontations to the lowest possible level.

A case in point is the recent conflict over Ukraine, which was still unresolved at the time of writing (April 2014). So far, at least, there has been no panic reaction like the one that followed the Communist coup in Prague in 1948, when NATO turned itself into a traditional military alliance in response to the destruction of democracy in a country that had already been abandoned to the Soviet sphere of influence at the Yalta conference three years before. Russia's illegal annexation of Crimea has been almost universally interpreted as a crude face-saving action by President Putin, who was humiliated by the overthrow of the pro-Russian government in Kiev, and not as the first step in a Russian project for world conquest. While any further Russian encroachments on Ukrainian sovereignty would undoubtedly lead to a prolonged period of tension between NATO and Russia, the alliance has already made it clear that it has no intention of sending Western troops into Ukraine. There is a distinct lack of enthusiasm for the whole notion of a new Cold War, and not simply because today's Russia, with only half the population of the old Soviet Union and much less than half of the military power, is too weak to hold up its end of it. NATO doesn't need a new Cold War to justify its continued existence: it has succeeded in finding other things to do.

———

Traditional peacekeeping operations have continued to occupy some Canadian troops in the post–Cold War world, and the UN-backed operation in Bosnia and Croatia in the mid-1990s saw Canadian troops involved in a considerable amount of actual combat. But the new fashion was for "out-of-area" NATO operations like the bombing campaign against Serbia in 1999, the International Security Assistance Force (ISAF) in Afghanistan, and the bombing campaign in Libya in 2011, all of which attracted Canadian participation. The Serbian and Libyan operations only involved the Royal Canadian Air Force and cost no Canadian casualties, but the major Canadian troop commitment to Afghanistan in 2003–2011 peaked at 4,000 soldiers and resulted in 158 fatal casualties—more than half of Canada's total losses in overseas military commitments in the past sixty years. The way it came about was instructive. In early 2003 U.S. president George W. Bush's

administration in Washington expected Canada to be part of the "coalition of the willing" that he was assembling for the invasion of Iraq—
but Prime Minister Jean Chrétien said no.

> Over the last few weeks the U.N. Security Council has been un-
> able to agree on a new resolution authorizing military action
> [against Iraq]. Canada worked very hard to find a compromise to
> bridge the gap in the Security Council. Unfortunately, we were
> not successful. If military action proceeds without a new resolu-
> tion of the Security Council, Canada will not participate.
>
> Jean Chrétien, House of Commons, Ottawa,
> March 17, 2003

"It was a very difficult decision to make, because it was the first
time there was a war where the Americans and the Brits were involved
and Canada was not there," Chrétien told the *Huffington Post* on March
19, 2013, the tenth anniversary of the invasion. "But my view was there
were no weapons of mass destruction, and we're not in the business of
going everywhere and replacing dictators. If we were to do that, we
would be fighting every day." A week earlier, he even boasted that it was
"a very important decision for the independence of Canada, because
unfortunately a lot of people thought sometimes we were the fifty-first
state of America. It was clear that day we were not."

In reality, Chrétien's motives were a good deal more complex than
that. In his Commons statement, Chrétien explained his decision in
terms of international law (since 1945 it has been a crime to invade a
sovereign country without the approval of the Security Council), but
this was almost certainly not his primary concern. His doubts about the
accuracy of the intelligence that the Americans were providing about
Saddam Hussein's alleged possession of "weapons of mass destruction"
were fully justified, but would he have seen that as a sufficient reason,
all by itself, to defy and perhaps seriously alienate the Americans? There

is reason to believe that another, entirely domestic consideration was the decisive factor in Chrétien's decision.

In terms of his dedication to upholding the authority of the Security Council, Chrétien's record was distinctly spotty. Newly chosen as leader of the Liberal Party in 1991, he opposed the invasion of Kuwait in order to push Saddam Hussein's army out of that conquered country, although the operation had been authorized by the UN Security Council. He even called the planned multinational military action "illegal." (Prime Minister Brian Mulroney sent troops anyway.)

The intelligence about Saddam Hussein's alleged pursuit of nuclear weapons which the United States produced in order to justify invading Iraq was not only wrong but, in some cases, deliberately fabricated. After it turned out that the "weapons of mass destruction," the excuse for a war that ultimately killed several hundred thousand people, simply did not exist, there was a concerted attempt by those who had generated the misinformation and equally by their gullible victims to pretend that nobody could have known any better at the time. That's nonsense. Even without any access to "classified" information, it was obvious to anybody with even a little experience that the intelligence was being cooked. If you were an insider, you would have had to work hard *not* to know.

I was the [Canadian] ambassador [to the United Nations] in New York, I had access to the reports of the UN weapons inspectors, and it was evident to me that the United States was putting exclamation points in places where they should have been putting question marks, that the evidence really wasn't persuasive. . . .

Hans Blix, the chief weapons inspector, and his people were basically going pretty much where they wanted to go in Iraq, and he wasn't finding anything, and I went to see him and I said to him, "What's happening?" He said, "I have asked the United States for the best intelligence they have and what they've given me, I go and investigate and I don't find anything."

That was one thing; another thing was when the president said in the State of the Union Address that there is uranium material being imported from Africa to Iraq. I have a colleague who worked at the International Atomic Energy Agency in Vienna. It took them one day to show that that was a forgery, yet the United States was building a whole case of going to war, in part, on such evidence. The person who signed the document who was supposed to be authorizing this transfer wasn't in office at the time the document was supposed to have been signed.

Paul Heinbecker, Canadian ambassador
to the United Nations, 2000–04

Heinbecker's reports from the United Nations were going directly to Prime Minister Chrétien, and he was also in regular touch with him personally: "I told him there was no prospect of UN Security Council approval of a resolution mandating attacking Iraq. It just wasn't going to happen—nobody in New York was convinced of the necessity of the action." So Chrétien knew that the "evidence" of Saddam's WMD was deeply suspect, and he also knew that the Security Council was not going to come up with a resolution that would legitimize what the Americans wanted to do. But what really tipped the scale for Chrétien was Quebec—and his final decision seems to have been made quite late in the day.

As late as December of 2003 Chrétien's government still had plans for Canada to send up to eight hundred Canadian troops to Iraq if the UN Security Council authorized an attack, and senior Canadian Forces officers were still participating in the Pentagon's war planning. Back home, however, opinion polls were revealing something quite alarming; Canadians didn't want to go to war in Iraq without a UN Security Council resolution that made it legal. The numbers were clear: the various opinion polls held in January 2003 showed that only 26 percent of Canadians supported Canadian involvement in an invasion of Iraq without United Nations approval—and only 7 percent of

Quebecers did. For a Liberal government facing a national election within a year, and concerned about retaining its share of the Quebec votes, this was bad news.

The Liberal Party's pollster, Michael Marzolini, chairman and CEO of Pollara, the country's largest Canadian-owned market research company, told Chrétien that he could get national support for a commitment to Iraq if he worked at it: "A small majority of people outside Quebec were in favour of joining the coalition even though a lot didn't like the war. We asked if they would support a government decision to participate and 46 percent said yes. About 48 percent said they would support the government if it decided to stay out. This meant we could have sold either position. Both were moveable to 53 percent with selling." But those were the figures for Canada as a whole. You couldn't sell it in Quebec, and that mattered a great deal to Chrétien.

The first sign that Chrétien was going to defy the United States came on February 12, 2003, when he responded to a United Nations request for some troops in Afghanistan by announcing in Parliament that Canada would send two thousand troops to that country, which had been occupied by Western forces since late 2001.

> It had caught us all completely off-side. We found out about an hour before. . . . If you had come into the Department of National Defense headquarters after that speech, most of us looked like deer caught in headlights. . . . We were shocked because we had other projects and this would tap us out. It made Iraq impossible. . . . I resigned because we were too stretched. It came out of the blue without consultation and without discussion. The minister said in a statement that I was in charge of planning for this deployment in Afghanistan. He was wrong. It was Iraq I was planning for.
>
> Major-General Cameron Ross, director general of
> International Security Policy, National Defence
> Headquarters, 2003

It only became clear in retrospect how this served Chrétien's purposes. By sending most of the available Canadian combat troops to Afghanistan he had effectively emptied the bank, leaving nothing for Iraq, and yet it would let him claim that he was doing something to help the United States elsewhere. That would mollify the Americans and the English Canadians—and the French Canadians wouldn't mind because Afghanistan was a perfectly legal, UN-approved operation in which there were, at this stage, very few casualties. He would already have been worried that a decision to join the United States in invading Iraq would damage the Quebec Liberal Party's hopes of unseating the PQ in the next provincial election in Quebec, but the massive anti-war demonstration in Montreal on March 12 confirmed it. A quarter-million people marched in the city, while only a tenth as many marched in big English Canadian cities.

The Parti Québécois, facing likely defeat at the hands of the Quebec Liberal Party in the next provincial election, sensed an opportunity to campaign against an unpopular federally condoned war and called a snap election on March 14. That just confirmed Chrétien in his conviction that Iraq was a war to avoid, and on March 17 he made his statement in Parliament. On March 19, 2003 the invasion went ahead without Canada. Most Canadians were happy about that—and nobody else seemed very upset about it. Not even the Americans.

President Bush cancelled a state visit to Ottawa that had been scheduled for May, and some Americans boycotted Quebec maple syrup, but it was not renamed "freedom syrup." Even the White House was not really feeling vengeful. When Chrétien ran into Andrew Card, the White House chief of staff, at a wedding a few weeks later, Card told him: "You have been very clear with us [about not going into Iraq without a Security Council Resolution]. You did not double-cross us. We were disappointed, but we knew that you had said that." As Chrétien reflected with some smugness: "Some of [the Americans] thought 'at end of day you will come along anyway,' and they were a bit surprised that I did not come along anyway. But they could not complain about the clarity of my position."

At home, Chrétien's decision was the catalyst that crystallized public opinion against the war: 70 percent of Canadians approved of it. The opposition in Parliament condemned his decision, with opposition leader Stephen Harper comparing it to the failure to confront Nazi Germany in the 1930s. (Godwin's Law: As an online discussion grows longer, the probability of a comparison involving Nazis or Hitler approaches unity— and whoever first mentions the Nazis automatically loses the argument.) But even Harper came around eventually: in 2008 he conceded that his support for the American war in Iraq had been a mistake.

In terms of Canadian casualties, Chrétien's decision probably didn't make much difference. If Canadian troops had been sent to Iraq instead, they would almost certainly have been based around Basra in the south of the country with the British army. The British lost 179 killed in Iraq, out of a force that totalled 43,000 during the invasion but rapidly dropped thereafter to 8,000 or less. Canada lost almost that many soldiers killed in Afghanistan, out of a force that was at all times significantly smaller than the British contingent in Iraq—but it should be noted that only four Canadian soldiers were killed in the ISAF operation before the force was moved from Kabul to Kandahar in late 2005. That decision was taken by Prime Minister Paul Martin, Defence Minister Bill Graham and the chief of defence staff, General Rick Hillier, long after Chrétien had left office.

And while the Afghanistan operation was authorized by the United Nations, in contrast to the lawless American invasion of Iraq, it was just as pointless and futile. Even within the broader lunacy of using regular armies to fight a "war on terror," both those wars made no strategic or political sense. This was more obvious in the case of Iraq, where Saddam Hussein had no contact whatever with the al-Qaeda terrorists and was indeed one of the Arab rulers whom they hoped to overthrow, whereas there actually were several hundred al-Qaeda members, mostly Arabs, in Afghanistan as guests of the Taliban regime before the 9/11 attacks on the United States. However, no Taliban member has ever been involved in terrorist attacks abroad (except in Pakistan), and it is very much to be doubted that Osama bin Laden told the Taliban leaders that he was planning to launch the 9/11 attacks. It would have been a dangerous breach of security, and, more important, it would have alarmed his hosts, who would rightly have anticipated that they would be blamed for the attacks and invaded by American forces. A brief military incursion to destroy the al-Qaeda camp in Afghanistan might have made sense, but the continued military occupation of the entire country for thirteen years after the surviving al-Qaeda members had fled across the border into Pakistan, a much better base for their operations, was an expensive irrelevance. But Canadians still don't do their own strategic thinking, and there is no evidence that any senior officer in National Defence Headquarters in Ottawa ever seriously questioned the absurd notion, dominant in the United States, that large conventional military forces were an appropriate instrument for dealing with a rather modest terrorist threat.

———

When General James Wolfe captured Quebec City in 1759 and added Canada to the British empire, his army was only 4,800 men. The Marquis de Montcalm's army was about the same size, and the battle on the Plains of Abraham caused only 260 British and French deaths (including those of both commanders). It was quite typical of pre-modern wars, in that the returns on a successful war more than justified the cost in money and lives in the eyes of the participants. In those days, nobody saw the institution of warfare as a "problem," and even losing a war was generally just a setback, not an irreversible catastrophe.

The advent of fully industrialized warfare in the early twentieth century changed this situation for good. In the First World War, the cost in lives and resources was so great (eleven million dead, and the equivalent of at least two years' national income for all the main participants) that it was a disaster even for the victors. All the governments on the losing side and one on the winning side (Russia's) were overthrown, and two empires that had existed for centuries were carved up and destroyed. Communism and fascism, radical political doctrines that had previously been marginal, gained power in great states like Russia and Germany.

Twenty years later, the Second World War killed at least four times as many people as the first, and left half the cities of the developed world in ruins. Canada, the United States and Britain had a relatively easy time of it, since their armies were only involved in major ground combat at the very end of the war and the North American countries were not even bombed, but in the last month of the war, nuclear weapons were used on cities for the first time. After the fighting ended, many of the surviving leaders of the defeated powers were tried and executed as criminals, and both Germany and Japan were occupied by foreign military forces for a decade.

We were all climbing a steep learning curve about industrialized total war, Canada no less than the great powers, and the initial response in almost every country was the same: to define the struggle as good against evil, for how else could the scale of the losses be justified? By the end of the First World War, Canadians genuinely believed they were defending democracy against tyranny. They even believed it at the end of the Second World War, although the biggest winner was our great ally, the Soviet Union. It was the right side of the brain, full of hate and hurt and righteous wrath, that wrote the vengeful peace treaty with Germany after the First World War and made the Second World War almost inevitable. But even in 1918 the left brain was also engaged, and its analysis of the problem of war (everybody now agreed that it was a problem) was very different.

The very same people who wrote the Treaty of Versailles also founded the League of Nations, which was a more or less rational attempt to fix a faulty international system. The fix was not well thought out, and the League of Nations fell at the first hurdle, but the underlying analysis was quite correct: it was a system problem. The traditional right of every sovereign state to wage war against any other sovereign state made militarization inevitable and wars very likely. That had been acceptable when wars were small-scale events that did little damage to civilian society, but now great-power wars had become intolerably destructive, so sovereignty had somehow to be restrained. These two ideas—the notion that war is a crusade against evil, and the hypothesis that it is actually a system problem—are mutually incompatible, of course, but that didn't stop intelligent people from believing them both.

The same bipolar vision prevailed after the Second World War: yes, the fascist dictators had been a particularly nasty set of men, who could fairly be described as evil. But it was also obvious that wars between the great powers would continue to occur, with or without fascist dictators, until the international rules were changed. But changed in what way?

Canada played a minimal role in this debate after the First World War, when it was mainly concerned with establishing itself as an independent country in the eyes of the world, and it was positively destructive in the 1920s, when it succeeded in establishing the principle that safer countries like itself (the "fireproof house") had the right to abstain from collective military action to enforce international law. But after the Second World War it played a different and quite useful role. Although we had a much easier time in that war, Canadian politicians and diplomats were well aware that the existence of nuclear weapons had made it even more urgent to create an institution and a set of rules that would lessen the danger of a Third World War—and in 1945, for the one time in its history, Canada was almost a great power. It was a transitory status, due solely to the fact that most of the real great powers were temporarily flat on their backs because of war damage, but we used our fleeting power well. Canadian diplomats played an important role in writing the Charter of the United Nations, which has served us far better than most people recognize.

Nobody in San Francisco truly believed that the United Nations could stop all the wars in the world. Its real purpose was to prevent any more wars between the great powers, for that kind of war was already killing in the tens of millions, and another time it would probably be in the hundreds of millions. Unfortunately, no matter what kind of new rules you write for the conduct of international affairs, the great powers cannot be forced to obey those rules, for there are by definition no greater powers. So the drafters of the Charter did the best they could, making it illegal for any country to use military force against another country no matter what the excuse unless it was explicitly authorized by the Security Council—and that turned out to be enough. No great power has fought any other great power for sixty-nine years now. That is around three times as long as ever before.

Smaller countries can fight each other, and many have. The Security Council does have the authority to use force against an aggressor in such cases, but it has only twice managed to agree to do so: when North Korea invaded South Korea in 1950, and when Iraq invaded Kuwait in 1990. Great powers can still attack lesser countries with impunity—the Russian invasion of Afghanistan and the American invasion of Iraq, for example. But the great powers do not fight each other any more.

This self-restraint is not really due to some newfound respect for international law on their part. They genuinely do not want to fight each other any more, no matter what the provocation, because they are acutely aware of the probability that any open warfare between nucle-ar-armed great powers could quickly escalate into mutual nuclear destruction. Nevertheless, their leaders still operate in a domestic polit-ical context where "backing down" and failing to defend "vital national interests" will expose them to savage criticism and quite possibly loss of power. What they need, therefore, is some means of backing away from a dangerous confrontation that will not result in accusations that they have betrayed the national interest.

The United Nations provides that means. Rather than give in to the threats of a rival great power and suffer an unacceptable loss of face, a national leader can draw back from the brink out of respect for international law and the (imaginary) authority of the United Nations. It seems a very slender reed on which to base the world's hopes of avoiding another, even more devastating great-power war, but it has already saved us several times, most notably in the case of the Cuban Missile Crisis of 1962.

There is, of course, no guarantee that this flimsy barrier against a return to the great wars of the past century will hold forever. Whether it does will depend to a large extent on a fear of great-power war that has been acquired through the experience of two such wars with modern weapons, and it is not certain that emerging, non-Western great powers that do not have that terrible history will be equally and adequately frightened of the consequences of not backing away from a confrontation. But the founders of the United Nations did the best they could, and they did better work than they knew.

And then, having done our best to end the cycle of great alliance wars, we panicked in the late 1940s and created another great alliance to stop the Russians (who weren't coming). Canada took a leading role in the panic, being one of the two countries that persuaded the United States to go down the road that led to the foundation of NATO, and we devoted most of our military efforts to the Cold War for the next forty years, doing peacekeeping on the side to assuage our nagging suspicion that we had taken the wrong road. After the Cold War ended with the collapse of the Soviet Union, we even went along with the conversion of NATO into a sort of freelance world police force, there being no longer any rival great power to put a brake on our ambitions. Some of the small wars we took part in could be justified in humanitarian terms, and we did manage to dodge the most flagrantly illegal one, in Iraq, but the pretense that "coalitions of the willing" or the "international community" (aka NATO) had the right to use force unilaterally undermined the always shaky authority of the United Nations. However, the declining enthusiasm of the United States for such wars may put an end to this policy before it does irreparable damage to the international rules of conduct that we worked so hard to devise and entrench.

It is a distinctly mixed record, and the best that can be said is that so far we have got away with it. When you're up to your ass in alligators, it's easy to forget that your original aim was to drain the swamp. But that is the job we embarked on almost a hundred years ago, and it's still very much a work in progress.

> However deficient in many ways the United Nations may be, I think it's an absolutely essential organization. There is no way in which ths effort cannot be made—it has to be made—knowing perfectly well that you're pushing an enormous boulder up a very steep hill. There will be slips and it will come back on you from time to time, but you have to go on pushing. Because if you don't do that, you simply give in to the notion that you're going to go into another global war again at some point, this time with nuclear weapons.
>
> Brian Urquhart, former undersecretary-general,
> United Nations

Amen to that.

PHOTO PERMISSIONS

Wounded Canadians after Paardeberg
Source: Library and Archives Canada/Credit: Reinhold Thiele/C-006097

Soldiers leave for War, 1915
Source: City of Toronto Archives, Fonds 1244, Item 727

B Company, Newfoundland Regiment, in front line, Suvla Bay, 1915
Source: The Rooms Archives, St. John's

The enthusiasm of the early days was long gone. . . .
Source: City of Toronto Archives, Fonds 1244, Item 816

Talbot M. Papineau, April 1916.
Source: Library and Archives Canada/Talbot Mercer Papineau fonds/C-013222

Sir Robert Borden chats with a wounded man...
Source: Library and Archives Canada/Department of National Defence fonds/PA-000880

How did people in the West feel about conscription?
Source: Library and Archives Canada/ The Toronto world [microform] – June 6, 1917– AMICUS 8693733 – Page 6.

Lester B. Pearson, spring 1918
Source: Library and Archives Canada/Duncan Cameron fonds/PA-110824

Members of 5ᵗʰ Canadian Mounted Rifles...
Source: CWM 19930012-528; George Metcalf Archival Collection © Canadian War Museum

Mackenzie King was a dumpy, fussy bachelor...
Source: Library and Archives Canada/Laurier House collection/C-080345

Sutherland Brown, Special Reconnaissance
Source: Department of National Defence, PMR 85 151

Mackenzie King inspecting guard of honour...
Source: Library and Archives Canada/Credit: Capt. Laurie A. Audrain/ Dept. of National Defence fonds/PA-152440

The Malton aircraft factory in Toronto
Source: Avro Lancaster 11736-6
McDonnell Douglas Canada, Neg MDCAN 11736-6

"I've been in a permanent state of exhilaration since March 8..."
Source: Public Archives: C 130882

Survivors of the H.M.C.S. *Clayoquot*
Source: Library and Archives Canada/Credit: Ernest Campbell/Dept. of National Defence fonds/PA-141316

Carriers in soft, flooded ground, Breskens Pocket
Source: Lt. Grant/DND, Public Archives Canada PA 131252

HMCS *Summerside* in heavy seas
Source: Library and Archives Canada/Credit: Gilbert Alexander Milne/ Dept. of National Defence fonds/PA-115481

Sherman tanks of Lord Strathcona's Horse...
Source: Library and Archives Canada/Credit: Paul E. Tomelin/Dept. of National Defence fonds/PA-115496

CF-101 Starfighter in 1977...
Source: Public Archives of Canada PCN77-510, photographer M/Cpl Knox

President Dwight Eisenhower meets Prime Minister Diefenbaker and Minister of Foreign Affairs Howard Green, 1960.
Source: Library and Archives Canada/Department of External Affairs fonds/PA-122743 © Government of Canada. Reproduced with the permission of Library and Archives Canada (2014).

By the end of 1962 the Bomarcs were all fully operational...
Source: DND/John Sherman

Canadian soldiers on NATO manoeuvres, 1984
Source: Kent Nason

INDEX

11th Infantry Brigade, CEF, 89–91

139 Squadron, RAF, 107

163rd (Canadien-Français) Battalion ("Poil-aux-Pattes"), CEF, 85

189th (Canadien-Français) Battalion, CEF, 85, 88

19th Army Field Regiment, Royal Canadian Artillery, 234

1st Battalion, RCR, 281

1st Brigade, CEF, 194, 195

1st Canadian Division, CEF, 44, 45, 52, 54, 55, 194, 195

1st Contingent, CEF, 45, 47, 80–81

22nd Battalion, CEF, 46, 85, 88, 123, 159

26th Reserve Corps (German), 54

2nd (Special Service) Battalion, RCR, 14–15,

2nd Canadian Armoured Brigade, CAR, 234

2nd Canadian Infantry Division, Canadian army, 195, 236

2nd Canadian Division, CEF, 81

38th Parallel, 278, 292, 299, 300, 303–4

3rd Brigade, CEF, 55

3rd Canadian Division, Canadian Corps, 126, 195

401 Squadron, RCAF, 195

47th Squadron Division, RAF, 143

67th Battery, Canadian army, 141

81st Field Regiment, RCHA, 281

Acadia, 34

Acheson, Dean, 293, 295–96, 298, 302, 308

Achilles, Ted, 272–73

aerial warfare, 106–10, 195–96, 202–4, 206, 210, 223–27, 280, 300–1, 308, 332–44, 383

Afghanistan, 370, 386, 390–93, 396

Africa, 134, 163, 164

Air Force Act, 107, 108

Alaska, 287

Alaskan boundary dispute, 10, 11, 12, 20–21

Alberta, 48–49, 117

Alderson, Sir Edwin, 82
Algeria, 54
Algoma East (riding), 372
Allison, J.Wesley, 58
al-Qaeda, 392–93
Alsace-Lorraine, 36, 137
Amazon forest, 287
Amiens, Battle of, 125–26
Amy, Edward "Ned," 3
Anatolia (Turkey), 153
Anderson, W.F., 144
Andropov, Yuri, 380
Anglo-French alliance, 189
Annis, Claire, 334
anti-ballistic missiles, 380
anti-Semitism, 180, 221, 250
anti-tank rifles, 102
Antwerp (Belgium), 239
appeasement policy, 169, 177–81
Arab revolt, 138
Arab-Israeli War, 319
Arcand, Adrien, 221
Archangel (Russia), 141, 142, 144, 145
Ardennes region (France), 214
armaments production, 77–78,
    204–8, 215
armistice, 126–27, 136, 141, 300,
    304, 305
arms control, 349, 370, 376, 386
    (See also nuclear deterrence;
    nuclear disarmament)
Army Council, 246
Arnhem Land (Australia), 286–87
Arras (France), 124–25
Article 10 (UN Charter), 157, 163
Article 2 ("Canadian article"), 273
Article 51 (UN Charter), 312

artillery, long-range, 64
artillery spotters, 102
ASDIC, 209, 211
Asia, 134
Asquith, Herbert, 25, 28
Aswan High Dam, 315
Athenia (ship), 186
Atholstan, Lord, 114
Atlantic, Battle of the, 229–32 (See
    also submarine warfare)
Atlantic Wall, 234, 250
atomic bomb, 252, 263, 277, 337
Attlee, Clement, 263, 271, 302
Austin, Warren, 297, 299–300
Australia/Australian troops, 20, 22,
    60, 69, 80, 103, 112, 125, 129,
    146, 160, 286–87, 318, 373
Austria, 35, 36, 49, 116, 117
Austria–Hungary, 136, 138
Austrian Air Force, 108
autocracies, 133–34
Avro Arrow, 344, 346
Axis powers, 189

Baghdad Pact, 315
balance of power, 32–33, 149, 162,
    199, 223, 259–60, 307, 355
ballistic calculations, 102
Baltic countries, 174, 192
Barker, William "Billy," 107–10
Barton, Bill, 352–53
Bay of Pigs (Cuba), 354, 355
Bayne, Francis, 281
Beatty, Perrin, 383, 384
Beauharnois Light, Heat and Power
    Company, 205
Beaumont Hamel, battle of, 60

Beauvoir (France), 235
Belarus, 136
Belgium, 65, 66, 67, 71, 214, 236, 239, 240, 275
Belmont (South Africa), 14
Benelux countries, 271, 275
Bennett, Richard B., 88, 164, 165
Berlin crisis, 354, 356
Berlin Wall, 377
Berlin, 67, 137, 253, 273–74
Bermuda, 44, 200
Bernadotte, Count, 319
Bevin, Ernest, 263–64
Big Five (UN), 258
Big Push, 125–26
bin Laden, Osama, 393
Bird, Will R., 92
Bishop, Billy, 109–10
Black, Herman, 92
"Black Pit" (mid-Atlantic gap), 211
Blackshirts, 221
Blitzkrieg, 193, 213–15
Blix, Hans, 388
Bloch, Jan, 63–65, 67, 73
"blooded" concept, 227–29
Boer War, 7–23, 26, 29, 51, 113, 296, 305
Bohlen, Chip, 272
Bolsheviks, 117, 136, 141–44, 180, 250, 267
Bomarcs, 250, 344–45, 360, 365–66, 367, 372
Bomber Command, 226
bombers, 102, 203, 223–27, 346, 369
Bonard Law, Andrew, 74
Bonner, Allan, 2–3

Borden, Frederick, 23
Borden, Henry, 95, 205, 207
Borden, Robert, 27, 29, 56, 45, 46, 73–75, 77, 79–80, 82, 92, 93, 94–95, 97, 110–18, 119, 123, 125, 126, 137, 143, 144, 145–46, 148, 150–51, 157, 205, 218, 244, 259
Bosnia, 386
Boston, 230
Bourassa, Henri, 8, 13–14, 41, 87, 112 , 116, 130, 221
Brantford (ON), 26
Bren guns, 205
Breskens Pocket, 240–41, 252
Brest (Brittany), 194
Brest-Litovsk, Treaty of, 124, 136
Brezhnev, Leonid, 380
Britain, Battle of, 196
British Admiralty, 210
British empire, 13, 16, 25, 30, 49, 61, 84, 86, 96, 143, 146, 152, 154, 155, 160, 161–62, 169–70, 171, 178, 180, 181, 200, 272, 393
British Expeditionary Force, 66
British High Command, 93, 229
British Military Medal, 93
British Royal Navy, 27, 40, 135, 160, 209, 210
British War Cabinet, 148
British West Indies, 200
Broadfoot, Barry, 198
Brock, Jeffry, 188, 291, 292, 299, 302, 358
Brodie, Bernard, 324, 326, 369–70
Brown, J. Sutherland "Buster," 157–58, 160–61, 162

Bruchési, (archbishop of Montreal), 84

Bruchmüller, Georg, 102–3, 124

Bruges (Belgium), 240

Brussels, Treaty of, 271

Bryce, Bob, 340

Buchenwald (concentration camp), 233

Bulgaria, 384

Bundy, McGeorge "Mac," 375

Burns, E.L.M. "Tommy," 89, 90–91, 161, 228–29, 319–20

Bush, George H.W., 385

Bush, George W., 386–87, 389, 391

Byng, Sir Julian, 92

Cadieux, Léo, 329

Calgary Highlanders, 236, 242

Calvin, Jim, 311

Cambrai (France), 101, 102

Camp David, 374–75

Campaign for Nuclear Disarmament, 360

Campbell, Craig, 186, 230–32

Canada–U.S. Permanent Joint Board on Defence (PJBD), 201, 332–33

Canada–U.S. relations (postwar), 329–44, 346–53, 357–59, 360–67, 371–92

Canadian Air Group, 381–82

Canadian Air Sea Transportable (CAST) Brigade, 382

Canadian Armed Forces Chiefs of Staff, 362

Canadian Army Corps, 228

Canadian Army Medical Corps, 71

Canadian Chiefs of Staff Committee, 272

Canadian Corps Heavy Artillery, 109

Canadian Corps, 82, 88–89, 90–93, 103, 125

Canadian Destroyers Far East, 299

Canadian Engineers, 141

Canadian Expeditionary Force, 44, 58, 74, 159, 196

Canadian Forces, 378–79, 381, 383, 389

Canadian General Staff, 23, 24, 25, 43, 154, 195, 227, 298, 341

Canadian Joint Staff Mission, 330

Canadian Military Gazette, 47

Canadian Military Mission, 267

Canadian militia, 160–61

Canadian Mission to the United Nations, 297

Canadian Mounted Rifles (CMR), 17

"Canadian proposal," 167

Canadian Scottish Regiment, 241, 252

Canadian Syren Force, 141, 142

Canadian Third Division, 234

Cape Colony, 9

Cape Helles (Gallipoli), 57

Cape Town (South Africa), 14

capitalist encirclement, 265

Card, Andrew, 391

Cardin, P.J.A., 187, 220

Carroll, John, 55

Carter, Jimmy, 380

Cartierville (Montreal Island), 114

Castro, Fidel, 355

Catholic church, 84–85, 115, 181, 221

Caucasus Mountains, 138, 234
CBC, 2, 383, 384
CCF party, 184, 245
Cecil, Lord Robert, 148, 169
Ceylon, 318
Chamberlain, Joseph, 9, 13, 21, 24
Chamberlain, Neville, 183, 190, 192
Chambly (corvette), 211
Chanak (Turkey), 154, 155
Charter of the United Nations, 247, 254, 258–59, 290, 312, 395
Chernenko, Konstantin, 380
Chiefs of Staff Committee, 298, 340, 347
children, 16, 17, 18, 19, 46, 50, 176, 243, 298
chimpanzees, 284–86
China, 26, 293–94, 299, 300, 301–2, 303, 315
Chrétien, Jean, 387–92
Churchill, Winston, 101, 177, 192, 201, 245, 268
CIA, 314
Citizen (Ottawa), 17, 18
Clark, Alan, 99–100
Clausson, Gilles, 243
Clavette, Al, 241, 252
Claxton, Brooke, 334
Clemenceau, Georges, 96, 128, 137
Clint, Mabel B., 57, 72–73
Coates, Robert, 359, 370, 376, 379, 380, 381, 384, 385, 386, 397
Cold War, 2, 266–67, 278, 312, 322, 331, 343
collective security, 149, 150, 151, 156, 163–67, 169, 175, 255, 256–57, 271, 294–97, 305, 312, 313

Collishaw, Raymond, 143
Colonist (Victoria), 117
Colorado Springs, 357
Committee of Imperial Defence, 27, 28
Commonwealth Air Training Plan, 190–91, 226
Communism, 180, 267, 269, 270, 271, 276, 293–94, 295, 297, 303, 304, 305–6, 314, 357, 380, 394
concentration camps, 233, 255
Congo, 322
Congress of Vienna, 34
Congressional Record, 303
Connaught, Duke of, 75
conscription, 75, 78–81, 95, 97, 110–20, 125, 129, 131–32, 159, 173, 184, 185, 187, 196–98, 217–19, 220–22, 237–38, 239, 243, 244–46
Conservative party, 45, 111, 114, 116, 117, 118, 152, 196, 198, 218–19, 220–21, 318, 341, 352, 363, 380–81, 383, 391
continental defence, 200, 330
continuous front, 63, 67–68, 100, 215
convoy SC42, 210–11
corvettes, 209–11, 230
Council of the League of Nations, 15, 155
counter-factual history, 133–40, 249–52
Courcellete (France), 85
Crimea, 312
critical system, 37–38, 385
Croatia, 386

Croix de Guerre, 93
Cronje, Piet, 15
cronyism, 80–82
Cuban Missile Crisis, 353–59, 360,
    363, 397
Cullen, Walter, 126
Cullum, A.E., 55, 56
Currie, Sir Arthur, 56, 92–93, 123
Curtis, W.A., 106
Cycle Corps, 126
Cyprus, 322
Czech Republic, 384
Czechoslovakia, 270

Dafoe, John W., 151, 152, 168
Daily News (Toronto), 117
Dandurand, Raoul, 155, 157, 186
Danzig (Poland), 180, 249
Dardanelles (Turkey), 59–60, 154
Darmstadt (Germany), 225
Dauphin (MB), 107
Davidson, Sir Basil, 58, 59, 60–61
D-Day, 234, 235 (*See also*
    Normandy landings)
de Gaulle, Charles, 34
de Montcalm, Marquis, 393
DEFCON alerts, 357, 359
Defence of Canada, The (film), 1–4
Defence Scheme Number One
    (invasion of U.S.), 157–62
democracy, 95, 123, 133, 138, 183,
    270, 301, 354, 376, 385–86, 394
Denikin, Anton, 143
Denison, T., 10
Dent, Len, 3
Denton, Faye, 206
Dept of External Affairs, 25, 71,

164, 165, 169, 175, 194, 201, 254,
    256, 260, 265, 268, 271, 277,
    279, 293, 298, 306, 318, 331,
    336, 340–41, 342–43, 348, 351,
    352–53, 357, 362, 373, 376, 382
Dept of National Defence (DND),
    3, 335, 351, 357, 358
depth-charges, 209, 211, 232, 346
Devonport (UK), 80
Dextrase, Jacques, 235, 236, 304
Diefenbaker, John, 320–21, 341–45,
    348, 351–54, 357–59, 360, 363–
    67, 371, 376
Dieppe, raid at, 196, 223
Dion, Wilfrid, 121
Directorate of Military Operations
    and Intelligence, 160
Doherty, Charles, 150–51
Dominion Police, 114, 120
Donkeys, The (Clark), 99–100
Dorchester riding (PQ), 118
Dover, 193, 202
Drapeau, Jean, 221
Dresden (Germany), 225
dual-key system, 362, 371
Dublin, 114
Duff, Mr. Justice Lyman, 119
Dulles, John Foster, 305, 315
Dullstroom (South Africa), 17–18
Duncan, Sara Jeannette, 26
Dunkirk, 180, 193, 195, 207, 214
Duplessis, Maurice, 186, 187
Dvina River (Russia), 141

E.A.C. Amy & Sons Management
    Support Services, 3
East Berlin, 253

East Germany, 322

East Prussia, 249

Easter Rising (Dublin), 114

Eastern Europe, 67, 123, 180, 181, 189, 208, 246, 250–51, 268–70, 306, 322, 346, 365, 385

Eberding, Knut, 243

Eden, Sir Anthony, 316, 317

Edmonton (AB), 48, 329

Edmonton Regiment, 192

Egypt, 80, 250, 314, 315–21

Eisenhower, Dwight D., 305, 306, 317, 334, 351, 380

Elizabeth I (queen), 173, 174

Ellesberg, Daniel, 354

Elliott, William, 144, 196, 202, 214, 239

English Canada, 87, 88, 97, 110–22, 129–30, 131, 132, 155, 162, 170, 171–74, 185, 187, 190, 191, 197, 218–19, 221, 238, 246, 306, 317, 320, 343, 391

English Channel, 67, 124, 195

Enlightenment, 284

Entente powers, 41

Episcopacy of French Canada, 84

escort convoys, 209, 210

espionage, 223, 261–63, 272

Esquimalt (naval base), 24

Essex East (riding), 169

Estonia, 136, 174, 384

Ethiopia, 163–69

European wars, short, 34–36

Everywoman's World (magazine), 116

executions (military), 122–23

Far East, 333

Fargo (ND), 157

farmers, military exemptions, 46

fascism, 139, 221, 252, 276, 394, 395

female pilots, 330

Festubert, Battle of, 56

field hospitals, 72, 73

fighter pilots, 195–96, 202–4, 330

Finland, 136, 174, 192

First Canadian Army, 234

"First Five Hundred," 59

first strike (capability), 327, 336, 338, 354, 356, 370

First World War, 1, 4, 5, 31, 33–145, 150, 153, 158, 161, 162, 171, 172, 180, 189, 190, 198, 213, 215, 227, 228, 229, 246, 247, 268, 283, 289, 290, 321, 349, 393–94, 395

Flanagan, Arthur, 19

Flanders (Belgium), 130, 151, 152

flexible response doctrine, 369

Flood, Daniel J., 365–66

Florizel (ship), 59

Foch, Ferdinand, 67

Focke-Wulf (manufacturer), 190, 202

Fokker D-VII (aircraft), 108

Ford Motor Company, 204

"forward basing," 355

Foulkes, Charles, 239–40, 243, 272, 298, 340–43, 347

France, 26, 35, 40, 44, 65–67, 139, 151, 152, 153, 189, 194, 195, 199

France and Low Countries, 193–94, 198, 213–15

Franco, Francisco, 252, 276

Frankfurt, 225
Franz Ferdinand (archduke of Austria), 49
Fraser, A.D., 56
Fraser, Blair, 305
freedom of the seas, 128
Freeman, George, 234, 305–6, 389, 391
French African Light Infantry, 54
French army, 65–66, 68, 95, 123, 136–37, 193, 194
French Canada, 84–88, 97, 110–22, 129, 130–32, 152, 153, 159, 166, 170, 172–74, 184–85, 186, 187, 197, 198, 199, 204, 218–19, 220–21, 238, 246, 298–99
Fresnes Prison (Paris), 233
Frink, M., 50
Front de libération du Québec, 378
Fuller, J.F.C., 80
Fusiliers Mont Royal, 235

Galicia (Eastern Europe), 116
Gallipoli (Turkey), 57, 59–60, 72, 317
Gallishaw, John, 60, 61, 62
Gaspé (QC), 85
Gault, A. Hamilton, 51
Gaza Strip, 315
Gazette (Montreal), 115
Gellner, John, 339, 347
Geneva, 155, 165, 166, 167, 350

George VI (king), 173, 174
German 26th Reserve Corps, 54
German General Staff, 65, 67, 99
German High Command, 213

German March offensive, 124–25
German victory, counter-factual history, 133–40
German–Soviet war, 250–51, 252
Gestapo, 232, 233
Gibraltar, 34
Gilbert, Bertrand, 233
Globe, 12
Gneisenau (warship), 202
Godbout, Adélard, 187, 221
Godega Aerodrome (Austria), 107, 108
Gombe National Park (Tanzania), 285
Goodall, Jane, 285
Goose Bay (Labrador), 333, 346
Gorbachev, Mikhail, 380, 381, 385
Gouzenko Affair, 263
Gouzenko, Ivor, 261–62
Graham, Bill, 392
Graham, George, 158
Great Lakes, 28
Greece, 71, 153
Green, Arthur, 77
Green, Howard, 349–50, 352, 362
Greenland, 210
Grey, Sir Edward, 28
Griesbach, W.A., 162
group-living predators, 289–90
Guatemala, 314
Guderian, Heinz, 214
guerrilla warfare, 16–17, 81, 278, 315
Gueudecourt, Battle of, 60
gunpowder, smokeless, 64
Gwatkin, Sir Willoughby, 43, 94

Hague, The, 64–65
Haig, Sir Douglas, 92
Halifax (NS), 24, 186, 230
Halifax Harbour, 232
Halstead, John, 336
Hamburg, 225
Hames, Clifford, 123–24
Hankey, Maurice, 28
Harkness, Douglas, 358–59, 362, 364–65
Harper, Stephen, 392
Harris, Sir Arthur "Bomber," 224
Hawken, "Hap," 241, 242
Heinbecker, Paul, 389
helicopters, 383, 384
Hellyer, Paul, 372, 378
Henry, R.A.C., 205
Héroux, Omer, 173
Heseltine, Michael, 382
Hickerson, Jack, 272
High-Frequency Direction-Finders, 209, 210
Highland Light Infantry, 241
Hillier, Rick, 392
Hiroshima, 261, 345
Hitler, Adolf, 168, 174, 175, 176, 177, 178–82, 189, 192, 195, 203, 207, 214, 247, 250, 252, 267, 276
HMCS *Clayoquot*, 230–32
HMCS *Skeena*, 210
Hoffman, Max, 99
Holland, 214, 236, 239–42, 275
Hollis, Christopher, 348
Holmes, John, 256, 266, 276, 297, 306, 318
Honest John missiles, 346, 372

Hong Kong, 217, 219–20, 221–22, 223
Hornbostel, Klaus, 232
horticulturalists, 284, 287
"hot lines," 385
House Committee on Appropriations, 365–66
Howe, C.D., 205–8, 211, 259
Hudd, Leslie, 51, 52–53, 54, 93
Hughes, Sam, 29–30, 43–45, 58, 79–82, 93
Hume, Alex, 19
Hundevad, John, 142
Hungary, 317, 322, 384
hunter-gatherers, 284, 286, 287, 288, 289, 290
Hurricanes (planes), 179
Hussein, Saddam, 387, 388, 389, 392
Hutton, Edward, 11

Iceland, 208, 211
Ignatieff, George, 249, 277, 278, 340–41, 342, 293, 295
Imperial Conference (1902), 21–22; (1907), 24; (1923), 155
Imperial Defence Conference (1909), 25
Imperial Federation League, 10
Imperial General Staff, 29, 195
Imperial German General Staff, 65
Imperial Munitions Board, 77
Imperial War Cabinet, 60, 95, 96, 97, 126
Imperial War Conference, 75, 145–47
Inchon (South Korea), 299

India, 75, 146, 160, 250, 318
industrialized military technology, 64, 68, 76, 195, 289, 393–94
Inglis (washing machine) Company, 204–5
intercontinental ballistic missiles (ICBMs), 308, 329, 338, 339, 346, 349, 355–56, 360, 365, 367, 369
International Security Assistance Force (ISAF), 386
international system, 31–32, 35, 128, 129, 145, 147, 148, 150, 156, 169, 170, 175, 257, 259, 395
Iran, 315, 387, 388–92, 396
Iraq, 71, 138
Is War Now Impossible? (Bloch), 64, 65
isolationism, 151, 152–53, 155, 165, 166, 167, 176, 185, 198, 199, 256–57, 279
Israel, 315–21

Istanbul, 59, 153
Italian army, 123, 136–37
Italo–Ethiopian settlement, 167
Italy, 35, 36, 107, 108, 153, 163–69, 189, 194, 228–29, 237, 252, 269, 360

Japan, 139, 189, 208, 217, 219–20, 251, 253, 267–68, 278, 292–93, 394
Jefferson, John, 19, 21
Jellicoe, John, 96
Jews, 176, 180, 221, 250, 252
Johnson, Lady Bird, 374, 375

Johnson, Lyndon B., 373, 374–75
Jupiter missiles, 360

Karelia, 141
Kemal, Mustafa (Ataturk), 153–54
Kennan, George, 272, 293
Kennedy, John F., 353, 354, 356–57, 360, 367, 369, 372, 380
Khrushchev, Nikita, 292, 312–13, 338–39, 354, 355, 357
Kierans, Eric, 377
Kim Il-sung, 278, 280, 291–92, 295
Kimberley (South Africa), 14
Kinmel Park (Wales), 158–59
Kissinger, Henry, 152
Kitchener, Horatio Herbert (1st Earl Kitchener), 59
Knowles, J.M., 132
Korea, 280 (See also North Korea; South Korea)
Korean War, 277–81, 291–305, 308, 312, 329–34, 337–40, 377, 395
Kruger, Rayne, 15, 16, 20
Kuwait, 388, 396

L'Événement, 113, 120
La Liberté, 113, 114
La Ligue pour la defense du Canada, 221
La Patrie, 10
La Réveil, 113
Labelle riding (QC), 13
Lacombe, Liguori, 184–85
Lacroix, Wilfrid, 184–85
Ladies' Patriotic League, 50
Laing, George, 224, 225, 226, 227
Lake, Percy, 23

Lalumière, Élie, 114, 115
Lancaster bombers, 206
Lansing, Robert, 146
Lapointe, Arthur, 85, 122
Lapointe, Ernest, 168, 184, 187
Larin, Napoleon, 55, 56
Larue, Lucien, 8
Latvia, 136, 174, 384
Laurendeau, Andre, 221
Laurier, Sir Wilfrid, 10, 11–13, 20,
    21–23, 24, 27, 40, 111, 118–19,
    151, 152, 186, 305
Lavergne, Armand, 113, 114
Le Devoir, 41, 116, 173, 347
Le Temps, 40
League of Nations, 129, 137, 149–
    51, 259, 264, 283, 289, 294, 321,
    395
Leavitt, Herb, 15
Lee-Enfields, 52
LeMay, Curtis, 326–27, 338
Lemnos (Greece), 57, 72, 73
Lenin, Vladimir, 267
Lessard, E.L., 121
Lévesque, Omer, 195, 202, 203–4,
    300–1
Levy, Jack, 37–38
Liberal party, 12, 111, 113, 116, 117,
    118, 152, 153, 184–85, 187, 191,
    196, 198, 205, 218, 245, 341, 363,
    366, 367, 371, 383, 388, 389
Libya, 204, 386
Liddell Hart, Sir Basil, 180
limited nuclear war, 346, 361–62
Limited Test Ban Treaty, 350
Lithuania, 174, 383
Lloyd George, 96

Lloyd George, David, 75, 89, 93,
    96, 123, 126, 137, 146, 154, 155
London (UK), 76
London Daily Mail, 153
looting, 16–18
Lord Strathcona's Horse, 16
Lovett, Robert, 272
loyalty, 11, 12, 18, 26, 60, 86, 129,
    132, 152, 171, 172, 185, 187, 359,
    360, 361, 367, 373
Ludendorff, Erich, 96, 99, 125
Luftwaffe, 202–3
Luxembourg, 275

Macalister, Ken, 232
MacArthur, Douglas, 292–93, 299,
    300, 303
Macdonald, Angus, 207
MacDonald, Donald, 377
Macedonia, 71–72, 106
machine guns, 51, 52, 54-55, 66,
    68, 86, 91-93, 101, 105, 108, 121,
    188, 219, 233
Mackenzie, C.J., 259
Mackenzie, William Lyon, 118, 152
Mackenzie King, William Lyon,
    111, 118, 152–55, 157, 164–71,
    172–73, 175, 176–77, 179, 184,
    185, 186, 187, 190, 191–92, 195–
    98, 199–202, 204, 207, 208, 211,
    217–22, 223, 227, 228, 236, 237–
    38, 242, 244–47, 256–57, 262–
    65, 270–71, 278, 279–80,
    330–32
Maclean's (magazine), 347
Mae Enga horticulturalists, 287
Malik, Yakov, 293

Malone, Richard, 239
Malton aircraft factory, 206
Manchuria, 301
Manion, Robert J., 171, 173
Manitoba Free Press, 151
Mann, Donald, 43
Manson, Paul, 383
Mao tse-tung, 293–94
Marchand, Jean, 377
Marshall Plan, 276
Marsil, Tancrède, 113–14
Martin, Paul, 169, 204, 373, 392
Marxist-Leninist ideology, 253–54
Marzolini, Michael, 390
Masaryk, Jan, 270, 271
Mason, James, 78
mass bombing, 225–27
massive retaliation doctrine, 325, 326, 327, 354, 369
Maus, Jairus, 52, 53, 57
Maxim machine guns, 64
McCrae, John, 127
McDonnell-Douglas of Canada, 344
McNamara, Robert, 365, 366, 369–70, 373
McNaughton, Andrew, 109, 194, 228, 272, 245–46
McPherson, Joe, 92
Mechanized Brigade Group, 381–82
Meighen, Arthur, 152, 196, 218–19, 220–21
Mesopotamia, 71 (*See also* Iraq)
Mewburn, S.C., 143
Middle East, 322, 333
Mignault, Dr. Arthur, 45–46

Milan, 34
Military District No. 4 (Montreal), 161
military exemptions, 46–47
military hospitals, 94
Military Service Act, 119, 131
military-industrial complex, 309, 379, 381
Militia Dept, 26–27

militia ideology, 80
Miller, Frank, 337, 343, 347
minesweeping, 230–32
Minorca, 34
Minshall, William E., 365–66
Minto, Lord, 9, 10–12, 20
Mississauga Horse, 47
Modder River (South Africa), 7
Molotov, Vyacheslav, 255
Monroe Doctrine, 22, 199
Mons (Belgium), 126
Montgomery, Bernard Law "Monty," 239
Montreal Star, 47, 114, 115
Montreal, 40, 47, 113–14, 115, 161, 207, 221, 261, 263, 377, 378
Montreuil-Bellay (France), 222
Moose Jaw (corvette), 211
moral equivalence theory, 266
Morris, Edward, 58–59, 60–61
Morrison, E.W.B., 17–18, 46
Moscow, 208, 312
Mount Royal Club (Montreal), 115
Mulock, William, 12
Mulroney, Brian, 380–81, 388
Munro, Ross, 237, 242
Murmansk (Russia), 145

Murngin people (Arnhem Land), 286–87

Murray, Ivor, 55, 56

Murray, L.W., 209

Mussolini, Benito, 163, 166–67, 169, 252

Nagasaki (Japan), 261

Napanee (ON), 30

Nassau summit, 364

Nasser, Gamal Abdel, 315–16, 319

"National" (coalition) government, 191, 218

national identity, 48, 89, 129, 172

National Research Council, 259, 261

National Resources Mobilization Act (NRMA), 197, 198, 207, 237, 244, 245, 246

national security "threats" (post-war), 160–62

National Steel Car, 206

Nationalists, 40, 113, 116, 143, 170–71, 273

NATO, 3, 272–76, 278, 293, 294–98, 302, 305, 306, 307, 309–13, 316, 319, 322, 336, 348, 349, 361, 362, 372, 373, 377, 382, 383, 384–86, 397

Nazis, 198–99, 222–23, 250, 276

Nazi–Soviet Pact, 174–75

neutrality, 25, 41, 66, 71, 77, 96, 134, 171, 192, 199, 222, 276, 350, 377

New Guinea, 287, 290

New Mexico, 226, 261

New York, 230

New Zealand/New Zealand troops, 20, 69, 78, 129, 146, 318, 373

Newfoundland Escort Force, 209

Newfoundland Patriotic Association, 58, 59

Newfoundland, 57–61, 69, 200, 210, 211, 333

Nicholson, Sir William, 29

Nielsen, Erik, 381–83

Nieuwpoort (Belgium), 67

Nile River, 315

9/11 attacks, 393

Nixon, Richard, 380

Nobel Peace Prize, 321

non-alignment, 322, 376

non-proliferation agreements, 370

NORAD, 322, 338, 339, 340–44, 345, 348, 356, 357, 359, 360, 367, 377

Normandy landings, 234–36, 237, 241, 251

Norstad, Lauris, 362–63

North Atlantic Treaty Organization. *See* NATO

North Bay (ON), 250

North Korea, 278, 279, 280, 291, 292, 293, 295, 299, 300, 303, 395

North Nova Scotia Highlanders, 243

North Pole, 333

North Vietnam, 374

North York (ON), 118

Northern Africa, 163–69, 228

Northern Europe, 192

North-West Rebellion, 14

Norway, 192, 202, 205, 382

nuclear deterrence, 323–28, 346, 348, 361, 369

nuclear disarmament, 348, 351–52

nuclear strategy, 323-27 nuclear test ban, 349–50, 370

nuclear warheads, 261–64, 308, 329, 344, 346, 352, 353, 360, 362, 367, 370, 371, 372

nuclear weapons, 307–9, 318, 332–34, 337–67, 369–72, 394, 395, 398

Nunn May, Allan "Alek," 261, 263

Nuremberg trials, 236

nurses, 72, 117 (*See also* field hospitals)

October Crisis (1970), 377, 378

Ogdensburg (NY), 199, 200, 210

Onega sector (Russia), 144–45

Ontario Conservative Party, 45

Ontario Liberal Party, 12

Ontario, 119, 174, 191, 345

Operation Rolling Thunder, 374

Orange Free State (South Africa), 9

Order in Council: (1899), 13; (1915), 74

Ortona, Battle of, 229

Osborn, John Robert, 20, 217

Ost Battalion, 234

Other Side of the Hill, The (Liddell Hart), 180

Otter, William, 14–15

Ottoman empire, 133, 138

Paardeberg, Battle of, 14–16

Pakistan, 315, 318, 393

Palestine, 138

Panikkar, K.M., 301

Papineau, Louis-Joseph, 87

Papineau, Talbot, 56–57, 87, 130, 132

Paris (France), 40, 65, 66, 67, 136, 146, 150, 222, 233

Paris (ON), 39, 49, 55, 57, 59, 174

Paris Ministerial Association, 50

Paris Star, 185

Paris, Treaty of, 34

Parti Québécois, 391

Passchendaele, Battle of, 123

patriotism, 30, 46, 47, 48, 49, 50, 58, 59, 61, 155, 174, 197, 198, 298, 311

Patterson, George, 280

peacekeeping, 300, 318, 321, 322, 386, 397

Pearl Harbor, 219

Pearkes, George, 342, 352

Pearl Harbor, 208

Pearson, Lester B. "Mike," 71–72, 123–24, 127, 176–77, 227, 257, 271–72, 273, 274, 279, 294, 295–96, 300, 306, 308, 312–13, 315, 316, 317, 318–20, 321–22, 342, 363, 366–67, 371, 377

Pelletier, Gérard, 377

Pelletier, Oscar, 8

Peltier, J.E., 7

Pentagon, 272, 330, 331, 333, 337, 340–41, 359, 389

People's Democratic Republic of Korea, 280

Perkins, Albert, 15, 16

Perley, Sir George, 82

Permanent Force, 24, 44, 161

Permanent Joint Board. *See*

Canada–United States Permanent Joint Board on Defence

Persian Gulf, 26

Peterson, Dale, 285

Petrograd (Russia), 114, 135 (*See also* St. Petersburg)

"Phoney War," 189, 190, 196

Pickersgill, Frank, 183–84, 193, 222–23, 232–33

Pickersgill, Jack, 171, 184, 190, 199, 223, 245, 246, 271, 305

Pier 90, 247

Pink, R.C.M., 107

Plains of Abraham, 393

Plan XVII (French mobilization plan), 66

poison gas, 54–55

Poland, 64, 174, 175, 176, 180, 189, 195, 233, 235, 249–50, 251, 267, 384

Polish Corridor, 180, 249

Pope, Maurice, 267

Port Said (Egypt), 319

Portugal, 222

"Post-War Canadian Defence Relations with the United States" report, 331

Potsdam Conference, 259

Power Law, 37–38

power politics, 149, 259, 264, 309

Power, Charles G. "Chubby," 121, 151, 187, 204, 238

Prague, 270, 385

Prairie provinces, 116–17, 118, 157, 246

Pratt, Art, 61

predicted fire, 102

primates, and warfare, 284–85

Prince Edward Island, 50

Princess Patricia's Canadian Light (PPCLI) Infantry, 51, 52, 56, 132, 159, 192, 311

Princip, Gavrilo, 36

Prinz Eugen (warship), 202

prisoners of war, 202, 225, 232–33, 234, 236

propaganda, 13, 21, 108, 180, 223, 274, 309, 315, 335

Pusan (South Korea), 299

Putin, Vladimir, 385–86

Quebec Chronicle, 113, 120

Quebec City, 14, 120, 132, 204, 393

Quebec Liberal Party, 12, 391

Quebec South (riding), 121, 151

Quebec, 50–51, 79, 84–85, 110–22, 129, 130–32, 161, 184–85, 186, 187, 219, 220–21, 298–99, 345, 389 (*See also* French Canada)

Queen Mary, 247

Queen's Own Rifles, 319, 320

Quimper (France), 222

radar, 179, 209, 210, 338

Radford, Naomi, 48, 73, 83, 84, 110, 119, 191, 329–30, 341

Ralston, J.L., 197, 201, 218, 237, 239, 244

Rand district (Transvaal, S.A.), 9–11

rapid-firing rifles, 64

Rasputin, 95

Rawicz (Poland), 233

RCAF Staff College, 347

RCMP, 115, 262, 265
Reagan, Ronald, 370, 379, 380
Rebellion of 1837, 118, 152
Red Army, 208
reflex strikes, 346
Reichswehr, 179
Reid, Escott, 194–95, 223, 260,
  268, 272, 275, 295, 298, 301
reparations, 137
Republic of Korea, 280
Republican Party, 334, 335
Rhee,Syngman, 278–79, 280, 292
Rhineland, 169, 178, 179
Rhodes, Beit & Co, 10
Richardson, Lewis, 37
Riddell, Walter, 166–69
Riga (Latvia), 102
riots/demonstrations, 20, 40, 88,
  113–14, 115, 118, 158–59, 221, 391
Ritchie, Charles, 254, 255, 256, 351,
  361, 364, 373–75
Roberts, Lord, 14–15
Robertson, Norman, 254, 260, 262,
  273, 348, 349, 351
Robillard, Leo, 204
Robinson, Basil, 357
Rockingham, John, 304
Rodgers, George, 121
Romania, 36, 174, 267, 269, 384
Rommel, Erwin, 234
Roosevelt, Franklin D., 199–201,
  255, 258, 268, 279, 280
"Rosie the riveter," 206
Ross, Cameron, 390
Rousseau, Jean-Jacques, 284
Roy, J.H., 85
Royal 22ème Regiment (Van Doos),

159, 304
Royal Air Force (RAF), 106, 107,
  143, 179, 202, 225
Royal Canadian Air Force (RCAF),
  107, 109–10, 161, 190, 195, 223–
  24, 334, 346, 347, 386
Royal Canadian Dragons (RCD), 17
Royal Canadian Naval Volunteer
  Reserve, 185–86
Royal Canadian Navy (RCN), 42,
  160, 166, 186, 188, 209, 210, 211,
  230
Royal Canadian Regiment, 44, 159
Royal Engineers, 101
Royal Flying Corps, 106, 123
Royal Newfoundland Regiment, 57,
  60
Royal Rifles of Canada, 219–20
Ruhr, the 178
Rumpler aircraft, 108
Rupprecht (crown prince of
  Bavaria), 92
Rush-Bagot Treaty, 28
Rusk, Dean, 373
Russia, 35, 36, 65–66, 95, 133, 136,
  141–45, 147, 202, 207–8, 235,
  382, 394
Russian Far East, 142
Russian Front, 234
Russian Revolution, 95, 102, 114,
  135, 267, 307
Russo-Japanese War, 268
Rutherford, Mabel, 42

Sabourin, Jean-Paul, 204
Sadler, Serres, 49, 236, 241, 247
Saint-Anselme (QC), 118

Salisbury Plain (UK), 51
San Francisco Conference (UN), 255, 247, 290, 395
Sarajevo, 36
Sardinia, 34
Saturday Night (magazine), 218
Scharnhorst (warship), 202
Scheldt Estuary, 239–43
Schleswig-Holstein region, 36
Schlieffen, Alfred von, 65
Schlieffen Plan, 65–67, 102, 140, 214
Scotland, 192
Scott, Gordon, 207, 208
Second British Expeditionary Force, 194
Second Canadian Corps, 240
second strike capability, 355–56
Second World War, 5, 134, 162, 170, 171–72, 174–81, 183–210, 213–15, 217–48, 249–52, 289, 298, 307, 321, 329, 337, 339, 394, 395
Seoul (South Korea), 299, 303
Serbia, 386
Seven Years' War, 33
Sévigny, Albert, 117–18
Sharp, Mitchell, 205, 376
shell production, 68–69
Shepherd, George, 19
Sherbrooke (QC), 118
Sicily, 228
Simon, Sir John, 177
Simonds, Guy, 236, 298
Sinai Peninsula, 315
Single Integrated Operational Plan (SIOP), 354
Sino-Soviet split, 306

Skelton, O.D., 25, 145, 164–65, 167, 175, 176, 187, 201
Slovakia, 384
Small Arms School, 159
Smith, Donald A., 19, 40, 126, 174, 185
Smith, Goldwin, 18–19
Smuts, Jan, 147, 169, 259
Snipe fighter, 108–9
Social Darwinism, 253
Somme, Battle of the, 69–70, 82, 83, 88, 89, 95, 123
Soroka (Russia), 141–42
South Africa, 69, 129, 146, 147
South African war. *See* Boer War
South Korea, 279, 280, 291, 292, 294, 296, 299, 300, 302, 395
South Vietnam, 374
South-East Asia, 251
Soviet Air Force, 329
Soviet embassy, 262
Soviet purges (1935–39), 267
Soviet Union, 174–75, 180, 189, 192, 208, 215, 253–57, 259–80, 291–95, 306–18, 318, 322, 383–84 (*See also* US–Soviet relations [postwar])
Spain, 32, 34, 252, 276
Spanish Civil War, 195
Spanish Netherlands, 34
Special Operations Executive, 223
Spectator (magazine), 348
Spitfires, 179, 203
Spry, Dan, 159, 194, 240, 247–48
SS *Sardinian*, 14
St. John's (NF), 59, 186, 209, 230
St. Laurent, Louis, 273, 277, 279,

280, 293, 297, 305–6, 317, 320, 335

St. Petersburg (Russia), 102, 384
(*See also* Petrograd)

Stalin, Joseph, 174, 247, 261, 264, 268, 269, 291–92, 312

"Star Wars" project, 370, 380

Starfighers, 250, 346, 348, 372

Star-Transcript (Paris), 19

Statute of Westminster, 155

Stephenson, Sir William, 262

Stettinius, Edward, 255, 263

storm-troops, 88–89, 102, 124–25

Strategic Air Command (SAC), 308, 333–34, 336, 338, 346, 348, 354

strategic bombing, 224–25

"strategic" nuclear weapons, 308, 369

Strathmore (AB), 48

Stuart, Ken, 227, 228, 235

Stuka dive-bombers, 214

submarine warfare, 96, 134–35, 186, 187–88, 199, 207–10, 230–32, 383

submarine-launched ballistic missiles (SLBMs), 369

Suez, 161

Suez Canal, 314–15, 316, 317

Suez Canal Company, 315

Suez crisis, 314–21

suffrage, 117, 118

superpowers, 307, 309–10, 370, 376

surprise attack, 100–1, 102, 141, 157–58, 292, 302, 316, 336, 337, 369

Sweden, 32, 192

Swinton, E.D., 101

Switzerland, 67

Sydney (NS), 210

tactical nuclear weapons, 345, 362

Taiwan, 294, 303

Taliban, 393

tanks, 100–2, 103, 213, 214, 215

Tanzania, 285

Tarte, Israel, 10, 12

Taylor, A.J.P., 307

Taylor, E.P., 205, 208

Ten-Year Rule, 178

Thatcher, Margaret, 100

Thériault, Gérard, 381–83

Third Canadian Division, 240

Third World War, 279, 379

Thirty Years' War, 32

Thompson, J.M., 91

Thomson, Dale, 279

Toronto, 121, 205, 206, 207

Toronto Military Institute, 10

Toronto Telegram, 117

total war, 76, 96, 147, 196, 224, 225, 324, 394

"totalitarian," 276

Transvaal (South Africa), 9–10, 113

trench warfare, 51–52, 60, 63, 64, 67–69, 100–1, 102

Trochu (AB), 42

Trondheim (Norway), 192

Trudeau, Pierre Elliott, 164, 221, 376–78

Truman, Harry S., 258, 263–64, 265, 266, 270, 276, 277, 279, 292, 293, 295, 302, 304–5

Truman, Margaret, 276

Tsar Bomb, 350

Tulgas (Russia), 141
Turkestan, 234
Turkey, 32, 59–60, 138, 153–55, 360
Turner, George, 89, 126

U.S. Air Force, 301, 308, 333, 334,
    336, 337, 338, 354, 356
U.S. Army, 273
U.S. Congress, 128
U.S. Defense Dept, 367
U.S. General Staff, 341
U.S. Joint Chiefs of Staff, 304, 336,
    341, 354
U.S. Navy, 160, 346
U.S. Senate, 151
U.S. State Dept, 272, 273, 275, 293,
    296, 364
U.S.–Canada Halibut Treaty, 155
U.S.-Soviet relations (postwar),
    354–57, 360, 361, 370, 379–81,
    384 (*See also* Cold War)
U-501, 211
U-806, 230–32
Ukraine, 136, 385–86
Ukrainian immigration, 116–17,
    118, 198
UN Disarmament Committee, 350
UN Emergency Force, 161, 319–20
UN General Assembly, 257–58,
    300, 319
UN Security Council, 256–58, 272,
    293, 294, 317, 387, 388, 389, 395
Union government, 116, 117, 118,
    196, 218, 219, 220
Union Nationale, 186
United Nations Temporary
    Commission on Korea

(UNTCOK), 278–80
United Nations Unified Command,
    294, 297
United Nations, 169, 293, 294–95,
    297, 299, 300, 305, 313, 314, 315,
    317–19, 320–21, 349, 389, 395,
    396–98 (*See also* Charter of the
    United Nations)
United States. *See* Canada–U.S.
    relations (postwar)
Uplands Airport (Ottawa), 110
Upper Canada, 158, 218
Upper Peninsula (MI), 158
uranium, 259, 261, 372, 389
Urquhart, Brian, 398
Utrecht, Peace of, 34

Valcartier (Quebec City), 43, 44
Valenciennes (France), 109
Vancouver, 77, 207
Vancouver Sun, 305
Vandenberg resolution, 275
Vansittart, Robert, 169
Venetia, 36
Verdun, Battle of, 69
Versailles, Treaty of, 137, 146, 163,
    177–78, 179–80, 290, 394
Vichy (France), 222
Victoria (BC), 77
Victoria (queen), 10
Victoria Cross, 109, 220
Victory Aircraft, 206
Vienna, 137
Vietnam War, 372–77
Vimy Ridge, Battle of, 90–92, 93, 95
Vine, John, 19
Vladivostok (Russia), 142, 143

Volga River, 14
von Bismarck, Otto, 36
von Falkenhayn, Erich, 99
von Fiala, Ritter, 107
von Holzendorff, Henning, 134–35
von Rundstedt, Gerd, 180–81
Voodoos, 346, 372

Walcheren Island, 239
Wales, 158
Wallace, Henry, 265–66
Walpole, Sir Robert, 32, 35
war economy, 205–6 (*See also* armaments production)
war guilt, 137, 163
"War in the Modern Great Power System" study, 37–38
War Memorial Opera House building, 255
War of 1812, 158
War of the Austrian Succession, 147
war on terror, 392
war toys, 19
Warner, Lloyd, 286–87
Warsaw Pact, 309, 378, 384, 385
Wartime Elections Act, 117, 196
Washington Naval Treaty, 160
Waterloo (ON), 113
Watt, Ted, 42
weapons of mass destruction, 350, 387, 388–89
Westphalia, Treaty of, 34
Wehrmacht, 213, 249
Weinberger, Caspar, 382, 384
West Berlin, 253, 273
West Germany, 273, 322, 382
Western Alliance, 270–71

Western Canada, 116, 117
Western Europe, 267, 268, 269, 270–71, 273, 276, 298, 306–7, 308, 309, 310, 325, 361, 372
Western Front, 7, 60, 67, 69, 71, 95, 101, 103, 108, 123, 124, 135, 189, 215
Westmount (QC), 118
White Russia, 143
Wilhelm II (emperor of Germany), 180
Willison, J.S., 12
Wilson, Woodrow, 128, 148
Wilson's Fourteen Points, 128
Windsor (ON), 169, 204
Winnipeg, 47, 79
Winnipeg Free Press, 168
Winnipeg Grenadiers, 217, 219–20
Wise, S.F., 144
Woerner, Manfred, 382
Wolfe, James, 393
women in armed forces, 72–73 (*See also* female pilots)
Woodsworth, J.S., 184
Woodward, W.C., 207
Working Committee on Post-Hostilities Problems, 330
"world conquest" myth, 180
World Peace Award, 374
world wars, 31, 32, 33, 34, 35, 76, 149, 156 (*See also* total war)
Wrangham, Richard, 285, 286

Yalta conference, 268, 270, 386
Yalu River, 299, 300, 301, 302
Yanomamo peoples, 287
Yeltsin, Boris, 385

Yeo-Thomas, Forest Frederick "Tommy," 232
Young, Syd, 344
Ypres, battles of, 82, 95
Ypres, First Battle of, 52–56, 57
Ypres, Second Battle of, 101

Ypres, Third Battle of, 68–69

Zabotin, Nikolai, 261
Zeppelin raids, 76
"Zombies," 198, 238, 246, 247

GWYNNE DYER has served in the Canadian, British and American navies. He holds a Ph.D. in war studies from the University of London, has taught at Sandhurst and served on the board of governors of Canada's Royal Military College. Dyer writes a syndicated column that appears in more than 175 newspapers around the world.